AF560308

Accumulation *and* Dispossession

Communal Land in Northeast India

Accumulation *and* Dispossession

Communal Land in Northeast India

Asok Kumar Ray
Bhupen Sarmah
Gorky Chakraborty

ACCUMULATION *AND* DISPOSSESSION
Communal Land in Northeast India
Asok Kumar Ray, Bhupen Sarmah and Gorky Chakraborty

First Published 2017

ISBN 978-93-5002-433-1

Published by
AAKAR BOOKS
28 E Pocket IV, Mayur Vihar Phase I, Delhi 110 091
Phones: 011 2279 5505, 2279 5641
aakarbooks@gmail.com

Laser Typeset at
Arpit Printographers, Delhi 110 032

Printed at
Printed and bound by Sapra Brothers, Delhi 110 092

Contents

Foreword

This book is an academic exercise to understand the growing incidences of grabbing and privatisation of communal lands in the hill areas of Northeast India. From the pre-colonial times to the contemporary era, multiple modes have been used for grabbing and dispossession of communal land which have not only brought about massive changes in the land relations in the hills but also annihilated the lived space of the tribal people. This has finally scrambled the land based identity of the tribal people in Northeast India.

OKDISCD undertook an ICSSR supported research project in collaboration with Institute of Development Studies Kolkata (IDSK) on *Land as a Private Property: Changing Patterns of Land Relations in the Tribal Societies of Northeast India*. This book is the final product of the project. With an inter-disciplinary approach, the book handles the central questions of accumulation and dispossession of communal land in Northeast India, the changing land-use and cropping patterns affecting the convivial land relations of the tribal communities in Northeast India against the larger theoretical, historical and institutional perspectives. This book has raised relevant policy debates on the communal land system and has given interesting academic insights, reflections, new interpretations and food for thought for the academic community and the research scholars working in and on this region.

Guwahati

Bhupen Sarmah
Professor and Director
OKDISCD
Guwahati

Introduction

A brief overview of the archaic land systems in the tribal societies in Northeast India bears testimony of a relational-communal character of land. This character unveils the fact that while devolution of property had been from the community to the individual, the devolution itself had been subject to community control. Thus, individual right on communal land did not exist on its own; it was subsumed within the community right and property was never, therefore, private in the feudal sense of the term. Although there were lineage preference, landlessness and slavery among some tribal groups of the region, the dominant egalitarian mode of production and the distribution system associated with this, left no room for communal land being privatised. The practice of shifting cultivation with primitive tools and instruments of production was subsistence in nature that could not rise to such a level which could host an economically lazy class who, without taking part in the production process, could enjoy the fruits of it.

This situation started to significantly erode with the advent of the British colonial power that targeted the natural resource endowments in the tribal areas for usurpation either by primitive accumulation or by accumulation by dispossession. One significant mode of primitive accumulation/accumulation by dispossession was structured subordination of the chiefs and the headmen of the tribal communities in the hills. This made the chiefs/headmen instrumental in land resource usurpation by the British. The process was started in the Khasi Hills that first came under the colonial administration in Northeast India and then in other hill areas of the region. Structured subordination also privileged the chiefs/headmen so much so that they could emerge as a nascent landed gentry from within their own communities. The colonial state being an aggrandising state, usurped community land first by plunder and destruction and then by extraction of as much rent as it could be possible from the land, forest and mineral resources in this region. In this way, they amassed huge wealth from the hills for draining out to Europe. These un-tribal features 'corrupted' the tribal communities and left wide-ranging ramifications for the community as a whole.

The land and natural resources of the tribal communities were progressively commoditised and were given a fetish character. The connotation of 'occupancy' got transformed into 'ownership 'of land. Communal land, thus, lost its sacrosanct entity as it progressively went towards individuation of land right in the hills of Northeast India. This subsequently privileged the first generation tribal elites, who claimed community land citing the provisions of customary laws and usurped wider areas of community land either through fencing, upgradation, and improvement through building permanent structures on land and so on. They made selective interpretation of the customary law, which became an alarming problem in the highlander communities. Introduction of plantation economy in the hills by the British led to further land concentration and landlessness of the tribals. In the contemporary hill scenario, it is not therefore surprising to come across a Garo or a Naga or a Karbi or an Aka, or a Dimasa owning huge areas of land, a situation unknown even a few decades earlier. As parallel practice, sale-purchase-lease-mortgage of land also became routinised in the tribal areas. Community lands were usurped for industrial and commercial uses that severed all connection with the tribal economy. These developments have now posed serious challenges to the theoretical and historical bases of the communal land system. There were critical roles both of the external and of internal agencies in the process of accumulation and in bringing about corresponding changes in the traditional institutions, conventional land use pattern and in the land-based identity of the tribal people.

There was great role of colonial jurisprudence in converting communal land to private land. Starting from the Bengal Eastern Frontier Regulation to the Chin Hills Regulation, there were uninterrupted efforts to colonise the communal land. The process of institutional accumulation was carried forward to the post-colonial period which following the colonial jurisprudence, introduced land reform acts in the different states of Northeast India. The institution of district council was introduced to protect tribal land from being alienated. But in reality it created more confusion in the communal land systems than solving them. Land issues under the district councils led to several judicial disputes in the Khasi Hills and state-district council conflict over their powers and jurisdictions. The district councils of Tripura and Manipur were modelled differently and there soon arose conflict between the district councils and the tribal communities. In Manipur, there arose serious conflict between the jurisdiction of the district council and that of the Manipur Land Revenue and Land Reforms Act on land issues in the hills.

The post-liberal institutional reforms demanded a distinct individual property right to be enshrined in the law of the land. This was not there in the communal land system in the hills. Besides, the market economy demanded the economy of scale through enhanced production of commercial species, growing industrial use of the hill lands and replacement of authority-based transactions to contract-based exchange relations. These exerted a powerful influence and greater pressure on the states of the region to formulate market-oriented policies and legislations. These policies and legislations dwarfed the social, economic and ecological significance of communal land and the prevailing agrarian practices in the hills. The post-liberal economy had multiple interests in communal land, which had so far no legal title. These included conversion of subsistence use of communal land to commercial and industrial use, enclavisation of communal lands by special zoning, indiscriminate commercial use of the land and water resources of the region for hydro-power, mining operations, infrastructure building, commercial cropping and so on. The post-liberal economy indulged in flexible accumulation through spatial fixation of capital on communal lands in the hills.

In this larger backdrop, the book is spread over five chapters.

Chapter one deals with the theoretical issues and history of land privatisation in the tribal areas of Northeast India. We have spliced together Marx's 'primitive accumulation' and Harvey's 'accumulation by dispossession' and fielded these theoretical instruments for larger understanding of the privatisation scenario of the communal lands in the hills of Northeast India. With these instruments, we have sketched a historic-epistemic road map of accumulation and dispossession of communal land in the hills of Northeast India from the pre-colonial, colonial, post-colonial to the post-liberal times. In this mapping, innumerable *modus operandi* of accumulation and dispossession of communal land were found in different hill areas of Northeast India at different phases of history. The processes of primitive accumulation and accumulation by dispossession privileged the state and the external agencies but did not elevate the hill region to a higher level of society and economy. On the contrary, these caused perennial annihilation of the lived spaces of the tribal communities.

Chapter two deals with the institutional modes of accumulation of communal land resources. This included both the customary institutions pertaining to communal land and the formal institutions of the state affecting communal land. This chapter makes a broad overview of the customary laws of the tribes governing communal land and then goes into the details of the colonial regulations and legislations through which the process of dispossession and accumulation of the communal resources went on unabated in different hills of the region. The colonial institutional legacy and the jurisprudential principles were carried forward to the post-colonial times in the states of Northeast India which created complex problems in the communal land system in the tribal areas. In the neo-liberal order, the institutional reform programme became much more oppressive and abiding to the states of Northeast India. The communal land qualifying nothing to the reform programme, received largely the *terra nullius* status and became subject to progressive annihilation, while at the same time, such community lands became the ideal space for indiscriminate extraction of water, mineral and forest resources by the state and the market forces.

Chapter three deals with the changes in the traditional cropping pattern and land use patterns that led to progressive privatisation of land. These changes responded to the shift of the state policies from food-secure subsistence economy to market economy. The policies of the states in Northeast India, were accordingly geared for increasing commercialisation of agriculture, contract farming, horticulture, plantation and agri-business in order to respond to the market economy. The shift in cropping patterns from the subsistence use did not benefit the poor tribals of this region. Industrial use of communal land became mainly extractive in nature. Northeast India, as such, is not a manufacturing region. The extracted (minerals, water, forest, etc.) resources were drained out elsewhere. The private companies, foreign direct investors and the corporate cronies did capital fixation in the hills in order to extract the minutest geological and hydro-resources available in the hills. The state governments of Northeast India assumed surrogate roles and made concerted efforts to make the respective states, the preferred destination of FDI and corporate investment; offered excessive policy subsidies to the investors in terms of tax, natural resources, infrastructure, etc. and tightened the governance norms in order to protect the lives and property of the investors. Such changes happened at the cost of the communal resources as a result of which, the community people were thrown to a tenuous situation.

Chapter four deals with land-based identity of the tribal communities Three aspects are problematised here: The first aspect is institution-driven identity that has shown how the coercive institutions of the colonial economy were used for accumulation and dispossession of communal land and broke the convivial and non-adversarial land-based identity of the tribal people. The second aspect is elite-mediated identity, which has shown how elite mediation in land matters scrambled the historico-anthropological construction of ethnic identity for the sake of private accumulation of communal land resources. It has also shown the ideological encounter of two types of elites—the Zealots and the Herodians—both having motives of aggrandisement and accumulation of land resources by application of the crafty *modus operandi.* The third aspect deals with the shift of community labour from its production-reproduction function to production function and wage labour as a result of privatisation of communal resources under the market economy. This gave the tribal labour a fetish character which replaced the fixed, self, referential and inward-looking place-myth with the market which trivialised the somatic attachment of the tribal people and endangered their land-based identity.

Chapter five is a conclusive chapter. It offers a reflective analysis of the privatisation narrative of communal land in Northeast India. Two analytical tools, namely, racial anthropology and political economy, have been used for the analytical purpose. In the process of colonial land grabbing, the roles of anthropology, race theory and theology were complementary. Racialisation of the hill communities by the colonial administrators and the missionaries served as the ideological state apparatus for primitive accumulation and accumulation by dispossession and for simultaneous commoditisation of the communal land economy. This had backing of the colonial state power. The 'Sword and Sermon' of the colonisers worked together for accumulation and dispossession of communal lands of the tribal communities.

There was a shift of the anthropological parameter towards the political economy parameter for accumulation of the communal land resources under the colonial economy. In this parameter, one can find the collective roles of revenue administration, power state, policy packages and economic models of the colonial and post-colonial state in resource capture in Northeast India. The political economy parameter became more pronounced with the advent of the market economy. All the state policies pertaining to land were geared towards the market economy, in which the communal lands were most affected. The state and the market in connivance, adopted such policies in order to build blocks of a neoliberal order. Under the neo-liberal regime, both land and labour received a fetish character. The communal land space was re-configured in which the natural movement of the community members was curtailed. Capital fixation on enclavised community space brought the pre-capitalist economy closer to the neoliberal economy and privileged the latter to exploit the minutest natural resource endowments available therein. This has invited tension between the social optima principle in communal land and the profit maxima principle of global capital. The latter, while clashing headlong with the community cause, did not refrain from the use of force, fraud and deceit to historically continue the processes of accumulation and dispossession.

1

Theory and History of Land Privatisation

Looking retrospectively, the concept of private property did percolate from the Greek to the Roman jurisprudence and then to other parts of the world. The Roman jurisprudence made two categories of things: (i) *Res mancipi* (consisting of land, certain rights of user over land, slaves, cattle and horses), transfer of which was made through an elaborate public ceremony called *mancipation* and (ii) *res nec nancipi* (thing that could not be so transferred). In the Roman law, the concept of *jus quiritium,* (acquisition right) was the privilege only of a Roman, which was above the law of the land. He could perform a number of acts about these things on which he asserted such a *jus*. He was the *dominus,* the *paterfamilias* and the housemaster (head of the household). (Max 1925: 208-209). The Roman jurisprudence received the status of '*corpus Juris civilis*' in the hands of Emperor Justinian and continued to be the law of the Roman Empire. It consisted of the Institutes (a student text book), Digest (selection from the jurists' writings), Codex (that summarised imperial edicts) and the Novels. (Max 1925: 227-228).

Corpus juris civilis endangered communal property and established the private property regime that came to dominate the economic history in Europe, Africa and Asia. From John Locke (1632-1704) to Adam Smith (1723-1790) and from John Stuart Mill (1806-1873) to Max Weber ((1864-1920) there were uninterrupted efforts to construct the theory of accumulation by the *homo-oeconomicus*. The history of economic philosophy from the 17th century onwards was, therefore, the history of intellectual construction of the grand theories of individual right and private property by a galaxy of thinkers.

Locke's notion of property right was rooted in the classical-liberal and utilitarian-laissez faire principles. His notion of property right presupposed a state of nature, devoid of any regulatory political authority—a divine injunction to make earth productive and profitable. He justified self-ownership of one's own labour in production, profitability and in private property. Wood, in contrast, viewed that it was not labour *per se*—but its *improvement* to ensure the earth's productivity and profitability—that formed the basis of private property in the 16th century English agriculture, culminating in the golden period of agrarian capitalism in the 18th century. (Wood 1998: 21). Adam Smith's theory of property right was foundational to the jurisprudential structure of society that, in turn, constructed his own vision of the free-market and commercial society, in which presence of the state was *sui generis*. John Stuart Mill gave a labour justification of initial capital formation and stated that capitalists themselves were the original labourers or descendants of the labourers that gave them the exclusive right to their capital and control over production. Things being so, they could now hire workers at a lower wage for production. Weber found the spirit of capitalism in the radical ethics of Protestantism and regarded capitalist accumulation as a moral act. The Protestant Ethics of "Calling" and "Thrift" and the Calvinist theory of individual wealth accumulation gave Weber the ideological justification for capital and profit accumulation.

This Western galaxy, producing patrician pedagogy, was seriously contested by Marx's concept of primitive accumulation. In the German Ideology, Marx and Engels stated that the "whole interpretation of history appears to be contradicted by the fact of conquest. Up till now, violence, war, pillage, rape and slaughter have been accepted as the driving force of history". Adam Smith described such accumulation as "*previous* to division of labour and hence preceded capitalist accumulation and is its point of departure." Primitive accumulation, to Marx on the other hand, "played approximately the same role in political economy as original sin in the Christian theology". "And from this original sin, dates the poverty of the great majority that, despite all its labour, has up to now nothing to sell but itself, and the wealth of the few that increases constantly although they have long ceased to work" (Marx and Engels 2010: 667-70; Fowkes 1990: 873; Marx and Engels 1945: 8, 37, 8). Marx, thus, found primitive accumulation as a temporal phase in the history of capitalism (Marx 1977: 713-714) and saw it as *class relation* in a non-capitalist, non-market forms of slavery, taxation, rent, labour service and servitude, contrary to Smith's concepts of capital as '*Stock*' and '*previous accumulation*'. Marx found "primitive accumulation," as a precondition for the origin of capitalism so that "accumulation of wealth at one pole was, at the same time, accumulation of misery, the torment of labour, slavery, ignorance, brutalisation and moral degradation at the opposite pole" (Christian 1990: 223). As an 'extra-economic' force, primitive accumulation separated the peasants from the land and commoditised both labour and land through appropriation of labour time and privatisation of land. Though he saw the capitalist transformation as historically progressive, Marx dispelled the myths about both its *birth* and its *mature* forms.

Lenin and Rosa Luxemburg were the trail breakers and made subsequent analyses of primitive accumulation in the context of the new wave of militarism, expansion of monopolistic firms in major capitalist states in the 20th century. Lenin analysed primitive accumulation in the light of 'monopoly capitalism' while Luxemberg saw it as a means to overcome the chronic problem of 'under-consumption'. Both, however, found violence as an extra-economic force though they disagreed on the relationship between primitive accumulation and expanded reproduction. For Lenin, the scramble would yield the 'ultimate' stage of unequal development, marked by war and revolution to establish conditions for expanded reproduction in the peripheries. For Luxemburg, the scramble would re-create the necessary organic relationship between expanded reproduction and primitive accumulation, escalating through relentless warfare until the final exhaustion of non-capitalist societies and capitalism. Three aspects of their analyses were remarkably prescient: the monopoly form of capitalism did become its 'ultimate' form; primitive accumulation remained a fundamental dimension of capitalism and both monopoly and primitive accumulation have continued to require endless militarisation. These three aspects explained the centre-periphery contradiction on a world scale and systematic transfer of surplus value from the periphery to the centre. Through these mechanisms, the centre could displace its own contradictions of accumulation to the periphery where primitive accumulation was more intense (Mayo, Yeros and Jha-2012: 186-187). As the process of primitive accumulation rested on "capitalisation of nature"(Paranjape 2013: 75), it was a brutal process, as Fawkes said, of forceful expropriation of the means of production from the pre-capitalist society by a small group of people. It appeared primitive because it happened in the pre-history of capital and in Europe it was largely responsible for expropriation of the small peasants (Fowkes 1990: 873-875).

Angelis proposed to embed Marx's primitive accumulation both in historical and in continuity arguments and compared Lenin and Luxemburg in this connection. He labelled Lenin's interpretation as historically and temporally defined and Luxemburg's approach as "inherent-continuous primitive accumulation (Angelis 2000). To Marx, this process was not natural but was clearly the result of a past historical development, the product of many economic revolutions, of the extinction of a whole series of older forms of social production and such history is "written in the annals of mankind in letters of blood and fire" (Marx 1977: 706, 179-180). His primitive accumulation exposed the nature of monopoly control over land space called 'enclosure'' that became critical in eventual structuration of production relations and social relations. Enclosure restricted the movement of the people to eliminate fear of the mob and the ethics of 'improvement' justified the 'enclosure' economy. Enclosure is not, according to Wood, simply privatisation and fencing of formerly common land but also extinction with or without a physical fencing, of the common and customary use-rights (Wood 1998: 24). Lodi saw the importance of 'enclosure' in the structuration of social relations and quoted Marx in this connection: in the history of primitive accumulation, " great masses of men are suddenly forcibly torn from their means of subsistence, and hurled into the labour market as free, unprotected and rightless proletarians." Thus enclosures are a "continuous characteristic of capital, not just a historical phenomenon" (Lodi 2007: 1442-1443). The continuous character of the English land enclosure was carried forward to India as a part of the colonial project of monopoly control over the land space.

Marx did not agree that industrial revolution was a sudden, fortuitous spate of mechanical invention in the post-1760 England, nor did he find the peasant and artisan production of the 16th century onwards as capitalist production that had no more than a snail's pace to capitalist development. He described the post-feudal mode of the 16th century onwards as a petty mode of production out of which *capitalism originated but did not triumph*. Capitalism triumphed only by destroying this mode. Habib wrote, Marx did not classify such non-capitalist commodity production as feudal, to bridge the entire gap of three-and-a-half centuries between c. 1450 to c. 1750, whereafter the industrial revolution began. This mode was the petty 'mode of production' with a 'snail's pace' which came out of massive primitive or primary accumulation from non-capitalist sectors of economies "through internal exploitation of the peasantry and external plunder, linked to global colonial dominance". "The 'snail's pace' within the Petty Mode, could now be changed into rapid growth of 'hot-house fashion 'in which force 'is itself an economic power" (Habib: 2011: 2-5). Millar also found the role of power of state and primitive accumulation to accelerate the hothouse fashion (Millar 1978: 387).

Barbara Harris-White on the other hand, found two tendencies on the agrarian questions in the 21st century: First, petty commodity production (PCP) as the robust backbone in manufacturing, trade and services which is not transitional but is constantly being replenished and reproduced. Second, the PCP of the pauperised class [in India] resulting in 'perverse transformation'. PCP thus, coexists with, but is not co-terminus to 'peasant capitalism'. In India, the 'intermediate classes acted as the rung above PCP and its existence did not imply teleology of development. Its existence was market-dependent (Harris-White 2012: 118-119, 125) In many cases, including in India, the poor petty production mode, in the absence of state and market support, tended to sink into "Penny Capitalism".

Marx described the multiple modes of primitive accumulation including "super-exploitation of labourers, dispossession of the peasants, discovery of gold and silver in America, the enslavement and entombment in mines of the aboriginal population, conquest and looting of the East Indies and the turning of Africa into a warren for the commercial hunting of black-skin, public debt and lending out of capital to foreign countries" (Bose 1988: 1169-70). "The colonial system ripened like a hot-house, trade and navigation. The colonials secured a market for the budding manufactures, and through the monopoly of the market, increased accumulation. The treasures captured outside Europe by undisguised looting, enslavement and murder were floated back to the mother-country and were there turned into capital" (Bose 1988: 1169-70) which to Fowkes were the "chief moments of primitive accumulation" that led to commercial war between the European nations" (Fowkes 1990: 915-916). He even despised the Glorious Revolution in Europe as an act of fraud, theft and direct seizure of state lands and branded the 'Bill for Enclosure of Commons' as a parliamentary form of robbery of the cultivable space and housing sites of the agricultural labourers (Fowkes 1990: 885, 886, 889-90, 915-16). Marx distinguished two modes of accumulation: the ideal mode of rational accumulation (surplus value) that excludes force, fraud, oppression, expedition and the primitive mode that includes these. He used primitive accumulation in locating the historical process of capitalist development in England. However, such accumulation also happened in many other countries beyond England, in Australia (McMichael 1980); Egypt (Richards 1977); China (Weber 2008); Tunisia (Bennoune 1979); West African forest kingdom of Asante (McCaskie 1983); Sub Saharan Africa (Emoungu 1992); USA (Weiss 1982) (Pedal 2011); Dakota, Minnesota, the Acholi in Northern Uganda, Southern Mexico (Kligerman 2010) and Nigeria (Olorode 2013) which destroyed the communal land resources all over the world.

The brunt of primitive accumulation was felt more stringently in the less developed countries and much more in the peripheries—the lived space of the tribal people. Primitive accumulation did not honour the principle of *Salus populi suprema lex est* (the safety of the people is the supreme law) and blocked a generic intellectual history of land ownership pattern to emerge that could resonate with the complexities of ethnic allusion and the varied metaphoric constructs associated with land. Most of the colonial administrators did not comprehend the nature and meaning of communal land resources and the ideology, the ethnic communities attached to land. They constructed the meaning of land based on commercial principles and so at the beginning, the colonial accumulators resorted to plunder, warfare, expedition and destruction as the usual modes of accumulation.

The classical theory that obscured the role of primitive accumulation in the emergence of capitalism was laissez faire that condemned "sloth and indolence of the poor "and associated moral philosophy by work ethics, that, if not pursued, would be punishable". "In a conscious attempt to justify the emerging capitalism, primitive accumulation used two parts comparable to two blades of a scissors. The first blade served to undermine the ability of people to provide for themselves. The other blade was a system of stern measures required to keep people away from finding alternative survival strategies" (Perelman 2001: 7-8, 9).

The modes of primitive accumulation were later made more institutionally structured. The three institutional expressions of such modes were the colonial jurisprudence, colonial bureaucracy and the colonial army. Purposeful rationalisation of accumulation and the cognitive shift in the meaning and ideology of communal land became eventually perilous to the ethnic communities. Precisely therefore, we could find a few more modes of primitive accumulation including peasant expropriation, forcible eviction, usurpation and enclosure of land, conversion of arable land into pastureland, diminution of village, de-population, price rise, increase of monopoly farms, theft of common property and so on (Fowkes 1990). The bloody legislations, including the early 16th century statutes in England, the Low Countries, and in Zurich (Perelman 2001: 8), the oppressive acts passed by Henry VII, Edward VI, Queen Elizabeth, James I and Edward III against the vagabonds and labours (Fowkes 1990) were the legal modes of primitive accumulation. Revolution of industry and capitalist farming that annihilated the peasantry (Fowkes 1990) was the third mode. Primary accumulation of capital from the spoils of the colonial system, from the silver of Mexico and South America, slave trade and plunder of India were the fourth mode. (Fowkes 1990). Through these different modes of primitive accumulation not only the common land was lost but livelihood of people based on these lands also obliterated. Marx observes "by 1750, the yeomanry had disappeared, and so had, in the last decade of the 18th century, the last trace of common land of the agriculture labourer". (Marx 2010: 676)

Primitive accumulation being the *ultima thule*, in India J.F. Stephen (Law Member of Government of India, 1869-1872) defended his efforts to create a new code of law and disrupt the Indian society for moral and material progress along the European lines (Owen 1987: 2). Therefore, Pathy found, piratical plunder of the third world resources from the 16th to the 19th century, consistently augmented the affluence and opulence of Europe (Pathy 1987: 2). Marx found that the East India Company in the earlier period made colossal direct plunder, exploitation and extortion that were more rewarding than the commercial gain of the company. Neglect of irrigation and public works, introduction of English land system, private property and criminal law, direct prohibition of or heavy duties on import of Indian manufacture, monopoly of the Company and financial oligarchy, destruction of Indian handloom, revenue and rent extraction from the cultivators and extraction of tributes from India (Dutt 2008: 88-91) were the different modes of British primitive accumulation in India.

In re-deploying Marx's primitive accumulation, David Harvey produced his thesis on 'accumulation by dispossession' in the context of neo-liberal global south. He surpassed the temporality of primitive accumulation and fielded the thesis of 'accumulation by dispossession' in the continuity trajectory. To Harvey, capital being aggressive and imperial, looks both beyond space and time that enhances historical materialism to historical-geographical materialism. Space and time are the basic categories of human existence, not separable from the material processes of social life. Thus every mode of production produces its own conception of space and time.

Harvey also found primitive accumulation as a permanent feature of capitalism and the neo-liberal onslaught has intensified it (Moyo, Yeros and Jha 2012: 18). He developed this theory in the era of volatile global capital with the chronic problem of over-accumulation in the 1970s. He interpreted this as a series of temporary spatio-temporal fixes that failed to deal with the problem of over-accumulation. The inability to accumulate through expanded reproduction on a sustained basis, to Harvey, could be temporarily addressed by accumulation by dispossession. He drew on the dual character of accumulation following Rosa Luxemburg with a difference: replacement of under-consumption thesis of Luxemburg by over-production. He saw the crisis of over-accumulation as a constant factor in capital accumulation in which accumulation by dispossession could act as a temporary safety valve by lowering the prices of consumer commodities that could push up general consumption (Harvey 2003: 139). Harvey has found the powerful presence of primitive accumulation within capitalism's historical geography and has shown how the credit and financial systems have created new avenues and opportunities for predation, fraud and thievery. He found the whole new mechanisms of the new developments, ranging from

IPRs, WTO negotiations and TRIPS to dismantling and auction of public assets and utilities at a pittance (Paranjape 2013: 87). Accumulation by dispossession, to Harvey, entailed accumulation through expansion of wage labour in industry and agriculture that gave rise to trade unions and working class political parties. Dispossession, on the other hand, was fragmented and particular—a privatisation here, an environmental degradation there, a financial crisis of indebtedness somewhere else. Dispossession also entailed loss of rights which went towards a universalistic rhetoric of human rights, dignity, sustainable ecological practices, environmental rights that became the basis for a unified oppositional politics (Harvey 2005: 178). Internally, the neoliberal state was necessarily hostile to all forms of social solidarity as these restrained capital accumulation (Harvey 2003: 75). Therefore, labour could be viewed only in market terms, not in social terms.

Harvey's discourse on privatisation in the neoliberal era added a new dimension to the concept of accumulation. In his *Brief History of Neoliberalism,* he found four main features of accumulation by dispossession: Privatisation and Commodification of public assets, public utilities, welfare provisions, public institutions, IPR and even warfare; *Financialisation* through speculation, predation, fraud and thievery through deregulation, stock promotions, ponzi schemes, structured asset destruction through inflation, asset stripping through mergers and acquisitions; management and manipulation of crises and the state allowance of transfer of assets to a small elite (Harvey 2005: 159-164).

In the neoliberal private property regime, competitive markets, and 'the rule of law' were propounded by the World Bank advocates. They despised communal property following Garrett Hardin's charge that the graziers over-exploit natural resources and communal property, destroy environment and bring collective tragedy (Whitehead 2003: 4227; Mukherjee 2013: 77). In this perspective, Harvey's accumulation by dispossession became a temporal or partial solution to over-accumulation. Privatisation of land became phenomenal with the global surge for earning quick buck from the land sector. This required transformation of the use-value of land into its exchange value and integration of the peasantry into the monopoly-controlled global agro-food system. In this scenario, land right remained no more the right of the communities and nature remained no more natural. Land was re-meaned and re-valued, resulting in dispossession of the communal right.

In the Third World countries, FDI had entered largely through the primitive route. On the other hand, the fiscal concessions, tax subsidies, land subsidies, policy incentives, labour sector deregulation and informalisation in the FDI recipient states accelerated up the process of dispossession of the poor and affected the tribal communities most. Thus, in spite of space-time compression and annihilation of space by time in the post-modern condition, Harvey found that "heightened competition under the conditions of crisis has coerced capitalists into paying much closer attention to relative locational advantages precisely because diminishing spatial barriers gave capitalists the power to exploit minute spatial differentiations to good effect" and "superior command over space becomes an even more important weapon in class struggle". Thus, Harvey found, "flexible accumulation typically exploits a wide range of seemingly contingent geographical circumstances, and reconstitutes them as structured internal elements of its own encompassing logic". Besides, since capital accumulation operates through market, the services of primitive accumulation are required almost by definition when the market is in crisis. During critical phases of capitalist crisis, primitive accumulation emerges to help transaction barriers to accumulation in two ways: (a) by facilitating the transition from the critically fated regime to a new regime of accumulation, and (b) by continuously negotiating the spatial expansion (both internal and external) of capitalism. During periods of transition and expansion, "new enclosures" are required for putting the normal course of capitalist reproduction back on track. Securing these enclosures through force and other "direct extra economic means" is the function of primitive accumulation (Harvey 1990: 293-294; Chandra and Basu 2011: 28).

Polanyi on the other hand, viewed that the major tragedy of the Industrial Revolution was not greed of profit but social devastation of the uncontrolled market economy. He observed that the social implication of a particular economic system in the 19th century was not due to economic determinism but due to the ideal system of the new economy that demanded abnegation of the social status of human beings (MacIver 1944: ix). Polanyi's view was a-historic and purposive as he intended to hide the gluttony for profit maximisation through primitive accumulation and accumulation by dispossession. The mutual constitutivity of accumulation and dispossession, in fact, became trans-historic and raised new concerns for understanding the specific nature of land dispossession in different spatial contexts. This scenario was proclaimed by Garrett Hardin in the neo-Malthusian way that individualism is cherished because it produces freedom, but the gift is conditional: the more the population exceeds the carrying capacity of the environment, the more freedom must be given up (Hardin 1998: 1243-1248).

The neoliberal trans-national investment also needed spatial-fix of the investment for certain relative economic advantages, including cheap resources and labour, more surplus working hours, investment-friendly state policies and a congenial investment climate. Such spatial fix was required for service industries and capitalist enclosures that in turn created a particular type of predatory social relation and pushed the great masses to the unorganised labour market as uprooted and rightless communities. Capitalist social relation in the enclosure, therefore, assumed a 'continuous character' of capital, not just a historical phenomenon (Lodi 2007: 1442-1443). The taxonomic transformation of the land-space into 'enclosure' also structured and re-structured the social relations within it.

Fielding the Concepts in Northeast India

We need to understand the historical setting of the archaic mode of production in the hills of Northeast India before fielding the concepts in Northeast India. The archaic land system in the hills of Northeast India resembled many features of the Asiatic Mode of Production (AMP) like its contraposition to the West European Mode of Production, its distinction from the primitive, ancient, feudal and modern society frame, absence of private property in land and presence of communal ownership, its relative stagnancy and immutability of economy and society which Engels attributed to the 'climate and nature of the soil'. Given the differences between the AMP and the European Mode of Production, Shiozawa found expropriation of surplus labour in the AMP to be the tribute receiving Oriental Despotic State and the system of tribute presentation *(tributeverhaltnis)*, the slave owners and the slave system, and the feudal lord and the serf system" (Shiozawa: 2013: 307-308).

In Northeast India, a textual exposition of the tributary mode of production is found in the Royal Chronicles in Assam (*Ahom Burunji*), Manipur *(Chaitharol Kumbaba)* and Tripura *(Rajmala)*. In fact, scholars have approved the presence of the "Tributary Mode of Production" as a special mode of production in the past royal kingdoms in this region.

Secondly, in the hills, there was great ecology-economy interdependency in the shifting cultivation economics and the communal nature of land ownership associated with this (Sharma 1990b: 3) which is evidenced by the archaeological relics in the region (Guha 1991: 1-2; Rao 1991: 114-115, 119, Barpujari 1990: 240; Heimendorf 1982: 42, Das 1993). It followed the simple logic that the lower the attainment in technology, the higher is the dependence on geography and nature and vice versa. The influence of geography, thus, stood inversely proportional to the degree of technology development (Thavaraj 1984: 29).

Thirdly, in Northeast India, shifting cultivation being an organic response to specific ecological condition, a reflex to the 'physiographic character' of land', was more a concession to conditions of land abundance and the character of the soil than an act of barbarism (Guha 1991: 4). Being essentially a techno-light and input-free, the vertical spread of shifting cultivation was feasible due to abundance factor alone. The social organisations evolved around this economy for this very reason assumed a uni-class character, in which the concept of labour emerged as a non-monetised collective endeavour. It is for this reason that, for example, "in the early Mizo society, there was no paid labour"(TRI 1982: 23) and the community rituals were routinised to represent the collective consciousness of the people.

The significance of geographical space did not disappear with the spread of capitalism. David Harvey took the geographical logic from the past to the post-modern condition for relative locational advantages to exploit minute spatial differentiations. He found "flexible accumulation typically exploits a wide range of seemingly contingent geographical circumstances, and reconstitutes them as structured internal elements of its own encompassing logic" (Harvey 1990: 293-294). This converted land from being a community space to a market economy space.

It is in this setting of communal land that the concepts of accumulation and dispossession need to be fielded in the hill economy in Northeast India. The analytical value of the theoretical contours of Marx's primitive accumulation and Harvey's accumulation by dispossession being what they are, the two are spliced together for a realistic understanding of the land privatisation scenario in the hill areas of Northeast India. An introspection into history makes it evident that privatisation and accumulation of natural wealth happened in different parts of the region with different modes, but an overall commonality ran down the line having remarkable resonance with the twin theories.

The incidence of accumulation of communal land was found in the domestic mode first and in the colonial, post-colonial and the post-liberal modes then. The domestic mode of primitive accumulation lay, as Sharma stated, in the Vedic concept of *pana,* which later came to mean coin and *dhana* (*w*ealth), appeared in the earliest portion of the *Rig Veda* as prizes, wagers or stakes won as a result of either war or competition. Acquisition of property involved war and '*Loptra*' or loot (spoils of war) that was the earliest source of property for the *Rig Vedic* people (Sharma 1976: 42). In the Asiatic economy, absence of private property in land was a conspicuous feature. In fact, as Dutt found, the key of the whole East was the absence of private property in land. The soil of India belonged to the tribe or its sub-divisions—the village community, the clan or the brotherhood settled in the village and was never considered as property of the king. Either in feudal or in imperial schemes, ownership of the soil was vested in the peasantry (Dutt 2008: 222-228). A section of the historians wrongly equated the territorial headship of the kings (benevolent despots) with their property right in land following the sanitised classics like the 'Manu's Hindu Code' that defined different stratified modes of acquisition for four different varnas or castes.

The Shastric legacy was flown into the pre-Gupta period when agriculture became a mode of acquisition permitted to the Vaishya varna only. After the 5th century AD customs overrode the Shastric law and all the four varnas were granted the right to ownership of land. However, only the Sudra varna and the Avarnas (Untouchables) were to actually cultivate the land who had no prescribed mode of acquisition recognised by law. Dis-possession and accumulation took place in the Gupta polity right in the heart of the forest dwellers' domain (Chaudhury 2004: 30) [except pasture lands, which Kautilya said, were the common lands and the king should never privatise pasture land by giving them to the noblemen (Kadekodi 2004: 3)]. Chattapadhyaya noted that in early medieval Bengal, the rulers occupied forest regions for providing space to the Brahmanas. King Lokanatha gifted land in the Subunga Visya for temples and for settlement of Brahmanas on forest land (Chattapadhyaya 1991: 28) which dispossessed the forest dwellers. Choudhury wrote that they did "not only represent a space which yielded varieties of resources and all important revenue for the state which, for the Mauryan state, the herders and hunters had to part with. The forest dwellers needed to be made to conform to what the state required and, thus, be subservient to the state" (Chaudhury 2004: 30) which was one of the Indian variants of primitive accumulation/dispossession. The royal grant of forest land;

grant of land to the Brahmins; transformation of forest land into kingdoms and Sanskritisation of space were some of the other modes of accumulation through dispossession. The caste mode of accumulation resulted finally in caste-class convergence, which went a long way to become a crystallised theory in the Indian social scape and very rightly Mukherjee found invagination of caste into the class structure in colonial India (Mukherjee 2000: 334).

This tradition was flown to medieval Assam where land was classified as: *Kshetra* (arable land), *Khila* (wasteland) and *Vastu* (building sites), most of which were collectively/ community owned. The Ahom rulers believed in state ownership in and absolute authority of the kings over land. During the Ahom period, land was tenured not on the basis of *revenue* but on the basis of *service* to the state. By virtue of this, the aristocrats, nobles, generals and administrators received large tracts of land. Under the Paik system, each member of the Paik was also given two *puras* (nearly three acres) of rent-free rice land for rendering personal service to the king as a soldier or labourer (Daimary 2012: 32-33). With land grants, the temple or priests also got the labour of so many paiks (Saikia 1965: 9). Guha found that royal grants to the Brahmanas and religious institutions were initiated by the Kamrupa King Bhuti Verman in the 16th century that continued up to the Ahom period (1228-1826) and the royal donee also got gifts of inhabited villages or a certain number of peasant families as farm labour to cultivate in a sparsely populated region like Assam. On the eve of Ahom colonisation, hundreds of such Agrahara grants were made all over the Brahmaputra valley, where Brahman settlements took place in the midst of tribal lands (Guha 1991: 40-41). The Kayastha, Daivajna and Bhuians, also received land grants in the 14th and 15th centuries for providing necessary protection to the weak kings against frequent Bhot and Bodo Kachari invasions (Guha 1991: 41). The 13th-14th centuries also marked some degree of feudalisation of land in certain areas (Guha 1991: 42). The typology of copper plate land grants emerged in the 17th century with the introduction of *devottar, dharmottar* and *brahmottar* land grants (Guha 1991: 48). The non-hostile Naga tribes inhabiting the hills close to upper Assam were also brought under the Ahom confederacy and as a gesture of strategic co-option, several Naga chiefs were given grants of Khats or land, and Beels or fishing waters in the plains, and were assigned Paiks (Singh 1994: 3). To keep the frontier tribesmen in good humour, a form of Posa, "an allowance for certain hill tribes inhabiting the hills in the northern frontier of Assam bordering Darrang and Lakhimpur, on account of commuted blackmail or in consideration of abandonment by them of their claims with regard to certain duars" (Chakravarty 1973: 122), was introduced. The Jaintia kings also made extensive land grants to the Brahmans in the early part of the 18th century that proliferated subsequently to as many as 32 odd land grant charters of the Jaintia raja. (Rynjah 2006: 95, 97).

The tributary mode during the initial Ahoms rule did not lead to a serious clash between the migrant Ahoms and the aboriginal Moran and Barahi tribes in the 13th century. With wet rice cultivation, the Ahoms were not interested in dispossessing these tribes of their dry lands that did not produce sufficient surplus to support several thousand Ahom migrants. The wet rice cultivation in Assam led to individual reclamation of land while land reclamation through collective efforts necessarily belonged to the community. One example of this is found among the Khampti tribe in which although the chief was the lord of the soil, the whole community tilled it on the cooperative system (Guha 1991: 42-43).

The next modes of expropriation were tax and revenue. The Paiks, who received land grants, had to pay a nominal house tax. Any Paik cultivating land in excess of his two *puras*, had to pay a certain amount of revenue. In the inundated areas, the cultivators had to pay plough tax. The hill tribes, who cultivated cotton had to pay hoe tax. There were other professional castes, who also enjoyed tax-free homestead and farm lands on the condition of supplying some quantity of products to the royal households and public storehouse (Daimary 2012: 32-33).

In the feudatory state of Manipur, the king claimed absolute proprietorship of all lands within his territory and he also made extensive land grants to Brahmins, Sepoys, priests, idols and to his own relatives (Das 1989: 48). Dun found that people could hold their lands on payment of usual tax in kind (Dun 1980: 59). Land revenue administration was initiated by King Pakhangba in 33 AD who divided land in four divisions called *Pana* and lands were divided into *Inkhol* (rent free lands occupied by households and gardens) and *Lou* (revenue paying land for rice cultivation). Immediately before the initiation of the survey operation the following types of land Patta were prevalent: *Sanalou Patta* (Patta for the king's paddy field); *Lairou Patta* (Patta for deity's land); *Kharposh Patta* and *Talablou Patta* (to certain types of state employees in lieu of cash salary); annual Patta and Ryotwari Patta. The first four types of Patta were revenue free. Such land grants gave rise to absentee landlordism and agricultural tenancy. The *Lairao Patta* made the *Sevait* a privileged class (Ray 1991: 168-169). The principle of land grant was service-based and there was no private property, as the granted lands were retrieved after the lifetime of the grantee. However, there was a unique type of newly colonised land called *Taona Lou* that had a quasi-private property character. Such land was held by the gentry constituting of the members of royal family (Singh 2009: 118-119).

In the other feudatory state of Tripura, the practices resembled those of Assam and Manipur. Caste-based land grants were in common practice. Sengupta found the earliest copper plate charter of the 6th century Tripura depicting a gift of land to Buddhist establishments and donation of jungle land for temple services to 200 Brahmins. This happened in the wake of agrarian expansion in Tripura (Sengupta 1991: 167-168). Such grants were of two types: rent paying and rent-free (Goswami 1994: 53-61). Land grants were also made to accommodate the massive influx of Bengali settlers by obtaining land from the poor tribes. Much later, transfer of tribal land to the non-tribals was prohibited through an amendment of the Tripura Land Revenue and Land Reforms Act 1960. But the lands occupied fraudulently by the non-tribals were legalised with the help of the local administration (Roy Burman 1991: 96-97). Earlier, there were no written laws regarding land settlement and land revenue and the kings made rent-free land grants for religious and charitable purposes. The paying part of Tripura was Chakla Rosanabad, that was under the Zamindari of the King. The hills were not the paying part. Accordingly, the hills became Independent Tiperrah and the Raja who was an ordinary Zamindar on the plains, reigned an independent province over 3,000 square miles of upland. The king of Tripura ruled the hills through the chiefs, who would collect the tributes and other requirements for the government. The most important sources of revenue from the hills were family tax, duties on forest products such as cotton bamboo, canes and the sale of elephants captured in the state. The dual status of the king was accepted by the British government subject to his submission to the British paramountcy (Chaudhury 1983: 38, 88).

In the hills, a form of house tax or family tax was imposed on the cultivators. In 1919, King Birendra Kishore Manikya enacted a law for assessment of house tax at different rates as for the Tripuris (Rs. 3.50); Jamatias (Rs. 3.50); Notias (Rs.10.00) and for the Kukis (Rs. 5.25). If a tribal did both *jhum* and settled cultivation he was to pay rent and half the house tax. In 1931and in 1943, a certain area of land was declared as tribal reserve for plough cultivation by five specific tribal groups. In 1931, the area reserved was 110 sq. miles and 1943, it was extended to 1950 sq. miles. These reserved areas covered an area of 42 per cent of the total area of the state for settlement of five classes of tribes including Puran Tripuri, Naotia, Jamatia, Riang and Halam. In this reserved area, no transfer was permitted to persons apart from those five tribes. The tribal reserves, however, did not adequately protect the tribal interest and the boundaries were vaguely described. The exclusion of 14 other tribes from such settlements was discriminatory. Such land consolidation by the King diluted the authority of the village councils, village chiefs and circumscribed the tribal right to use of land and forest (Ayer 1995; Dutta 1986: 130-131).

J.B. Ganguli found that at the beginning of the 19th century, the conditions prevailing in Hill Tipperah strongly resembled the feudal socio-economic system. The *Jhum* land was communal and the chief of the tribe had overall control of the use of land by the individual families for *jhuming*. The Raja of Tripura collected House Tax (*Ghar Chukti Kar)* from the *jhumia* families through the chiefs, the rate of which varied from tribe to tribe. The Kukis were sometimes excused from all money payment conditional upon their rendering military service to the king. The Tipperah also paid lower tax for rendering personal services at the palace and carried out the orders of the Raja. The tribal *jhumias*, in addition to the high rate of house tax, also paid the high rate of duties on the production and export of main cash crops that far exceeded the official rates leading to extortion of surplus from them. This was the beginning of the process of primitive accumulation (Ganguli 1987: 221-223). The *Parbatya prjaganer Ghar Chukti Kar Sambandhiya Ain* was passed in the 1329 Tripura Era (1919), which was repealed subsequently (Chakravarti 1994: 126).

The Rajmala of Tripura Kings evidenced that the tribal people used to pay *Raj Kar* or royalty every year in kind such as homemade clothes, ivory, animals, etc. Some of the tribes served the state instead of royalty or tax. Besides, customary cess of *Awab* was imposed on the tribal people (Bhattachacharjee 1977: 190-193). This marked the transformation of the once tributary mode of production to taxation mode indicating simultaneous transformation of economic anthropology to political economy in the hills of Tripura. In the 1296 Tripura Era (1886), the law of Landlord and Tenant in the independent state of Tripura paved the way for the growth of individual proprietary cultivation. The Bengali settlers, tribal chiefs and the influential and resourceful people in the king's court took advantage of this. In 1880, the Maharaja of Tripura took measures to replace shifting cultivation by wet-field agriculture and reserved vast areas of land for *jhumia* settlement. The King followed a dual system of land tenure for shifting and settled cultivation. The chiefs collected the tributes and taxes that were handed over to the King's capital in the annual meet at the Durga Puja festival.

The chiefs subsequently started to earn cash income from commercial farming in addition to tax exemption. They also acted as local contractors and agents of the traders, forest tax farmers and money lenders. At the beginning of the 20th century, the rulers of Tripura offered very attractive terms for the prospective tea entrepreneurs in the state. The whole process of primitive accumulation was found in the steady rise of wage labour, unequal land distribution, and steady fall of land for productive use and shift of tenancy right of the tribal settled farmers to other tribals or non-tribals (Ganguli 1987: 224, 226, 227, 228). The tribal reserves were broken owing to the influx of the immigrants after the merger of Tripura within the Union of India in 1949 (Chakravarti 1994: 126-127).

In Northeast India, the domestic mode of primitive accumulation led to a state of perennial dispossession and the historic legacy of primitive accumulation was routinised in course of time. The petty mode of production in the hills could not excel. In this mode, the rich land, forest, water and mineral wealth in the Northeast rested in the lap of nature. These were never private wealth of any individual; the community had only the usufruct right over these resources and tribal land economy emerged *ipso facto* as a non-accumulative economy. The domestic mode of accumulation in the Northeast emerged largely from the surplus generating wet field cultivation in the valley areas. But this was also not of scale and hence, as Ganguli wrote, it could not be raised by some dramatic increase of capital formation (Ganguli 2006: 10-11). For example, the king of Manipur restricted the average size of a farm to around three acres of land which yielded very little surplus that limited the possibility of accumulation of wealth by the agricultural farmers. In the manufacturing sector also, occupational mobility was under strict restriction. Hence, saving and accumulation were negligible (Ganguli 2006: 326). In such a situation, the other way of primitive accumulation was slavery in the forms of Paiks in Assam; slavery and *Lallup* in Manipur; and slavery of different kinds in Tripura, including, the debt-driven slaves and their wives and children in the hills (Ganguli 2006: 57-58). Besides, there was the great role of subjugation and plunder in the early accumulation process. The Ahom kings subjugated the Dafla, Lakma Naga and Mikir tribes of Arunachal Pradesh through expedition, plunder and burning of their villages. They were then reduced to submission before the royal force and were compelled to serve the Ahom Army. Later on, due to perpetual plunder by the frontier tribes, the royal rulers felt the futility of using force against them and the former had to accept the rule of the Singpho chiefs over the areas east of Namrup (Choudhury 1983: 89-94).

The Burmese ravages in the region resulted in wanton robbery of wealth, burning, looting, violating the chastity of the young and old women and killing. The historiography of colonial intervention in Assam highlighted this barbaric nature of oriental behaviour and the jural order as contrasted against the civilised Western judico-administrative system. The East India Company's rule in this region made meticulous recording of Burmese atrocities that ended with the Treaty of Yandaboo. (Sharmah and Dutta 2013: 75-76, 77). Once the treaty was concluded, the incredible natural resource endowment of the region became the target of the colonisers and they resorted to similar practice of plunder or capture of resources like coal, limestone, petroleum, salt, platinum and even gold found in the region (A Mittal Publication 1984: 23-26). The forest resources became a great source of profit-revenue from the hills. It was reported that the total area of reserved forests in Assam in the year 1921-22 rose to 5,584 square miles and an area of about a hundred square miles was finally deforested. Some "interesting sal taungya" plantation was started alongside in the Garo Hills and Surma Valley (A Mittal Publication 1984: 108).

While fielding the concept of privatisation of communal land, it is necessary to demystify the prevailing notion of ownership of land resources in the tribal areas of the region. Prof. Lal Dena, referring to Manipur, once raised a very pertinent question: "To whom does the land belong? To the Manipur maharaja, tribal chiefs during the colonial period or to the succeeding Manipur state in the post-independence period? During the colonial period, Shakespeare, the political agent, issued 'boundary papers' to the tribal chiefs in the name of the Maharaja. This implied that at least formally the whole land within the boundary of Manipur belonged to the Maharaja (Laldena 2011). Prof. Laldena's question has a historical continuity of a major debate on actual ownership of the communal land. The assumption of royal right over customary rights of land also appeared in the mainstream economic and social discourses. The colonial rulers toed with the thesis of kings' ownership whereas the dissenting view was that it was the community ownership. Islam wrote that "under the Mughal Constitution each group of landed interest had some kind of customary right in land. The English administration thought that land was a solid property as in England. But they were not certain as to who owned that landed property. The zealous revenue officers dug into old records to find definite answers or clues about the ownership of land. Contradictory results emerged from their researches. Some declared that the state was the sovereign owner of land; ryots paid their rents through the agents called Zamindars. According to them, the Zamindar was only a "conditional officer annually renewable and revocable on defalcation. But some others declared land to be the absolute property of the Zamindars" (Islam 1979: 6). The discourse was resolved finally by the Permanent Settlement vesting the Zamindars with absolute property right in land. Yet, the notion of 'wealth-power' equation obsessed many people, including, even J.N. Das who, following E.W. Dun, considered the rulers of the region, including, the Raja of Manipur and the ruler of Cachar as the owners of lands.

Our view is that privatisation of wet-fields in the valley, improved means of production, organised revenue administration, landlord-tenant relations and proto-feudal forces in the valley areas of the region might have thoroughly mystified the notion of land ownership system in the hills and the notion that 'land belongs to the ruler' remained thoroughly a contested notion in the hills. The tributary mode of production in this region did not affect the communitarian land system in the hills. The British ended the tributary mode and introduced the Hill House Tax instead. Historico-epistemologically, the customary rights over the archaic land systems were built first on the principle of primacy of occupation and then on the basis of inherited or the acquired rights to lands (the latter turning to inherited land on the death of the person acquired) under the overall stewardship of the chiefs, headmen or the community councils. At this stage, the productive forces were simple, land was abundant and the scale of production did not exceed beyond subsistence. There is a view that private property is systemic and incipient in some tribal societies of Northeast India. But it is not sufficiently supported by historic evidences and even if incipient private property in some tribes was found, this not necessarily featured the archaic economic and social milieu of the tribal communities.

As the tribes in this region were at different stages of historical progress, their systems of land ownership exhibited multiple features. Some land systems were more developed than the others depending on the degree of dependence/ independence on nature and on historical stages of development of the means of production. Secondly, the form of land ownership in the archaic tribal societies needs be understood essentially as a social arrangement, not in terms of class polarisation. Thus for example, the concepts of public and private (*Ri Raid* and *Ri Rynti*) land system of the Khasis led some continental scholars to hastily jump to the vapid conclusion that Khasi society is class polarised.

To de-mystify them, it is necessary to lay bare the nature of the two concepts. In the Khasi society, public land was meant for the exclusive use of the political rulers, priests and the village community. These people had no ownership over public land and its ownership rested with the community concerned, i.e. village, *raid* or state. It was inalienable and the occupancy right was reserved for the members of the community only. The forest land, boundary land, land owned by war and land of the extinct families were in the category of public land. Sacred groves also fell in this category. Private lands included lands owned by particular clans and those that were individually acquired in course of time turned into ancestral land. The conspicuous feature in the Khasi land system was that private land was the individual property of the *clan* concerned, with the right of inheritance vested in the youngest daughter (*ka-khudduh*) of the group under the care and protection of the mother's brother and could not be partitioned without the consent of the clan along with their brothers or mothers' brother. The clan organisation of the Khasis, though not hierarchical, had a number of segments within it, each having its *ka Khuddah* and its own system of rights and obligations. The self-acquired land was the absolute monopoly of the individual owner, but once it became the ancestral land, it was also subject to the same checks and balances as the clan land and the youngest daughter of the group getting the major share and her brother or mother's brother acting as the protector. Therefore, the ultimate control over *Ri Kynti* land—both ancestral and self-acquired—was in the hands of the clan council (*Darbar Kur*).

The pattern of rights and ownership of the two types of land system corresponded to the political and kinship organisations of the Khasis. Public land was kept for meeting the needs of the political functionaries, for providing free land to the landless for cultivation and for supplying the community needs for firewood, timber, thatch and pasturage. Land in the Khasi tribe therefore did not belong to any individual but belonged to the society in whose territorial jurisdiction it fell and the landlord-tenant relationship was never present throughout the Khasi Hills (Nongbri 1987: 73-76; Datta 1987: 83; Sen 1987: 1992).

Similarly, among the Nagas, as Barpujari (Jr.) saw, land was originally held in common although rights over land were individual and communal. There was no absentee-landlordism and no class of landless peasants. The wealth of the country was measured with the needs of its people (Barpujari 1987: 194). Barpujari (Sr.) found communal land ownership of land in a system of joint ownership of the territory among the families in the Khel (Barpujari 1990: 237). Among the Nagas, therefore, clan, lineage and family own the land and every Naga household is considered to be equal in respect of land and wealth (Aier 1987: 208-209).

In the Chin Kuki-Mizo groups of tribes, the chiefs enjoyed custodial right and their land right was only notional as they would only allot lands to the villagers for cultivation as *homo giftus*. They, however, had the responsibility to see that no land was transferred to the outsiders. This vigilance of the chiefs was necessary to uphold the social, cultural and economic bond of the community and the integrity of the economy. There was also the system of communal labour in the practice of shifting cultivation. Besides, the villagers enjoyed many rights with corresponding duties under the rule of the chiefs. They had the right to free movement within the village territory, hunt any animal and gather minor forest produce. No commercial use of forest products was allowed. The concept of right, as we understand in the positive law, could not appear in the economy of shifting cultivation because at the end of each *jhum* cycle, the chief and his followers normally used to leave the *jhum* field without leaving behind any vested interest in it. There was only temporary usufruct right over *jhum* land. After the end of every *jhum* cycle, the chief might re-allocate the land in a different manner. Shifting cultivation, therefore, could be "frequently associated with the tradition of communal ownership of land... They can hold the land so long as they make effective use of the same. As soon as they stop their operations, their right ceases"(Datta 1987: 177). Besides, the social function of land was very significant. In performing the social function, in every village the chief used to keep some village, areas as village commons. Moreover, production from *jhum* land was not of the scale that could bear the burden of an economically idle class (Datta 1987: 178) and hence there could not evolve, by custom, a more centralised political system to support a private property regime.

Colonial Accumulation

Primitive accumulation became an agenda of the colonial modernity. The colonial power rationalised it by political organisation, military-bureaucracy, jurisprudence and ideology. These designated the British crown as the landed proprietor, who could grant lands through the colonial agents to the private producers. This established the tight inter-relationship between primitive accumulation, abstract space, the legal concept of *terra nullius* and the colonial conquests during the first phase of capitalist expansion throughout the globe (Whitehead 2003: 4230). Bhambhri wrote that "India was plundered by the Rubber State of British imperialists and the long bleeding process of the colonial phase of history led to the complete distortion of material and social structure... from the beginning of the 17th century (Bhambhari 2013: 71).

The first imperial expropriation of the communal land in India was made by the East India Company through, as Dutt wrote, extreme revenue extraction from the peasants, transforming the traditional land system through assessment and registration of ownership and replacing it by the English economic and legal institutions. The plunder of India in the second half of the 18th century, the building of modern England and the spoliation of India made possible the industrial revolution there" (Dutt: 2008: 227-228, 98-112). Things culminated in the introduction of Permanent/Temporary Settlement and Ryotwari System. Bagchi wrote, "In India both in Permanent Settlement and in Ryotwari areas, payment of tax to the treasury became the first charge and the essential condition for the landlords (Zamindars) or small holders (Ryots) right to the fruits of land" (Bagchi 2010: 248). The method of revenue realisation was coercive and crude. In this connection Huq wrote that "the collectors by their own authority arrested the debtor and confined him. If the dues were not paid within a reasonable time, he was to be put up in the stocks, had his ears pulled and a peon was ordered to lay hold of him by the neck and run him backwards and forwards in the public cachery"(Haq 1964: 37). The individuation of landed property through the Permanent Settlement or Ryotwari system marked a brake in the extant structure of landed property of India. "The Regulation of 1790 was the real beginning of the Permanent Settlement that required the revenue farmers to issue written undertakings (pattah) to the tenants. In many cases the tenants claimed hereditary rights of occupancy, which the 'pattah' would deny to them. Because of the fraudulent practice of the intermediaries, the vast majority of the hereditary occupants failed to secure the true record of rights and became mere tenants-at-will" (Bagchi 2010: 249). Things culminated in the Land Acquisition Act of 1894 that empowered the state to apply the principle of eminent domain in acquiring communal land in the public interest. This Act was the major instrument also in post-colonial land acquisition from the tribal community.

The initial phase of colonisation of nature was carelessly destructive that was a part of military operations. Pouchepadass stated that colonisation bred the "emblematic figure of the pioneer, whose symbols were the axe and the gun, both being tools of destruction for substitution of the civilised order for savagery". "They renamed the regions, trees, animals and landscape elements after those with which they were familiar in their countries of origin. As far as forestry was concerned, their idea was plantation of a few commercially viable species while the species commonly used by the local population were extremely numerous. Such an overseas concept destroyed and reshaped the landscape". Later, they realised the profitable use of land for plantation, commercial cultivation and animal husbandry (Pouchepadass 2002: 123-125). Before receiving sovereign legitimacy, the British rule was in the state of primitive accumulation. Queen Victoria assumed sovereign legitimacy to rule India when the 'The Royal Title Bill of 1876' was passed in England, (Thorner 2002: 3). Having thus established sovereignty, the colonials resorted to force, fraud, plunder and capture of resources to build the colonial edifice. Agriculture and forestry were the two available *in situ* resources although forests received only peripheral significance in the colonisation narrative in the first instance. The overseas practice of augmentation was replicated in the colonization projects in different parts of the country in different ways. In Punjab, it was the canal colonisation scheme, in Rajasthan, it was the Rajasthan Colonisation Act, in Bengal, it was the Permanent Settlement and in Assam, it was the Ryotwari system.

Forest became important only when the colonials realised it as the lucrative source of profit and revenue. For the tribal societies, on the other hand, forest was more important than merely an economic chattel—it was also important space for their corporate living and cultural identity, a space of symbiotic ecology and a collectivised social space. The unwritten nature of the use and ownership right over such resources gave the British an added advantage for capture. While, therefore, in the first phase colonial privatisation was done without attending much to any norms or regulations, in the second phase regulatory norms were introduced in the forestry sector: what George Stigler called, 'Regulatory Capture' where "regulators do not exist to realise the idealised public good, but to serve themselves and their affiliate industries"(Dietrich 2006: 1445). Such regulatory capture was initiated through positivistic jurisprudence based on *res nullius* and through creation of resource enclaves like Reserved Forest and Protected Forest. Lord Dalhousie's 'Charter of India Forest' -1855, the Indian Forest Act 1875 (as revised in 1878) and the first forest policy in 1894, were the institutional penetrations for regulatory capture of the forestry resources. Dalhousie's forest policy stipulated timber monopoly, promoted ideology of scientific forestry to rationalise timber production and forest conservation (after 1878) that classified forests as 'Reserved' and 'Protected'. The Indian Forest Act was amended in 1927 to regulate the law relating to forests, forest produce, forest transport related duties and penalties. Section 55 of the act empowered the state government "to constitute any land as reserved forest by issuing a notification, after which no rights should be acquired in or over the land comprised in such a notification except as concession or under a grant of contract in written made or entered into by (or on behalf of the government) some person in whom such right was vested when such notification was issued, and no fresh clearing for cultivation or for any other purpose shall be made in such land except in accordance with the rules as may be made by the state government in this behalf". Governmentalisation of forest through enclaves, deconstructed the hitherto existing community space and their natural rights by the twin jurisprudential instruments of *res nullius* and *lex loci*. By the first instrument, the colonials annihilated the natural right of usufruct and by the second instrument, they established their 'legal' rights- backed by institutional power of the colonial state. This first displaced and dispossessed the tribal people and then annihilated the place (integrated ecology including human beings, their social and emotional and cultural location), by converting it into a lumpen, society-less, culture-less, private space for commercial plantation and timber operation. This was the threshold to a colonial private property regime in the forestry sector. The colonial debate on forest policy as seen by Ramchandra Guha, centred on three categories of officers: the annexationists led by Baden Powell, who advocated that the state should take over the forest for public benefit in which the state could play the role of benevolent landlord; the sympathisers of the local communities, who argued for the passive role of the state in forest affairs and the third category of officers, who looked for a middle path by advocating for active role of the state in protecting forests and in taking care of the people's needs. The discourse that the state should respect the customary rights and privileges became the basis for the Forest Act of 1878 (Murari 2004: 183).

The colonial modus operandi for accumulation in Northeast India was hexangonal. This included penetration of policy, capital, ideas, institutional force (militarisation), bureaucracy and the multi-ethnic routes. The multi-ethnic routes were not very smooth in Northeast India. There were so many tribal movements against colonial accumulation. In order to contain those, the colonials took another soft route of primitive accumulation, for example in NEFA, of appeasement, presents and gifts to keep the tribesmen happy and content. The officers and explorers on tour gave extravagant gifts; in Lohit, for example, opium was distributed as a 'political present'; in Subansiri, ugly and unsuitable gifts of cloth impaired the natural taste of the people; and everywhere, rum was the most popular way of establishing friendly relations. The custom has continued to the present time, but in a modified form, and of course, giving of opium and rum has now been stopped (Heimendorf 1982: 35-36; Elwin 1964:203). Commercial plantation was also another mode of accumulation of communal land.

The process of primitive accumulation scrambled the debates on rights. In this debate, the state engulfed, what Roy Burman wrote, the proto-political jurisdictional rights in the pre-state or state indifferent societies rooted in ethics and obliterated the division between jurisdictional rights and economic rights. He felt the necessity of differentiating between proto-political jurisdictional rights of pre-state and state indifferent tribal and the analogous people in respect of land and market-oriented commodity character imputed to the same at the intervention of the state. For uninterrupted functioning of temporo-spatial jurisdictional rights, there was some coordinating mechanism that existed in diverse forms. In many cases, the coordinating mechanism was the eldest male member of the lineage or the group that drew upon some symbols or by rational calculations of fair share and in some other cases, the coordinating mechanism was self-regulation of individuals (Roy Burman 1998: i-ii).

Parallel to this scramble, the colonisers criminalised the tribes. In the Foreword of the book, *History of Assam Rifles*, by Colonel L.W. Shakespeare, W.J. Reid pictured the tribal society of Assam as a "society organised upon war footing" who "ambuscades an alien village—even its women when drawing water from the stream—to burn its homes and massacre its inhabitants" which "have been regarded as sporting enterprise". Then he viewed that the "most obvious methods of stopping these marauding raids were by retaliatory incursions into tribal territory". "The punishment that was required could be inflicted most rapidly and economically by a Special Police Force led by a civil officer. So originated, the military police has developed into the five battalions of Assam Rifles" (Shakespeare 1977: v-vi). A similar account of the tribes was given by S.E. Peal about the tribes inhabiting the hills south of Seebsaugor (Manas Publication: 1988: 330- 331). Starting from the British annexation of Assam in 1825-26, the saga of the Assam Rifles ran down the history through a series of expeditions on different hill areas of Assam and on other parts of Northeast India and even beyond in the Chin Hills of Burma. The Assam Rifles adopted a primitive way of accumulation of resources in the tribal areas of Northeast India and helped colonial accumulation of forest resources, much of which, were also plundered and destroyed. Lord Robert's Account, recorded similar plunder in the military advance up the Barak valley. For construction of the first bridge to advance, "the 42nd A.L.I. set at once, some felling bamboos and trees, others cutting them to required length, while others waded to their chests in the stream and drove the uprights into the river bed to which the bamboo flooring was then rapidly attached"(Shakespeare 1977: 67).

In the Abor Expedition of 1912-13, the Military Police Column, while passing through the thick belt of jungle had cut its way in places by the use of *Kukris*. Jungle cutting was done for transportation of coolies and for clearing up some of the difficulties on the line of communication (Dunbar 1984: 151, 155). A series of expeditions from 1871-72 to 1889-90, to the Chin Lushai Hills resulted in final annexation of the country and capture of their resources. As many as eleven army expeditions were sent during nearly two decades of the later part of the 19th century into the Chin Lushai land. Clearing and cutting of vegetation for army passage to the tribal territories was a common practice. The colonial intervention in the hills was also strategic. In the Naga Hills, there was no possibility of enough revenue and enough raw materials that could interest the British. Lord Dalhousie, therefore, dismissed the idea of permanent occupation of the Naga Hills. Lord Dalhousie's Minute of February 21, 1851, categorically asked for only a *line of frontier defence, not a forward policy* that remained valid for fifteen years till it was replaced in 1866, when it was found that the Naga incursions were a threat to the tea, oil and coal fields of Assam (Bhattacharjee 1987: 380-381). The colonials took the path of "expedition in order to draw maps, to assess resources, to develop friendly alliances, to punish those, who defaulted, to extract tributes and to bring regular administration in the area". "In January 1832, the first British men to visit the Angami region—Pamberton and Captain Jenkins—marched into the area". "A stockade was taken at the point of bayonet" (Elwin 1969: 114). When Manipur was *annexed* in 1891, such mode of primitive accumulation was justified "on the ground of moral right" and "recognition of the tribal chiefs, who enjoyed considerable powers and privileges within their chiefdoms. Their main concern was to collect the Hill House Tax and extract forced labour through tribal chiefs"(Laldena 1991: 71, 81). There are many other cases on record, of subjugation of tribal chiefs through the "recognition mode" under the surveillance of the martial power of the colonisers. The Kohima Column, Silchar Column and the Tammu Column were displays of martial power of the colonisers.

Commercial plantation led to large scale accumulation of land. Guha found that "the Charter of 1833, for the first time allowed the Europeans on a large scale to hold land in India, either on long-term lease or with freehold rights and thus paved the path of colonial capitalism in the region"(Guha 1991: 194). He referred to Jenkins' report in 1833, on the necessity of "undertaking some public work as an immediate measure to generate a flow of cash into the money-short economy that could create absolute property right in land". He insisted on free-hold land with payment of a fixed and unalterable rate of rent just to attract a class of European planters in Assam's wastelands suitable for commercial crops. Thus, discriminatory land revenue policy was favoured to evict the tenant cultivators through heavy tax and to make them work for cash crop-oriented capitalist farmers. Things took the final shape in the Wasteland Rules of 1838 (Guha 1991: 149, 154). These rules were revised in 1854, to provide ninety-nine years' lease on more liberal terms. This resulted in huge land transfer to the planters. Goswami found that from 1928 to 1954 the European control of tea estates was dominating and the percentage of area under European control became more than the Indian control. In this sector, a 'managing agency system prevailed that was subsequently abolished by Indianisation of the Government of India (Goswami 1988:164-65). Guha further wrote that by 1871, more than three lakh acres of wastelands were settled with planters in Assam proper alone. In the decade ending 1881, the same leaped up by 63.8 thousand acres and in 1901-02, land area under tea increased to 204,682 acres (Guha 1991: 186, 188-89, 191). The plantation economy constructed privatised enclaves in Assam and the new economic class was fielded to play within these privatised enclaves. The plantation economy was "marked by system of land tenures that set off vast tracts of wastelands as a distinct category from the land under traditional cultivation". "While the tea planters had access to both types of land, the wastelands were barred from traditional agriculture. Consequently, the planters could exercise their option freely and encroach upon land under traditional crops, if suitable tracts of wastelands had already been exhausted or there were exceptional advantages in this course" (Dasgupta 2008: 177-178).

The transition from subsistence agriculture to commercial plantation happened parallel to dispossession of the communal land and plantation encroached upon many shifting cultivation areas. The colonials also thoroughly discouraged shifting cultivation as the 'petty mode of production' in the hills of the Northeast and expanded lands for commercial cropping. For the colonials, land was significant for its revenue and profit-yielding value which could be achieved first by the jurisprudential dismissal of communal land rights and then by the actual initiation of plantation on the wide stretches of land. Therefore, the greater the land under plantation, the more was the degree of privatisation. This also resulted in land speculation and over-accumulation of wastelands and the "Wasteland

Settlement policy facilitated land grabbing through fee sample grants" (Guha 1997: 14)

The extension of the tea estates affected the Lushai society in two opposite ways. On the one hand, tea extension on Southern Cachar and South East of Sylhet during 1826-73, put a check on the mobility of the Lushais and on their hunting and *jhuming* rights. The East India Company established the 'Kheda System' for catching elephants in the forests and the Kheda personnel and the military department clashed with the Lushai chiefs' jurisdiction. Prosperity of the tea estates, therefore, provoked the Lushai raid almost every winter. On the other hand, establishment of trade marts in the Lushai Hills in the post-Lushai Expedition of 1871-1872, made many chiefs affluent. They could bring annual rent and sales tax from giving the lease of trade mart to the British. During this period, some Lushai chiefs also became official Zamindars under the Permanent Settlement (Bengal Regulation 1793) who paid annual rent of their lands to the treasury in cash (Chatterjee 1993: 153-154).

Karlsson observed that "tea came to trigger changes that had far-reaching consequences for the region as a whole, including large-scale transformation of environment.... A vast landmass was cleared of forests and planted with tea seedlings in straight rows, thus reshaping the landscape into a disciplined, mono crop plantation" (Karlsson 2011: 31). " Most of these areas were declared off the limits of the tea planters through the 'so-called Inner Line System" (Karlsson 2011: 32). The concept of wasteland was confusing but included, as Chakraborty stated, highlands, forests, marshes, *chars,* land covered with grass and reed and/or any other uninhabited area. The colonial administrators "wished to bring these so-called wastelands under the purview of the sovereign authority by using force and using the twin principles of *res nullius* and *terra nullius* and found nothing unusual in pre-fixing 'waste' to any uninhabited and/or unused land and its eventual appropriation for revenue generation" (Chakraborty 2008: 192-3).

The Zamindari system introduced in Goalpara patronised a section of the affluent families (jotedars) who accumulated huge surplus through the idyllic process of rent appropriation from the farmers. It is from this section of the people that the first generation elites emerged as social and political leaders of the tribal and the semi-tribal communities. The British adopted the Assam Land Revenue Regulation of 1886 in the Manipur valley and the Chin Hills Regulation in the hill areas where in place of land revenue, hill house tax at the rate of Rs. 3 was charged. In Manipur, the valley areas were the main source of revenue, although the Cadastral Survey during 1958-1970 also included 12 villages in the hill district of Churachandpur with a reported area of 20,762.26 acres (Ray 1991: 168-171) as revenue villages.

Manipur was seen as a strategic zone of the eastern frontier and its utility depended upon its natural resources and the efficiency of its military force. (Pamberton 2000: 48). A similar arrangement was made in Assam for capture of land, mineral and water resources. The revenue from export goods included "stick lac, moon silk, moonga cloth, manjeet, black peeper, cotton, ivory, bell metal vessals, mustard seed, iron hoes, thaikol fruits" (Pamberton 2000: 80-81). The vast tract of unoccupied and fertile land in Sylhet attracted the colonials to extend the Permanent Settlement for revenue purposes, the improvement of which was made principally due to detachment of Sylhet Light Infantry stationed there (Pamberton 2000: 201, 202).

In 1886, the law of 'Landlord and Tenant' converted the communal land of Tripura into individual property that deprived the ordinary tribal people. The *jhumia* colony scheme acquired 26,101 hectares of land and was allotted to the immigrants from Bangladesh. Over a period of time, the immigrant settlers further accelerated the process of expropriation of the lands of the tribal farmers (Nongkynrih 2009: 22-23). The Khasi chiefs had the authority over the subjects, not over the lands. The British imposed only House tax, and except for the permanently cultivated lands in the hills, no land revenue was imposed and no land settlement took place. So, the extent of government authority was not precise. Land in the Khasi Hills was, thus, the absolute property of the cultivators

(Chaube 1999: 59-61). The British purchased and acquired some lands as the tenant of *Ri Kynti* owners through the Land Acquisition Act of 1894. There were 31 such villages in the Khasi hills known as British villages and some more areas of Shillong city were taken at different periods as cantonment land, normal area, administered area protected forest area, etc (Chakrabarti and Changsun 2004: 108).

In the Jaintia Hills, the British made a series of changes in the land system after 1835. In 1859, Bengali Amins were sent to measure the hals of Raj lands, lands of the Dolois and the subordinate officers. In 1860, house tax of Re. 1 was imposed on the villagers; in 1867, orders were issued for measurement of all cultivation lands in Jaintia Hills; in 1882, an inquiry was made into the land tenure system, the report of which was submitted in 1884, by Mr. Heath. He set forth the possible schemes for taxation on lands; in 1884, government orders were issued; in 1885, an inquiry was made in the plots of Raj land; in 1886, forms of *chitha* and *jamabandi* were invented and the Dolois were appointed as collectors of revenue; in 1901, a decennial lease system was introduced and these lands were leased out to private holders on rent; in 1916, the owners of hali land either limited their claims to permanent terraced lands with good terrace or they included in their claim land in valleys which was intermittently cultivated and on which small rough banks or terrace had been rapidly and cheaply made; in 1929, on intermittently cultivated lands, rice was grown with bone meal yearly and terraces were improved and in 1933, government orders were issued for allotment of 33.33 per cent in the area (hali land) to cover any margin of error in calculation. Besides, land revenue was collected from the Garo hills, a small area of Sadiya and Baliapara Frontier Tract and Naga Hills as well (Cantle 2008-09: 107-117; Bareh 1985: 269; Mittal Publications 1984: 53).

Most of the hill areas of the region were thickly forested where forest, not agriculture, could yield quick buck and handsome revenue and profit. The colonials resorted to timber trade and plantation of commercial species. The ever-green forests of Cachar were felled. In 1896, Dhaleswari Reserved Forest of 22164 acres was deforested; Sonai Reserve was deforested and 1800 acres of area was immediately settled; huge areas were settled for cultivation on taxation basis (Bhattacharjee 1996: 164-165). The Hill areas were not taxable. House tax, dao tax and grazing duty were collected from them. The British discovered rubber in 1862, which the traders from Bengal collected from the hill people in the important transit stations of Cachar district. An import duty of Rs. 10 per maund was imposed on rubber brought from Manipur and the Lushai Hills. They also captured elephant tusks and opium for revenue generation through issue of license (Bhattacharjee 1996: 169-170).

Although land augmentation was another mode of accumulation, in Northeast India it was not much possible due to the terrain and 'land fixity' and limited output. This was also because "the products of this land was *sui generis* and could not be produced elsewhere" (Patnaik 2014: 9). The other strategy adopted by the colonial state was therefore, "imposition of 'income deflation' on the population to squeeze local demand, either to obtain the goods needed for metropolitan capitalism, or to divert tropical land away from its existing use to produce goods required by metropolitan capitalism" (Patnaik 2014: 10). To break the *sui generis* character of land product, the colonials introduced cash crop that was labour light. This squeezed income, restricted local demand of food crops and caused forced income deflation. Deindustrialisation and the colonial tax system were the other instruments for income deflation and reducing local absorption of goods needed in the metropolis (Patnaik 2014: 9-10). The basic industries established in Northeast India were the extractive industries like coal, timber, limestone etc. that served the metropolis which also squeezed income and food security of the local tribal people.

Post-Colonial Trends in the North East

The unimodular land reforms agenda of the post-colonial Indian state was imposed on the shifting cultivation areas. The customary land ownership system received a marginal berth in the land reform agenda while the state arraigned the hill cultivators for surplus yielding cash crop cultivation. Amidst the backdrop of contradictory debates of the wasteful perspective and the efficiency perspective of shifting cultivation, the Indian state sided with the former and undertook a series of policies and programmes for weaning the tribal people away from the practice of shifting cultivation. In this connection, we briefly examine three important reports:

(i) In the 'Report of the Inter-Ministerial National Task Force on Rehabilitation of Shifting Cultivation Areas', Government of India encouraged cash cropping on shifting cultivation land. The fallow management was brought within the larger framework of forest management in which a pilot project was recommended for cultivation of the best-fit species in agro-forestry. For successful fallow management, individual land tenure or tenure in favour of a group of households were required for the pilot project. This privileged the new middle class from among the tribals of the region, who took advantage of the loopholes of the institutional arrangements and concentrated communal land in alarming proportions.

(ii) The 'Report of the National Commission on Backward Areas in Northeast India' recommended individualisation of communal resources. This led to a gradual but steady process of depeasantisation and landlessness among the tribal people. The Dhebar Commission found inadequate knowledge of the authorities about the real conditions of the tribal areas and the complicated legislation for this state of affairs.

(iii) The 'Draft Report of the Committee on State Agrarian Relations and Unfinished Task of Land Reforms' upheld the importance of Common Property Resources and found diverse use of these resources for urbanisation, industrialisation, mining, developmental projects and for residential/homestead purposes which annihilated

> the communal property perennially. While privatisation of communal land was reinforced by the state policy of metropolitan growth paradigm, common property resources were patronized as a necessary category.

The error of equating of common property resources with communal property has always been problematic. Roy Burman demystified the error and said that "common property resources should always be seen as a transitional stage between open access to resources and private property, on the assumption that every agent is actuated only by self-interest" and even "the protagonists of private property resources, namely the classical and neo-classical economists, had recognised the need for and role of CPRs" (Roy Burman: 1987; Kadekodi 2004: 14). On the other hand, the communal property has always been subject to primitive accumulation and/or accumulation by dispossession.

In this framework a few modes of dispossession of communal land resources in Northeast India are discussed below:

a) Dispiriting Petty Production

The petty production mode of shifting cultivation did not receive official patronage for its non-surplus nature, non-transformability of the subsistence farmers, weak structure and system, failure in commodity production, market imperfection and for the absence of economy of scale. The mood for dispiriting petty production of shifting cultivation came from the need of an economy of scale, which the non-affluent and subsistence farming class could not afford to bring about. In India, dispiriting petty production became the common alibi of colonial projects and the post-colonial economic reconstruction projects. In Northeast India, the more recent policy attack on shifting cultivation came from the Draft Perspective Plan for Development of the Forestry Sector, 2007-08 to 2012-13. Among other things, the Draft held shifting cultivation responsible for land degradation and soil impoverishment. Grazing in forest was held responsible for soil compaction, damage of forest plantation, natural regeneration and for threat to forest conservation. In 1961, the National Council of Applied Economic Research blamed shifting cultivation in Tripura for steady destruction of the remaining forests'. 'The Government of India, in addition to the 'forest policy', also adopted a separate 'soil conservation' policy in Tripura on the ground that shifting cultivation was causing soil erosion. In 1955, L.M. Srikant, the Commissioner for Scheduled Castes and Tribes, suggested that on account of the great national importance of forests and conservation of soil and economic development of the tribal people, it was necessary to help the hill people practising shifting cultivation to switch over to permanent cultivation.

The Draft National Policy for Tribals mentioned the need for training, extension and sensitisation for the tribals for alternative economic activities. This policy was not well-conceived by the authorities as they had inadequate knowledge about the real conditions of the tribal areas. This exposed their vapidity in understanding the basic economics of shifting cultivation and the incipient collective consciousness of the people associated with this practice (Ray 2005: 171). Though the Policy prohibited transfer of land from tribal to non-tribals, it stipulated assigning the patta system for forest tribal villagers for the land under their tillage since ages. It also stipulated for access of the tribals to village land records. Both these concepts were alien to the tribals. The policy also required the state to launch development projects and to take adequate care to keep the tribal lands intact and when not possible, allot land to them even before a project could take off. It is ironical that the Draft policy was conceptualized in line with the mainstream agrarian epistemology of the official economists and the policy makers. They ignored the fact that the tenural mode does not fit in with the dominant 'usufruct mode' in the shifting cultivation economy (Ray 2005: 172). This ready-made solution of land allotment also did not take into account the very land-based cultural ontology of the tribal people.

To handle the problem of shifting cultivation, the Draft National Policy also promoted rationalisation of land tenure by giving the tribals the right to land ownership and by encouraging them to raise cash crops and horticultural plantations. Rationalisation of the land tenure system also did not fit in with the dominant 'usufruct mode' of shifting cultivation economy (Ray 2005: 172) and the community process involved in it. The National Afforestation Programme of the MoEF, GoI and the National Mission on Horticulture targeted the *jhum* lands and appropriated the same for non-agricultural and commercial use.

In Tripura, the process of dispiriting petty production started during Maharaja Bir Chandra Manikya, who undertook a comprehensive scheme for plough cultivation in the hills. Under this scheme, a memorandum was issued that geared the entire state machinery towards assembling the villagers for demonstration of plough cultivation by skilled cultivators brought from Bengal. Subsidised input supply, financial grants and technical assistance were provided to the royal subjects. Modern demonstrational farms were also set up in localities, where these types of support were not available. In 1953, a pilot programme for the settlement of the *Jhumias* was undertaken in the Belonia Subdivision. At the end of 1955, the scheme was made extensive. *Jhumia* settlement colonies were established with land, money grants and cash subsidies. Various facilities were provided for cottage industry and education for the settlers. Alternatively, about four acres of land were to be allocated to each family to promote settled cultivation. A regulated *jhuming* right, called the '*Toungya* system' within the reserved forests was also granted (Barooah 2007: 50-51; Chaube 1976: 213-214).

In Karbi Anglong, the state government and the District Council encouraged wet cultivation and individuation of communal land. There was the great role of the outsiders in the spread of wet cultivation in whose instance individual ownership of land was promoted on the tribal lands. The administration also promoted individual ownership through establishing settled and permanent villages. The District Council was instrumental in opening up a few model villages of a minimum of 50 houses conducive for planning and development. In pursuance of this model, each family was provided with 5 to 10 bighas of well-irrigated land, including 1 bigha of homestead land. The administration undertook certain schemes for cash crops, horticulture, rubber and coffee as alternatives to *jhum*. The Assam Plantation Crops Development Corporation gave a fillip to the plantation programme and the government of Assam undertook a big project for *Jhumia* rehabilitation (Bathari 2009: 149-150). As alternative measures to shifting cultivation, various schemes for commercial plantations were undertaken and were included within *Jhumia* Settlement Schemes. In Tripura, the schemes of plantation included coffee (Coffee arborea), arecanut (Areca catechu), black pepper (Piper nigrum), rubber (Hevea braziliensis), betel (Piper betel), kathal (Artocarpus heterophyllus) and orange (in North Tripura) (Gupta 2000: 621-623).

Das's study of the land system of Mizoram in 1986 found that the major part of the cultivated land was covered by *jhum* land. (Das 1986: 139). Subsequently, orchards or fruit trees increased the demand for passes for "garden-lands" so much so that during 1981-83, 3150 passes for garden-land were issued by the Directorate of Revenue and Settlement in Aizawl and Lunglei districts (Das 1986: 145). The Lushai Hills District (Jhuming) Regulation 1954, The Pawi-Lakher Region (Jhum) Regualation 1956, The Pawi-Lakher Autonomous District (Jhum Regulation) Act 1983 and The Pawi Lakher Region (Jhum) Regulation 1986 were also critical in dispiriting shifting cultivation. Das also found that The Pawi-Lakher Region (Jhum) Regulation altered the system of lottery and introduced allotment to the holders in the last cycle of *jhuming* that provided some kind of permanent right in the *jhum* plot that would ultimately become heritable, transferable and valuable property (Das 1986: 151).

In Mizoram, the New Land Use Policy was adopted with the major objective of dissuading the farmers from shifting cultivation. Some of the core objectives of the NLUP included : keeping 60 per cent of Mizoram's total land area under rain forest; weaning away farmers from destructive *jhum* practices and assist the *jhumia* workforce in being employed in sustainable economic venture to create productive assets in each family and improve income for both urban and rural poor through sustainable farming, non-farming, micro enterprises including promotion and modernisation of small-scale and cottage industries.

In a Seminar on Land Use Planning and Watershed Management for Control of Shifting Cultivation, organised by the Soil and Water Conservation Department (State Land Use Board), Nagaland, the major recommendations for formulating the 8th Five Year Plan proposal on *jhum* control, included, among other things, farm technology (mixed farming); alternative to *jhum* cultivation based on scientific land use; optimal use of soil and water; cash crop; high production and high economic return from plantation of rubber; ridge and furrow technique; bench terracing, contour bunding; three-tier system (improved varieties of crop suitable for zone upto 30 per cent slope on terraced land, horticulture on slope on 30 to 40 per cent by making contour bunds and silvi-pastoral system on steep slopes beyond 40 per cent). Bulldozing land for construction of terrace supplementing with adequate manures and fertilisers for fertility restoration and restructuring land tenure system to suit technology adoption on watershed basis were recommended. In the 1970s, the North Eastern Council urged the planning for resource management through expanding scope of commercial plantation of tea, rubber, coffee, oil-bearing seeds, livestock and poultry, fishery, etc. The Council identified among other things, the community land system, shifting cultivation, and subsistence agriculture as the constraints on the way. It was stated that the strategy of agricultural development should be based on the twin principle of self-sufficiency within the state and development of high value and low volume weight farm products for sale outside the state (Patel 1978: 96-100).

In the 1980s, development priorities of Arunachal Pradesh were laid on agriculture and allied activities and communication. Introduction of the scientific method of cultivation, diversification of agriculture, settled cultivation, terrace cultivation, combining traditional *jhuming* with permanent cultivation, combining afforestation in the form of improved *jhuming* in the upper hill region were also encouraged. As per the recommendations of S.M.S. Shivaraman (Advisor of the Planning Commission), leguminous crops were planted and trial centres were opened, the area of which was recommended for increase. Nandriu variety of banana, Singapore variety of jackfruit and Bangkok variety of silk were also recommended. These came as important directives on the Administration of NEFA-1967 (Chowdhury 1983: 232-234).

It was assumed that capitalist agriculture could be possible on elimination of shifting cultivation. So the non-surplus economy of shifting cultivation came under serious attack both by the state and the market which created a strong policy alibi for commercial crop production. Later on, the neo-liberal state further dismissed shifting cultivation as a petty mode of production. The cumulative policy attacks on shifting cultivators increased their dependency on the state and the market and were compelled to adopt the predatory mode of production. In this process, they were entrapped invariably in the nexus of the agricultural marketing agencies, middlemen, moneylenders and the agro-product industries at local, national and global levels. Dispiriting petty production also involved a drastic scramble in the extant concept of labour and its non-class connotations resulting in degradation of the petty producers to daily-rated wage labour and of their collective identity and ontology.

The proscriptive policies against petty production were not formulated after a careful review of history and economic anthropology of shifting cultivation. All that petty production could do was not bad. Ranajit Guha wrote that in 18th century England and France, the small holdings (*petty production*) were well recognised as these were the essential conditions for large-scale capitalist enterprise in agriculture. Above the abstract theory, it was also common experience that agricultural improvement in 18th century England had been the work of a number of pioneers, publicists, country gentlemen, owner occupiers and large tenant farmers rather than large land holders (Islam 1979: 79-80). The abstract theory was backed by the state to become real. In Northeast India, the state did not do that and instead ruled it out straightaway.

b) Land Augmentation

Increase in land augmentation (increase in the area of land), land augmenting investment and technological progress in irrigation constituted another mode. This required substantial state expenditure in improving the capacity of public works, like the Canal Colony scheme of Punjab. In the hills of Northeast India, however, land augmentation of this kind did not take place because of the *sui generis* nature of the products. But introduction of cash crop broke the *sui generis* character of the land product in the hill region.

The export-oriented plantation economy in Northeast India emerged due to augmentation on which European finance capital could operate. Certain specific land spaces in Assam, North Bengal and Southern India were identified for commercial enclaves for tea plantation in the 19th century. The plantation system resulted in structural transformation of the modes of production from a peasant mode to an expanded cash crops production system (Viswanathan and Shah 2013: 36). Some lands in the Adi areas of Arunachal were occupied for tea cultivation without a fixed land boundary. In an application for land for plantation in the middle of the 19th century, the boundary specified was to the East: as far as will complete the area; to the West: Road to Bhooi Punji; and to the North and South: the high hills. These unspecified boundaries created suspicion among the Adis of their lands being threatened with usurpation on which they had customary and traditional rights. This happened particularly in areas bordering the present-day Arunachal Pradesh, Nagaland and Mizoram (Dutta 1986: 139). This was one example of primitive accumulation through land augmentation in the hills of Northeast India.

c) State/District Council vis-a-vis Customary Law

Territorial autonomy, not, land alienation, was the first love of the autonomy movement in the hills for the District Council. Although the Bordoloi Sub Committee was greatly concerned with the issue of the protection of tribal land and the Sixth Schedule to the Constitution of India entrusted power to make law relating to land and forests to the District and Autonomous Councils, the first generation councillors did not problematise the issue of land alienation in the tribal areas as much as they did the issue of territorial autonomy. The legislative competence of the ADC being thoroughly limited, the ADCs could not make any major breakthrough in regard to land legislation to really protect the tribal land resources. But as the ADC was also a state creation, the state-ADC unholy nexus led to land alienation. Policy protection of tribals was stymied by usurpation of the same as strategic requirement of the state what Roy Burman called 'state-sponsored feudalism'.

In some tribal societies on the other hand, the traditional land holding system was patronised by the state. For example, by custom the Kuki chiefs were not the owners of land (they were only trustees), but the Directorate of Settlement and Land Records of Manipur in the 7th Five Year Plan described them as virtual owners and proposed to extend survey and settlement operations in the hills by pursuing the chiefs. Besides all persons having land pattas from the government, were recognised as land owners as per the Land Revenue and Land Records Act 1960. As the community is not recognised as a 'person', the chiefs, who were thrown out after independence by the tribals as colonial legacies were called back by the same people to prevent the state's takeover of all lands. In some areas, where people refused to part with land, the officials settled these with the chiefs (Roy Burman 1987). This exposed the indecision and confusion of the state on settling the exact nature of the land ownership of the chiefs.

In the Jaintia Hills, the traditional power and control of land by the *Siyem* and Doloi was scotched by the British. They converted all the Rajhali (private lands of the erstwhile *Siyem* of Jaintia) into government land. The users of the land were given individual pattas for a limited period of ten years subject to tax payment. They divided the land into (i) Hali lands or irrigated paddy lands; (ii) Highlands or private lands like Hali private lands; (iii) unclaimed lands or government wasteland. The Hali lands were sub-divided into: Raj lands, Service lands, Village Puja lands and Private lands. After Indian independence, the management and control of Hali lands was transferred to the District Council, which initiated some changes. 'The Jaintia Hills Autonomous District Council replaced the old periodic lease of Raj Hali lands by a new form of lease that was made applicable to all Hali lands. The period of the lease was not mentioned in the patta but it said that the land is settled with the lessee'. The lease patta granted by the District Council was a lease in perpetuity on which a landholder had permanent, heritable and transferable right of use and occupancy. The new regulation gave tax-free patta to the lessee (Nongkynri 2009: 28-29).

The Report of the Land Reforms Commission for Khasi Hills, defined the *Ri Raid* (community land) under the management and control of the community and such land came completely within the jurisdiction of the community concerned. The community may be (a) a village for a village *Ri Raid* land, (b) a group of villages constituting the *Raid* for *Ri Raid* land of the *Raid*, (c) the *Elaka* itself for the *Ri Raid* land. Describing the right to use the *Ri Raid*, the Report said that if a person vacates or does not make use of the land under his actual occupation for three consecutive years, the land reverts to the community, village, *Raid* or *Elaka* as the case might be. There is no proprietary, heritable or transferable right on the *Ri Raid* land. It further elaborated that the right to use the *Ri Raid* is based on the membership of the person in the specific village. A person belonging to Khasi society does not enjoy the right to use the above said land, if that person is not a member of the village, *Raid* or *Elaka* (a cluster of more than one village). Non–Khasis are not allowed to use the *Ri Raid*. The village headman or the head of the *Raid* does not have the authority to grant permission for such use to a non-Khasi. According to their customary law, community land is collective property and the residents of the village are users of the land. To understand the practice of community land, a few examples were discussed that provide the 'field-view' of the Commission (Nongkynri 2009: 25).

The Land Reforms Commission in Meghalaya admitted that the time honoured system of administration of *Raid* land is no longer observed. Indiscriminate issuing of pattas by the *elaka* authorities caused loss of land to the real tillers of soil. Outsiders of the village or *Raid* obtained pattas and grabbed the land and the villagers or people of the *Raid* lost land. The Commission, however, was of the view that in the interest of the landowning class themselves in particular and of the rest of the Khasi population in general, the customs and usages governing the administration of *Ri Kynti* land be systematised and codified. Three important points of the Report were: (a) The *Ri Kynti* in the olden days took rent in kind for seasonal cultivation of the land by other people. (b) It is as much a fact of ancient custom for *Ri Kynti* owners to have full proprietary right over the lands. (c) A Khasi *Ri Kynti* owner does have the sanction of custom to levy rent from a person, who takes land to lease for seasonal cultivation. This practice was in vogue before the advent of the British (Sen 1987: 95, 97). On the other hand, Section 14 of The Assam Land and Revenue Regulation 1886 stipulated that the state government may make rules for allotment from the land referred to in Section 12 (power to make rules for the disposal of government lands and ejectment therefrom of unauthorised occupiers) for the use of tribes or families practising *jhum* or migratory cultivation, of areas suitable for such cultivation, of sufficient extent, and situated in localities reasonably convenient, for the purpose of the persons to whom they are allotted, and for regulating and controlling the enjoyment of lands so allotted by persons permitted to resort to the same. But no rules have hitherto been framed by the state government under this section (Saikia 1986: 73).

The autonomous district council in Mizoram brought

significant changes in the traditional land management and control. In Mizoram, a Land Settlement Certificate was issued to the people for permanent settlement, subject to approval of Mizo District (Agricultural Land) Act 1963 and the Mizo District (Agricultural Land) Rules 1971. The same Act and Rule were also applicable to a pass or permit granted before the commencement of the Act of 1963 requiring that such a pass or permit be registered afresh for grant of fresh annual patta on payment of the prescribed fee. The Act allowed two types of allotment: temporary and permanent. The Jhuming Regulation Act of 1954 and the Mizo District Forest Act of 1953 came to govern the settlement of land tenure system of *jhum* and forest lands of Mizoram. Assessment of land revenue is done under the Lushai hills District (Revenue Assessment) Regulation 1953 (Barooah 2001a). In the Garo Hills, Jhum Regulation of 1954, Garo Hills Autonomous District (Land & Revenue) Regulation 1954, District Council Forest Act 1958, *A' Wil* Fees Act, 1960, and the Land Reforms Branch of the District Council empowered the District Council so much in the matters relating to all aspects of land and forest so that these amounted to scotching the customary rules and practices. The District Council took over the power of realizing *A' Wil* fees themselves instead of by the Nokmas and shared only 25 per cent of the same with them. While the District Council exploited the forest resources on silvicultural principle, and on royalty-payment-permanent-coupon system, it allowed the *A'khing* members to access forest products only for domestic consumption. The District Council also took up plantation and afforestation of commercial species and alienated the traditional *Mahari* ownership and in its place promoted individual rights. The Jhum Control Scheme of the State Soil Conservation Department also changed the traditional land use pattern. This led to growing privatisation of land for commercial farming (Kar 1982: 239-243).

The Chakma Autonomous District (Agricultural Land) Act-1982, empowered the District Council to control and allot land and for the improvement of agriculture within the Chakma Autonomous District. Before this act, the land holding system was based on Section 4 (3) of Pawi Lakher Region (Agricultural Land) Act 1959. Under this section, temporary passes and Permanent Settlement Certificates (PSC) were issued to the people. All other land registrations passed by the PLRC namely, Pawi Lakher (Land and Revenue) Act 1960 and Pawi Lakher (Revenue Assessment) Regulation 1960, were applied to the land system of Chakma district. But now all lands are governed by the Chakma Autonomous District (Agricultural Land) Act 1982, which issues periodic patta and PSC. The act provides initially for periodic patta convertible to patta for permanent settlement only after the Lapse of three years from the date of issue of the periodic patta. The Act of 1982, applies to all lands within the district, except the land included in the state reserve forest. The lands of all government and public roads and all lands of the Council came under reserved forest (Barooah 2001b: 21-39).

Among the Mara tribe in the Saiha district of Mizoram, the village land was the chief's estate. Ownership was permanent and transferable for him. It was hereditary and was handed down from generation to generation. The villagers had no right to part with any part of the village land for *jhum* cultivation without the permission of the chief. As the chief owned the village land, he received certain dues from all the products from the land. He also settled all the cases of selling and disposing of land or the cases of village land disputes. After independence, the Autonomous District Council of Aizawl-Lungleih area and Autonomous Regional Council in Pawi-Lakher Region were established. These introduced a totally new pattern of land holding system among the Maras. Under the changed system, the entire land came to belong to the District Council in Mizoram. An individual needed to seek an allotment order from the concerned authority in order to possess it. For homestead or cultivable lands, one needed to obtain a certificate of allotment either in the form of annual or periodic patta. The District Council in collaboration with the village councils, came to execute allotment of land to the villagers. Lands were allocated under different systems, for example, *jhum* lands were allocated with a periodic patta for a certain period of time only. Some people were issued simple passes, whereby they obtained a temporary right of use and occupancy over a plot of land for a specified period, prescribed in the pass. A person could be issued LSC on showing the details of boundary areas and after assessing the revenue to be paid annually.

All types of lands in Mara district were not transferable except the land held under LSC or patta. Periodic patta and *jhum* land could not be transferred. There was a general restriction imposed by the Mizo District (Transfer of Land) Act, 1963 and by the corresponding acts of Pawi, Lakher and Chakma district on sale, mortgage, lease, barter, gift or lands otherwise transferred by a tribal to a non-tribal or by a non-tribal to another non-tribal, except with previous permission of the administrator. A Mara requires the consent of the District Council for transfer of LSC land (Barooah 2001c: 23-34).

In the Garo hills, the changes in the customary practices of *A'khing* land marked a sharp shift towards permanent cultivation; Lands acquired by reclamation from the jungle or by transfer from the previous owner in the form of inheritance; annual patta issued by the Garo Hills Autonomous District Council, making the patta holders owners of that land; There are some cases of migrant non–tribals occupying lands with a legitimate patta issued by the District Council; and Families and individuals are disposing of it. In some cases *A'Khing* land is gifted and mortgaged; Commercialisation of land-based activities, mal-distribution of landed possessions, institution of paid labour, mal-distribution of income among the fellow villages and loss of reciprocity in socio-economic relations; Acquisition of land in and around Tura for government and semi-government purposes against large sums of compensation to the Nokmas (Nongkynrih 2009: 29-31).

In Manipur, the *sui generis* nature of District Council outside the Sixth Schedule was conspicuous. But the trend is different from that in Meghalaya. In Manipur, the main grievances of the hill people relating to land grabbing was against the MLR&LR Act 1960, which was extended to the hill areas and many tribal villages were converted into revenue villages in the hill districts of the state. From the early 1970s, therefore, popular resistance against the Act of 1960, was started in the hills. The hill people considered that the hill areas should be brought under the Sixth Schedule of the Constitution that could save the tribal land from being taken over or grabbed in spite of the fact that the District Council under the Sixth Schedule reserves the right of monopoly control over all lands, including, community lands. In the same way, the land reforms acts as state made acts, also empowered the state to have monopoly right over land. Within this contesting institutions, when the MLR&LR (Sixth Amendment) Bill proposed to insert a new Section 13 (B) stating that "the state government may make rules for regulating and controlling *jhum* or migratory cultivation for protection of environment, catchments areas of irrigation, hydro-electric and water supply project and prevention of landslides near national and state highways and major district roads," it ignited the tribal communities to intensify their demand for expelling the MLR & LR Act in the hills and the same Sixth Schedule was invoked for all the hill districts of Manipur. In this movement, the All Tribal Students' Union of Manipur (ATSUM) took the lead role (Shimray 2008: 110-111).

d) Development-Induced Land Alienation

In the current development paradigm, there is growing surge of land capture for urbanisation, industrialisation, commercialisation and for accommodating the population pressure on the urban areas in the hills of Northeast India. The major developmental initiatives were evinced on three major resources of the region, including water, mineral and forest resources. Development –induced land alienation has increased either because of growing industrial use of communal land or plantation of commercial species on land or because of growing mining operations in the hills. These initiatives led to capture of communal land resources of the region. In the tribal areas, the specific problem emerged from the customary basis of land holding as the owners could not produce any documentary evidence to defend their land from being acquisitioned by the state or the corporate. Water resources have become the major target of the power sector investors and investments have been made in several areas of the Northeast for hydro-electricity generation. This has caused massive dispossession of the communal land in different parts of the region, particularly, in Arunachal Pradesh. This has also problematised the current development discourse and the state policies of opening up and de-regulation and provoked civil society activism in the region. The discourse is centred essentially around the current paradigm of development. The modern state (representing the private interest and the corporate cronies) viewed such development as most essential in public interest, whereas, the tribal communities found such development as a major threat not only to their economy and society but also to their 'public interest'. Displacement has been the inevitable fate of the community, whereas, annihilation of the social space as a result of development infrastructure invited the doomsday of the tribal society in Northeast India.

Secondly, the alibi for 'national interest' has always denied the social, economic and existential interests of the smaller communities. But what is small for the state is not small for the small communities, some of whose demographic figure is as small as that of a small locality of the big state. The repulsion of the tribal communities against the statist paradigm of development has ignited the media and the civil society in Meghalaya (mining operation uranium, coal); in Manipur (hydro-electricity, mining operation, forest and sanctuaries); in Arunachal Pradesh (hydro-power, commercial plantation); in Tripura (commercial plantation, hydropower, forest, Wet-rice cultivation); in Nagaland (terrace cultivation, mining, plantation) and in Assam (plantation, hydro-power). The development induced displacement has become more critical in the Northeast due to the predatory policies and retreat of the state from its welfare role, its pro-market approach and its commitment towards private property regime that have led to adopt energy policy, mineral policy, plantation policy that offered to foreign direct investors and private corporations, enormous amount of policy subsidies in their favour.

e) Elite Capture of Land

The role the tribal elites played in resource dispossession were extremely critical in Northeast India. Initially, these elites were the chiefs/headmen of the tribal villages; the first generation educated; the scrupulous power seekers and the 'Actually Powerful'. They sat on the saddle of traditional culture and kinship relationship. Their strategic social location and spectator posture of the community, legitimised their acts of resource capture. The colonials took such an elite route and instrumentalised them for larger misappropriation of community resources. Referring to Khasi Hills, Baden Powell wrote that "the greatest part of the hills consists of estates of the chiefs. They pay no tribute, but have resigned their mines, minerals, forests, elephants, and natural products, and receive half the profits from these sources. ....The people are extremely well-to-do, and make money by trade in the staple which the hills produce" (Powell 1990: 455) Similarly, in the Mizo society, the chiefs, locally known as 'Lal', became actually powerful from the time of receiving *Ramri Leikha* from the British. The Kuki chiefs became powerful too, after receiving the settlement right from the British and so on.

But these elites could not grow into the affluent enterprising and industrial class. Lack of capital formation and market availability did not allow an industrially affluent society to emerge in this region although these elites bettered their fate out of land resources, embarking on their customary position. The liberal paradigm of development, emergence of private property regime, monetisation of the tribal economy, trade and business opportunities allured this class. The lesson they imbibed from the modernist paradigm was that of accumulation, hitherto uncommon in the tribal society. Thus, although they did not formally dis-member themselves from the community, their hedonistic pursuits made them virtually secede from the community. This we may term as 'secession of the rich'. This was the threshold for the emergence of landed elites in the region.

In the Khasi and Jaintia tribes, Sen found emergence of absentee landlordism that had made one section of people the sharecroppers and the landless agricultural labourers. A few memoranda submitted to the Land Reform Commission in Meghalaya mentioned the exorbitant land rent as a result of which the landless people were rack rented by the *Ri Kynti* owners, who collected 30 or 40 per cent of the produce of the land if taken in kind or an equivalent, if in cash. The final result being that land came to be concentrated in only a small percentage of absentee landlords, while the overwhelming majority became landless. Privatisation of land happened also due to encroachment of land by the powerful section of the community. Sen further observed that, their society "in the pre-British days may be described as a society in the process of evolution into a more elaborate state form. It had been gradually *deviating* from the basic characteristics of a tribal society and emerging as a sort of peasant society with most of its functional ramifications, although some of those elements characterised a feudal order. In this intermediary stage, there appeared a rudimentary form of social stratification with all the economic and political implications". He noted, "the administration of both Khasi states and Jaintia kingdom was, therefore, so structured as to suit the need of a stratified society, which was not as rigid as obtained in class-based societies. Even then, it was such as to suggest the existence of a landed gentry, who would naturally wield political power. There are also reasons to believe that this landed gentry would use the customary land tenure in a fashion, which would help perpetuate their rule"(Sen 1987: 94,98).

In the Khasi society, the *Bakhraws* were the landed aristocrats belonging to the powerful clans, who usurped the *Ri Raid* lands. Nongbri noted that this class made land private property through permanent improvement. Occupancy right favoured the rich, when the poor farmers could not improve the land due to resource scarcity. The rich could employ a large number of workers and inputs for better harvest. They opted for cash cropping. Such people were the middle class or the upper middle class, who continued to live in the towns and gave their lands to sharecroppers for cultivation and appropriated a share of the produce. Thus occupancy right caused class cleavage between those who own and occupy and those who do not (Nongbri 1987: 78).

In Meghalaya, Misra wrote, "with the increase of population, improvement of transport facilities and growing demand for cash crops, there was a marked tendency for persons to occupy and claim as much *Raid* land as they could. People possessing ready cash were apt to enclose big areas in a *Raid* land to the exclusion of everybody else in the village. The traditional social system became conducive to allow the *Bakhrawbatri* the much needed primitive accumulation. The customary land tenure recognised the permanent and heritable right of a person over the *Raid* land if it was not kept fallow for three years at a stretch. Thus, the *Bakhrawbatri* having the necessary capital and legal sanction acquired as much private land as they thought could be profitably cultivated" (Misra 1989: 690). Chakraborty found a similar trend of usurpation of *Ri Raid* land by the tribal elites. Cultivation of cash crops and horticulture; land leased-in by outsiders for mining operation and monetisation of the economy led to the emergence of tribal elites and private property (Chakraborty 2008: 70-71). Patricia Mukim blamed the customary law itself for privatisation of community land. She found male appropriation of community lands that are administered by the *Dorbar Shnong/Dorbar Raid* (Village Council) or *Dorbar Hima* (Chieftainship) and *Rangbah Shnong/Sordar* whose heads are men alone. They, in collaboration with other members of their council, converted large areas of land into privately owned land. This happens, especially, in the case of forest land. In this process, the women's status in Khasi society reversed from owners of land to mere inheritors of ancestral property with all its social encumbrances (Mukim 2009: 49-50).

In the similar way, Ms. Lyngdoh found that the *Siyems* and *Ki Mantri* begun to realise the profit by issuing patta to *Ri Kynti* land. Gradually the *Siyem*, the elected head of the people, began to use his power by issuing *Ri Raid* land, (that belongs to the community) flouting the customary law. In the customary law, *Ri Kynti* (private) land was the privilege only of some clans. But in course of time, people begun to develop vested interest upon the *Ri Raid* land, claiming them as their own private possession. That is how, the *Ri Kynti* of the present day came into existence. As the number of people as well as clan increased, so also *Ri Kynti* land multiplied and today it appears with different names in different places (Lyngdoh 1992).

Karlsson found that a distinct interest group called the 'Land and Forest Owners Association' came up and showed concern about their private property rights by asserting them as 'prudent resource managers' and this association became the most vocal opponent to the Supreme Court ban on timber. In a letter to the Minister of Environment & Forests, Government of Meghalaya, it was stated that *jhuming* and charcoal production are a much larger environmental problem than logging is (Karlsson 2011: 110). This trend started in the Garo hills of the early 20th century colonial Assam, noted Karlsson, when a new rightist movement was started under the banner of the Sangma Movement with its leader, S.R. Sangma, against the Bijni Zamindari trespass in the Garo areas. The focus area was later expanded by including the demand for re-opening of these areas or compensation for the areas the government had declared as forest reserve and for abolishing the hated colonial practice of forced labour. It was stated that Sangma had added these issues to mobilise popular support for the land claim that he twisted into a personal one. Sangma argued that the disputed land not merely belonged to the Garos, but more precisely to his wife, Thokje Gabil Momin. Karlsson, following Ranajit Guha's term, described Sangma's strategy of turning the colonial dominance through law against itself as an example of the 'modality of inversion' (Karlsson 2011: 142-145).

In the spree of commercial plantation, wide ranging changes were observed among the Tangkhul Nagas of Manipur. Land that was traditionally classified into different categories, started losing the community character as a result of elite capture. A similar practice was found among the educated Nagas, who imbibed new ideas for improving their agriculture, various arts and crafts and exploitation of the forest resources. The economic development in Naga society caused social division of labour that served to modify the tribal organisations of settled agricultural villages (Khashim 1987: 54-64). It is noteworthy that among all these selected cases, community land was reclaimed citing the provisions of customary laws since the same permitted an individual (*Raid* family in Meghalaya for example) to lay private claim on community land if permanent changes were brought about in that piece of land. This alibi, which was traditionally permitted for a small piece of land (although the 'smallness' was unspecified), was used by the tribal elites to usurp bigger areas of communal land either through fencing or upgradation or through improvements. They made a selective interpretation of customary law for land usurpation, which was actually meant for usufruct rights. Therefore, the erstwhile temporary users now became the *de facto* landowners. Moreover, these landowners (many among them) do not cultivate themselves but lease-out land to others for cash crop cultivation and collect a land tax known as *loushan* or *luisha* from the cultivators. It is due to this that today, as Khasim wrote, in areas like Ukhrul, Hundung, Phungyar and many other places, purchasing, leasing and mortgaging the community-held land have become a common practice (Khasim 1987: 54-64).

A number of studies were made on land concentration by the tribal elites of Northeast India, particularly in Khasi-Jayantias of Meghalaya. Prominent among these studies include (Vincent, 1979) (Mathew and Nair, 1983), (Datta and Datta, 1986), (Datta, 1984) etc. exhibits that it is, thus, no longer surprising to come across a Garo or a Naga owning a thousand acres of land. Nowhere in these areas, customary practices would have permitted such concentration of land, but new linkages brought the hitherto unknown phenomenon like absentee landlordism, realisation of rent from land, sharecropping, land mortgages, landlessness and so on (Karna 1990: 30-38). Baruah found that the enterprising individuals among the Karbis come together to form committees and then with the blessings of official agencies secured land deeds either from the headman or the Autonomous District Council. The results being that 'an influential, educated and well-connected Dimasa individual owns over 700 bighas of land in the name of homestead plantations (Baruah 2005: 48-61). Similar situations have also been found among the Akas of West Kameng district of Arunachal (Fernandes and Bharali 2005) and the Angamis in Nagaland (D'Souza 2005).

Land in the Kuki tribe once created a serious controversy. The government equated the Kuki land owning system with the Zamindari system. The Kuki chiefs sent constant protest notes against the government and defended their egalitarian nature of the land ownership system. When in 1949, the Congress Committee of Manipur took a resolution against the Kuki chiefs, the latter made a strong protest against this resolution. The Kuki chiefs never regarded *changseo* and *samal* (customary tributes of rice and games) payable to the Kuki chiefs as taxes.

The government, however, tried to regulate the customary dues enjoyed by the Kuki chiefs. The money value of the customary dues was fixed at Rs. 5/plus three tins of rice. The Chief Commissioner of Manipur was, however, of the opinion that "no general rule should be laid down in this matter"(Letter of the Deputy Commissioner 1952). The Acquisition of Chiefs Rights Act 1967, also faced organised opposition from the Kuki chiefs. In 1984, the Sadar Hills Kuki Chiefs Organisation of Manipur categorically claimed that chieftainship is a vital organisation of the Kuki ethnic (group) and the chiefs' rights over their land never affected the community, rather their rights act as effective protection of tribal territory. In the hills of Manipur, the complex nature of land ownership created a lot of confusion in extension of the Manipur Land Revenue and Land Reforms Act. The original Act of 1960 was not extended to the hill areas. Section 1(2) of the Act categorically stated that 'it extends to the whole Union Territory of Manipur except the hill areas thereof'. This left the land ownership system in the hills unchanged. The Act was subsequently extended to the hill areas through Section 1 (3) of the Manipur Land Revenue and Land Reforms (Amendment) Act, 1975. During the first fifteen years, the departmental survey operation was extended over a total area of 7562 hectares in all the hill districts of Manipur. The major opposition to the extension of the Act came repeatedly from the Kuki Chiefs. The government also took an adamant stand on this issue. While the government insisted on abolition of the chieftainship system of the Kukis, the Directorate for Settlement and Land Records in Manipur, during the 7th Plan patronised them for extension of the survey operation through them. This gesture of the Directorate provided the Kuki chiefs ample opportunity to claim compensation for any land acquired in the process of cadastral survey. The Tribal Land Protection and Restoration Committee of Manipur was of the opinion that the Manipur Land Revenue and Land Reforms (Second Amendment) Act 1976 provided adequate legal safeguards against alienation of tribal lands. But even after this amendment, alienation of land continued. In a memorandum submitted to the Chief Minster, the members of the Tribal Land Protection and Restoration Committee of Manipur in 1976, expressed satisfaction over the hope of getting agricultural land for wet field purposes. But they regretted that the hill people got a negligible proportion out of the ten thousand hectares of land distributed so far. This memorandum blamed the state for alienation of land from the tribals. Alienation from the bottom was effected through sale of land by the chiefs to the non-tribals.

The Act of 1976 created apprehension that abolition of chiefs rights would lead to alienation of lands to the non-tribals. Under the provision of Section 158 (C) of the Manipur Land Revenue and Land Reforms Act, many non-tribal farmers formed farmers' cooperative societies or service cooperative societies. Many tribals mortgaged their lands with such cooperatives for a period from 3 to 6 months after the expiry of which they lost their land to the non- tribals. In this background, the members of the Tribal Land Protection and Restoration Committee defended the chiefs as protectors of land (Ray 1991b: 61-63).

The Kukis of Southern Manipur, on the other hand, were in

favour of giving up their land ownership on two conditions: (i) a compensation @ Rs. 3,000 per hectare to the Kuki chiefs in case of government acquisition of their lands for public purpose and (ii) a compensation at the rate of 5 tins per household per year be paid for a period of thirty years as customary tributes to them. The criticality was that if the chiefs were protectors of communal land, their claim of compensation trivialised their moral claim. In fact, in a petition of the Chiefs' Union of Churachandpur to the Chairman of the Hill Areas Committee, the chiefs insisted that their rights, titles, and privileges over their land should be at par with article 31 (a) of the Constitution of India. The government side also considered the Kuki chiefs as owners of land for the purpose of acquisition of land for public purpose. The government, thus, acquired 30 acres of land from some of the chiefs and individual owners for the location of Border Security Force at Thingkhangphai Lourup village and the chiefs of Thingkhangphai, Songpi and Gangpimual villages were given compensation at the rate of Rs. 3,000 per acre of land (Roy and Kamkhenthang[a] 1991). In fact, some chiefs indulged in selling the trees of the village forest for easy income as they could no longer extract annual tributes from the villagers. In some cases, the state acquired land for public purpose by convincing the chiefs and on paying money to them. In New Phangsang village in Churachandpur district, the chief gave about thirty acres of land to the Manipur Plantation Corporation for coffee plantation with the result that the community lost the usufractuary right in such land (Roy and Kamkhenthang[b] 1991). A number of such cases are there in the Singhat sub-division of Churachandpur district of Manipur where lands were sold out to some people who had established villages after purchasing such land. In this way, at certain point of time, the chiefs assumed the grabbers' role through the government route.

Concentration of communal land in fewer hands, therefore, assumed alarming proportions in the hill areas of Northeast India. The market economy further helped the tribal elites to graduate from the rudimentary 'class-in-itself' stage to the 'class-for-itself' stage. Elite capture has also received policy patronage.

The Report of the National Committee on Development of Backward Areas, Planning Commission, GoI, November 1981, expressed concern about the risk of tribal exploitation and pleaded for protective and promotional measures like restriction on the entry of outsiders for purposes of trade (as in Arunachal Pradesh) etc. But it is the same government which opened up the communal land for mineral exploitation, forest felling, water resource privatisation by the corporate bodies and foreign direct investors.

f) Afforestation and Governmentalisation

The colonials perceived the forest initially as jungle. Mr. Andrews, who came to work in the tea industry of Assam wrote a letter to his mother in England on July 18, 1865, in which he wrote, "there is nothing visible but mud and jungle here in Assam. I am alone in the jungle, a sort of a small king among the 400 niggers, counting women and children". Andrew's representation echoed the sentiment of colonial administration of the 19th century. "The denseness of its jungle, the stiff precipices, the torrential streams", in British colonial eyes, "created a sharp geographical line separating the known from the unknown, civilisation from slavery" (Saikia, 2005). This continental perception was in sync with the Indian tradition of polarisation of Jungle and Civilisation reflecting the Rig Vedic construction of conflictual dualism between the *Grama* (village) and *Aranya* (forests). In the colonial discourse, this dualism provoked brutalisation and plunder of forests. Both in the Indian and in the colonial elite discourses, forest as a socio-spatial entity was considered as the 'other' of civilisation. The perception and elite discourse on forest were always guided by the forces of political economy. Thus, when it was found that the forests were also resource-giving and lucrative entities and that these would also yield revenue, income and profit-destruction and plunder were qualified with jurisprudential accumulation. This was based on trans-valuation of forests and its incredible resources that were to be annexed, colonised and be brought under the state control by juridical means. And for this, the forest-dependent people like the *jhum* cultivators, hunter-gatherers, grazers and the Transhuman communities were to be subjugated by state forces and be out-competed from the forests and then it would be easier to capture their social space for resource accumulation and profit-revenue generation. While grabbing and destruction of forest resources was a part of the colonisation project and destruction of forest at times also symbolised "political victory"(Handique 2004: 30), the conservation-protection-trade-profit-revenue was a part of the consolidation of the empire. From symbolism to empire building and from empire building to empire consolidation, the forest resources were continuously purged upon through the primitive as well as the parliamentary mode & Forest as a major source of revenue, impacted the minds of the colonial policy makers and the administrators in due course of time.

Colonial re-imagining of jungle as forest was based on the progressive image of profit-revenue yielding. The horror image of jungle was surrendered in favour of the gentrified image of forest and the colonials changed the plunder consciousness towards political economy gains from forest. Revenue consciousness from the forest resources was then transferred to the post-independence rulers. The first national forest policy was proclaimed in 1952 that gave higher stress on production forestry. This was followed by the Wildlife (Protection) Act 1972 and the Forest Conservation Act 1980. The two acts perpetuated the historical injustice towards the forest-dependent communities. These acts found that environmental protection and rights of tribal communities were irreconcilable concepts. On the other hand, plantation of commercial species threatened the livelihood security of the tribal people. The second national forest policy of 1988, for the first time, acknowledged the symbiotic relationship between environment and community and highlighted the need to involve tribal communities in forest management. This was the time when the struggles against commercial forestry were going on in different parts of the country. In the 1970s, the Forest Department in Manipur was forced to modify its plan for plantation of pine when the ecological researchers discouraged it. The Gauhati High Court's Law Research Institute recorded in the early 1980s, that in some parts of Arunachal Pradesh, the Environment Protection Committees restricted entry of timber contractors in their forests and supply timber to the plywood industries against the usufractuary rights of the tribal communities. The state used the eminent domain on the natural right of the local communities and this invited wider legal and political economic debates (Kadekodi 2004: 2).

The Scheduled Tribes and Other Traditional Forest Dwellers (Recognition of Forest Right) Act of 2006 was vehemently critiqued by Roy Burman (2008). He found that the population groups included in the act were ambiguous and restrictive. This act excluded the nomadic tribes and the transhumant communities in Arunachal Pradesh, who also rely on forests; denied the use of grazing grounds and water bodies (Section 3); this act has no effect on Nagaland and Mizoram (protected under Articles 371(A) and 371(G) of the Constitution) and on the Sixth Schedule areas of the North East. The migrants and outsiders in Reserved Forests were also excluded from the ambit of the act. The large number of Nepali migrants settled in the KK Reserve Forest range of Manipur and Bangladeshi refugees in N.C. Hills did not fall under the definition of population as per the act and ipso facto, lost their rights in the forests. He further stated that the 'reserved forests' in the Northeast were notified without legal rights for settlement and there was a historic clash between the forest department and the indigenous authorities over the control, management and use of forest resources and shifting cultivation. As most of the tribes in this region received forest rights from the colonial government, their settlement patterns and village structures also changed considerably. The Supreme Court demanded stringent forest protection leading the state governments to evict the 'encroachers'. But in the context of the non-settlement or improper settlement of forest rights, it resulted in forcible illegal eviction of some 300,000 forest dwellers. The Court had passed a series of orders against communities' right to manage their own resources. In 1998, the Supreme Court passed a sweeping order to all North Eastern states to stop felling of any trees in any forest (including community or private forests) till the already felled timber was sold and ordered that all forests, including those under ADCs, had to be managed in accordance with the Forest Department's working plans or schemes. This was also against the interest of the community. The VIth Schedule Areas and community institutions in the Northeast enjoy protection of customary rights and indeed, it is the court, a Committee of ultra-wildlife conservationists viewed, and not the Forest Rights Act, that is the most immediate threat to these institutions. Roy Burman, however, lauded Section 3.1 (g) of the Act that provided recognition to the Forest Dwellers' rights for conversion of pattas or leases or grants to titles. But in some ex-Princely States, the feudal rulers had issued pattas in favour of tribal chiefs, vesting them with the right of possession of vast tracts of tribal lands. In Manipur, it has not been possible to extinguish this incongruity, because continuation of the same was a part of the merger agreement.

He found the second positive content of the act in its recognition of the community as a legal person eligible to claim forest rights. But treating the community at par with individual or a family {Sec. 4 (6)} and restricting an area of four hectares seems to have mutilated its positive intent. But in Northeast India, community access, control and management of forest tracts go much beyond four hectares. The Act laid down the process for determining the nature and extent of forest rights. The JPC recommended community control of forests to counter monopoly of the forest department, and gave the Gram Sabha sole authority and responsibility for settling forest rights of the Forest Dependent STs and other traditional forest dwellers within the local limits of its jurisdiction under the Act. But involvement of Panchayati Raj and forest department officials in the process, diluted the spirit. Moreover, the actual determination of rights is made by sub-divisional committees and the rules include the state agencies in the list of aggrieved persons, who can appeal against the decision of the Gram Sabha.

Moreover, involvement of the Government-Centric Committees further diluted the process, although the decision of the DLC stands final.

In the tug of war between the community (backed by the NFP-1988) and the eminent domain of the state, production, forestry and revenue interest found preponderance. And therefore, one can find in Tijit, a small township at Mon district of Nagaland, four Veneer Mills and two plywood factories in place. They peel about fifty old trees a day and many more trees are sent to other plywood factories in nearby Assam. The farms are owned by non- North Easterners and most of the employees are non-Nagas (Bhattacharji 2002: 194, 197, 198). This exhibited a phenomenal increase of 'green capitalism' in the hills of Northeast India.

g) Neoliberal Accumulation

The neoliberal economy forcefully integrated the peasantry into the global market system and made them more reliant on purchased inputs in the deregulated markets that only helped the private accumulation process (Ghosh 2011: 38-39). Samir Amin found primitive accumulation and monopoly 'enclosures' to accelerate the dispossession of the peasants the world over. The current dominant discourse on 'reform of the land tenure system' and 'new investments in agriculture' manifest collective imperialism (of the World Bank, numerous cooperation agencies). A growing number of non-governmental organisations understand land reform as acceleration of the privatisation of land and agribusiness (Amin 2012: 11-26). Utsa Patnaik found that the peasantry of the global South is under attacks by capital on land. Primitive accumulation appeared in different forms and under different circumstances under global capital (Patnaik 2012: 236). The assertion of state ownership of land was prompted by the drive for accumulation. So Marx depicted the state as a growth on top at the expense of the local communities and an "excrescence of the society" (Gailey 2003: 53).

The neoliberal processes of primitive accumulation and accumulation by dispossession were carried over to different parts of Northeast India in different ways: (i) the practice of *sale-purchase-lease-mortgage* has received frequency in the hills in which a section of the elite class has become the major player (all states of Northeast India); (ii) the state has resorted to progressive transfer of communal land, water and mineral resources for commercial and industrial use to the private and corporate cronies and to the foreign direct investors (in Arunachal, Manipur, Meghalaya); (iii) computerisation of land recording system (not received momentum in Northeast India as yet); (iv) spatial fixation of capital for exploitation of the minutest geographical resources. The MNCs are setting up pharmaceutical industries by exploiting the local herbs and medicinal plants on a massive commercial scale (Lama 2013: 7). As many as five Bhubaneswar-based private companies have leased as much as 351 ha. of hill land for chromite and limestone mining in Ukhrul district in Manipur, where they have invested capital for flexible accumulation. The same practice is found in Meghalaya for mining operations; (v) enclosure economy has stepped in Nagaland through SEZ for real estate, IT Park, etc.

Conclusion

A brief introspection into the history reveals the dual role of primitive accumulation and accumulation by dispossession of communal land in the hills of Northeast India from the pre-colonial to the post-liberal times with different modus openadi. The pre-colonial domestic modes were land grants, land gifts, land donations, taxation etc. that perennially dispossessed the people. The colonial modes of accumulation were numerous including destruction, force, fraud in the beginning, later followed by penetration of policy, capital, ideas, institutional force and bureaucracy. The post-colonial Indian state adopted a septagonal modus operandi of accumulation that were, however, not uniform in their application in all the hill areas of Northeast India. Things depended on the temporal needs, strategic requirements and the push and pull factors of the changing political economy in the hills at different points of history. The above account shows that the process of accumulation and dispossession of communal land in the hills of Northeast India had a strong resonance with the grand theories of primitive accumulation and/or accumulation by dispossession and with the historical continuity of accumulation in all ages. This process did not elevate the hill region to a higher level of economy but caused perennial annihilation of the lived spaces of the tribal communities.

REFERENCES

Amin, Samir (2012). Contemporary Imperialism and the Agrarian Question. *Agrarian South: Journal of Political Economy* 1(1).

Angelis, Massimo De (2000). *Marx's Theory of Primitive Accumulation: A Suggested Reinterpretation*. UEL. London: Department of Economics Working Paper No. 29, May. University of East London.

Aier, I. Lanu (1987). Emerging Urban Land Pattern in Nagaland, in B.B. Dutta and M.N. Karna edited, *Land Relations in Northeast India*. New Delhi: People's Publishing House.

Bagchi, Amiya Kumar (2010). *Colonialism and Indian Economy*. Delhi: Oxford University Press.

Bareh, Hamlet (1985). *The History and Culture of the Khasi People* (Revised and Enlarged Edition). New Delhi: Spectrum Publications.

Barpujari, H.K. (1990). *The Comprehensive history of Assam*, Vol. 1, Guwahati: Publication Board, Assam.

Barpujari, S.K. (1987). Naga Attitude Towards Land and Land Revenue, in B.B. Dutta and M.N. Karna edited, *Land Relations in Northeast India*. New Delhi: People's Publishing House.

Baruah, Sanjib (2005). *Durable Disorder: Understanding the Politics of Northeast India*. New Delhi: Oxford University Press.

Barooah, Jeuti (2001a). *Customary Laws of the Mizos of Mizoram with Special Reference to Landholding System*. Guwahati: Law Research Institute, Eastern Region, Guwahati High Court.

Barooah, Jeuti (2001b). *Customary Laws of the Chakmas of Mizoram with Special Reference to Landholding System*. Guwahati: Law Research Institute, Eastern Region, Guwahati High Court.

Barooah, Jeuti (2001c). *Customary Laws of the Maras of Mizoram with Special Reference to Landholding System*. Guwahati: Law Research Institute, Eastern Region, Guwahati High Court.

Barooah, Jeuti (2007). *Customary Laws of the Tripuris in Tripura with Special Reference to Their Land Holding System*. Guwahati: Law

Research Institute, Eastern Region, Guwahati High Court.

Barpujari, H.K. (1990). *The Comprehensive History of Assam*, Vol. 1. Guwahati: Publication Board, Assam.

Bathari, Uttam (2009). Land, Laws, Alienation and Conflict: Changing Land Relations Among the Karbis in Karbi Anglong District in Walter Fernandes and Sanjay Barbora edited, *Land, People and Politics: Contest Over Tribal Land in Northeast India*. Guwahati: North Eastern Social Research Centre.

Bhambhri, C.P. (2013). The Indian Transition, *Social Scientist*, Vol. 41 No. 1-2, January-February.

Bhattacharjee, J.B. (1987). A Critical Analysis of the Angami Policy of Lord Dalhausie. Kohima: Proceedings of Northeast India History Association. (Eighth Session)

Bhattacharjee, Jayanta Bhusan (1977). *Cachar Under British Rule in Northeast India*. New Delhi: Radiant Publications.

Bhattacharji, Ramesh (2002). *Lands of Early Dawn: Northeast India*. New Delhi: Rupa & Co.

Bose, Sutapa (1988). The Problem of Primitive Accumulation, *Economic and Political Weekly*, Vol. 23, No. 23 June 4.

Bennoune Mahfoud (1979). Primary Capital Accumulation in Colonial Tuniaia, *Dialectical Anthropology*, Vol. 4, No. 2 (July). Springer E-journal.

Cantle, Sir Keith (2008-2009). *Sir Keith Cantle's Notes on Khasi Land*. Shillong: Chapala Publishing House.

Chakraborty, Gorky. (2008). Land Administration in the Char Areas of Assam: The Task Ahead in Asok Kumar Ray and S.B. Chakrabarti edited, *Society Politics and Development in Northeast India: Essays in Memory of Dr. Basudeb Datta Ray*. New Delhi: Concept Publishing Company.

Chakrabarti, S.B. and C. Changsun (2004). Customary Right and the Question of Land in Arabinda Basu, Biman K. Dasgupta and Jayanta Sarkar edited, *Anthropology in Northeast India: A Reader*. Calcutta: Indian National Confederation and Academy of Anthropologists; Indian Anthropological Society and National Museum of Mankind.

Chakravarti, Mahadeb (1994). Land System in Tripura: The Tenural System and Transfer in J.B. Ganguli edited, *Studies in the Economic History of Northeast India*. New Delhi: Har Anand Publications.

Chakravarty, L.N. (1973). *Glimpses of Early History of Arunachal*. Research Department. Shillong: Arunachal Administration.

Chandra, Pratyush and Deepankar Basu (2011). Neoliberalism and

Primitive Accumulation in India: The Need to Go Beyond Capital, in Pratysh Chandra edited, *Neoliberalism, Primitive Accumulation and Politics in India,* Radical Notes 5, Delhi: Aakar Books.

Chandrasekhar, C.P. and Jayati Ghosh (2006). *The Market that Failed: A Decade of Neoliberal Reforms.* New Delhi: Left Word.

Choudhury, J.N. (1983). *Arunachal Pradesh from Frontier Tract to Union Territory.* New Delhi: Cosmo Publications.

Chatterjee, Suhas (1993). History of Mizo Economy. Jorhat, Proceedings of Northeast India History Association, 1993.

Chattopadhyaya, B.D. (1991). *Aspects of Rural Settlements and Rural Society in Early Medieval India.* Calcuta: K.P. Bagchi & Co.

Chaube, S.K. (1976). *Hill Politics in Northeast India,* Calcutta: Orient Longman.

Chaube, S.K. (1999). *Hill Pollitics in Northeast India.* London: Sangam Books (updated version).

Choudhury, Nalini Ranjan (1983). *Tripura Through the Ages: A Short History of Tripura from the Earliest Times to 1947 AD.* New Delhi: Sterling Publishers.

Choudhury, B.D. (2004). State's Perception of the 'Forest' and the 'Forest' as State in Early India, in B.B. Chaudhury and Arun Bandopadhyaya edited, *Tribes, Forest and Social Formation in Indian History.* New Delhi: Manohar.

Christian, David (1990). Accumulation and Accumulators: The Metaphor Marx Muffed. *Science & Society,* Vol. 54, No. 2 (Summer, 1990). Guilford Press. http://www.jstor.org/stable/40403070.

D'Souza, Alphonsus and Christina Kekhrieseno (2005). "Social Change in Northeast India: A Comparative Study of Three Tribes" as quoted by Pereira, Melville, "Globalisation and Changing Land Relations in Northeast India", Proceeding of a Seminar on Impact of Globalisation on North East, at Himalayan Research Institute, March 10-11.

Daimary, Luke (2012). *Status of Adivasi/Indigenous Peoples Land Series 5: Assam.* Delhi: Aakar Books.

Das, Gurudas (1993). Tribal Formation and Their Economic Base. Proceedings of Northeast India History Association, Shillong: Thirteenth Session.

Das, J.N. (1986). *A Study of Land System of Northeast India* Vol. VI: Mizoram. (Mimeographed). LRI Eastern Region. Guwahati: Guwahati High Court.

Das, J.N. (1989). *A Study of Land System in Manipur.* Guwahati: Law Research Institute, Eastern Region, Guwahati High Court.

Dasgupta, Keya (2008). The Coming of Tea in the Brahmaputra Valley, in Asok Kumar Ray and S.B. Chakraborty edited, *Society Politics and Development in Northeast India: Essays in Memory of Dr. Basudeb Datta Ray.* New Delhi: Concept Publishing Company.

Datta, B.B. and P.S. Datta (1986) in B.N. Bordoloi edited, *Alienation of Tribal Land and Indebtedness.* Guwahati: Tribal Research Center.

Datta, P.S. (1984). "Emerging Differentiation in a Traditional Tribal Economy", *Social Research,* Vol. 4, No. 3-4, July-December.

Datta, Parthsarathi (1987). Future of the Past: A Few Words in Anticipation of Land Ownership Pattern in Mizoram, in B.B. Dutta and M.N. Karna edited, *Land Relations in Northeast India.* New Delhi: People's Publishing House.

Dutta, S. (1986). The Anglo-Adi Relation (Upto 1922), Proceedings of Northeast India History Association, Pasighat: Northeast India History Association.

Dutta, N.C. (1986). Land Reform in Tripura, in Atul Goswami edited, *Land Reform and Peasant Movement: A Study of Northeast India.* NewDelhi: Omsons Publications.

Dietrich, Alexa S. (2006). Coercive Hegemony, Deep Capture and Environmental Justice in Puerto Rico. *Development and Change,* Vol. 42, No. 6, November.

Dun, E.W. (1980). *Gazetteer of Manipur.* Delhi: Vivek Publishing House.

Dunbar, George. (1984). *Frontiers.* New Delhi: Omsons Publications, (Reprint).

Dutt, Rajni Palm (2008). *India Today.* New Delhi: Peoples Publishing House, 10th edition.

Dutta, B.B. (1987). Land relations in Khasi Hills in B.B. Dutta and M.N. Karna edited *Land Relations in Northeast India.* New Delhi, Vikas Publishing House.

Dutta, J.C. (1994). A Study of Awabs as in Practice in Hill Tipperrah and in the Zamindaris of Chakla Rosanabad, in J.B. Bhattacharya edited, *Studies in Economic History in Northeast India.* New Delhi: Har Anand Publications.

Elwin, Verrier (1964). *A Philosophy for NEFA,* Shillong, (reprint).

Elwin, Verrier (1969). *The Nagas of the Nineteenth Century.* Bombay: OUP.

Emoungu, Paul-Albert N. (1992). Education and Primitive Accumulation in Sub-Saharan Africa, *Comparative Education,* Vol. 28, No. 2.

Fowkes, Ben (Translated) (1990). *Karl Marx-Capital: A Critique of Political Economy*. UK: Penguin Books.

Fernandes Walter and Gita Bharali (eds.) (2005)."*The Socio-Economic Situation of Some Tribes of Bishnupur and Palizi*" as quoted by Pereira, Melville, "Globalization and Changing Land Relations in Northeast India", presented at a seminar on Impact of Globalisation on North East, at Himalayan Research Institute, March 10-11, 2005.

Gailey, Christine Ward (2003). Community, State and Questions of Social Evolution in Marx's "Ethnological Notebooks", *Anthropologica*, Vol. 45, No. 1.

Ganguli, J.B. (1987). The Problem of Tribal Landlessness in Tripura, in B.B. Dutta and M.N. Karna, edited, *Land Relations in Northeast India*. New Delhi: People's Publishing House.

Ganguli, Jalad Baran (2006). *Economic History of Northeast India*. New Delhi: Akansha Publishing House.

Ghosh, Jayati (2011). Social Process in the Indian Accumulation Story. *Social Scientist*, Vol. 39, Nos. 1-2, January-February.

Goswami, D.N. (1994). Land System of Gobinda Manikya as Reflected in the Land Grants in J.B. Bhattacharjee edited, *Studies in the Economic History of Northeast India*. New Delhi: Har Anand Publications.

Goswami, P.C. (1988). *The Economic Development of Assam*. Guwahati: Kalyani Publishers.

Government of Manipur (1981-1982). *Manipur: Handbook of Settlement Training*. Imphal: Directorate of Settlement & Land Records.

Guha, Amalendu (1991). *Medieval and Early Colonial Assam: Society, Polity and Economy*. Calcutta: K.P. Bagchi & Co.

Guha, Amalendu (1997). *Planter Raj to Swaraj*. New Delhi: Indian Council of Historical Research.

Gupta, A.K. (2000). Shifting Cultivation and Conservation of Biological Diversity in Tripura, Northeast India, *Human Ecology*, Vol. 28, No. 4, December.

Habib, Irfan (1985). Studying a Colonial Economy Without Perceiving Colonialism, *Modern Asian Studies*, Vol. 29, No. 6.

Habib, Irfan (2011). Capitalism in History in Shireen Moosvi edited, *Capitalism, Colonialism and Globalisation*. New Delhi: Tulika Books.

Handique, Rajib (2004). *British Forest Policy in Assam*. New Delhi: Concept Publishing Company.

Hardin, Garret (1968). The Tragedy of the Commons, *Science*, December 13, Vol. 162, No. 3859.

Harris-White, Barbara (2012). Capitalism and the Common Man: Peasants and Petty Production in Africa and South Asia, Agrarian South, *Journal of Political Economy* 1(2).

Haq, Mazarul (1964). *The East India Company's Land Policy and Commerce in Bengal, 1698-1784.* Dhaka: Asiatic Society of Pakistan.

Harvey, David (2005). *A Brief History of Neoliberalism.* Oxford: Oxford University Press.

Harvey, David (2003). *The New Imperialism: On Spatio Temporal Fixes and Accumulation by Dispossession.* Oxford: Oxford University Press.

Harvey, David (1990). *The Condition of Postmodernity: An Enquiry into the Origin of Cultural Change.* Oxford: Blackwell Publishing.

Heimendorf, C.V.F. (1982). *Tribes of India: The Struggle for Survival.* New Delhi: Oxford University Press.

Heimendorf, C.V.F. (1982). *Highlanders of Arunachal Pradesh.* New Delhi: Vikash Publishing House.

Islam, Sirajul (1979). *The Permanent Settlement in Bengal: A Study of its Operation 1790-1819.* Dhaka: Bangla Academy.

Iyer, Gopal K. and S.V. Bhave (1995). Report on Tripura, Workshop on Land Reforms-Agenda for the North East, Gauhati, papers on the North Eastern Scenario, Land Reforms Unit, Mussoorie: Lal Bahadur Shastri National Academy of Administration. April, 3-5.

Kadekodi, Gopal K. (2004). *Common Property Resource Management; Reflection on Theory and the Indian Experience.* New Delhi: Oxford University Press.

Kar, Parimal Chandra (1982). *Garos in Transition.* New Delhi: Cosmo Publicaitons.

Karlsson, Bengt G. (2011). *Unruly Hills, Nature and Nation in India's North East.* New Delhi: Orient Blackswan.

Karna, M.N. (1990). The Agrarian Scene, *Seminar,* No. 366, February.

Khashim, Ruivah (1987). Land Ownership and Its Problems Among the Tangkhul Nagas in Dutta, B.B. and M.N. Karna edited, *Land Relations in Northeast India.* New Delhi: People's Publishing House.

Kligerman, Nicole S. (2010). The Violences of Capitalism: Privatisation and Land Tenure in Uganda, Minnesota, and Mexico: Macalester College, *Latin American Studies Honors Projects.* Paper 4. http://www.macalester.edu/dotAsset/92e2eaad-1b64-4b32-bce8-d1e8c41316e3.pdf.

Lal Dena (ed.) (1991). *History of Manipur 1826-1949.* New Delhi: Orbit

Publications.

Lal Dena (2011). Land Alienation and Self-Government in the Hill Areas of Manipur, www.manipuronline, accessed on -09-03-2011.

Lama, Mahendra P. (2013). Labour and Employment in the North-Eastern Region, in *Labour and Development*, Noida: V.V. Giri National Labour Institute, Vol. 20, No. 2, December.

Letter from the Office of the Deputy Commissioner (1952). Imphal No. 133-48/DC, Imphal, dated 24.04. 1952.

Lodi, A. Haroon Akram (2007). Land, Market and Neoliberal Enclosures: An Agrarian Political Economy Perspective. *Third World Quarterly*, Vol. 28, No. 7.

Lyngdoh, Alfreda L. (1992). *Land Use Pattern and the Changes Therein in West Khasi Hills District–A Case Study of Mawthawniaw Village.* Guwahati: Institute of Social Change and Development, Assam Sachivalaya. (Mimeographed).

MacIver, Robert M. (1944). Foreword to Karl Polanyi's *The Great Transformation*. Boston: Beacon Press.

Manas Publications (1988). *Selection of Papers Regarding Hill Tracts Between Assam and Burma.* Delhi: Manas Publications (Reprint).

McCaskie, T.C. (1983). Accumulation, Wealth and Belief in Asante History. I. To the Close of the Nineteenth Century, *Africa: Journal of the International African Institute*, Vol. 53 No. 1.

McMichael, Philip (1980). Settlers and Primitive Accumulation: Foundations of Capitalism in Australia. *Review* (Fernand Braudel Centre), Vol. 4, No. 2.

Marx, Karl and Frederic Engels (1945). *The German Ideology.* Calcutta: Modern Publishers.

Marx, Karl (1977). *Capital Vol. I.* Moscow: Foreign Languages Publishing House.

Marx, Karl (2010). *Capital Vol. 1.* New Delhi: Leftword.

Mathew, T. and M.K.S. Nair (1983). *Tribal Mode of Production (in Meghalaya) in Transition.* Shillong: Department of Economics, NEHU, (Mimeo).

Max, Radin (1925). Fundamental Concepts of the Roman Law. *California Law Review*, Vol. 13, Issue 3.

Mayo, Sam, Paris Yeros and Praveen Jha (2012). Imperialism and Primitive Accumulation: Notes on the New Scramble for Africa, Agrarian South: *Journal of Political Economy* 1(2).

Millar, James R. (1978). A Note on Primitive Accumulation in Marx and Preobrazhensky, *Soviet Studies*, Vol. 30, No. 3, July.

Misra, Bani Prasanna (1989). Agrarian Relations in a Khasi State, *Economic and Political Weekly*, Vol. 14, No. *20*. May 19.

Mittal Publications (1984). *Report on the Administration of Northeast India, (1921-1922)*. New Delhi: A Mittal Publications.

Mukherjee, Ramkrishna (2000). Caste in Itself, Caste and Class, or Caste in Class. *Journal of World-Systems Research*, vi, 2, Summer/Fall 2000, 332-339 Special Issue: Festchrift for Immanuel Wallerstein – Part I

Mukherjee, Pampa (2013). Common Property Resources, Institutions and Governance-Understanding Elinor Ostrom, *Man & Development*, Vol. XXXV, No. 1, March.

Mukim, Patricia (2009). Land Ownership Among the Khasis of Meghalaya: A Gender Perspective in Walter Fernandes and Sanjoy Borbora edited *Land, People and Politics*. Guwahati: Northeast Social Science Research Centre.

Murari, Atulya (2004). Forests, Development Ideology and Peasant/Tribal World: Madras Presidency, Nineteenth and Early twentieth Centuries, in B.B. Chaudhury and Arun Bandopadhyaya edited, *Tribes, Forest and Social Formation in Indian History*. New Delhi: Manohar.

Nongbri, Tiplut (1987). Khasi Land Tenure System in B.B. Dutta and M.N. Karna edited, *Land Relations in Northeast India*. New Delhi, Vikas Publishing House.

Nongkynrih, A.K. (2009). Privatisation of Communal Land of the Tribes of Northeast India: A Sociological Viewpoint in Walter Fernandes and Sanjoy Borbora edited, *Land, People and Politics*. Guwahati: Northeast Social Science Research Centre.

Olorode, Omoloyo (2013). Privatisation is a Looting Agenda; Obasanjo, Okonja Iwela are Liars, September 7, saharareports.com/report/lecture-privatization-looting-agenda. E-journal.

Owen, Roger (1987). Anthropology and Imperial Administration, Sir Alfred Lyall and the Official Use of Theories in Social Change in India after 1857 in Talai Ashad, edited, *Anthropology and Colonial Encounter*. New York: Humanity Books.

Pamberton, R.B. (2000). *The Eastern Frontier of India*. New Delhi: Mittal Publications (Reprint).

Paranjape, Suhas (2013). Capitalisation of Nature and Accumulation by Dispossession in Choube, N.P., Debabrata Panda and Girijesh Pant edited, *People's Struggles and Movements for Equitable Society*. Delhi: Daanish Books.

Patel, A.R. (1978). Focus on North Eastern Region: Planning for

Resource Management, *North Eastern Economic Review*, Vol. II, No. 2, Guwahati.

Pathy, Jagannath (1987). *Anthropology of Development: Demystification and Relevance.* Delhi: Gyan Publications.

Patnaik, Utsa (2012). Some Aspects of the Contemporary Agrarian Question, Agrarian South: *Journal of Political Economy* 1(3).

Patnaik, Prabhat (2014). Capitalism and Global Poverty, Silver Jubilee Special Lecture. Guwahati: OKD Institute of Social Cahnge and Development.

Pedal, Felix (2011). Investment-Induced Displacement: Analysing the Neoliberal Power Structure, Guwahati: Seminar on "Neoliberal State and its Challenges", Omeo Kumar Das Institute for Social Change and Development, 20-21 December.

Perelman, Michael (2001).The Secret History of Primitive Accumulation and Classical Political Economy, *The Commoner* No. 2, September.

Pouchepadass, Jaques (2002). Colonisation and Environment in Alice Thorner edited, *Daniel Thorner, Land, Labour and Rights, 10 Daniel Thorner Memorial Lecture.* New Delhi: Tulika..

Powell, Baden (1990). *Land System of British India,* Vol. III. New Delhi: Low Price Publications, (Reprint).

Proceedings of the Seminar on Land Reforms in Tribal Areas of Northeast India (1987). Northeast India Council for Social Science Research in Shillong during April 24-25.

Rao, S.N. (1991). Megalithic Practices Among Khasis and Nagas of Northeast India in Jayprakash Singh and Gautam Sengupta, edited, *Archaeology of Northeast India.* New Delhi: Har Anand Publications.

Ray, Asok Kumar (1991a). Rural Studies: A Case for Manipur in R.K. Samanta edited, *Rural Development in Northeast India.* New Delhi. Uppal Publishing House.

Ray, Asok Kumar (1991b). Land Reforms and Economic Development in the Manipur Hills in Malabika Dasgupta edited, *Land Reforms in Northeast India.* New Delhi: Omsons Publications.

Ray, Asok Kumar and H. Kamkhenthang (1991a). Land Reforms and Organizational Problems: The Chin- Kukis of Manipur, Seminar on 'Organising the Rural Poor for Land Reforms'. Hyderabad: NIRD, June 14.

Ray, Asok Kumar and H. Kamkhenthang (1991b). Land in the Hills of Manipur, Selected Readings on North East, Mussoorie: Lal Bahadur Shastri National Academy of Administration.

Ray, Asok Kumar (2005). *Contemporary Discourses on Democracy*. New Delhi: Om Publications.

Reid, Surg-Lieut-Col. A.S. (1976). *Mizoram Gazetteer*. Calcutta: Firma KLM Pvt. Ltd. on behalf of Tribal Research Institute, Aizawl, (Reprint).

Richards, Alan R. (1977). Primitive Accumulation in Egypt, 1798-1882, *Review* (Fernand Braudel Centre), Vol. 1, No. 2. New York: Research Foundation of SUNY.

Rao, B. Janardan, Tiplut Nongbri and Livinus Tirkey (2010). Problem of Tribal Society, Some Aspects. New Delhi: RGICS Paper No. 47.

Roy Burman, B.K. (1987). Society, Ecology and Land Reforms in Tribal India, Paper presented at the 'Seminar on Agrarian Structure, Land Reforms and Agricultural Growth', Almpra: G.B. Pant Institute in November.

Roy Burman, B.K. (1998). Introductory Note in Dr. B. Janardhan Rao, Tiplut Nongbri and Livinus Tirkey, Problems in Tribal Society, Some Aspects, RGICS Paper No. 47. New Delhi: Rajiv Gandhi Institute for Contemporary Studies.

Roy Burman, B.K. (2008). Ambiguities, Incongruities, Inadequacies in Scheduled Tribes and Other Technical Forest Dwellers (Recognition of Forest Rights) Act 2006, A Case For Constructive Engagement. *Mainstream*, Vol. XLVI, No. 15. 29 March.

Roy Burman, Jagat Jyoti (1991). Impact of Land Reforms in Tripura, in Malabika Dasgupta edited, *Impact of Land Reforms in Northeast India*. New Delhi: Omsons Publications.

Rynjah, Diangunmon (2006). The Jaintia Land Grants, Proceedings of Northeast India History Association, Aizawl.

Saikia, Yasmin (2005). The Tai-Ahom Connection, www.india-seminar.com/2005/550.

Saikia, K.N. (1965). *The Assam Land and Revenue Regulation 1886*. Guwahati: Lawyers Book Stall.

Sen, Soumen (1987). Land as Property: Its Significance in the Traditional Society and Polity in Khasi-Jayantiya Hills, in B.B. Dutta and M.N. Karna edited *Land Relations in Northeast India*. New Delhi, Vikas Publishing House.

Sengupta, Gautam (1991). Tripura Sculpture—An Overview in Jayprakash Singh and Gautam Sengupta edited, *Archaeology of Northeast India*. New Delhi. Har Anand Publications.

Shakespeare, Colonel L.W. (1977). *History of Assam Rifles*. Calcutta. Firma KLM (Reprint)

Sharma, R.S. (1976). *Forms of Property in the Early Portion of the Rig Veda, Essays in Honour of Prof. S.C. Sarkar*. New Delhi: People's Publishing House.

Sharma, Tarun C. (1990b). On the Pre-historic Background of Social and Political Institutions, in Jayanta Sarkar and B.Dutta Ray edited, *Social and Political Institutions of the People of Northeast India*. Calcutta: Anthropological Survey of India.

Sharmah, Bhupen and Binayak Dutta (2013). *History of Judiciary in Assam:* Law, Law Courts and Laweyrs. Gauhati: DVS Publications.

Shimray, M.K. (2008). Tangkhul Land Use System: Land, People and Politics in Walter Fernandes and Sanjay Barbora edited, *Land, People and Politics: Contest Over Tribal Land in Northeast India*. Guwahati: North Eastern Social Research Centre.

Shiozawa, Kimio (2013). Marx's View of Asiatic Society and His Asiatic Mode of Production in *Development Economics*, Vol. 4, Issue 3, Institute of Development Economics, Wiley Online Library.

Singh, Ch. Priyo Ranjan (2009). Land, Development and Identity: Agrarian Relations and Social Issues in Manipur in Ch. Priyo Ranjan Singh edited, *Tribalism and the Tragedy of the Commons: Land, Identity and Development: The Manipur Experience*. New Delhi: Akansha Publishing House.

Singh, K.S. (ed.) (1994). *People of India, Nagaland*, Volume XXXIV, Anthropological Survey of India.

Soil and Water Conservation Department (State Land Use Board) (1988). Dimapur: Proceedings of the Seminar on Land Use Planning and Watershed Management for Control of Shifting Cultivation, Sponsored by the Ministry of Agriculture 8-9 March.

Thavaraj, M.J.K. (1984). The Concept of Asiatic Mode of Production: Its Relevance to Indian History, *Social Scientist*, Vol. 12, No. 7 July.

Thorner, Daniel (2002). The Royal Title Bill of 1876, in Alice Thorner (ed). *Daniel Thorner, Land, Labour and Rights, 10 Daniel Thorner Memorial Lecture*. New Delhi. Tulika.

Vincent, Kaushal (1979). Socio-Economic Study of Bhilymlong. Madras: Christian Literature Centre.

Viswanathan, P.K. and Amita Shah (2013). Trade Reforms and Crisis in India's Plantation Industry: An Analysis of Tea and Rubber Plantation Sectors, *Social Change and Development*, Vol. X, No. 2, Guwahati, Assam.

Webber, Michael (2008). Primitive Accumulation in Modern China, *Dialectical Anthropology*, Vol. 32, No. 4 (December).

Weiss, Rona S. (1982) Primitive Accumulation in the United States: The Interaction between Capitalist and Non-capitalist Class Relations in Seventeenth-Century, *The Journal of Economic History*, Vol. 42, No. 1.

Whitehead, Judy (2003). Space, Place and Primitive accumulation, *Eonomic and Political Weekly*, Vol. 38, No. 40, October 4-6.

Wood, Ellen Meiksins (1998), The Agrarian Origin of Capitalism. New York: *Monthly Review*, Vol. 50, Issue 3, (July-August).

2

Institutional Dispossession of Communal Land

Within the alpine terrain of Northeast India, the pristine land institutions responded to the prevailing modes of production. The low level of the productive forces in the alpine terrain did not produce specialised, separable, complex and formal institutions, in which situation, the clan or the chieftainship institutions simultaneously represented social relations within the community and production relations within the economy. This was essentially a non-class arrangement that provided the basis of the institutional epistemology of the communal land system in the hills. The lat-long differences in economic formation in the hills and the valleys in Northeast India shaped the institutional order in respect of land differently in the hills and in the valleys. Therefore, while the Ahoms developed the technique of wet rice cultivation on flat fields, their tribal neighbours practised shifting cultivation (Guha 1991: 63). The powerful clans in Manipur valley captured the wet field economy (Kamei 2009) and in Tripura, the surplus generating wet field cultivation led to the rise of a strong monarchy in the 15th century (Ray 2010: 49), while the tribals in both the states remained tied up with the economy of shifting cultivation in the hills. With lat-long differences in economic formations, Northeast India had blissfully mothered (i) the bi-focal economy in the valley and the hills; (ii) the twin mode of production and (iii) the twin institutional order. The official pedagogy on this *critical duality* remained thoroughly mis-understood by the state and the policy makers that in due course of time opened up larger theoretical debates. The debates were troubled on the claim of the absolute ownership of the kings over the land. Dun, for example and later on, Das, found the Raja as the absolute proprietor of land in Manipur, (Dun 1980: 59.60; Das 1989: 14), while Roy Burman expressed a dissenting view and contested the Raja's superior landlordship over the communal land in the hills (Roy Burman 1991: 30-31). He interpreted the overlordship of the kings in the hills as symbolic of political allegiance which did not impair the communal land institutions in the hills.

In this generic background, we take up the institutional issues of the hill lands. The economic formation in the two ecological terrains in the region was featured by mutual inter-dependency of the hills and valleys that led to a tributary mode of production relations in the hills. The tributary mode being a benign pre-capitalist mode of production, in Manipur for example, this led to the emergence of the 'ritual theatre state' and the allegiance shown by the hill people to the Raja was accepted in the political order in a lord-subordinate relationship with annual presentation of tributes and participation in a cyclic friendship ritual in the capital, known as 'Mera Haochongba' (Arambam 1986: 222). A similar practice was found in Tripura, when the tribal people would offer annual tributes to the Raja during Durga Puja. This mode allowed the tribal chiefs/ headmen considerable institutional and functional autonomy in relation to the communal land. The pride and prejudice around the rudimentary private property formation in the valley economy was, thus, juxtaposed to the communal, non-hierarchical land owning system in the hills with the maintenance of clear and distinctive recognition of the *dominium* in the hands of tribal communities.

Given the extreme diversity of the customary laws on land, a uniform communitarian ethos ran through the land institutions in the hills. Hodson, thus, found among the Nagas the prevalence of a customs of equal distribution of water on terrace lands and the lower fields, lest the latter should suffer. (Hodson 1989: 105-106). In land disputes among the Mao Nagas, oath on the earth was usual; in timber disputes the oath on the axe was employed and in cases of inter-clan or inter-village quarrels, the oath on the cat was necessary. Moreover, in both private and public cases, the water ordeal was followed (Hodson 1989: 109-110). The non-adversarial justice dispensing system, which included the land disputes, was abiding to all members for upkeeping communal harmony. Among the Ao, Angami and Chakesang tribes, within the matrix of clan ownership of land and forest, there emerged village holding, clan and lineage holding and individual holding. Besides chiefs's ownership was found among certain tribes within the main framework of communal possession and clan ownership. All the subsequent settlers in a village were tenants, though they acted as full members of the village community. An individual member of another clan was also permitted by the village council to settle in a village, to clear and reclaim a tract of forest. Land could be borrowed by an individual, and if he did not belong to the founder clan, he was entitled only to use the right as long as he wished to reside. He could not transfer his holding without permission of the council and should he go elsewhere, the land would revert to the village. (Elwin 1964: 64).

Among the Ao's, lineage and clan lands were formed through amalgamation of lands received from the heirless clan members after their death. The *jhum* lands were hereditary and followed the male line which was ultimately linked with the kinship and descent groups. (Singh 1994: 78-79, 80-81: Ao 2010: 52). The clan elders controlled communal property of the Angamis. The terraced fields, wood plantations, gardens, house sites and parts of *jhum* land were individual properties. A certain portion of *jhum* land and festival grounds were clan or village property on which the cultivator was settled by general consent. Sometimes a deserving cultivator could put an area marker of his choice with no intention to deprive other clan members. A series of cultivation on the same plot by the same man would result in his right to the land that possibly led to the rise of institutions of private property as *prescriptive* right. In some villages, collective farming was practised. Bequeathing of property to any person outside the clan was prohibited and inheritance followed the male line (Bhattacharya 1990:109-111; Singh 1994: 69). Among the Chakhesang Nagas land, forest and water resources were managed by the individuals as well as by the lineage and clans. Family land and purchased land was under the absolute ownership of a person. Community land was owned by the village council. Use of clan (*khel*) land was restricted only within the clan with demarcated boundaries which could not be disposed of without consent of the village council. *Jhum* cultivation was under both individual or clan ownerships. *Jhum* land was also given to the tenant cultivators. The people largely depended on terrace lands, individually owned and demarcated by boundaries. But the traditional headmen and the village councils had the overall control over land, power of adjudication and justice-dispensing power on land issues. Clan and village lands could not be sold or transferred. Recently, individual land is being sold without the approval of any authority and common property is also being sold for collective economic benefit with the consent of the village council (Singh 1994: 182; Baruah 2011: 25-40).

In Arunachal Pradesh, there are three broad types of land ownership: clan, community and individual ownership. Among the Monpas, Heimendorf found, cultivable land, pastureland and forest land being common land. In Kamla Valley, one can find the community land system (Heimendorf 1982: 43, 156). The clan/communal ownership could not be legalised when its use was limited to hunting, gathering and shifting cultivation. Communal ownership did not obtain a permanent character when land was abundant. With the exhaustion of natural resources and food gathering, the community had to shift to a new place in search of livelihood. Communal ownership became permanent when migration to a new place became difficult for non-availability of vacant land (Roy and Kuri 1996: 21). The early pastoral and transhumant communities in Arunachal Pradesh moved in bands and instead of lineage or clan organisation, they developed the chieftainship system to regulate the hunting and gathering activities and to distribute the fruits of labour. Animals at this stage, became the property (which resembled the *Rig Vedic* tradition of cattle being the wealth of which the king was the protector. He was not the protector of land (Sharma 1996: 40, 45; Thakur 2003: 29).

The diverse land rights in customs in Arunachal Pradesh had a general uniformity in most important counts. The elementary land right, included, use and occupancy right of any person, while undisturbed and continuous use and occupancy of land over a longer period would accord him a permanent and heritable right. As social commerce developed, this right ripened into a property and became an object of transfer. Now in Arunachal Pradesh, there is individual usefructuary and occupancy right over *jhum* land. But several tribes practise sedentary cultivation on a massive scale (Das 1989: vii, 9). The Apa Tanis and Khamtis do only permanent cultivation and the Adis and Mismis have evolved a method of *jhum* cultivation on permanent, well-defined and well-demarcated plots, whereby they return exactly to the same plot at the end of each *jhum* cycle, and the rights over which became permanent, heritable and transferable (Heimendorf 1985: 26). On the other hand, the Nishis and the Mismis practise *jhum* cultivation. People acquire land right by clearing jungles for which no permission of any organisation or village elders is needed; by inheritance from the previous owner; and by transfer from the previous owner. There is no distinction between inherited and self-acquired property. A cultivator does not necessarily return to the same *jhum* plot that leaves no possibility of permanent right over it. Besides, there are common hunting grounds and clan fisheries although there is no common burial ground. Inheritance is patrilineal. Transfer, mortgage and sub-let of land are uncommon but gifts are popular. Wet-rice lands are transferable to the men of the same tribe. Sale, though uncommon and prohibited to non-Nishis, exists and the sale price is paid either in *Mithun* or in cash without any documentary proof. And yet, there is no high concentration of land among them (Das 1989: 24-25; Baruah 2007: 26). The Mismis also do permanent cultivation, the fields of which are cleared and well-demarcated for each family. These lands are family owned and are cultivated individually. Rights on these plots are permanent, heritable and transferable. Unlike the Nishis, the Mismi families return to the *jhum* plot at the end of the *jhum* cycle. The nature of right is use and occupancy right. By clearing jungle and continuous use and occupation, one can become the owner of the same. Besides, there are village commons. The *jhum* land is transferable to the persons of the same tribe and a permanent resident of the village. Transfer in all forms is allowed except mortgage. Homestead land is transferable. Gifts and mortgage are rare and bequest is unknown. Sub-let and *Adhi* system are in vogue though not extensively. The Mismi inheritance is patrilineal on equal share basis (Das 1989: 107-108; Baruah 2007: 32-40).

The Khamptis practise the wet rice cultivation on individual ownership basis. The land is acquired in the same way as the Nishis. The village chief, in consultation with the village council, may allot new homestead land to a permanent resident from the village commons. Joint cultivation is done on certain common lands for raising funds for common purpose. Homestead land is permanently owned and is heritable, if not saleable. If abandoned and left permanently, it reverts to the chief for re-allotment. Their custom of inheritance is patrilineal on equal share basis, except the eldest, who bears bigger family responsibilities. Clan or village lands are collectively inherited and can also be individually inherited if decided by the village council. Transfer by sale is frowned on in Khampti society. There is no mortgage, written lease, sub-let and transfer of land to non-tribals though donations for public purposes are allowed. (Das 1989: 115; Baruah 2007: 28-30).

The Apa Tanis also predominantly practise wet-rice cultivation. Heimendorf found three types of formal ownership: individual land, clan land and common village land. Individual ownership did not lead to private accumulation (Heimendorf 1962: 40). The hill slope forests are reserved for firewood, house building materials and pasture. Right over homestead plot is permanent, heritable, and transferable. Certain lands are also kept for common use of burial and hunting. There is no separate grazing ground and common fishery. Ownership and inheritance follow the rule of male primogeniture. The use and occupancy right is transferable only to the same tribe. Sale, mortgage and sub-letting are uncommon but when sub-letting is done, a rent is realised. Residential plots are transferable though not to any outsider. Transfer of clan land needs permission of the clan members and the first buying preference goes to one's own relatives and clan members, for which a negotiator is engaged (*Kris dune*). The village council *(Buliang)* is responsible for enforcement of land-related customs (Das 1989: 35-41). The Adis have permanent use, occupancy and heritable rights over the *jhum* land, well demarcated by boundaries. People shift but do not abandon a *jhum* plot. An individual member of the village community can acquire the right to forest land with approval of the village council. Compact homestead lands belong to individual families. Timber extraction needs permission of the owner but gathering of firewood and timber for house-building is permissible. There is no village commons. They follow the principle of patrilineal inheritance on equal share basis. Transfer of *jhum* land and permanent cultivation land are possible but there is no sale deed for that. Sale, gift and mortgage and lease are restricted to the people of the same tribe and same village. Homestead land is not transferable but a person loses all rights over it on abandonment (Das 1989: 74-75, 83-84).

Assam, Manipur and Tripura have some commonalities in regard to hill land. In Assam, Das found that the Dimasas have individual ownership of *jhum* land which they procure by individual selection. They do not reclaim the land. So, individual right over *jhum* land does not emerge. Transfer of land does not take place as there is fixity of tenure (Das 1982). Baruah, on the other hand, found that village land is community owned, of which, the *Khunang* (headman) is the sole repository. He allots land to the individual families. One can become owner of land by inheritance, acquisition or by purchase. Transfer of land is subject to restrictions imposed by the village council or the

Khunang. The custom of gift, will, debt, mortgage, lease, loan and sale prevails among them (Baruah 2007: 42-67). In the Karbi tribe, *jhum* land is communal property. The *Me* (village council) under the headman, selects the *jhum* sites for distribution to the households. The headman does not own the land. Land transfers are prohibited to outsiders and non-tribals. *Sukti Bandhak* (agreement of mortgage), *Khoi Bandhak* (temporary mortgage), *Mena* (unclaimed land given to non-tribals for reclamation and cultivation for certain years) and *Adhi* (half-sharecropping base settlement with a cultivator) are the different types of land holding systems of the tribe. Besides, sale, mortgage, lease, gift, will, debt and loan are in practice. These customs might have been influenced by the surplus generating agricultural economy in the valley (Baruah 2007: 37-50; Bahari 2009: 149-150).

In Manipur hills, four broad types of the land ownership system are found: clan ownership, chiefs' ownership (that follow the law of male primogeniture), individual ownership and community ownership (Das 1989: 77). The Kuki chiefs have notional ownership of *jhum* land, who allot the same to the community members, who enjoy rent-free usufruct right. The *jhum* cultivation is labour reciprocal. The chiefs enjoy the customary tributes of the hind legs of slain animals and basketfuls of paddy from the community members. But the land ownership system of the Kuki group is not similar to the Athenian, Roman and medieval equation of landed property with political power (Ray 2010: 40). There are two types of chieftains: the clan chief and the village (territorial) chief, who are notional owners or trustees of land. But while the clan chiefs strictly adhere to the principle of primogeniture, the village (territorial) chiefs get the *derivative* right of land as the younger batches of the clan chiefs. The principle of primogeniture is followed by other members of the community but they depend on the chief for allotment of land (Jain 1991). Customarily, shifting cultivation would go with shifting the village. Village forests are used for hunting, gathering and for firewood collection. A Paite (in the Kuki group) can have self-acquired land on paying cash or kind to the chief with a request for the same. The chief may gift land to an individual who wins his favours for good deeds. He in turn gets a portion of flesh of the game killed. The chief allots rent-free homestead land to each family, which is heritable but not transferable. He can give the same to an outsider temporarily. A person can cultivate the plain areas with the chief's consent on payment of cash or kind and that land becomes the property of that person. For use of wood lands, the chief gets a nominal fee. He also gets the best part of the game hunt in the forest. There is the village commons that the chief can donate for public purposes. The Paites follow both primogeniture and ultimogeniture for inheritance but the ancestral property goes to the eldest son. As such no land can be transferred without the consent of the chief. Sale and gift are practised but lease, will, and mortgage are restrictive (Das 1989: 105-107, 147; Baruah 2007: 47-55).

Among the Tangkhuls the *Awanga* (headman) owns the land but practically land is held by the community. Any cultivator can acquire rent-free right by jungle-clearing with the consent of the village council. There are five zones of land among the Tangkhuls: village settlement area; woodland; terrace land and wet-rice land—all are individually held and the rights over these are acquired by use and occupation. The common land (called *Masala)* for *jhum* cultivation is at the disposal of the village council. The southern Tangkhuls own *jhum* land individually (Ruiva 1989: 55). Among the northern Tangkhuls, individual land is inherited by the eldest son. A landless individual may also get a plot from his relatives and other households against payment of a tax called *Ramsahai.* Lease of land is done on agreement between the owner and tenant. Individual land can be sold in consultation with the clan members and clan head. Buying preference usually goes to the insiders. In the southern Tangkhul area the *Awanga* is the founder of the village land. A number of clans, who settle with the *Awanga,* share *Ramsha* (absolute individual right) in the name of the chief of the clan. The ancestral land cannot be sold or transferred. Transfer through sale, mortgage, lease, gift, loan, debt and inheritance is prevalent within the same village, not outside the village. The Tangkhuls follow the rule of male primogeniture. The traditional Tangkhul land holding system was discussed at a meeting of all headmen on December 14, 2006. Two views emerged there: one view was that customary law was enough for them, while the other view favoured a change over to a legalized land system. (Das 1989: 66-67).

The Kabuis have a three-tier system of land ownership: (a) *Nampao* (clan head) is the owner of the village, clan or community land; *Rampao* (intermediary owner of individual family land) and *Laopao* (tenant cultivator) enjoying *prescriptive* right under the overlordship of the *Rampaos*. Below the *Laopao* there is an under-tenant. There are five kinds of land among the Kabuis (i) Homestead zone allotted by the chief in consultation with the village council; the owner having permanent, heritable and transferable right. (ii) Forest belt or woodland zones belonging to the village community. (iii) *Jhum* land zone is the property of the *Rampaos*. A *jhumia* can acquire permanent right over *jhum* land by repeated cultivation of the same plot under the landlordship of *Rampaos*. (iv) Wet rice and terraced lands are permanent, heritable and transferable and (v) Village common lands. Transfer through sale, gift, mortgage, lease of the *jhum* plots is prevalent though not to the non-tribals. Inheritance is patrilineal with equal share. The youngest son inherits the parental house and the parents live with him. Hodson has found that the Kabuis were exposed to Manipuri influence and came into close contact with the Kukis. (Hodson 1989: 102-103; Das 1989: 86-102; Das 1985: 141-142; Baruah 2007: 24-41).

Land of the Khasis is classified as *Ri Raid* (public land) and *ri-kynti* (private land). *Ri Kynti* is obtainable through agreement with the *Jait* system (the ruling clan). Public lands include *Ka ri Raj* or *ka ri Siyem* (crown's land or *Siyem*'s land); *Ka ri Lyngdoh* lands (priest's land); *Ri snong* (village lands) cultivated by ryots of the village only on the basis of occupancy that is not transferable and *Ki lawkinthang* (sacred groves). Private land is sub-divided into *Ri kur* (clan) lands and *Ri Kynti* acquired by a man individually, or in case of a woman, inherited from her mother. Misra (1990) has made the following classification of land of the Khasis.

Table 2.1: Land Classification of the Khasis

Authority	*Type of Land*	
	Forest	*Others*
1. Syiem	Ri Siyem (U, H)	Ri Bam Siyem Ri lapduh (U, H)
2. Lyngdoh	Ri Law Lyngdoh (U, H)	Ri Lyngdoh (U, H)
3. Clan/s	*Ri Law Sumar (U, H, T, O)*	*Ri Kur, Ri Khain, Ri Duwar (U, H, T, O)*
4. Individual	*Ri Law Sumar (U, H, T, O)*	*Ri Nongtypmen, Ri Khorid, Ri Dakhol (U, H, T, O) Ri Spah U, H, T, L), Ri Longdung (U, L), Ri Raid (U)*
5. Community	*Ri Law Snong (U)*	*Ri Pud*
6. No man's land	-	-
7. Prohibited land	*Ri Law Kyntang, (U), Ri Law Adong, Ri Law Sang*	

U- usufructuary, H- heritable, T- transferable, O- ownership, L- leasehold

In the Khasi hills, clan land cannot be transferred without the consent of the clan durbar. Inheritance must follow the law of entail, by which the property descends from the mother to the youngest daughter. Daughters, other than the youngest daughter, are entitled to maintenance from the produce of such family lands. (Gurdon 1975: 87-88; Misra 1990: 62). Cantlie put the succession to the *iing Khadduh* (the house of the youngest female) in the following order (Cantlie 2008-2009: 11-13, 15):

1. Mother's youngest daughter.
2. Youngest daughter's youngest daughter, however, low so ever.
3. On failure of the youngest daughter's stock, the next youngest daughter of the mother.
4. Her youngest daughter however low so ever.
5. Failing all daughters and their female stocks, the *iing*

> *khadduh* would be absorbed in the *iing khadduh* of the mother's family. Male inheritance is allowed, if all the members except the male, die. If the property is divided and the females of a stock holding a separate share all die, a surviving male takes the property.

But female ultimogeniture as the archaic system was under strict control of the Khasi nobility, and the former could never have survived, as Misra wrote, had it gone against the Khasi nobility. (Misra 1979: 888).

The Khasi Darbar adopted a codified body of land laws in 1925, according to which *Ri Kynti* is a part of private land of an individual or a family or a particular clan; *Ri Shnong* is a village land, belonging to the first occupants which may be inherited or occupied by the members of that community; *Ri Khain* is a portion of that land owned and cultivated by members of a clan; *Raid* is an area belonging to a resident member in the territory on it or its vicinity; *Ri Seng* is a portion of land that remains undivided and undisturbed among the various members inheriting plots of land from the predecessors; *Ri Lyngdoh* is a part of land owned by the *Siyem* and managed and supervised by the priest incharge or a representative from his house; *Re Siyem* is land owned by *Siyem* or his family and is managed by the members of that clan; *Law Kintang* is a reserved forest for sacrificial purpose; *Law adong* is assigned to a section of forests reserved for public use but not for any immediate use; *Law Lingdoh* is a sacred forest; *Raid* is a commune; *Re Lapduh* is a plot of land, of which family owners have become extinct, such lands are without claimants and the *Siyem*'s duty is to keep or dispose of it. *Hima* means the state ruled by a Lynddoh, or *Sirdar* or *Siyem*.

Community land is not transferable and is controlled by the *Raid Durbar* (community assembly). The community members have use-right, occupancy right, and sometimes even heritable right, but only on approval of the *Raid-Durbar*. If an individual user exercises these rights after three consecutive fallow years, the land automatically reverts to the community assembly for re-allocation (Bareh 1985: 268).

The Garos have clan land (*Nokma*) and individual land. The ownership right over *A' Khing* land (*jhum* land) goes to the heiress, which passes on to her heir's daughter in the next generation. The managerial right goes to the husband (*Nokrom*), who can pass on his rights to his sister's son only by getting him married to his heiress daughter. Thus, among the Garos, cross cousin marriage (FSS and MBD marriage) has emerged (Nongbri 1995). Garo inheritance follows female ultimogeniture. The youngest daughter, called *Nokna* is selected by the parents for this. If the mother has no issue, she may adopt a girl as *Nokna* from her maternal line and if she dies before selecting, the father has the right to select. The wealthy parents may also give some property to the other daughters. (Sangma 1987: 149-154).

A-mate A-khing land (individual land) is acquired by purchase or donation. Besides, there is community land called *A-jinma* or *A-joma* land, over which the *Mahari* (clan) has a voice although consent of all members of motherhood is necessary for any decision on land. The caretaker or the *Nokma* of *A-joma* acts according to the wishes of the *Chra* (nearest male relative on the wife's side) and the *mahari* (clan) (Marak 2000: 140, 141, 173-180, 187).

The Lushai chiefs (Lal) in Mizoram were notional owners of lands and enjoyed customary tributes called *Fathang*. The chiefs would follow a hierarchical order in land distribution. While he would retain the best land for himself, the *Ramhauls* (expert *jhum* cultivators) would get the next best part followed by *Zalen*, (service provider to the chiefs). The community members enjoyed usufructuary rights. Inheritance followed the principle of male ultimogeniture. The women could own and inherit property, only when a person was sonless when preference would be the youngest daughter. Sale, gift, exchange, allotment were allowed, though not to a non-tribal and from a non-tribal to another non-tribal. (Shakespeare 1912: 54; Das 1986: 165-168; Chatterjee 2008: 43-44, 49). Among the Chakmas, ownership of ancestral property would go to the male head of the family. Joint property (Ismaili) being common pool was acquired by all the family members. The villagers were allowed to gather firewood and straw for domestic consumption from the village common land. No villager could encroach upon the village commons. The homestead land was vested in the village council that could be allotted to the individuals for house building, against payment of tax. The property was inherited by sons. The daughters, following the *Dabha* system, were entitled to a portion of the patrimony and in the absence of son, daughters and surviving widows inherited it equally. In the absence of daughter, the widow had the right to inherit and if the daughters married against the will of the parents, they would lose this entitlement. The male head of the family could gift or distribute the land, except that of joint property to any person other than the progeny with the consent of the heirs. (Baruah 2011: 21-29).

The Riangs of Tripura practise shifting cultivation, the site of which is selected by the village leader called Choudhry, in consultation with the heads of the family. The entire *jhum* cluster is divided into family-wise plots with boundary marks. *Jhum* land is always cultivated through labour interchange that led to a strong community life. A migrant family also can get homestead land permanent cultivation land. Ownership of land is, however, individual. Inheritance follows the male line on equal basis. In the absence of any son, land goes to the nearest male relation. A father may also give some land to his daughter. The settled cultivation lands belonging to individual heads of families, are transferable through sale and gift, though not to the non-tribals. Widows and divorcees are eligible to maintain family property and a widow-headed family is also entitled to *jhum* plots and community labour. A widow loses these rights on remarriage (Das 1990: 146-147; Baruah 2009: 19-41). The Tripuri tribe has a similar mode of selection of *jhum* lands. The *jhum* cluster is divided into family-wise plots with boundary marks. The forest land in the periphery is always kept under *jhum* cultivation and the forest resource of such specific forest land is vested in the concerned villagers only, where no outsider can access. This type of forest land is called *daikung*, which has been incorporated in the land management records. The khas land of a Tripuri hamlet is controlled by the village council and the headman is the sole authority to allocate household land to an individual family. The inhabitants of the hamlet have access to community orchards or water areas. The Tripuri inheritance is patrilineal on equal share basis. The married sons are bound to maintain his minor brothers and sisters till they attain adulthood and get married. The married sons, who are an separated from the parents, also get an equal share. An adopted son inheriting the property has the same obligations. A widow has the right to enjoy the deceased husband's property that expires if she remarries. (Das 1984: 72; Das 1990: 42-67).

In A Nut Shell

Within the archaic mode of *jhum* economy in the Northeast, individual right was subsumed in the communitarian tradition and, therefore, property was never private, although the formal ownership remained in most cases with the headmen or chiefs. The relation of production in *jhum* economy had the moral foundation of community labour, sharing, social exchange and 'custodial responsibility' of the chiefs and headmen over land that Roy Burman viewed, did not mean "property right over means of production" (Roy Burman 1987). Community land had two dimensions—community ownership and community usufruct. Different though in meaning and implication, these had a common message, i.e. absence of privatisation. This was precisely because, in the East, the Western type of primitive communism in land did not develop into landed property and feudalism owing to incompatible climatic and geographical conditions (Dutt 1986: 85), and low level of productive forces. Certain vital customary laws like *non-reclamation* of *jhum* land in certain tribes and the custom of *reversible right* among some others, might have positively contributed to the egalitarian spirit in land. Moreover, the *jhum* with the primitive tools and instruments of production, could not reach the economy of scale. Thus, although the internal organisation of most of the tribes contained strong elements of an emerging landlord-serf relationship, the value attached to land was less likely to change substantially due to the interplay of endogenous factors. This also built the ethics of egalitarian land system and labour cooperation. Ganguli categorically stated that *Jhum* (shifting cultivation) was a typical case of stationary economy, where production was predominantly for self-consumption, not for accumulation (Ganguli 2008: 116). Within this economy, there emerged three broad types of traditional and working land ownership systems—individual, clan or communal and chief's ownership. The latter did not create a vertical divide in the community. Thus, Guha found shifting cultivation more as a "concession to conditions of land abundance and the character of the soil than as a device of barbarism". However, permanent terrace cultivation coexisted with *Jhuming* and Apatanis and Monpas of Arunachal, the Maos and the Tangkhuls of Manipur, the Angamis of Nagaland and, the Khasis of Meghalaya widely practised terrace cultivation. Barring a few exceptions, the absence of ploughs became a general feature of the hill economy. (Guha 1991: 3-4). He found that shifting cultivation in Assam was suited to the central belt of the riverine tract and the belt of the submontane tract and such lands must have been held only as a tribal or communal territory. This was the material reason behind the formation of convivial economic and social relations and non-adversarial justice dispensing systems in the hills. The most unique feature was the multiple land ownership system within the same ecological zones; diverse customary laws relating to land; unique village structure; predominant *jhum* economy with hunting, fishing and collection as subsidiary food system (Guha 1991: 63).

The question of ownership of tribal land became confusing in the Northeast precisely for two reasons: the kings of Assam, Tripura and Manipur claimed absolute ownership of all lands while to the tribal communities, land had an egalitarian character. The king of Tripura converted the tributary mode of the tribal population towards taxation mode through the *Ghar Chukti Kar*. Secondly, the customary land ownership system in the hills of North Eastern India was further confused with colonisation. Boundary demarcation of communal lands and giving such lands to the chiefs and headmen through various instruments like Agreements, sanads, settlements etc. made them new-landlords in the hills. This vitiated the sacrosanctity of their custodial rights. The rights of the chiefs/headmen now onwards became the *derivative* rights, subject to predatory conditionalities.

The British classified the inhabitants of the Garo hills as Zamindari Garos (living as ryots under the Zamindars in Assam, some of the Garo chiefs living in the outer hills flanking the southern plains, were extracted by the Bengal Zamindars); tributary Garos (who were paying tributes to the British) and the Independent Garos, who were not paying tributes. This artifactual division of the people of the same community dilated their genuine customary practices relating to land. In 1872-73, the Garos were subjugated and in 1874, the Garo Hills district was annexed to Assam. This was followed by a boundary demarcation between Goalpara and the Garo Hills, known as Beckett's Boundary. The Government of India Act-1919, declared the Garo hills as 'Backward Tract' and under the Government of India Act 1935, it was declared as 'Partially Excluded Area'. The Khasi Hills were relatively independent, governed by respective chiefs (*Siyems*). The Khasi chiefs were brought under the British administration after a number of agreements in 1830, 1856, 1858, 1859, 1863, 1877, 1892, etc. Following these agreements and in exercise of the powers under the Land Acquisition Act of 1894, the British administrators straightaway purchased some areas and acquired some land as the tenant of *Ri Kynti* owners, so much so that 31 Khasi villages came to be known as British villages. Besides, lands were taken at different periods under different heads like cantonment land, normal area, 'Administered' Area, Protected Forests, etc. There were also some individual leases for a certain specific purpose for a term of 99 years and 10 years in respective cases (Chakraborti and Changsen. 2004: 102, 106). The customary laws were re-interpreted by them.

The colonials passed a comprehensive act on regulation of house tax in 1919 in Tripura, debarred shifting cultivation and made them cultivate on wet lands. The Raja of Manipur, who had tributary relations with the tribes, became the labour agent during the First Anglo-Burmese War. With gradual consolidation of the British rule, the Raja's relations with the tribes started to drift away from being ritualistic to being the *de facto* ruler of the tribes. The process was further expedited in the changing socio-economic context of the country, till the critical pentagon of *sale-mortgage-rent-exchange-transfer* came to be practised in the tribal economy in Northeast India as a new development in the history of the tribes.

Denial of land rights to the women community in the customary laws, as we understood them, appears to be a major flaw within the customary laws in the hills. Although little interpretation is found on it, one can find existence of only some marginal and concessionary rights to the tribal women under the customary laws in the hills. In fact, in the gathering economy, the women community had a greater stake in land than in the agricultural economy. But the concessionary rights of women in customary laws grossly trivialised the egalitarian ethos of communal land system as it created social division within the tribes. Rights denial to the women's community in the tribal world of the Northeast has recently been linked with the grand narrative of resource dispossession of the women's community the world over by some social activist groups. The pre-colonial and the colonial state exhibited an enormous amount of gender insensitivity in the matter of land rights, the legacy of which was carried forward to the post-1947 period (Sharma 2012: 149).

With modernisation the prescriptive right, derivative right, concessionary right, custodial right, usufructory right, occupancy right and heritable right were discarded as markers of institutional imperfection and such rights were considered as *res nullius* so that acquisition of communal land could be easy on the part of the state with the jurisprudential stamp of *res nullius*. Besides, the scramble happened from inside the society, by the moneylenders and the crafty outsiders in the hills. In Arunachal Pradesh, for example, land is sold or mortgaged with the moneylenders on the basis of oral contract.

A non-tribal may approach the government to allot land in the name of his tribal wife, adopted tribal son or a tribal servant. A tribal woman married to a non-tribal may also apply for land. Such a purchase is not documented. Besides, money economy and cash transactions have replaced the customary transactions in the tribal societies (Agarwal 1986: 179-180). The similar role of moneylenders and crafty individuals are found in Assam, Manipur and Tripura.

We find significantly different accounts of the customary laws of the tribes of Northeast India in the two great works of the Law Research Institute of the Guwahati High Court—one by J.N. Das and the other by Jeuti Barua. This difference might be attributed to the differences in the two economic and historical epochs of the early 1980s and 2000 onwards. Within the gap of three decades, spectacular changes have taken place in the land economy of the tribal communities of Northeast India. The penetration of market economy considerably diluted the customary laws of the tribes of this region. This gave rise to the nascent form of private property in the hitherto communal land system in the hills, in which the state, market and the elites were the three major players. There was also the great role of institutions, including, a new set of land administration of the state, land revenue acts, Land Possession Certificate (LPC) and land patta system, JFM, CFM, etc. that gave the message of individuation of the communal land in the era of market economy. The participatory forest management discouraged shifting cultivation and the growing incidence of forest resource grabbing by affluent sections became more pronounced in this era for spatial fixation of capital. Barua's studies captured some of the changes that so happened in the tribal land system.

The country discourse did raise serious scepticism on the future of the customary land ownership systems in Northeast India in spite of the constitutional safeguards and policy commitments to save the customary laws of the tribes. The customary land ownership system from the British days, has been interpreted and understood in many ways and have received different interpretations depending on the role of different interest groups operating from behind and their strategic locations in the communities. On the other hand, the liberal state of India always chose to see land in the rights-based frame, in which positive law prevailed over social customs, although it simultaneously celebrated the principle of 'Tribal Panchsil'. But in the changing context, the customary land ownership system in this region got entrapped in the critical triangle of the state, market and the land speculators and land became the victim of push and pull of these forces till the practices of sale, purchase, lease, mortgage and sub-renting progressively seeped in and eventually routinised in the tribal societies to build another trajectory of accumulation by dispossession. This process was sharpened with the advent of globalisation. Under globalisation, there was a growing trend towards homogenisation of the land ownership system based on positive law. This trend, side by side, has freed the communal land system from its pristine productive and reproductive uses and fetishised the same under name of economy. This brought about major changes in both the cropping pattern and the land-use pattern. The lower bands of the hills became more susceptible to privatisation and accumulation that are found in Meghalaya, Tripura and parts of Manipur (Churachandpur and Sadar Hills). Thus, even customary law is regarded as one of immemorial antiquity based on common consent (Baruah 2007: vi), it no longer remained antiquarian and consensual.

The Colonial Institutions

The colonial land institutions were meant for expropriation of land-based resources through establishing ownership rights, control over land use and unfair division of the products of land. The colonial administrators introduced the Roman jurisprudential distinction of *possession* and *ownership* as the two distinct legal forms. Private property was protected by positive law, which was later incorporated in the legal process of 'eminent domain', a concept developed by the famous Dutch jurist, Hugo Grotius in the year 1625. The instrument of eminent domain privileged colonial land grabbing in the tribal areas of the Northeast region. Territorial expansion of the colonials was also done through deceptive capture and coercive modernisation of which Fitzjames Stephen, the legal adviser to the Viceroy's Council, was the great advocate. He opposed the Ilbert Bill 1883, intended to equate the white and the native in law. The idea was to justify imperial absolutism and to capture communal resources through the two jurisprudential instruments of "*lex loci* and *res nullius*" (Pandey and Pathak 1995: 1974-75).

In course of time, the colonials in Northeast India acquired both *imperium* and *dominium:* sovereign power and ownership/ possession. The two major ways of acquiring the *dominium* of tribal land resources were conquest of tribal inhabited territories and dispossession of their land. The tribal land system was then *integrated* with colonial institution and finally, with the world system of capitalist modernisation. Formal institutions were forced upon the tribal societies only from the stage of *consolidation* of the nomothetic empire. They developed land codes in line with British Common Law that dismissed the communal land systems. Institutional economics set the fundamental political, social and legal ground rules to govern property rights of tribal communities and to routinise primitive accumulation through the jural route. This became trans-historical and blurred the distinction between *imperium* and *dominium.*

The *differentia specifica* of the legal rules from the customary ones were essentially effective-enforceable and cognitive-non-adversarial, on the one hand, and positive- adversarial and normative-convivial on the other. The uni-jural regulatory regime of the colonisers stymied customary rights by colonial concepts of possession and dispossession. The possessional functions, included, individual title deeds, tax-revenue rights, commercial and profit-making rights and natural resource rights while the dispossessional functions included de-recognition of the customary rules, derecognition of community as legal person, annihilation of communal land resources and *terra nullius* status to communal land. Application of the *lex loci* made the colonisation process complete in the hitherto stateless communities and henceforth communal land came to be governed by institutional economics, backed by colonial epistemology and political power. The formal rights to land was a colonial construct and, thus, when Baden Powell wrote *Land System of British India,* he categorically stated that "when the land revenue settlement operations of a district are concluded, when rights have been recorded, and the interests of all classes set down in due form" (Powell 1892: 2).

In Northeast India, after colonisation there was not much formal title of right, except some selected British areas, like Shillong. Therefore, allocation of much of the land resources was done through wrongful accumulation and grabbing. This let loose serious contradictions between the 'formalist' and the 'substantivist' or between the 'institutional' economics of the colonisers and the 'processual' economics of the tribal communities. The colonial bureaucrats could not universalise the institutional model in tribal land systems due to odd geographical terrains and apprehension of tribal upsurge. They therefore, allowed the customary laws to govern the tribal land systems but under strict colonial surveillance. Their strategy was to control the tribal economy *politically* through giving conditional allowance to the tribal headmen, subject, again, to overall colonial surveillance. Therefore, in the Khasi Hills, "the British established the right to carry a road, in whatever direction it might think proper, across the whole extent of country lying between Cherra and plains of Assam, and they were at liberty to construct bridges, erect halting bungalows, stockades, guard rooms or storehouses, at any point along this line of road. Among other things, the Khasi chieftains, in consideration that no revenue or tribute was extracted from them, were required to furnish, on being paid, the articles like timber, stone, slate and lime for the use of any establishment"(Pamberton 1991: 239-240). The land revenue being the least viable, the colonials imposed hill hearth tax, hill house tax, hoe tax, etc. on the subsistence hill cultivators of this region. The Mikirs of Assam were the first to be assessed on a graded House Tax system.

Such a taxation system was not of scale but had a strategic purpose to check the shifting habits of the people that often created governance problems. They sought to settle the tribes on a particular geographical location and in defined house sites so that their number could be monitored and conveniently governed. The political economy significance of the House Tax was transformation of the erstwhile Tributary Mode to the Taxation Mode and change in the erstwhile relation of production of the tribes. The Taxation mode in the hills being revenue light, the larger chunk of profit-revenue was drawn from commercial timber. And so the forest revenue administration trivialised the customary rights through a strategic combination of *conservation-dissolution* and artificially enclavised the forest space based on the *Pareto Optimal* principle, well guarded by authoritative forest administration. This criminalised the usufrauct right of the tribal people.

In Assam, the Permanent Settlement grounded the concept of private property in the rice producing land that created new structures and institutions. The British readily inherited the distinct landed interests group of the Zamindar class already in place during the Mughal rule. This class was recognised as the new landed class, although they were in fact revenue collectors, who received land grants, not land titles. (Powell 1882: 97-98). Politically, it was considered that the confirmation of hereditary rent collecting agents as the sole proprietors would bind them to the government and economically, it was expected, that the Permanent Settlement would encourage the investment of capital on land and growth of a middle class, commercial and agricultural wealth and increase tax paying ability of the population, which would compensate the government's sacrifice of the prospective increase in land revenue (Islam 1979: xi, 78). To Wallerstein, therefore, the single-most important change imposed by the modern world-system was establishment of a systematic legal basis of land title and ownership of land (Wallerstein 2010: 6-14).

A number of tribal areas in the hills were brought under the permanent settlement including the Khasis, Zamindari

Garos and a small section of the Mizos. Chatterjee wrote, during 1879, some Lushai chiefs became the official Zamindars under the Permanent Settlement (Bengal Regulation 1793). Raja Machuilal, son of illustrious Lalchukla, was the chief, who paid Rs. 210 annually to the Sylhet treasury (Chatterjee 1994: 39). The major attraction of the colonials in the hills being the forest resources; they enclavised the forest areas as Reserved Forests and Protected Forests that dispossessed the tribal people in the same way as agricultural land was enclavised in the late 18th and early 19th century England to dispossess the peasants by hired labour (Devi 1966: 33).

Jurisprudential dispossession caused conflicts between the pre and the post-accumulative institutions and, as Pandey and Pathak viewed, invalidated the assumption that modernity would subsume the traditional economy, politics and the legal systems. Lack of clearer understanding of anthropology of customary law created two traditions by the end of the 19th century: modernisation of tradition and traditionalisation of modern. As such, empire building and annexation of the tribal land in Northeast India happened in a state of vacum in formal jurisprudence, in which case, the doctrines of *res nullius* and *lex loci* as abstract constructs were used to place communal lands under the sovereign jurisdiction (imperium) of the British. Initially, the British treated all communal lands as *res nullius*. On consolidation of the empire, both *res nullius* and *terra nullius* were legalised through *lex loci*. The recent incarnation of *terra nullius* is *Khas land*, a governmentalised term often used for acquisition of tribal lands, which raised a serious controversy between the state, judiciary and the community. Later, they tried to build a modern judicial system by incorporating the native needs but at the same time, elevated the textual over the customary 'through revival of shastric scholarship which was a continuation of modern textual jurisprudence' (Pandey and Pathak 1995: 1974-75).

Two things happened as a result. One was obliteration of the stereotypes like the "status-contract, formal-informal, tradition-modern and great-little" (Pandey and Pathak 1995:

1975). The other was institutionalisation of *res nullius*. In this connection, Roy Burman refuted the state or king's ownership right, which was an Anglo-Saxon concept implanted by the colonial masters and found expression in *res nullius* and *terra nullius*. In India, the concept of *res nullius* came to prevail as a legacy of colonial rule and in some parts of the country, this concept was applied in the post- independence period. And the areas where the concept were applied were the resource-rich tribal areas. This concept is also used during the land survey and settlement operations in the hills. (Roy Burman 1998: iii, iv). He referred to the eminent historian Nilkant Shastry, who conceded that even in ancient and medieval India, sometimes the kings tried to apply the concept of *res nullius* that led to overthrow of dynasties (Roy Burman 1998: iii).

Grounding the concept of private property in the hills created a dilemma for the paternalistic and non-regulatory administration of the British. But as things demanded and to accommodate variations in the Hills, in the Lushai hills, a Superintendent was posted as its head and the Political Officers were placed in each division in the Northeast Frontier Agency, who enjoyed more discretionary powers than a Deputy Commissioner in the plains (Singh 1987: 106-107). In Manipur, the hill tribes came to be administered by the President of the Manipur State Darbar that ended the erstwhile tributary relation of the hill tribes with the King.

The colonial rulers made the state a powerful *gesselschaft* to become the 'universal landlord' (Powell 1882: 26). But at the same time, they had the apprehension that a big floating population, engaged in shifting cultivation and pastoral economy could be a potential threat to the law and order and that a sedentary population could be a sound base for political stability. These reinforced the state's aversion to these two modes of subsistence (Chaudhury 2004: 96-97). Driven by revenue motives, a host of acts and rules, including the Settlement Rules of 1870, (implemented in 1883), the Land and Revenue Regulation-1886 and Settlement Rules in 1887, Ryotwari system in the Manipur valley areas (through the

Assam Regulation of 1886), the Rules of 1880 on land revenue and Landlord and Tenant Act in Tripura, Assam Forest Regulation-1891 were framed to redefine ownership of communal land and institutionalise the absolute property right of the state on land. On the other hand, market operations led to resource drainage from the tribal region to the metropolis. The drainage followed a process of commoditisation (with no reciprocal exchange), distinct from commercialisation (with reciprocal exchange) leading to expropriation and annihilation of the community (Nadkarni, Pasha and Prabhakar. 1989: 26).

The reproduction-function of communal land was denied in this process. Besides certain types of spatial enclaves in the Northeast like 'Reserve Forests' and 'Protected Forests' reviled the natural right of the forest dependent communities and certain other types of enclaves created by Inner Line Regulation and the Chin Hills Regulation in the hills restricted entry of the outsiders. The colonial distinction between enclaves (inflated with riches) and the community space (progressively emptied) amounted to primitive accumulation of the social, cultural or civilisational space of the tribal communities in Northeast India.

The juridical mode of accumulation went with the twin assumptions that communal rights were imperfect and that acquisition of such rights was necessary in 'public interest', a term which remained thoroughly controversial in jurisprudence. This broke the individual-community conflation of communal land which Roy Burman found was critical while appraising land relations and the land reforms planning in the tribal areas of the Northeast India (Roy Burman 1991: 27). He refuted the jurisprudential principle of *res nullius,* as, empirically, there cannot be any original assertion of individual right over nature's endowment without hedging the rights of any group entity. He substantiated the argument by an example from Nagaland: When timber is extracted from a person's field for sale outside, a Naga commission is collected from the buyer, which is used for the common purpose of the village. He further contested the concept of *res nullius* that established the proprietary claim of the Raja over land which provided historical legitimacy of conquest to the Rajas of Assam, Manipur and Tripura (Roy Burman 1991: 28). Secondly, lack of written record of land ownership facilitated acquisition of tribal land by force and fraud which the customary laws failed to robustly oppose. In fact, the customary laws of the tribes were repeatedly diluted by the British, paving the way to individual ownership of the chiefs and headmen till the Committee on the Development of the Backward Classes set up by the Planning Commission, Government of India in 1981, recommended the legal right of individuals over land to incentivise improvements and increase productivity (Roy Burman 1994: 42).

On the other hand, the philanthropologic gesture of 'Tribal Panchsil' appreciated the sacrosanctity of the tribal land system, which threw the Indian state into a dual institutional dilemma in post-colonial economic reconstruction that demanded huge resources located largely in the tribal areas and the moral commitment towards the tribal communities. And yet, the Draft National Tribal Policy, proclaimed after 60 years of Indian Independence, once more raised the issues of land alienation and protection of forest rights. This time, the institutional dilemma was between India's commitment to the global market and policy commitment to the tribal autarky.

The treasury view of land revenue administration in Northeast India did not appreciate the bi-focal nature of the economy in the valleys and tended to institutionally homogenise the land economy and land revenue administration. The states of Northeast India, particularly Assam, Manipur and Tripura—the homes of bi-focal economy—did not enact separate land legislations for the hill areas, except the instrument of the Sixth Schedule having different incarnations in the three states. This let loose perpetual conflict between the state and the Autonomous District Council in the matters of land legislation and taxation.

On the social front, the self-aggrandising tribal elites acted as the third force in the land game, often leading to an unholy nexus with the state institutions. And today, this community champions the cause of land registration to radicalise their ideological standpoint ignoring the five golden principles of communal land: non-accumulative system; subsistence economy; harmonisation of agriculture with nature; production of social surplus and reproduction function of land.

Neoliberal Institutionalisation

The rationality principle of methodological individualism built the epistemological edifice of neoliberal privatisation and corresponding institutionalisation. The first generation structural adjustment programme proclaimed investment-growth equation. The second generation adjustment sought for Growth-Institution equation that required rule of law, defined and secured property rights, 'investment climate', security of lives, property and assets of the investors and policy and legislative reforms. The Growth-Institution equation demanded robust legislative and policy reforms and discarded communal land as symptomic of poor institutions responsible for the failure of the economy and hindering investment and economic growth. Institutionalisation of property rights in the neoliberal development theory went one step further for cementing finite neo-positivistic construction of property rights dismissing the natural right in land. A World Bank Document on India gave the following policy options for land reforms: (a) elimination of restrictions of land market and land lease, replacement of rent ceiling, allow land lease, drop restriction on subdivision and on sale of land to non-agriculturists, review legislation on compulsory land acquisition and allow farmers or their representatives to negotiate directly with investors for transfer of land. (b) provide option for wide range of ownership pattern; tenural security and title deed, a menu of tenural options, including the communal ones and allow groups to make need-based choice with possibility of making future transition to individual holding. (c) complement restrictions on tribal land alienation; providing individual or collective property rights for productive development and for avoiding distress sales; right of first refusal or community consent for sales (World Bank 2007: xiv, 93, 95). In response to the neoliberal land reforms programme, the states of Northeast India assured institutional guarantee to the foreign direct investors, provided resource subsidies and necessary infrastructure, tightened governance norms and enforceable contracts to facilitate "transformation costs" (Aron 2000: 99-105). This reduced the states to 'debtor states' romanticising with hydro-dollar, green capitalism and black capitalism. In this process, the North Eastern states finally sunk into the predatory market economy.

On the other hand, a section of land grabbers took advantage of the informal land market for idyllic accumulation. This raised the apprehension as Aron did, of higher transaction cost of goods, services and capital (Aron 2000: 103) and challenged Alesina's "Correlation Matrix" for institutional variables and growth (Alesina 1997: 112) on the basis of which the World Bank and foreign investors made spatial fix of investment in hill areas of Northeast India. A section of the tribal elites came to defend land reforms agenda to suit the neoliberal order and took advantage of the loopholes of the acts for fastidious land transactions. The land revenue acts of the states insisted on 'legal person' for ownership, the documentary proof of which was conspicuously lacking. This eased up elite capture by showing such lands as *terra nullus*.

We take the discussion back to the major colonial regulations to understand the issues of primitive accumulation and accumulation by dispossession.

The Bengal Eastern Frontier Regulation, 1873 (Inner Line Regulation)

The Bengal Eastern Frontier Regulation, 1873 was an enclavisation project that insulated the hill tribes from their neighbours in the plains. The economic and commercial objectives of the Regulation were four-fold: laying down rules of possession of land and control trade in forest products; regulate the trade of Indian rubber between the hills and the British traders; control the extension of tea plantation into the hill areas and to regulate the transfer of land in these areas. The Act, thus, had a political-economy purpose. This "unkind line" drawn by the colonial rulers "dismembered the hills from the rest of Assam" (Bezbaruah 1958: 95, 97), broke the organic unity of the people of the land and restricted British Subject or the non-natives of the Districts acquiring any land beyond the 'Inner Line 'without sanction of the government. The Regulation was extended to Kamrup, Darang, Naogaon, Sibsagar, Lakhimpur, Khasi and Jaintia Hills, Naga Hills and Cachar.

This regulation encouraged the tribal people to bring Simul timber and India rubber to the fairs at Darrang and Udalguri. Besides, rubber exported from Cachar was also collected from the forests of Manipur and the Lushai Hills revenue generation, trade regulation, protection of the Zamindari rights, capture of communal resources through reservation of forest and monopoly right over the resources in the hill were the chief purposes of the Inner Line Regulation. The monopoly control over resources, replaced the above Regulation, by Regulation I of 1882 and Regulation II (as extended by III of 1884). These Regulations prohibited extraction of forest products by all including, the Garos without license from the Deputy Commissioner. Increasing forest reservation extinguished rights of the Garos from the forest areas. The government gave monetary compensation to some and privileged the use of forest products, except the reserved varieties to others (Ratankumar 2004: 296; Dutta Ray 1985: 227-228). In the Khasi hills, no inner line was needed because the chiefs had resigned their natural resources, and received half the profits from these. The Schedule Districts Act of 1874 was enforced in the hill districts, where the Inner Line Permit was not yet extended. The Regulation was also extended to the Lushai Hills to check frequent Lushai raid on extended tea gardens along the foothills that threatened shifting cultivation and hunting grounds.

Besides the Inner Line, the 'Outer Line' was promulgated where administration was to be conducted in an ordinary way while between the inner and outer lines, it was to be administered only politically, i.e, with loose political control in the affairs of the frontier hills. In the 'Outer Line', the tribals could be reprised for raids on and damage to the plains' people, their cultivation and cattle; and for human sacrifice (Singh 1987: 108).

The protectionist version of the Inner Line Pass was contested by Muhkim (Muhkim 2013) and Chakravarti found the commercial purpose of this act, such as acquisition of land for plantations (Chakravarti 2013). It was one of the early primitive modes for extraction of resources from the hill region.

The Assam Land and Revenue Regulation, 1886

The Assam Land and Revenue Regulation gave a stronger institutional shape by codifying the Assam Settlement Rules 1870, without imparing the features of the earlier system which the colonials introduced. This led to the rise of a new agrarian class. The purpose of this act was to introduce absolute property right in land and to bring more lands under plough cultivation and plantation for revenue and profit. The Regulation established the rights of proprietors, land holders, settlement holders and to make the right a legally derivable concept (Saikia 2003: 40-41) and gave permanent, heritable and transferable right of use and occupancy to a person, who had held a plot of land continuously for the past ten years and had paid the requisite revenue. The Regulation empowered the state government to make rules for allotment of land for use of *jhum* cultivation and for regulation and control of enjoyment of land so allotted by persons permitted to resort to the same (Saikia 2003: 40-41).

This regulation was extended to the Garo Hills, Khasi Hills, Jaintia Hills, Mikir Hills, Naga Hills, Lushai Hills and the NC Hills. In the Hill districts of Assam, however, this regulation was applied with certain exceptions. In the hill areas, in lieu of revenue, an annual tax on each adult male person cultivating during the year of assessment, or on each family or house of persons taking part as aforesaid, was imposed. The revenue system in the hills was not uniform. Virtually no land revenue was imposed in the hills except in a very few specific areas of the Jaintia Hills and the submontane region of the Garo Hills. Assessment was made on houses, not on land. The Line System was introduced delimiting certain areas as closed to the immigrants and a Line System Committee was formed in 1936 to enquire into the working of the system which recommended ejection of unauthorised occupants from the 'closed' villages but suggested a larger unit of prohibited areas. Subsequently, no settlement or transfer of land by patta was allowed to the immigrants and squatting of land was to be evicted. In 1945, a practical measure for the protection of the tribals was adopted. The tribal belt or block in the sub-montane areas was created in areas with more than 50 per cent of tribal people. The Regulation of 1886 was amended accordingly to protect the backward classes, including plain tribals, hill tribals, tea garden tribes, Santhals, scheduled castes and Nepali cultivator graziers. The latter were subsequently omitted from the list of protected classes (Das 1982).

The Land Acquisition Act of 1894

In the common law system of UK, land was acquired for 'public purpose's which was followed throughout the Commonwealth nations, including India (Rathakrishnan and Kumar 2013: 31). The Land Acquisition drive was started for the private sector in 1863, with the alibi for 'public purposes' by application of the principle of 'eminent domain'. This principle privileged privatisation of land and made India a supplier of cheap raw materials for the British Industrial Revolution. The state sided with the capitalist classes and annihilated customary rights of the tribal people. The Act was amended in 1962, permitting the state to acquire land for a company for industrial purposes again inter pretext of public purpose. The Land Acquisition (Companies) Rules were made in 1963. The Collector and the Senior District Agricultural Officer had the power of enquiring whether the acquired land was agricultural or not, without consulting the cultivators. Further, amendment of the Act was made in 1984 that inserted the words, "or for a company" after the words, "any public purpose" (Rathakrishnan and Kumar 2013: 31). This amendment blurred the distinction between public and private that was enveloped in the modernist-positivistic jurisprudence. Many of the lands acquisitioned for such purposes were in the areas of the tribal constellation (Guha 2000: 86).

The courts have constantly differed from the legislative determination of 'public purpose'. In successive cases, the Supreme Court held that 'public purpose' was elastic and could only be developed through judicial inclusion or exclusion in keeping with the changes in time, the state of society and its needs. Moreover, courts have held that acquisition benefiting particular individuals or entities could satisfy the requirements of public purpose. The Act provides that compensation for land acquisition must be computed at the market value for the land acquired and must include payment of any damage made by the person interested as a result of acquisition. A solatium of 30% of the market value of the land is to be paid in addition to the compensation for compulsory acquisition. The Act prohibits the intended value of the land for computing market value. That is, if agricultural land is acquired for commercial use, the compensation will be based on the prevailing market price of agricultural land (Wahi 2013: 49-51).

But there is no clear basis of determining the affected parties and the definition of 'affected persons'. Very often, only the minimum subsets of landowners are identified as affected for compensation. Encroachers, sharecroppers and landless labourers, who have an interest in land are not compensated. The unregistered agriculturists are also not eligible for compensation. The process of acquisition is very time-consuming and the district collector/tehsildar have enormous discretion in adjudicating objections to acquisition and compensation. Often the awards are ad hoc and unacceptable to the local community. Finally, there is no clear formula for calculation of compensation though the judiciary in several cases have ruled that the compensation be paid more than three times the original amount. The amendments in 1962 and 1984 preserved the state's authority for acquiring land which in most cases did not follow the consultation or negotiation process. The state's action is considered as the best and onus to prove it unjust/wrong is left to the public. In many cases, the consultation process is avoided by invoking the urgency clause. In the speculative land market, the market value of the same remains under imperfect market conditions and monetary compensation does not augment social compensation for acquisition. (Kumar 2011: 23).

The Chin Hills Regulation, 1896

The Chin Hills Regulation (Regulation IV) of 1896 was promulgated for maintaining law and order and control over the tracts of the Chin Hills. It had authorised the Superintendent or the Deputy Commissioner of the Lushai Hills to order eviction of an undesirable outsider from the area and to tax the residence, permanent or temporary, clans and villages. It was extended to the NC Hills, the Garo Hills, the Khasi and Jayantia Hills (excluding the Shillong municipal and cantonment area where only the provision for taxation would apply), the Naga and the Mikir Hills.

This regulation imposed Hill House Tax in the hill areas. The Superintendent of the Chin Hills was empowered to appoint and remove any headman, define the local limits of his jurisdiction and to declare what clan, or village, or both should be subject to him. Although the superintendent was to be guided by the local customs as far as practicable, he was more concerned with keeping peace and order within the tract. Section 35 of the act stipulated that 'Taxes shall be levied on all clans and villages at such rates and in such manner as the local government might prescribe and Section 36 stipulated that an order for the payment of any fine or tax or for the delivery of any property, or for the performance of any act might be enforced- (1) by the seizure of movable property or standing crops of the person against whom such order is made, or when the order is made against a clan or village or family of Chins, of any person belonging thereto, or (2) with the sanction of the Superintendent or of an Assistant Superintendent, by simple imprisonment, for a term not exceeding one year, or the person against such order is made". The Regulation also contained punitive measures against any chief for abusing the powers conferred upon him by this regulation or for neglecting to obey any reasonable order of the Superintendent. Administrative control over the headmen under this regulation stymied the customary land rights.

Rules for the Administration of the Lushai Hills

The administration of Lushai Hills District was vested in the Chief Commissioner of Assam, the superintendent of the Lushai Hills and his assistants and in the chiefs and headmen of the villages. The latter were held responsible for the behaviour of their people, and the superintendent and his Assistants were required to uphold the authority of the chiefs to the best of their ability.

The rules also regulated the succession to villages of deceased chiefs, appoint guardians to minor chiefs, authorise the partition of existing villages, formation of new villages and to appoint chiefs or headmen and fix the number of houses in such villages. The Superintendent was empowered to determine the boundaries of lands to be occupied by chiefs, and to settle disputes between them regarding such lands. He had authority to punish chiefs and headmen, and, subject to confirmation by the Chief Commission, to depose them for misconduct. The formation of new villages was made possible through the grant of Boundary Paper to the chiefs, called *Ramri Leikha*. This 'structured-subordination' mode was used to capture and control communal lands through the chiefs. Das noted that in the colonial structure, the institution of chieftainship and associated management of resources prevailed to some extent yet the basic allegiance of the chieftains went towards the colonial state rather than to the community"(Das: 1982). For the purpose of *Ramri leikha*, the whole territory of Lushai Hills Districts was divided into 16 circles, with an officer in charge and one interpreter posted in each circle. The circle officers were responsible to the superintendent of the district. The British policy was not to interfere directly in the internal affairs of the Lushais but the Superintendent (of Lushai Hills) on behalf of the government, was empowered to interfere in the demonstration of the chiefs, only when they went beyond their respective jurisdictions (Datta 1995).

Ramri Leikha created another mini-enclave for resource accumulation. The British rulers instrumentalised, particularly, the Sailo chiefs for controlling the recalcitrant Luishai tribes, who were making sporadic attacks on the British territories. The British also increased the number of chiefs by selecting them from different clans and offered *Ramri Leikha*. These chiefs served the British in the Lushai Wars and were called *Hnamchawm* chiefs. Besides, there were some Hualngo and Pawi chiefs, established by the Sailos, to hold charge of sub villages belonging to the latter. The British recognised them as independent ones. By giving the chiefs the power to control their own community and the policy of non-interference towards them helped smooth administration over the tribe with less cost. The Superintendent of Lushai Hills prescribed a village with more than 80 households adequate for separate existence. Formation of hamlets was prevented and these were either destroyed or were amalgamated with the main village. While the *Ramri Leikha* recognised the hereditary rights of the chiefs, these rights needed confirmation by the Superintendent on each succession.

The hereditary right of the chiefs to the *Ram* was strengthened in 1937 by recognising the law of primogeniture (Deb and Lahiri 1982: XIII). *Ramri Leikha* took away much of the traditional rights and status of the chiefs. Chatterjee wrote that, McCall, the Superintendent of Lushai Hills, transformed the loyalty of the Lushai chiefs from the Superintendent to the British Raj. William Carey's Regulation and Shakespeare's Settlement Policy brought a sea change in the chieftainship organisation; they were made the representatives of the British and had to remain under strict surveillance and control of the Superintendent. The land-related rights that were abolished were (i) right to seize food stores and property of the villagers, who wished to transfer their allegiance; (ii) proprietary right over land; (iii) right to freedom of action in relation to making their sons chiefs under their own jurisdiction (Chatterjee 1975: 69-70).

Box 2.1: The Format of Ramri Leikha

Name of the chief............................of——————————— village.

The boundary of your village is already given below. You must not cross this boundary in any direction. You can establish a village anywhere within this boundary Whoever does jhooming within your village boundary shall, pay usual basketful of rice to you. On your part you pay house tax to the government. You will also adjudicate all disputes.

If you obey government orders, all these will be your RAM in your life.

If for any reason your RAM is too big for your requirement, this order can be rescinded. On your death, I shall decide who will be your successor, though normally they will be from your descendants.

Superintendent of Lushai Hills.
Aizawl.

The British introduced wet cultivation on patches of flat lands with Santhal labourers and collected land revenue. On the town lands of Aizawl and Lunglei, the chief's right to choose house sites was restricted and no one was allowed to possess more than one plot, where the house occupied by him actually stood. A small area around the house was also allotted for gardening of which nobody could claim inheritance right. Mortgage and letting land were also illegal. In case of acquisition for public purposes, land compensation amounted to the value of materials of the building, which stood on the land. In course of time, this restriction was extended to other stations. Land revenue was collected only for the land held by the Christian missions and from the shop sites of Aizawl and Lunglei (Ghuman 2010: 130-131). Through these instruments, the British could "intercept the tribal outrages and avoid undesirable consequences of the British rule over the tribes"(Rosanga 2008: 305-308). The petty chiefs were amalgamated with the big chiefs. In 1911-12, settlement of hamlet rules were laid down for those wishing to take up permanent cultivation and later this right of cultivation was made hereditary on conditional basis. The wetfields within the chiefs' jurisdiction were also made transferable to the individual households and the actual cultivators were to pay paddy tax to the chiefs. Shifting of households within the chiefs' jurisdiction was also prohibited and the colonial authorities advocated for government ownership of all the lands in Mizoram. In this way, the colonials incorporated the more powerful Lushai clans within land administration in a cheaper and more sanitised way. The instruments of *Ramri leikha* and similar other instruments corresponding to this also served as the political and ideological tools for annihilation of the community space.

Land Administration in the Naga Hills

In the Naga Hills, at the beginning of the British administration, there were 170 estates, paying a total revenue of Rs. 1,787. Extension of railway tract caused transfer of the Naga Mauzas assessed for revenue to Naogaon, Sivsagar and N.C. Hills Districts. This reduced the revenue available from the Naga Hills. However, House Tax remained the main source of revenue that was collected by the gaonburas on commission basis. Besides royalties from coal mines, forest products, grazing fees, fees for prospecting license were granted to White Hall Petroleum Corporation and Burma Oil Company. Income Tax from government employees and excise duty were the other sources of revenue in the Naga Hills (Mathew 2007).

The Naga Hills was a forest division of Assam from where not much revenue was derivable. But for revenue gain, large forest tracts in the Naga Hills were reserved for construction of the Assam Bengal Railway and measures were taken to determine the nature and extent of land rights over these places as per the Assam Forest Regulation 1891. The forest region of the Naga Hills was classified as Reserved Forest (exclusive right of the state); Protected Forest (limited right of the Naga villagers) and Unclassified State and Village Forest (Naga villagers had considerable control and use right) after the British departure. The state authority encouraged indiscriminate felling for higher forest revenue in the 1960s. It was also followed by illegal timber export, felling of private and village forests for saw mill factories. The clandestine timber trade gave birth to Naga business elites. Subsequently, the state introduced the Coupe System that required the contractors to deposit security money before felling. Transit pass and challan system were issued by the forest department. These measures led to considerable increase in issue of transit passes. Then a revenue sharing arrangement by agreement with the Zeliangrong Council and still later, a subsidised regeneration scheme were introduced (Singh 2001: 239-242). The Naga headmen were also subject to structured subordination. Robb wrote that the British introduced election of the Naga headmen, perhaps, because it would take time to convert the Nagas from their democratic and independent habits into a state of subordination to the council of elders. Bailey and Elliott were instrumental in this. Elliott envisaged introducing village or tribal system with headman being paid twenty per cent of the revenue collected, with the hope that authority would accrue to them and they would be able to control and guide the villagers with the assistance of government when necessary in support against disobedience and disrespect (Robb 1997: 261).

The Land Administration in Khasi, Jaintia and Garo Hills

The British initially did not introduce land revenue administration in the Khasi Hills. Revenue was raised from judicial fines and tolls levied on all goods in the village market. But in the British Khasi villages and the Jaintia Hills, government was entitled to receive as revenue at least such portion of the produce as went into the hands of the former rulers. Subsequently, they explored the possibility of land or house tax (Phira 1989: 6-8) by persuading the Khasi chiefs to lease their waste lands to the government for a royalty for coffee and tea plantation and pursued the Sirdar of Jeerung to make the richest Sal forest over to the government" (Joshi 2004: 313-314).

In the Garo Hills, the Scheduled District Act of 1874 conferred some powers to the chiefs in the matters of police, civil and criminal justice and in revenue administration within the Elaka. With little plans to colonise the hills, the British planned to win over the traditional power elites by bestowing them with certain rights of a nascent feudal order and so the British administration allowed them to become authoritative, which enabled them to usurp community land for commercial plantation, collect market tolls and to lease out mining activities to outsiders. Limestone quarries being handsome revenue sources in the Khasi Hills, the British concluded treaties with Khasi chieftains through grant of Sanads that gave the right to the British to exploit the quarries. The limestone quarries were leased out to the highest bidders. In the Jaintia Hills, the British became exclusive receivers of rents and royalties. (Dhkar 1983: 152).

In the Khasi Hills, as Karlsson wrote, the British treated the *Siyems* as territorial heads that undermined the traditional land tenure system (Karlsson 2011: 170). The British government clothed them with the sanctity of law for land grabbing and the mode of land grabbing became three-fold: some were ceded under the agreements, some obtained from *Ri Kynti* owners by outright purchase and some were acquired according to law (Phira 1989: 12). The sanads provided for complete subordination to the Government of Assam (Hidayatullah 1979: 19).

Box 2.2: Format of Sanad

YOU...................... having been elected of the state of .... in the district of the Khasi and Jaintia Hills, this sanad ratifying your election and appointing you *Siyem*, is conferred upon you on the following condtions:-

I. You shall be subject to the orders and control of the Deputy Commissioner of the district of the Khasi and Jaintia Hills, who will decide any dispute that may arise between yourself and the Chief of any other Khasi State. You shall obey implicitly any lawful order which the Deputy Commissioner, or other officer authorised on that behalf by the local government, may issue to you.

II. You are hereby empowered and required to adjudicate and decide all civil cases and all criminal offences, except those punishable under the Indian Penal Code with death, transportation or imprisonment for five years and upwards, which may arise within the limits of the State, in which your subjects alone are concerned. In regard to the offences above excepted, you shall submit an immediate report to the Deputy Commissioner of the Khasi and Jaintia Hills, and faithfully carry out the orders he may give concerning their disposal. And you shall refer all civil and criminal cases arising within the limits of your State, in which persons other than your own Khasi subjects may be concerned, for adjudication by the Deputy Commissioner of the Khasi and Jaintia Hills, or by any other officer appointed by him for that purpose.

III. The local government shall be at liberty to establish civil and military sanitaria, cantonments and posts in any part of the country under your control, and to occupy the lands necessary for that purpose, rent free. If government wishes any time to construct a railway through your territory you shall provide the land required for that purpose without compensation, save for occupied land, and shall render to the local government in this behalf all assistance in your power.

IV. You hereby confirm the cession to the British Government by your predecessors of all the time, coal and other mines, metals and minerals found in the soil of your state, and of the right to hunt and capture elephants within your state, on condition that you shall receive half of the profit arising from the sale, lease or other disposal of such lime, coal, or other minerals, or of such right. On the same condition you confirm the cession to the British Government of all waste land, being lands at the time of cession unoccupied by the villages, cultivation, plantation, orchards etc. which the British Government may wish to sell or lease as waste lands.

V. You shall not alienate or mortgage to any person any property of the state, movable or immovable, which you possess or of which you may become possessed, as Chief of the State.

VI. You shall not without the sanction of the government lease or transfer or allow to be leased or transferred to person, other than your own Khasi subjects, any land or lands in your jurisdiction.

VII. You shall cause such areas as may be defined by the local government for that purpose to be set aside for the growth of trees to supply building timber and firewood to the inhabitants of the state. You shall take efficient measures to secure those areas against destruction by fire and by *jhuming*.

VIII. You do hereby confirm the agreement given by your predecessor, regarding the trial by the Deputy Commissioner alone of suits for divorce and other matrimonial cases arising between the Native Christians, who have been married in accordance with the provisions of the Indian Christian Marriage Act XV of 1872.

IX. If you violate any of the conditions of this Sanad, or in the case of your using any oppression, or of your acting in a manner opposed to established custom, or in the event of your people, having just cause for dissatisfaction with you, you shall be liable to suffer such punishment as the local government, subject to the control of the Government of India, may think proper to inflict.

X. According to the conditions above enjoined, you are hereby conferred *Siyem* of the State of .... in the Khasi Hills. In virtue whereof this Sanad is granted to you under my hand and seal this...... day of 19.

In the Jaintia Hills, the British took a policy of light and judicious taxation to keep tranquillity and good order, in view of frequent rebellions of Jaintias against the British. No formal land revenue administration was introduced as the Jaintia Parganas were temporarily settled. The first regular settlement was made in 1838-1840, that continued at different intervals till 1918-1919. In the Khasi hills also, no land revenue administration was introduced but a class of land known as *Rajali* land was assessed for land revenue since 1883 at the rate of 12 annas per bigha. The hill districts were largely covered by House tax (A Mittal Publication 1984: 63, 64). The British administration was extended to the Jaintia Hills but the villages continued to be ruled by the Dolois, whose nomination/election was confirmed by the British. The tributary mode practised during the Raja's time was continued by the British. Later, this was replaced by a rough system of assessment of House Tax of Re. 1 per household. House Tax resulted in two rebellions, when on top of House Tax, a central Income Tax was levied. When the second rebellion was controlled, Income Tax was modified but House Tax continued to be levied. Sir Keith Cantlie classified land in Jaintia Hills as *Raj land,* service land, village puja land, private land and high land. High land was divided into *Hali land,* unclaimed land or government waste. Mr. Heath's report of 1884 mentioned *Hali land* and High land. *Hali land* (low land) was divided in *Raj Hali*—private land of Jaintia Rajah and *Buniaz* (private *hali land*) granted by the Rajah to the Dolois or Sirdars in lieu of salary. High land was sub-divided into government waste and private high land. All other high lands were considered as government lands following the principle of *terra nullius*. After Heath's Report, the lands in the entire Jaintia Hills were declared as absolute property of the government. Taxation system however was house tax, not land revenue. Subsequently, *Raj Hali* land was assessed to land revenue; government waste land also could be assessed to land revenue if these were brought under permanent cultivation. The high land under *jhum* cultivation, betel nuts and orange groves were revenue free. The settlement of Jaintia Hills was done in 1889 and periodic lease for *Hali* land was issued. The next settlements were done in 1901, 1911 and in 1941 (Phira 1989: 12-17).

The other revenue sources were sale of the tribute goats, forest and forest products revenue, rents on fishery, coal mines and limestone quarries, income tax, Stamp duty and land revenue. All the coal mines of Jaintia Hills became the sole properties of the British in 1855, which were leased out to the private individuals and companies run by the British and other businessmen. Lime quarries were also declared property of the state. In 1860, the House Tax was imposed on three classes of houses with different rates and later a uniform rate of Rs. 2 per house was fixed. Many people shifted to their relatives' houses and pulled down their own houses to evade tax. The British revenue suffered as a result when the British re-classified first and second classes of houses with tax rate of Rs. 3 and 2-8 annas respectively. Different *elakas* were treated differently for the purpose of House Tax, depending on the crops grown (Gassah: 1994: 46, 49-53).

The Garos were divided in three groups: Tributary Garos (paying tribute to the British), Independent Garos (who paid no tribute to the British) and the Zamindari Garos, under the Zamindars of Bengal and Goalpara, who expanded their territories and revenue areas into the Garo areas. Being unsatisfied with the share from the Zamindars, the British abolished the Zamindars and the *Sezawls* were entrusted to collect revenue of the Garo Hills directly from the chiefs. Due to growing raids of the Garos on the Zamindari plains, the British detached the Garo tracts from the Zamindars and introduced separate administration for Garos under the Regulation X of 1822. David Scott concluded engagements with 121 Garo Chiefs and realised nominal tributes from them as a token of acknowledgement of British supremacy (Das 1994: 8). The Independent Garos were brought under British control after an expedition and were made tributaries to the British. This time, the British imposed separate House Tax on each Garo household. Only in later years, some provisions of the Assam Land and Revenue Regulation were imposed in the Garo Hills. Mr. Kelso made a revenue survey of the boundary with Goalpara district and the line drawn by him was accepted as the Northern Boundary of the Garo Hills. The Zamindars, who continued to claim their right to tribute and cess from the Garos, were abolished in 1869 on payment of compensation. Garo Hills was divided into ten Mouzas divided as Hill Mouzas and Plain Mouzas. The Hill Mouzas were under shifting cultivation, where no revenue was assessed but House Tax was imposed. Land revenue was imposed on Plain Mouzas for permanent wet rice cultivation. The *A'khing* land was demarcated by boundary line and Certificates of Possession *(dolin)* were issued to the Nokmas. This gave proprietary right to the Nokams on *A'king* land. In the plain areas, a Jotdar class emerged who took excessive rent from the tillers.

Land administration in the Garo Hills was governed by customary law and Executive Orders. In the Plains, it was governed by the Settlement Rules promulgated from time to time and the Assam Regulation of 1886. Cadastral survey was conducted in the plains during 1905-08, that classified land into homestead (*basti*), wet-cultivation fields (*rupit*) and high lands (*faringati*). Record of rights was prepared and periodic lease was issued for lands under permanent cultivation or permanent homestead. The period of lease was ten years with heritable and transferable rights of use and occupation of land. The plain Mouzas were re-surveyed in 1916-17 and fresh leases were re-issued for another ten years. The leases were renewed in 1927 and in 1937, till the Garo Hills Autonomous District Council took over the administration of land (Marak 1998: 138-140; Phira 1989: 18-21). The diehard privilege of annuity payable to the Zamindars, was discontinued by "the Gouripur (Gholla) Zamindars' Annuity Right Abolition and Extinguishment Act, 1979 (Phira 1979: 133, 134; Bhattacharjee 1978: 23,32).

The Agreement with the Wahadadar of Chelyla Poonjee in 1829; Rajumn Singh of Nungkhlon in 1834 and document of possession to *A'khing* Nokmas in the Garo Hills (Pamberton 1966: 245; Mazumdar 1990: 4) became the different instruments of social engineering and different modes of primitive accumulation or accumulation by dispossession.

The next mode of accumulation by dispossession was the revenue administration mode that annihilated the customary land rights of the tribal people of Northeast India.

Land Revenue and Land Reforms

Rooted in Adam Smith's *Wealth of Nations*, the concept of land revenue continued to exist in the later history as the principal mode of state revenue. The land reforms agenda in India, Pathy wrote, was pushed first by the Indian industrial capitalists, who decried the economic justification of the Zamindars (who amassed huge wealth in the names of temple, servants and animals). The Congress Agrarian Reforms Committee Report of 1949 made major recommendations, among others, for abolition of intermediaries and confer permanent, heritable and transferable rights in lands to tenants (Pathy 1987). The feudal relations, nevertheless, came to exist which the Indian industrial lobby failed to eradicate (Dutta 1968: 32).

The land reforms became largely reform of revenue rather than of re-distribution. The concept hovered round Part III of the Constitution of India, which also enshrined the Grotian concept of *'dominiun eminens'* by which the state could "use, alienate, and destroy any property for public utility, while making good its laws to those who lose it" (Sampat 2013: 41). The Constitution makers enshrined this concept as a Fundamental Right (Krishna Ananth 2011). This produced the state-community controversy in the hills of Northeast India between normative-legalistic or naturalist-positive concepts of property rights. The Constitution always suffered a dual dilemma about distributive justice with normative foundation to the land reforms programme on the one hand and enhanced agricultural productivity that needed a latifundio economy and increased land privatisation on the other. The latter was addressed in Article 31 of the Constitution. This article, however, invited ceaseless conflict between the parliament and the Supreme Court that culminated in the 44th Amendment abolishing the fundamental right to property and inserting Article 300A that provided that no person shall be deprived of his or her property without the authority of valid law (Wahi 2013: 49-51). Amidst these criticalities, the communal lands were ruthlessly privatised that often went unnoticed in the dominant judicial-constitutional discourses of the country. Thus, though Justice Naolekar in his Foreword to the *Customary Laws of the Lais in Mizoram* said that law of the land also included common law (Baruah 2007: vii) and the doctrine of eminent domain had annihilated it in private interest in the heartlands of India.

The colonials did not prepare a record of right (ROR) to reflect the true agrarian relations of India. Nayak demystified the popular belief that land records of the colonial period were a reliable means to understanding agrarian relations in India. He said, it was meant to accommodate the wealthy and powerful sections of the Indian society. The ROR, in this case, had presumptive rather than conclusive value. The courts relied on oral evidence rather than on records of presumptive value and the latter was left to the courts to decide when it came to conclusive proofs (Nayak 2013: 71-73).

In the 1950s, 1960s and 1970s, two significant models of land reforms in the mainland were tried out: the tenancy model (Kerala and later West Bengal) that had distributive dimension and gave prime importance to record of rights to the tenant and Green Revolution model (Punjab and Haryana) in which ROR for the farm owners was based on latifundio economy. This model responded to the "research studies on the Green Revolution by the Rockefeller Foundation (New York) and the Mexican government in 1943, that was rooted in the political economy of global agri-business" (Ghuman 2010: 130-31) to cause socio-economic inequities, depeasantisation and crisis of the community land.

The Computerised Land Records (CLR), introduced during the Seventh Plan, had two ambitious schemes for strengthening revenue administration and updating land records with redistributive aim. But from the Eighth Plan onwards, the redistributive aim begun to get scrambled and by the Tenth Plan period, land reform was factored in the neoliberal agenda. The Eleventh Five Year Plan made a clear policy departure by liberalising ceiling and tenancy laws and envisaging a modern management system of land records for securing property rights, encouraging investment on land and for ensuring efficient land market. Land administration switched-over from registration of deed based on presumptive land records to "Torrens" system for conclusive land title. This system required amendment of the Registration Act 1908, the Stamp Act 1899, the state laws relating to survey and settlement for conclusive title and other legal changes that were techno-managerial in nature (Nayak 2013: 71-73).

The very nature of the border states and the capital-light land sectors in the hills of Northeast India did not invite large ideological, judicial and constitutional debates on land reforms in post-colonial India. The land reforms in this region had to encounter other kinds of problems arising from the phenomenal post-partition immigration from East Bengal (1947) and Burma

(1935). The former affected Tripura and Assam most while the latter was problematic in the hills of Manipur, Nagaland and Mizoram. In this larger backdrop, we propose to discuss in brief the land revenue and reforms acts in the states of Northeast India.

Land Reforms in Nagaland

The East India Company took control of the salt wells in the Naga Hills and the British relations with the Eastern Nagas started out of the Company's right over these wells. Land revenue was not realised then. In 1847, Captain Butler made some chiefs to pay a House Tax of Rupee one and later a settlement was made with Rengma Nagas to pay house tax. This was not effective. The Angami tract of the Naga Hills faced a series of British expeditions starting from the first Angami Expedition in 1839, till the occupation of Kohima in 1878, when sixteen Naga villages accepted the British protectorate. Thirteen of them paid revenue of Rs. 1,032. It was anticipated that eventually the British would raise Rs. 2 per house to draw a revenue of Rs. 2600 from the Angami, Kutcha Naga, Rengma and Lhota Nagas. Major Michel, the then Political Officer, viewed that the assessment of one rupee, plus one maund of rice per house was far too high. Subsequently, the rate of assessment was raised and a house tax of Rs. 2 was imposed per house. Hunter reported that land revenue was very small from Naga Hills and was levied only on two villages. In 1869-70, the proprietors paid a total land tax of 55^{P}, 9^{s}. In the following year, it reduced. The principal item of revenue was House Tax, which in 1870-71, stood at 429^{P} 18^{s} (Hunter 1990: 197; Barpujari 1994: 77-78; Alemchiba 1970: 185). The British then erected boundary pillars in recognition of the traditional boundary between the Ahoms and the Nagas marked by permanent embankment known as *Ladoingurh* and the *Naga Bund,* which was marked with a revenue triangular masonry pillars, indicating the Southern Revenue Boundary of the then Sibsagar district. The Inner Line Regulation of 1876, also coincided with the *Naga Bund* in this sector. Particularly, after the construction of the Assam-Bengal Railways in 1899, vast tracts of Naga territories were transferred to Assam in 1901, 1903 and 1923, without the consent and knowledge of the Nagas. Simultaneously, many large tea gardens were established within Naga territory. Following this, were the alterations and shifting of Inner Line deep inside Naga Hills purposefully to exclude all the tea gardens. Gradually, the annual tax that was paid by the plain people to 23 Naga villages as an annual 'customary tribute' for using the land was taken charge of by the British Assam Government, who then collected and handed over the tax to the Naga villagers. Many of the Naga territories were transferred for administrative convenience and for the tea gardens against a nominal token to the Nagas in recognition of the land ownership (Longkumar and Jamir 2012: 45).

But by the mid-19th century, land conflicts between colonial planters and the Nagas had started as the British brought new settlers to the newly acquired land (Longkumar and Jamir 2012: 45). Sections 1, 2, 69, 94 and 144A of Assam Land Regulation 1886 were applied in the Naga Hills. Section 144A laid down that "all rents, fees and royalties due to the government for use or occupation of land or water (whether the property is government or not) on account thereof... shall be recoverable as arrears of land revenue". Besides, the Bengal Eastern Frontier Regulation 3 of 1873, nullified the ownership of land to the Nagas to safeguard colonial interest (Longkumar and Jamir 2012: 43). Later, the land tenure system of the Naga Hills came to be governed by the Chin Hills Regulation of 1896. At the beginning of the British administration, there were altogether 170 estates in the Naga Hills paying land revenue. Fluctuation in the number of revenue paying estates continued from year to year. Hill House Tax as the main source of revenue, received exceptional care for its realisation. In 1908, the government made efforts to control export of forest produce from the Naga Hills and issued trade licenses to selected persons (Mathew 2007: 262, 267). The Chin Hills Regulation continued in the Naga Hills till the Naga Hills Jhum Land Regulation was enacted in 1946. Till 1970, the land tenure system in Nagaland (consisted of the then

Kohima and Mokokchung district) was guided by the same regulation, while the land tenure system in Tuensang area (a part of the NEFA till 1957) was guided by Baliapara/Tirup/ Sadiya Frontier Tract Jhum Land Regulation, 1947. On the other hand, the Act 73 created the State of Nagaland in 1963 that provided that no act passed by the parliament of India will have any legal force in Nagaland until it is made specially applicable by a majority vote in the Nagaland Legislative Assembly in respect of the following:

1. Religious and social practices,
2. Naga customary laws and procedures,
3. Civil and criminal justice so far as these concern Naga customary laws and
4. The ownership and transfer of land and its resources.

Article 371A (1) (iv) of the Constitution of India stated that "notwithstanding anything in this Constitution, no act of parliament in respect of ownership and transfer of land and its resources shall apply to the State of Nagaland, unless the Legislative Assembly of Nagaland by resolution so decides". Thus, land reforms measures were not introduced in the state except in the Dimapur Mouza, which was a part of the state of Assam. Only some of the administrative headquarters (town areas) were cadastrally surveyed in Nagaland. As such no land revenue was imposed and no systematic record of land was maintained. The ownership and transfer of land resources were vested in the traditions and customs. ((Ghosh 1986: 185-187). The Nagaland Land (Requisition and Acquisition) Act 1965, was used for speedy land acquisition for certain public purpose. The compensation payable to the owner was determined by the collector on average 15 per cent of market value (Longkumar and Jamir 2012: 46). The Nagaland Jhum Land Act 1970, defined *jhum* land as a land of shifting cultivation or grazing land on which a member or members of a village or community have customary right. The Act accepted the customary right of a village or community on the *jhum* land and prevented sale or transfer of *jhum* land outside the village or community without the permission of the Deputy Commissioner on the recommendation of the village or area council. This Act mentioned the following types of ownership: Village/ community ownership, clan ownership and individual ownership (except Sema and Konyak areas) (Ghosh 1986: 185-187). Such lands had no record of right and were governed by customary laws and the village councils had authority to interpret those. The Act of 1970, recognised the individual right to transfer *jhum* land only within the village and community boundaries. Therefore, the Act has recognised both the customary land rights and established the authority of the government over the land (Sharma 1999: 56-57). It criminalised removal of forest produce from *jhum* land, imposed penalties against removal of the same and treated such removal as a "forest offence" liable to prosecution (Longkumar and Jamir 2012: 46).

Bordoloi viewed state ownership of land in Nagaland insignificant, except that the State of Nagaland could acquire land under the Act which the state did not usually resort to and when required to acquire land for any public institutions, government rather approached the village council, which when satisfied could gift the required area of land to the government. It may be mentioned, in this connection, that the British conquered Naga areas were subsequently handed over to the British civil administration by the troops, and, thus, some land areas became government property, that included areas where administrative headquarters were set up on lands (Bordoloi 1990: 61).

What are significant in Nagaland are absence of absentee landlordism, landless peasants and presence of customary communal labour by the 'field companies' of men and women of the same age group. But the institutional measures of switching over to terracing, money inducement and technical assistance, irrigation projects and community development project, setting up of seed farms and established Agricultural Research Centre (Singh 1972: 167) have led to trivialisation of the communal land system.

Baliapara/Tirap/Sadiya Frontier Tract Jhum Land Regulation 1947.

The Baliapara Frontier Jhum Land Regulation 1947 recognised the customary right to the tribes to cultivate *jhum* land for not less than five years prior to this regulation. Government accepted village, community (including the residents of a village as a whole, the clan, sub clan, phratry or kindred) and individual ownerships only in respect of land under permanent and semi-permanent cultivation and land attached to the dwelling houses. This Regulation established customary right to *jhum* in favour of an individual cultivator, when he customarily inherited such land; if he purchased land prior to this Regulation and such purchase was not contrary to local custom or, if he purchased it subsequent to this Regulation, provided such purchase was not contrary to any local custom or any provisions of this Regulation or, if a resident of a permanent village brought the land under cultivation, not cultivated at any time within 30 years preceding his bringing the same into cultivation provided that such land is within the cultivable reach of his own village. The customary law, thus, came to be governed by the Regulation and all other lands including *jhum* land became vested with the state (Agarwal 1990: 44-46).

The Jhum Land Regulation 1947 became contentious for a couple of reasons: the Assam Forest Regulation 1891 as applicable in Arunachal considered *jhuming* as a privilege, not as a right; the state government had overriding powers of regulation in areas not being the property of the government. Government might also assume management of such areas in public interest or could acquire such areas for public purposes under the Land Acquisition Act 1894. *Jhuming* being considered as a privilege in the Forest Regulation, the latter was graduated to customary right under Jhum Land Regulation (Sinha 2006: 33). The customary land rights came under a controlled legal regime and such rights were subject to tax and rents. The natural right of the tribals over the forest produce was reduced to mere use right. The legal regime, thus established, ignored the nature-man symbiosis. Moreover acquisition of *jhum* land for public purposes had no formal acquisition proceedings except that an opportunity was given to the right holders to show cause against such acquisition and reasonable compensation was to be paid for this under the Act of 1947. Land so acquired shall, if relinquished by the government at any time, be returned to the village, community or individual, from whom it was acquired on refund of such compensation to the government as the latter might decide. This provision was in exercise of the eminent domain of the state.

In Arunachal Pradesh, a proposed land act of 1983, could not get through. But this empowered the government to carry out the survey and settlement and prepare a record of rights (Bordoloi 1990: 22-24). The Arunachal Pradesh (Land Settlement and Records) was passed in 2000, to provide a comprehensive law for land revenue administration incorporating customary rights on land. But this Act strongly embedded governmentalisation of rights over land. The provision of government compensation encouraged some of the tribals to surrender their cultivable land under individual possession. Moreover, adoption of *pani kheti* or terrace cultivation led to emergence of absentee landlordism. In many cases, people engaged in other occupations and possessed inherited, purchased or acquired land rented out those to sharecroppers (Agarwal 1990: 47). Accrual of individual rights was possible only within a governmentalised frame. Similarly, right to mines, quarries, mineral oil, natural gas and petroleum, trees, jungles natural products growing on land set apart for forest reserves, brush wood, trees planted and reared by the government and local authorities by the side of any road also became government property and set another case of primitive accumulation.

The Arunachal Pradesh (Land Settlement and Records) Act, 2000, was particular about recognising a "person" for entitlement of ownership. This Act also homogenised individualisation of land right notwithstanding the diverse land ownership patterns. But while an individual person could accrue ownership right from the government for agricultural purposes, Section 88 (2) of the Act of 2000, stated that no rights shall accrue under sub-section (1) in respect of land which: (i) are a part of the bed of a river, nallah, a stream, or a public tank, or (ii) have been acquired by the government for any purpose according to the provisions of any law in force for the time being relating to acquisition of land, or (3) objections to accrual right under sub-section (1) may be filed before the competent authority within such time and in such form and manner as may be prescribed by any person, who has interest in the land either in his individual capacity or as a member of a village community.

The objection to accrual right over agricultural land under the Act of 2000, came closer to 'show cause' against government acquisition of *jhum* land for public purposes in the Regulation of 1947. In both cases, the government remained *non-litiger* and shifted the onus of rightful claim of the land to the owner. Moreover, the duality in the land law-giving legal protection of people and lands and power of eminent domain of the state for acquisition of land for 'public good' became ambiguous. Moreover sub-section 7 of Section 88 of the Act of 2000, did not entitle sub-soil right to the people. The tenancy right in any land was left unregulated. Section 93 (1) left the interest of a tenant in any land to be decided in accordance with such terms and conditions as agreed between the parties. By this section, the government abdicated the social responsibility for protection of tenancy rights.

The Tripura Land Revenue and Land Reforms Act 1960

In the feudatory state of Tripura, the Maharaja had a dual status-as the zamindar of Chakla Rosanabad and as the chief of Independent Hill Tripperah (based on the grant of Sanad in 1904).The tenural pattern in Tripura, in the past, did not provide ownership rights and presence of intermediaries due to infeudation and sub-infeudation resulted in fragmentation of rentier interests that led to new mode of land alienation. The king encouraged plough cultivation and permanent settlement. The Tripura Tenancy Act of 1886 AD stipulated rent from each *kani* on 25:75 percentage share basis between the tenant and the land owner. The Tripura Tenancy Act of 1886 AD (amended in

1945) promulgated occupancy rights of tenants on continuous possession of the plot for seven years and on regular payment of rents. But they did not have ryot status. They were liable to eviction against recruitment of another tenant willing to cultivate on inferior terms with higher rent and strict rules. There was no documentary proof of the tenants and even the High Court of Tripura remained silent on this fact. This inadequacy in the land system led to mass immigration by the end of the century. This was also responsible for mortgage, sublet and transfer of Ryotwari interest which, in turn, was responsible for emergence of absentee landholders. They attracted a substantial number of tenant cultivators and realised rent from them by letting out their 'Taluks' in small plots. (Chakravorti 2004: 137-138). This led to growth of individual proprietorial cultivators in Tripura, who augmented lands of the tribals having no legal title on land. Thus, in the changing tenural system, communal right was overtaken by principles of individual proprietorship (Bhowmick 2009: 67).

The king encouraged the Bengali peasants to settle down as tenant cultivators and huge areas of tribal lands were brought under tenant cultivation through the crafty process of accumulation. The first *Jhum* Settlement of 1888, creation of Tribal Reserve Area in 1931, to settle the tribals permanently there for commercial cultivation of cotton and oil-seeds on *jhum* fields created a distinct class interest in Tripura. Choudhury wrote that cotton and oilseeds produced from the *jhum* fields were exported on a big scale. One-fourth of these crops were given to the Raja as rent. Karpas Mahals were created for collection of cotton and oilseed revenue. The *Izaradari* system was introduced for collection of oilseed and cotton revenue and two Englishmen acted as the joint *Izaradars* of the Karpas Mahal (Choudhury 2003: 47-48) From the hills, the other major source of revenue was forest. This revenue was export revenue collected from the people of the neighbouring British districts. Such revenue was also collected through the *Izaradars*. Khuski Mahal was created for surface export and Bankar Mahal was created for collection of tax of forest export through river ways.

Nadi Kar office and Bankar Ghat were created for collection of tax (Choudhury 2003: 44).

The Tripura Land Revenue and Land Reforms Act was passed in 1960. Two sections of the Act were prescient for understanding the nature of protective measures in favour of the tribals under this Act, Section 187 and Chapter IXA.

Section 187 of the Act intended to protect the tribal land from being alienated to the non-tribal people. It allowed land transfer from a tribal to another tribal with due permission of the DM & Collector, who is to obtain recommendation of the Tribal Advisory Committee. Despite this, a large chunk of tribal land was occupied fraudulently by the refugees. Das stated that notwithstanding the law to the contrary, benami transfer of land to the non-tribals took place and in spite of the provisions of Section 131 of the Act, a non-tribal of a scheduled village could so manage it that an under ryot would be a non-tribal (Das 1985: 97, 103).

Section 187 of the TLR & LR Act recognised only the individual ownership duely registered while most tribal lands were not registered. Non-registered community land was considered state property or became khas land which made the state take-over of tribal land easy for refugee rehabilitation. Most of the remaining lands were in the Bengali-majority villages in the documents, though these were recorded in the name of the tribal families. This amounted to illegal or Benami transfer that was not attended by Section 187 (Deb Burma 2008: 121-122) During the settlement operation, lands so occupied, were legalised with the help of local administrators (Roy Burman (jr.) 1990: 97) and in most cases, the landless tribal people were allotted Tilla lands, not suitable for paddy cultivation (Deb Burma 1990: 102). By Regulation 44 of 1793, all the previous leased and encumbrances attached to a plot sold at public auctions were cancelled. This opened the flood gate for fraudulent and *benami* transactions. Some Bengali refugee leaders even set up 'land cooperatives' like the Swasti Samity in north Tripura violating the Tribal Reserves regulations, and took over large swathes of land in connivance with the bureaucrats. *Benami* purchase provoked many tribal youth to join the Sengkrak movement. In settled agricultural areas like Khowai and Sadar, 20 to 40 per cent of the tribal lands were alienated by the end of the 1970s, when tribal insurgency gathered momentum. In some parts of south Tripura, as much as 60 per cent of the tribal lands were alienated (Himal 2004).

Chapter XI-A was inserted by amending the Tripura Act-1960 in 1975, which intended to control transfer of land by non-tribals living in tribal dominant villages. While Section 187 applies to the entire state and to both the scheduled and non-scheduled villages, Chapter XI-A applies only to the scheduled villages. This Chapter also intended to protect the rights of the under-ryots of a non-tribal ryot in a scheduled village. Das wrote that as the scheduled villages are subject to Section 131 (of the Tripura Act 1960), a non-tribal of a scheduled village having an under ryot on his land and intending to transfer it cannot in the first instance offer to a co-sharer or a tribal owner of adjacent land but must first of all offer it to the under rayat whether he be a tribal or a non-tribal. But the incidence of the non tribals living in the scheduled villages increased (Das 1984: 64; Das 1990: 87, 94, 99-100, 103). While Section 14(3) of the TLR & LR Act-1960 gave preference for allotment of land to the members of the cooperative farming societies, landless agricultural labourers, *jhumias* and members of the Scheduled Tribes and Scheduled Castes, Section 15 (1) empowered the competent authority to evict any person occupying government land on the charge of trespass. Such a trespasser was liable to pay a penalty six times the annual assessment on such land and upon payment of such a penalty the trespasser could have the right of tending, gathering and removing any ungathered crops.

The issue of land lease in the tribal areas became serious after the transfer of power and settlement of Bangladeshi refugees for wet-rice cultivation. The Tripura Land Revenue and Land Reforms Act, left serious loopholes through which lands could be transferred from the tribal to the non-tribal. The only condition was that one needed to obtain written permission from the DM or Collector. This stymied Section 187 of the state act.

Section 11. (1) of Chapter III of the Tripura Act stated, all lands, public roads, lanes and paths and bridges, ditches, dikes, and fences on or beside the same, the beds of rivers, streams, nallas, lakes and tanks, and all canals and water courses, and all standing and flowing water, and all rights in or over the same or appertaining thereto, which are not the property of any person, are hereby declared to be the property of the government. Subsection (2) stated that, unless it is otherwise expressly provided in the terms of a grant made by the government, the right to mines, quarries, minerals and mineral products, including, mineral oil, natural gas and petroleum shall vest in the Collector. Section 12. (1) vests right of all trees, jungles or other natural products growing on land set apart for forest reserves and of all trees, brush wood, jungle or other natural products, wherever growing, except in so far as the same may be the property of any person in the government. These sections are the classical displays of the jurisprudential principle of *terra nullius,* amounting virtually to primitive accumulation.

It is interesting to note that Section 178 of the Tripura Land Act was not in sync with the *jhumia* rehabilitation colonies, where the alottees were given private ownership of land with the rights of permanent use, occupancy and inheritance for plough cultivation which only the relatively solvent section could adopt, while poor tribals became agricultural labourers. The poor tribes lost not less than 26,101.2 hectares (64,470 acres) to the rehabilitation colonies- 5,499 hectares (13,572.65 acres) of it being private and the rest being common. No notification was issued or compensation paid for the commons since the TLR&LRA-1960 had turned them into "state property". Over and above these 70,910 acres, in 1981-82, the state acquired 3,697.03 acres—1,164.05 acres of it for plain land Bengali immigrants and 2,532.98 for East Pakistani refugees. Thus, the total land for refugee rehabilitation was 74,607.03 acres- 17,269.68 acres of it private and 57,337.35 common. It was taken from 22,394 persons (https://docs.google.com/viewer?a=v&q= cache).

Much more land was alienated with no legal procedure.

According to one study, the tribes lost 20 to 40 per cent of their land. Thus, the real number displaced was probably more than 50,000 persons. In the early 1970s, the Dumbur dam submerged over 23,530.55 acres and more land was used for its power house and the rest for infrastructure. Most of it was communal land that was not compensated. Its project files mentioned about only 2,558 individual land owning displaced families (13,000 persons) but studies found that 8,000 to 9,000 families (40-50,000 persons) were displaced. Of the 28,999 cases filed for land restoration till 2001, in only 8,636 cases the decision went in favour of restoring the illegally alienated land. But very little of it was restored in reality because most of it was in the middle of Bengali colonies that the tribals dared not demand its return. (https://docs.google.com/viewer?a=v&q=cache). Besides, the tribals displaced from the Reserved Forests could not go back to their homes because of judicial restrictions. Similarly, a large number of *Jhumias* and poor tribal families occupied Khas land for a fairly long time without any legally valid occupancy documents (Chakravarti 2002: 265-267, 269).

Gumti hydel project submerged 26000 acres of land, including, 24000 acres of cultivable land and displaced 5000 tribal families (Banerjee 2005: 328, 332). It also submerged fertile valley area of 46 sq kms. The displaced tribes resorted to illegal logging in the rich forests of the area. (Himal 2004; Dasgupta 1992; 206).

The great change in the land economy of Tripura indicated a parallel change in the mode of production relations of the tribals from tributary to taxation mode. It is on record in the *Rajmala* of Tripura (Chakravarti 1994: 123). The shift also resulted in commodity fetishism of land and labour in Tripura. The results being a steady rise of wage labour, steady fall in the total area available for productive use, passing away of tenancy right from tribal household to another household—tribal or non-tribal and growth of monopoly power in the landed class over the landless labour (Ganguli 1989: 228). This scenario of the Tripura Land Revenue Act overlooked the community process and imposed the state process on communal land.

The Manipur Land Revenue and Land Reforms Act 1960

On merger with the Indian Union, the Assam Land and Revenue Regulation 1886, was imposed on Manipur. This Regulation introduced the system of annual patta, periodic patta and revenue-free (*Khorposh*) patta. The Manipur Land Revenue and Land Reforms Act was passed in 1960, to replace the Assam Act. Annual patta was abolished by this act. Two sets of land laws, the Manipur Land Revenue and Land Record Act 1960 (in the valley areas) and Hill Areas (House Tax) Act 1966 came to prevail in the state. The Hill Areas were exempted under Section 1 (2) of the 1960 Act. Section 158 of the Act also prohibited sale or transfer of tribal land to the non-tribals without the permission of the Deputy Commissioner.

The Manipur Land Revenue and Land Records (6th Amendment) Bill inserted Sections 158-A, 158-B, 158-C and 158-D that removed the exemption under Section 1(2) of the Act of 1960. The 7th Amendment Bill-1992 removed restriction of land transfer in the hills and made the revenue tribunal the highest authority under the Act in matters of land transfer against which no further appeal should lie from the court. Thus, on revenue matters, one cannot go to the High Court or Supreme Court. (Kipgen and Singh 2009: 341-342). This provision empowered the state government to extend this section of the Act to any of the hill areas of the state. Thus, the Hill districts do not automatically become "hill areas". According to Section 2 (1) of the Act, "hill areas" mean such areas in the hill tracts of the state of Manipur, as state government by notification in the Official Gazette, declared to be hill areas. "In the five Hill Districts, there are 1558 villages out of which, 1454 are hill areas, satisfying the provisions of Section 2 (J) of the Manipur Land Revenue and Land Records Act-1960" (Das 1989: 76). The state government has since notified the following areas as hill areas:

Jiribam Sub Division (mainly plain areas having 142 villages out of 166 villages in hill areas (including 24 hill villages). In 1962, the following villages in the Hill districts were included in the plain areas of Imphal district.

1. In Tengnoupal sub division, 190 villages came under hill areas
2. In Tamenglong District, 190 villages came under hill areas
3. In Senapati District (Mao Maram), 312 villages came under hill areas
4. In Churachandpur district, 225 villages came under hill areas
5. In Ukhrul District 244 villages came under hill areas
6. In the remaining 89 villages in Churachandpur district in 1962
7. In 14 villages of Senapati district in 1965.

So far the act is applied to about 665 villages out of which 550 villages are situated in the three plain districts and the remaining 115 are situated in the plain areas of the hill districts. Most of these villages are located in Churachandpur and Senapati districts.

Under such a situation, the annual patta holders were asked to convert themselves to land owners by paying premium and those, who did not do so within a specific date were declared stateless or encroachers of government Khas land. Though Section 2 of the original Act says that it does not apply to the hill areas, the other part of the section says, "Provided that the state government may, by notification in the official Gazette, extend the whole or part or any section of this Act to any hill areas of Manipur also as may be specified in such notification." The MLR & LR Act 1960 was amended in 1975 that empowered the state government to extend the whole or any part of this act to any of the hill areas of the state. But owing to lack of cadastral survey, it was not possible to extend this act to the hill areas. The MLR & LR (Second Amendment) Act 1976 officially claimed to provide adequate legal safeguards against alienation of tribal lands. The Manipur (Village Authority in Hill Areas) Second Amendment Bill No. 4 of 1993 defined 'Hill Areas' as such areas in the 'Hill Tracts' of the State of Manipur as the State Government might by notification in the Official Gazette, declare to be the hill areas, vide notification No. 181/2/61 dated January 25, 1962. Administrative reconstruction of the Hill Areas let loose many such ambiguities and created misunderstanding and mistrust among the people of the hill districts. In a seminar on "Democratization Process Among the Zomis" held in Shillong, during March 19-20, 2013, there was a heated debate among the hill participants on this point. This provision encouraged many plains people to purchase lands from the tribals and got those registered with the land department. Of late, the Manipur Land Revenue and Land Reforms (Seventh Amendment) Bill 2015, allows the Act to extend to any hill areas of Manipur, which resented the All Manipur Tribal Students Union. This led to a mass protest against the bill and seven persons were killed and thirty people were wounded by the security forces in Churachandpur district of Manipur on September 1, 2015.

Box 2.3: Transfer of Tribal Land to Non-Tribal

In the last part of the 19th and the first part of the 20th centuries, the Nepalese were settled in the hills through land grant of the Manipur State Darbar. The Darbar, in turn, used to collect Grazier Tax from them. The second wave of land transfer started with induction of Nepalese as soldiers in the 4th Assam Rifles Division in Manipur in 1913. Kangpokpi-Kanglatongbi Gorkha Reserve was created in 1919-1920 for the Nepali settlement. With commendable skill in agriculture the Nepali farmers got permission from the Agent of Manipur for wet-rice cultivation in 1945. In 1946, the reserve was shifted in view of extensive cultivation by the Nepali farmers. But the Darbar allowed the Nepalese to stay back for cultivation. About four acres of land were also given to each willing Nepali farmer in Kangpokpi areas over which they got property right.** During British times, the Gorkha Ex-Army men's Colonies in Keithemanbi and Kanglatongbi came up. Besides, many Nepali farmers were encouraged to settle in the foothills of Kanglatongbi-Kangpokpi forest range in Sadar Hills, who in due course managed to get individual patta land. The third wave of transfer of tribal land to the Nepalese happened through informal routes of sharecropping, particularly, in Sadar Hills of Senapati District, where 90 percent land belonged to the Kuki tribes and 10 percent land belonged to the allied Naga groups.

Village Thonglang Akutpa is situated in the Kangpokpi block of Senapati District. This village is inhabited by four clans of Liangmei Nagas, namely, the Charunama, Ngonamai, Marumkangmei, and the Makuimai. Besides, there are some minor clans in the village. Half of the village land is community-owned, where shifting cultivation (locally called Maluanglu) is practiced and the other half is owned by individuals of the different clan groups, where terrace cultivation (locally called Taduilu or Taninglu) is practised. The clan land (terrace land) is distributed to the individual clan members.

There are a sizeable number of Nepali neo-migrants residing in the neighbouring villages on payment of some kind of annual tax (locally called Lam pan) to the village authority or the clan members. If they reside in community land, they pay such taxes to the village authority and if they reside in clan land, they pay the tax to the respective clan members. These Nepali cultivators use to lease-in the terrace land of the clan members of this village on yearly share-copping basis. The owner provides paddy seed for cultivation. The owner can also employ other Nepalis to work on the paddy field for the next year. The entire deal remains unwritten although the Nepali cultivators cannot sell, mortgage or sub-lease the parcel of land to anybody.

The practice of leasing-out of terrace land has increased due to new choice of the educated youth for the service sector in the towns and cities where they migrate. This caused a serious shortage of family labour for cultivation. The older people can no longer cultivate. So they lease out of land to the Nepalese. This led to de-facto transfer of land to the non-tribal Nepali farmers.

** K.S. Singh edited, *People of India, Manipur*, Vol. XXXI

The major public discourse on land reforms in the hills of Manipur got bifurcated. The rich section favoured extension of the act in the hill areas; sought for cadastral survey and conclusive title of land for either land speculation or for using the land title as collateral against institutional loan. Amidst the bifurcated public discourse, the provision for land mortgage to a cooperative society (Clause (c) of Section 158 of the Manipur Act 1960) left legal loopholes that allowed the unscrupulous non-tribal people to form cooperative societies and to obtain tribal land by way of mortgage without requiring to obtain consent of the authorities.

Box 2.4: Manipulating the Act

A valley based cooperative farming society formed by non-tribal people has encroached into tribal lands in Tharlon village in Tamenlong district in Manipur. This society made an agreement with the Chairman of the village authority for mortgage of *jhum* lands for contract farming when such land remains in the rest period of the *jhum* cycle. The cooperative society promised the share of the dividend to the chief of Tharlon village. In the Society's view, such land on which the Society would operate is community land' whereas in Tharlon village, there is no community land at all. All lands are owned by individuals. There is no khas land in the village either. The villagers had no knowledge about the mortgage agreement between the Chairman of the village authority and the cooperative society. This agreement amounted to doling-out tribal lands to the non-tribal cooperative society and is likely to create serious land disputes when cultivation would resume on the *jhum* land after the rest period.

Revenue record in the hills of Manipur is another area of serious contention. There are a huge number of villages in the hills that pay both Hill House Tax and land revenue to the government. A great number of land records of the hill of villages Chura Chandarpur district are maintained by the revenue office in the plains and the revenue is collected by the neighbouring valley district of Bishenpur while those villages regularly pay Hill House Tax to the government as well. This became the root cause of the overlapping census in 2011. Although cadastral survey was made in some hill villages, these did not mean transforming those villages into valley villages. This process has reduced the importance of hill district administration in land matters in the state and distorted the revenue map in the hills.

Box 2.5: Revenue Map is Distorted in the Hills

Extension of the Manipur Land Revenue and Land Reform Act-1960, in the hill areas and inclusion of a sizeable number of hill villages within the purview of the Act strained the relationship between the hills and the valley in Manipur. In Churachandpur district twenty-seven villages namely: Torbung Loklaphai, Lukhumbi, Chinglangmei, Langseitampak, Samulamlan, Lainom, Jalenphai, Matiyang, Lalumbung, Theikhakpi, Tuiringphaisen, Thampilen, Ukha-Tampak, Phoisanphai, Maichammun, Torbung, Kulbung, Saiton Khullen (Seitol), Saiton Khunnou, Ngairong, Sagang, Haotak Khullen, Haotak Phailam, Kangvai Phouljang, Moirangmantak, Kangthei and Khodang fall under two autonomous district council constituencies of I-Khousabung and 20-Sagang under 57-Henglep and 59-Saikot Assembly Constituencies (ST Reserved). The residents of these villages have patta land under the MLR & LR Act and pay land tax to the Revenue Department at Bishenpur District. At the same time eighteen villages out of the twenty-seven also pay Hill House Tax at Churachandpur district Headquarters.

The land patta holders are deemed to fall under the valley district of Bishenpur though the revenue boundaries of these villages do not coincide with the administrative boundaries of the district council. These villages were double censued in Churachandpur district and Bishenpur district in 2011. There is also double taxation in eighteen villages that pay both hill house tax (in Churachandpur) and land revenue (in Bishepur) districts.

Mr. Letpu Haokip, The Chairman of the Committee on Protection of Tribal Areas (Manipur) stated that a number of Hill Districts' land records are maintained and land revenue is collected by the neighbouring valley district while these villages regularly pay Hill House Tax. This was at the root of double census in 2011. There is growing apprehension that the revenue department of Bishenpur district will gradually swallow up the customary land ownership of the tribes till the MLR & LR Act-1960 will completely replace the customary land rights of the tribal people in time to come. The subsequent attempt to redraw the district boundaries on the basis of revenue record and overlapping census operation in 2011, are manifestations of grabbing tribal land. The process is still on when about 50 acres of Jairolpokpi village in Churachandpur were illegally acquired under the MLR & LR Act, where the Act does not apply at all. The bid to introduce Panchayati Raj in the Hills, where the district council exists, is another bid to grab tribal land.

Land Reforms in Mizoram

During the British rule, there was no regular land revenue in the Lushai Hills, except house tax. The Assam Land and Revenue Regulation 1886 was not extended to the Lushai Hills district. In 1898, Col. J. Shakespeare, the then Superintendent of the District, formulated the Land Settlement policy, which envisaged that each chief would get a certain area within which his people or subjects could move about and cultivate land as they liked. As such, the Lushai Hills were brought under the Inner Line Regulation-1873, to regulate the intercourse between the Hills and the Plains. In 1898, delineation of village boundaries was made within which lands were distributed to the people.

After transfer of power, the District Council was formed in Mizoram on April 25, 1952, and the Lushai Hills District (Reduction of Fathang) Act was passed in 1953. After the Assam Lushai Hills District Acquisition of Chiefs' Rights Act, the Autonomous District Council of Aizawl-Lunglei Area and Pawi Lakher Regional Council (PLRC) took charge of land administration in 1954. Under the Mizo District Council, the Deputy Commissioner was entrusted to make laws in respect to:

a) 'The allotment, occupation or use, or the setting apart, of land, other than any land which is a reserved forest, for the purpose of agriculture or grazing or for residential or other non-agricultural purposes likely to promote the interests of the inhabitants of any village or town.
b) Provided that nothing in such laws shall prevent the compulsory acquisition of any land, whether occupied or unoccupied, for public purposes by the government of the state concerned in accordance with the law for the time being in force authorising such acquisition.
c) The management of any forest not being a reserved forest.
d) The regulation of the practice of *jhum* or other forms of

shifting cultivation.

e) The establishment of village or town committees or councils and their powers.

f) The inheritance of property.

On grant of UT status, the Lushai Hills Autonomous District Council and PLRC were dissolved and three district councils were constituted: Pawi, Lakher and Chakma District Councils. Das wrote that there was no state legislation for the whole Mizo district. He mentioned as many as 20 legislations, (except the Rules and Amendment Acts) passed by the three district councils at different times from 1953 to 1983.

The first five acts related to permanently cultivated lands and permanent residential house sites on which permanent, heritable and transferable rights would apply, whereas for shifting cultivation lands, only annual use right would apply. The basic proposition in these acts being that all lands belonged to the state (Das 1986: 22-23, 27, 28).

The Mizo District (Land & Revenue) Act 1956 introduced Pass Holder's Right and Settlement Holder's Right. A pass holder had use right for the specified period. He had no right to transfer, inherit or sublet the land beyond the period of the pass. A settlement holder had heritable and transferable right of use and can sublet the land subject to payment of tax and revenue and the terms of settlement. There were also provisions for recording land records and 'Liability for Revenue Default' (Das 1986: 35). The Mizoram (Land & Revenue) Rules introduced a periodic lease that was not found in the Act. A lease holder, as defined under the Rules, was one who did not acquire the status of a Settlement Holder. He had only use right as specified in the lease terms. But whether a lease holder has acquired heritable and transferable right was not spelt out in the definition of 'Leasee' (Das 1986: 38).

The Mizo District (Agricultural Land) Act 1963 introduced two types of land rights 'Patta Holders' right' and 'periodic Patta' Holders' right'.

(a) 'Patta Holder's Right': This act converted the 'permit'

or pass system to 'Patta' for agricultural land. Section 7 of the Act gave a 'Patta Holder' heritable and transferable right of use, occupancy and subletting as per the terms and conditions imposed by this section. It also gave him power to evict unauthorised possession and to appeal for order for such eviction. A 'Patta-holder'could enter into an engagement with the District Council to pay land revenue, taxes, cess and rates as assessed under Section 7, although it did not give him legal ownership (Das 1986: 42).

(b) "Periodic Patta Holders Right": It was introduced by the Mizoram District (Agricultural Land) Rules and was defined as one, who has not acquired Patta Holder's right. Das wrote that this patta offered a right distinct from the patta. It gave less right than that given in Section 7 of the Act. This difference in right created by the rules was the crux of the problem. (Das 1986: 43-44).

Under the Mizo Hills District (Agricultural Land) Act and Mizo Hills District (Agricultural Land) Rules, settlement operation was taken up first in the wet-rice cultivation areas. A Land Tenure System Committee was constituted for the purpose. The Permit system was introduced on the wet-rice cultivation from which revenue could be drawn. A number of Periodic Pattas were surveyed to bring them under regular settlement. Under the Mizo District (Land Revenue) Act, House Passes were settled to individuals and a number of house sites were brought under land settlement within Aizawl and Champhai town areas.

The Mizo District (Transfer of Land) Act-1963 intended to check land transfer to non-tribals. The Lushai Hills District (Revenue Assessment) Act 1953, made provisions for tax on both land and people—a British legacy of personal residence surcharge. Land was divided into different classes with different rates of tax. There was no system of land revenue till the Land Revenue Act (1956) and Agricultural Land Act (1963) were passed (Das 1986: 50-51). The Pawi Lakher Regional Council

(PLRC) enacted separate legislation in 1959 and 1960, respectively. On abolition of PLRC, three district councils came up—each for Pawi, Lakher and Chakma districts, which passed separate agricultural land and revenue laws. The general picture of the land system in Mizoram drawn from different acts and rules were: all lands belong to the state; land was categorised into agricultural and non-agricultural; agricultural lands included permanent and *jhum* land; patta/periodic patta with specific rights to the holders of patta/periodic patta; abolition of pass system; classification, valuation and assessment of agricultural land; classification of non-agricultural land into residential and non-residential sites; maintaining land register with record update; restriction of transfer of land from tribal to non-tribal and absence of cadastral map of villages under district councils (Das 1986: 55-59).

After grant of statehood Mara and Lai District Councils were created. But all laws that were in force before the grant of statehood were to continue there until altered, replaced or amended. Subsequently the following important land legislations were made in Mizoram:

(1) The Mizoram (Land Survey and Settlement (Operation)) Act, 2003.
(2) The Mizoram (Restriction on Use of Transferred Land) Act, 2002.
(3) The Mizoram (Prevention of Government Land Encroachment) Act, 2001.
(4) The Mizoram (Taxed on Land, Building and Assessment of Revenue) Act, 2004.

Under the New Land Use Policy in Mizoram, land ownership was statutorily vested in the government that would formulate laws to govern different types of ownership; the Village Councils were to manage land for various purposes within their territorial jurisdiction for the period of three years since the interception of the Policy. After the lapse of three years, the regular land registration and record of rights would be made by the government only for those persons, who successfully developed their lands and *jhum* and forest laws were to be governed by the Jhum Regulation Act of 1954 and Mizoram Forest Act 1955.

The other major contours of the Policy were: control of shifting cultivation; allotment of suitable land to individuals for permanent use for a permanent source of income; rapid socio-economic development with ecological harmony; self-sufficiency in food grains through wet rice cultivation; horticulture, forestry, livestock development, small-scale and cottage industry and other subsidiary schemes.

In Mizoram, revenue administration and land recording work were geared up after 1987. Piecemeal and village/area wise operation at various pockets were adopted for the survey. Computerised data entry works for the Pilot Project was started in July 2007. The LSC holders were vested with legal ownership of land, including, rights and interest arising out of it (Das 1986: 37). Thus, the policy intended to create a class of permanent settlers enjoying almost permanent occupation subject to the condition that "*the state will continue to be the legal owner,* the initial decision whether a particular family was capable of retaining the piece allotted will be taken only after the evaluation of its performance over a period of five years" (Mahajan 1994: 294).

The criticalities of this policy lay in getting clearance of good performance on the land from an expert agency after which the government would enter into permanent relations with such families. It implies that if the performance is not satisfactory, or the land remained unused then the current allottee would be deprived of the land and the same would be handed over to another family. The second criticality is that what would happen to the family, who is to vacate the land after five years of unsatisfactory performance? The same risk factor would diehard for the next grantee for another five years. The capital starved new allottees would also fail in good performance and lose their allotment. Moreover, there are no mutually agreed good performance indicators. The ownership of the family would, thus, remain contingent upon good performance. In reality, the terrain being what it is, has is hardly any land available, which can be allocated to the people. Had such pieces of land been available, then the *jhum* system itself would have ended long ago. The government cannot create a enough number of such pieces of land for permanent occupation in limited time. This needed to be looked into more closely before announcing the complete winding up of *jhum* within the targeted period. There was no mention of what would happen to the families during the interval between shifting from *jhum* cultivation to settled land-use. The subsidy proposed to be provided might not meet the two ends (Mahajan 1994: 284). The more pertinent questions are the expectations for economy of scale, higher output from such land, marketable surplus, long-term changes in land use pattern and consequent land relations in the Mizo society.

District Councils and Land Reforms

The Bordoloi Sub-Committee Report felt the need of protection of tribal land from being alienated, control of immigration and allocation of land to outsiders. In forest management, it was felt that the legitimate desires and needs of the hill people be accounted as a policy. The tribes should also have the right of deciding for themselves whether to permit *jhum* cultivation or not and no general legislative bar could be imposed without taking local circumstances into account (Hansaria 2005: 230-231). The Assam Government prohibited transfer and alienation of land from a Khasi to a non-Khasi in Shillong and the Khasi States as per the notification No. RS. 167/46/114 dated August 23, 1948. Rules were accordingly made effective from September 1, 1948. Sale, barter, mortgage, lease or transfer of land of a Khasi to a non-Khasi was restricted except with the previous sanction of the provincial government. A non-Khasi found in possession or occupation of land otherwise than in accordance with the provisions of the rules, was to be evicted forthwith and the crops be confiscated (Phira 1989: 102-103). In 1953, the United Khasi and Jaintia Hills District passed the (Transfer of Land) Act to prohibit sale, mortgage, lease, barter, gift or transfer of land from a tribal to a non-tribal, or by a non-tribal to another non-tribal, except with the sanction of the District Council. The law on alienation of land was made comprehensive in Meghalaya Transfer of Land Act, 1971 (Meghalaya Act I of 1972) and made provision for registration of every transfer of land made after the commencement of the Constitution and before the commencement of this Act by a tribal to a non-tribal and by a non-tribal to another non-tribal within a period of two years from the commencement of this Act. This Act exempted (a) any transfer of land as security for any loan from bank, cooperative society or any other credit institutions, which the state government might, by notification, specify in this behalf; (b) the letting out on rent of any building standing on the land and (c) any transfer of land to, or in favour of, Government or District Council (Phira 1989: 109-112).

The land implications of the Sixth Schedule were laid down in Section 3 (1) (a) of the Sixth Schedule. Under clause (a) of paragraph 3(1) the District Council could make laws in respect of allotment, occupation or use, or the setting apart of land other than any land which is a reserved forest for the purpose of agriculture or grazing or for residential or other non-agricultural purposes or for any purpose likely to promote the interest of the inhabitants of any village or town provided that nothing in such laws shall prevent compulsory acquisition of any land, whether occupied or unoccupied, for public purposes by the government of the state concerned in accordance with the law for the time being in force authorising such acquisition. (b) the management of any forest not being a reserved forest; (c) the use of any canal or water course for the purpose of agriculture; (d) the regulation of the practice of *jhum* or other forms of shifting cultivation; (e) the establishment of village or town committees of the councils and their powers; (f) any other matter relating to town and village administration, including, village or town police and public health and sanitation; (g) the appointment or succession of the chiefs or headmen; (h) the inheritance of property; (i) marriage and divorce and (j) social customs.

Section 8 of the Schedule stipulated the powers to assess and collect land revenue and to impose taxes. The Regional

Council and the District Council were empowered to assess and collect revenue in respect of such lands in accordance with the principles for the time being followed by the government in assessing lands for revenue in the state generally. The Regional Council and the District Council were also empowered to levy and collect taxes on lands and buildings, and tolls on persons residing within such areas. The District Council was also empowered to issue licenses or leases for prospecting for and extraction of, minerals and share of annual royalties as agreed between the state government and the District Council. Any dispute over royalty was to be referred to the Governor for determination whose decision should be final.

The provisions of the Sixth Schedule had multiple explanations in different states and invited many litigations. In Sunil Dev vs. state of Tripura 2002 (1) GLT 538 it was decided that under clause (a) of paragraph 3 (a), the District Council can make laws controlling the occupation or use of any land within the tribal area, fixing minimum ceiling limit of allotment, prohibiting conversion of agricultural land into non-agricultural and preventing diversion of land. It can compel the land holders to keep some portion for grazing and social forestry. It can set up its own infrastructure to supervise the proper, fruitful and beneficial occupation and use of land. It can also make laws compelling the land holder to keep some place vacant within its boundaries for free flow of air and light and constitute a community farm for the benefit of the poor section. In Tarima Kanta Das vs. Karbi Anglong District Council, 1989 (1) GLR 147 and Udaldas Panika Prahlad Chandra Das vs Karbi Anglong District Council, 1990 (1) GLR 78 it was stated that land comprised in autonomous districts does not belong to the District Council and it is owned by the State government (Hansaria 2005: 45). Therefore, the extent of legislative competence of the District Council became contentious and created an obsession among the councillors to act like state legislators. Justice Hansaria, commenting on the legislative power of a District Council and referring to the case of District Council of United Khasi and Jaintia Hills vs Sitimon Sawin,

(1971) 3 SCC 708: AIR 1972 SC 787: (1972) 1 SCR 398, that had come up for consideration before the Constitution Bench of the Supreme Court, stated that:

Section 3 of the United Khasi and Jaintia Hills District (Transfer of Land Act, 1953) had prohibited sale, mortgage, lease, barter, gift or transfer in any other way of land by a tribal to a non-tribal, or by a non-tribal to another non-tribal, except with the sanction of the District Council. The question was whether this provision was within the law-making power of the District Council as conferred by Paragraph 3 (1)(a). This clause has empowered a District or Regional Council to make laws with respect to the allotment, occupation or use, or the setting apart of land for the purposes mentioned in the clause. The Supreme Court pointed out that unlike the Parliament and the State Legislatures, the District Councils are not intended to be clothed with plenary power of legislation. Their power to make laws is expressly limited by the provisions of the Sixth Schedule which has created them. It was then held that the bracketing together of the words allotment, occupation or use, or the setting apart of land' in clause (a), without using words like 'transfer' or 'alienation', was clearly indicative that the Constitution makers had intended to restrict the power of the District Council only to make laws with respect to actual use or occupation of land allotted or set apart for the purpose stated therein; and this power was not intended to extend to transfer of land.

The Court felt that the construction it was putting was not only in accord with the real sense discernible from the plain meaning of the language used in the clause, but it also served more effectively the manifest purpose, policy and the scheme underlying the provisions of the Constitution, namely, protection of the hill people against exploitation by the more sophisticated outsiders from the plains. The Report of the Sub-Committee on the Northeast Frontier (Assam) Tribal and Excluded Areas clearly supported this construction according to the Supreme Court. However, Justice Hidayatullah has regarded this judgment as against the history of this area

(Hansaria 2005: 45-46). On the other hand, Division Bench of the Gauhati High Court upheld the validity of the United Khasi-Jaintia Hills Autonomous District (Management and Control of Markets) Act, 1953, which inter alia provided for settlement of markets. The High Court was of the view that under Paragraph 3 (1) (a) the District Council could make laws in regard to land, its use and allotment for any purpose likely to promote the interests of the inhabitants, which purpose could include the holding of a market. Reference was also made to Paragraph 8 which had empowered the District Council to levy or assess taxes or tolls in respect of these lands (Hansaria 2005: 46-47).

Land (including forest) being the most critical issue in the Sixth Scheduled areas, the conflict of power between the institution of *Siyemship* and the District Council became inevitable. The root of the conflict could be traced when, as Chaube wrote, the members of the Khasi National Durbar submitted a memorandum, known as Solomon Memorandum, to the Statutory Commission complaining against the Sanad system since 1859 that completely subjugated the siems to the Deputy Commissioner and enabled the local government to grab land of the Khasis and entitling a chief to make profit out of the lease, sale, or other disposal of the minerals of the Khasi Hills. The Memorandum demanded rescind of Sanad and restoration of their ancient rights; establish a central Durbar as a federation of all the states and of the Khasi National Durbar. A counter representation signed by the landlords was made to the Statutory Commission denouncing the representative character of the Solomon Memorandum. In a stormy public meeting, presided over by Sib Charan Roy, MacDonald Khar Kongor, another landowner and Mukhteer (criminal lawyer) announced that the practice recently innovated of leasing out communal lands by *Siyem* was only possible through the usurpation of the constitutional rights of the people, which the British authorities had most emphatically disallowed, but the present political officers seemed to be under a misconception that the *Siyems* were Zamindars or landlords. The meeting denied the existence of any valid right of the chiefs in land implying the futility of revising the rights of the chiefs (Chaube 1999: 70-71).

Clause 1-A of the *Siyemship* (Administration of Justice) Order defined the *Siyem* as the customary head of the Khasi tribal institution of an administrative area of the United Khasi-Jaintia Hill District. On the other hand, appointment and succession of the chiefs became the power of the District Council that subordinated the *Siyem* to the district council. In the meantime, in Joramanik *Siyem*'s Case, vide T. Cajee v. Jormanik *Siyem*, AIR (1961), SC 276, the Supreme Court confirmed that the *Siyem* was an official of the District Council and the District Council conferred the status of an additional District Council court on the *Siyem*'s Durbar. Besides this judicial authority, the *Siyem* had some customary right over clan lands, unreserved forests belonging to the clan and the markets. This led to frequent accusations against *Siyem* as appropriating substantial parts of their revenue and litigation and conflict between the District Council and the chiefs (Chaube 1999: 107). Dutta found that the relationship between the 25 Khasi states and the functionaries of the autonomous District Council was strained and so the latter failed to get cooperation of the chiefs, who were given limited magisterial powers in the Council. Thus, most of the local authorities did not exercise their functions, particularly, the tax-related functions, while the *Siyems* of the Khasi Hills continued to function as independent rulers and realised revenue from market and fines for administration of justice. They also received fifty per cent of rent from exploitation of natural resources (Dutta 2002: 62-64).

The protective acts were scrambled due to the conflict of power between the ADC and the *Siyems* and repeated amendments of the foundational act. In 1953, the UK J Hills District Council adopted all the laws then in force in the state of Assam under the Assam Land and Revenue Regulation of 1886. But those were hardly enforced. The result was, though the District Council obtained house tax and land revenue from the Jaintia area, in the Khasi areas such collection could not be made as control over land remained with the *Siyems* and headmen. In the same year, the District Council brought all the markets of the district under its control and four kinds of markets—private ownership, *Siyemship, Doloiship* and *Sirdarship*—were made to pay half of their revenue to the District Council. By a subsequent amendment, payment on all markets other than the private, was abolished. Jaintia markets, being privately owned, paid 50 per cent of their income, while there was no effective control over the *Siyemships'* market. Besides, revenue from grazing lands in Jaintia Hills came mostly to the District Council while the same from the Khasi Hills went to the *Siyems*. Besides the Management and Control of Forest Act, 1958 could not be enforced due to opposition from the *Siyems*; so also introduction of House Tax failed in the Khasi Hills due to opposition of the *Siyems* (Chaube 1999: 109-110).

The laws passed by the Khasi Hills Autonomous District Council came into conflict with the state law and the latter came down heavily on the Council Transit Passes under the UKJ Autonomous Hill District (Management and Control of Forest) Rules, 1960 as it came into conflict with the Meghalaya Forest (Removal of Timber) Regulation Act, 1981. The Khasi Hills Autonomous District Council (Inheritance of Self-Acquired) Property) Bill 1980 could not get the assent of the Governor, as a similar bill was approved by the President of India in 1986 (Ebanoris 1988: 93). Secondly, the Act of 1971, was repeatedly amended in 1975, to add the Rabha and Kachari residents in Meghalaya for the purpose of the Act. In 1977, amendment was made to insert the word Koches. This amendment also provided for acquisition of land by the state government where a person intending to sell is not able to do so due to prohibition under sub-section (i) of Section 3 of the Act and where land cannot be disposed of to a tribal owing to adverse price terms or at the market value of the land. Such takeover of land is made against compensation as per the Land Acquisition Act, 1894. The Act was again amended in 1979 (Phira 1989: 17). In Jaintia Hills, however, the Autonomous District Council had already introduced a form of lease known as 'hot hali' that conferred permanent, heritable and transferable right of the leaseholder on the *Raj Hali* lands. The District Council also issued *'hot hali'* lands to the holders of the *Buniaz* (private) hali land. Such lease was, however, not issued to private (*Buniaz*) high lands (Phira 1989: 17). The Maghalaya Transfer of Land (Regulation) Amendment Act, 2012 allowed transfer of land through sale, gift, exchange, mortgage, lease, etc. that conferred rights on a non-tribal to use and derive benefit from the land as owner.

Besides, the Khasi Hills Autonomous District Council issued No Objection Certificates (NOC) for mortgage of land to financial institutions. It also issued land records to private individuals. The Khasi Hills Autonomous District passed (Allotment, Occupation and Setting Apart of Land) Bill in 2005. The United Khasi & Jaintia Hills Autonomous District (Management and Control of Forest) Act narrowly focused on timber and missed out the non-timber assets. The Meghalaya Transfer of Land Act created many loopholes and it was reported that the clause was inserted by which land could be transferred to any entity if it is in the tribal interest. But there was no clear definition of tribal interest. Educational institutions came under this exemption to please the private players that invited serious civil society reaction.

Box 2.6: Private University Act and SOMALA

The Meghalaya Private Universities (Regulated & Establishment & Maintenance of Standard) Act 2012 invited fresh problems and ignited serious public reaction and civil society activism. The Social Organisations of Meghalaya Against Land Alienation (SOMALA) demanded revocation of the notification issued on August 24, 2012 on the ground that this notification had relaxed and modified the earlier notification of March 30, 2011 which was decided to keep on hold for the present all the proposals for Transfer of Land to non-tribal entities in terms of Section 4(1) e and 4 (1) f of the Land Transfer Act pending consideration of the amendment to the Meghalaya Transfer of Land Regulation Act 1971. But no steps was taken for amendment of the Act. The government modified the notification of March 30, 2011 by another notification of August 28, 2012 "enabling the private universities to acquire land in

Meghalaya" without referring the matter to the joint committee constituted in June 2010 for its view. The acquisition of land by the private universities would affect the agricultural land which is the mainstay of the indigenous people. They made a demand before the government to scrap the notification till such time that the MTLR Act is amended as promised by notification of March 30, 2011.

The policy objective to give land to private entities needs to be viewed in the present context in which both the institutions—the Sixth Schedule and the Meghalaya Land Transfer Act, 1971 became dysfunctional in really protecting the land of the tribal people from being alienated and the welfare state did roll back and allowed crony capital to operate on land. Besides, though the policy statement that the mining lease would be regulated by Section 3 of the Company Act 1956, the nature of such a regulation came under serious public criticism. But the state did not change the rule of the game of transfer/sale/lease or sublet to various private agencies. This scenario in the Sixth Schedule areas of Meghalaya represents a *sui generis* case of primitive accumulation of communal land resources by the private cronies of the state.

In North Cachar Hills of Assam, the District Council took over the land in 1952 and passed the North Cachar Hills Land & Revenue (Adoption of Assam Land Revenue Regulation) Act in 1953. This act reiterated the old provisions of the Assam Regulation and, in due course, most of the matters dealt in the Regulation became applicable in the district. But there were no *jhum* land rules in the Regulation. These lands continued to be governed by customary practices (Das 1982: 131-132). In North Cachar Hills, therefore, the *jhum* lands were assessed to house tax. The District Council introduced annual lease, use and inheritance right during the year of issue of the same, but disallowed transfer of land without prior permission of the District Council, which made the latter the virtual owner of communal land. Moreover, the land settlement policy of 1954, gave a landless indigenous person the first preference in settlement of government land which intended to bring all lands progressively under wet-rice or special cultivation (Das 1982: 143-145; Sharma 1999: 48-49). The Sixth Schedule (Amendment) Act, 1995 inserted paragraph 3A that provided power to NC Hills Autonomous Council and the Karbi Anglong Autonomous Council to make laws on fifteen subjects. Sub-paragraph (3) of Paragraph 3, was amended in its application to the State of Assam that stated that save as otherwise provided in sub-paragraph (2) of Paragraph 3A, all laws made under this paragraph or sub-paragraph (1) of paragraph 3A shall be submitted forthwith to the Governor and, until assented to by him, shall have no effect"(Hansaria 2005: 44).

Large tracts of plain land in Karbi Anglong are covered with wet rice cultivation. It was cadastrally surveyed and recorded the rights. Periodic and annual leases were also prevalent. In this portion, the *'Paikas'* system and *Adhi* system were also prevalent. These systems produced a class of intermediaries and absence of tenancy and land ceiling legislations in the district leading to land concentration in a few hands (Das 1982: 149-150).

The Mikir Hills District (Jhuming) Regulation, 1954 disallowed any shift of village within the District Council from its existing site without the previous permission of the Executive Committee and prohibited *jhuming* and cutting forests within a radius of half a mile of the village site. Rotation and period of *jhuming* in certain parts of the village land and the areas to be cultivated by an individual cultivator were to be fixed by the Committee. The Regulation was amended in 1966 and allowed *jhum* in a particular restricted area of the village; people's selection of individual plots and prohibited *jhuming* within two chains of a perennial stream and one chain of a PWD or a District Council Road. No land revenue but a Hill House Tax was assessed on *jhum* land. The Karbi Anglong Autonomous District Council took several legislative measures to protect the right of the tribals over land; stop transfer of land from tribal to non-tribal; prohibit the *Paikas* system, regulate forest, *jhum* cultivation and grazing, etc.

But Bordoloi wrote that mortgage, land transfer from tribal to non-tribal, temporary alienation and unfair practices surfaced in Assam's landscape and the tribals got nothing in return except the reclaimed plots of land after the expiry of the agreement period (Bordoloi 1990: 30-31). Such practices rendered many tribals landless. Bhuyan gave a long failure inventory of the District Council in Karbi Anglong. These include: lack of adequate legislative powers; non-implementation of the Jhuming Regulation and the Grazing Regulation; the District Council authorities did not like to see the elected bodies of Town Committees so far constituted; incompetence of the Council in forest administration; failure to control illegal transfer of land from tribe to non-tribe; non-implementation of House Tax Regulation (Assam Land Revenue Regulation of 1886), etc. (Bhuyan 1999: 55-56).

The constitutional powers given to the District Councils under the Sixth Schedule, in respect of land, its occupation and use; management of forests and regulation of shifting cultivation; social customs and succession of chiefs and headmen broke the relational character of communal land and the larger social space associated with this. The spherical limitation imposed by district councils artifacted the community space and the customary right of the chiefs/headmen in relation to land became derivative rights.

The Manipur (Hill Areas) District Councils Act 1971

The Manipur (Village Authorities) in the Hill Areas Act 1956 axed the powers of the Kuki chiefs to a large extent. The Act was amended in 1983, to stop transfer of land from the tribals to the non-tribals. The Manipur Hill Areas (Acquisition of Chief's Rights) Act 1967, intended to abolish the chieftainship system which faces stiff resistance from the Kuki chiefs. In the meantime, the Manipur Land Revenue and Land Reforms Act 1960, was extended to several plain areas of the hill districts in 1975 that declared these areas as *khas* lands to become state property. This restricted the tribal people to cultivate on it. In the mean-time, in the Kangpokpi-Kanglatongbi range in Manipur, a large number of Nepali farmers settled and became sharecroppers first and later managed to get 'patta' lands in this range.

Both the Acts were opposed by the Kuki chiefs, who defended the Chieftainship institution through a memorandum to the Chief Minister of Manipur in 1976, which mentioned that the hill people got a negligible proportion out of the ten thousand hectares of land distributed so far. The same memorandum blamed the top authorities for sale of land from the tribal to the non-tribal people. The government equated the Kuki chiefs with the Zamindars, that the Sadar Hills Kuki Chiefs Organization of Manipur contested this charge in 1984, arguing that they are the protectors of tribal lands, not Zamindars (Ray 1991: 61-64).

Extension of the Manipur Land Revenue and Land Reforms Act to 89 villages of Churachandpur district and 14 villages each of Tamenglong and Senapati districts were resented by the tribal leaders of Manipur and, based on the Recommendations of the National Commission to review the working of the Constitution March 31, 2002, sought for extension of the provisions of the Sixth Schedule to the Hill Districts of Manipur (Sanga 2012). In a National Conference on Problems of the Hill Tribes at New Delhi in November 1990, two critical points were raised from the state of Manipur: one, the Manipur Land Revenue and Land Reforms Act 1960 should not be extended to the hill areas and two, the Sixth Schedule should be extended to the hill areas, thereof, (Report of Group I. National Conference 1991). The Sixth Schedule, according to many hill leaders, could be a protective institution against the land acquisition drive MLR & LR Act in the hills. Many social organisations of the Kukis, including, the Kuki People's Forum, Kuki Chiefs' Association Tengnoupal, United Chiefs' Committee, Council of Protection of Tribal Areas of Manipur (CoPTAM), Gunpi Area Chiefs' Association, Kana Area Chiefs' Association, Kuki Women's Association for Human Rights, Dingpi Area Kuki Chiefs' Association and the Thadou Students' Association also opposed extension of the MLR & LR Act in the hill areas. The Manipur (Hill Areas) District Councils Act was however passed as a from *sui generis* act in 1971 and the Rules came out in 1972.

In five fundamental counts, the District Council of Manipur

differed from the Sixth Schedule. (i) Unlike the states of Assam, Meghalaya and Mizoram, no area was declared as a 'tribal area' in Manipur; (ii) the District Council did enjoy equal power with the Sixth Schedule; (iii) the District Council of Manipur was equipped with the powers to control and administer in as many as seventeen subjects but in the field of legislation, it enjoyed only very limited powers confined, so far as they concerned the members of the scheduled tribes, to succession and appointment of chiefs; inheritance of property; marriage and divorce and social customs; (iv) these legislative powers are merely recommendatory powers; (v) the budgetary powers of the District Council under the Sixth Schedule is wider than that conferred by the Manipur (Hill Areas) District Council Act.

This Act was a half-hearted Act and remained ineffective in protecting tribal land from being transferred to the non-tribal farmers; the election of the council was also irregular. It also failed to hedge the Manipur Land Revenue and Land Reforms Act from being extended to the hills. Later on, the Sixth Schedule Demand Committee and the All Tribal Students' Union made big advocacy for the Sixth Schedule in the hill areas of the state. In recent years, the movement for the Sixth Schedule has been rejuvenated in the hills.

Box 2.7: Whither Customary Rights!

Mr. R. Sanga, an academic activist, and a spokesman of the United Chiefs' Committee of Manipur is of the view that the chiefs own the lands on behalf of the entire community. He referred to the land documents offered by the British to the chiefs which demarcated the land boundary of the villages.. This is sufficient proof that the tribal chiefs were not under the jurisdiction of the King of Manipur. Separate Acts were passed for the customary land administration for the hill areas of Manipur. There is also constitutional protection to the tribal people and tribal land. Ignoring these, the Manipur Land Revenue Act 1960 is being extended to the hills and hill lands are being acquired through this act. There have been growing cases of double taxation (Hill House Tax and Land Revenue) and double Census in many tribal villages. The new move for introducing Panchayati Raj Institutions and

Urban Local Bodies in the hills is at odds with the already existing District Councils in the hills. Besides, the state government also failed to address the forest-related grievances of the tribal people so far. Rather the state has allowed the forest contractor and timber traders till the recent past and many tribal land areas are being declared as reserved forests and sanctuaries. These amounted to state encroachment in tribal land and forest.

Moreover, about 59 ha. of tribal land was acquired for improving and widening Sinjawal-Dialkhai of Guite Road and Singngat-Behiang of Tedim Road by Border Road Organization and Border Road Task Force which added to the crisis of dispossession of tribal land. Compensation claimed for such acquisition was refused. The members of the Thanlon Sub-divisional Chiefs' Association claimed that the land acquired by BRO/BRTF belonged to the village chiefs whose land documents were issued. Demarcation was made by the competent authority in the pre-independence India. The Chiefs' Association now demand extension of the Sixth Schedule in the Hill Areas which the state government and valley people oppose.

The Tripura Tribal Areas Autonomous District Council Act 1979

The context of introducing the district council in Tripura were demand for protection of tribal right to land; refugee influx in tribal areas; failure of Tripura Land Revenue and Land Reforms Act to safeguard the right of the tribal people to land; failure of Tribal Development Blocks to protect tribal interest; minoritisation of tribes in their own land; migration of tribals to Maimama forest in East Pakistan and to different forest areas of Assam; political activism of TUJS for land, language and local autonomy and prohibition of *jhum*.

The demand for tribal autonomy was still ignored and finally the government had to yield to the movement pressure. The Constitution was amended (49th Amendment Act 1984) to extend the provisions of the Sixth Schedule to the tribal areas of the state of Tripura (Das 1982: 148). Modelled on the pattern of the Sixth Schedule, the District Council in Tripura had no legislative power in the matter of land, forest and *jhum* regulation. It had power of exclusive control and administration of the district council. The district council was given the power of exclusive control over the following matters:

- Allotment, occupation or use or setting apart of land for agricultural or other purposes, but land under Reserved Forest is excluded;
- Forest other than Reserved Forest;
- Use of canal water course for agriculture;
- Regulation of *jhum*;
- Village or town committee or council;
- Any other matter relating to village or town administration including police, health and sanitation.

The question of allotment of land became contentious as the Allotment of Land Rules of 1980, had no provision for restriction on allotment of land to a non-tribal in any specified area. The pertinent point was, if the District Council had power to make laws on allotment of land, it should also be given power to amend the Allotment of Land Rules of 1980, without which mere control was not adequate to protect the interest of the tribals. The only protection of the villages of the autonomous district and those including the Second Schedule of the Tripura Land Revenue and Land Reforms Act 1960, was a second or third preference to the tribals in the matter of transfer of land from non-tribals. This protection could easily be given either by adding a few clauses to Section 187 of the Tripura Land Revenue and Land Reforms Act 1960 or by suitably amending Section 31 or 32 of the Tripura Tribal Areas Autonomous District Council Act, 1879. Retention of two separate legal entities for the same purpose led to duplication, overlapping of functions, administrative complexities and avoidable strain on the public exchequer (Chakraborti 2004: 119, 121; Das 1990: 109, 110). Das found that the meaning of absolute control was not clear because Section 32 specified certain other matters, on which the district council could make bye-laws like inheritance, marriage, divorce and social customs of the tribal people (Das 1984:122).

The Sixth Schedule to the Constitution (Amendment) Act 1988 granted further autonomy to the District Council of Tripura. As a result, the customary land ownership became subordinate to the District Council. The District Council behaved like a mini-state in making laws on property rights and shifting cultivation; in assessing and collecting land revenue and imposing tax and in giving license for mineral extraction and so on. The District Council tried to stop transfer of land belonging to the tribals to the non-tribals but it did not restrict the incidence of intra-tribal transfer from which the tribal elites accumulated huge land and created a vertical division within the communities.

A Critique of the District Council

Though the Bordoloi Sub-Committee intended to protect the customary rights of the tribal people over land, in the beginning, the land question did not form the core of the public debate on the Sixth Schedule. The debate was mainly concentrated on political autonomy of the hill areas from the hegemony of the plains of Assam. Therefore, while territorial autonomy was given, land privatisation ran parallel in the Sixth Schedule areas of Meghalaya with progressive transformation of the *Ri Raid* land to *Ri-Kynti* land and land concentration became more serious in the Sixth Schedule areas of Meghalaya than in the colonial era. In the Khasi Hills, the local elaka authorities indiscriminately leased-out *Ri Raid* land to urban Khasis and non-Khasis grabbed *Raid* land by means of patta (Sen 1987: 92-99). In the Garo villages, a class of landed gentry, mainly absentee in nature, emerged (Mazumdar 1987: 181-191).

The institutional efficacy of the Sixth Schedule and its operational history in the hills of Northeast India, specially, in relation to alienation and privatisation of community land, remained thoroughly doubtful and challenging. Five major institutional bottlenecks were visible in the institution of the Sixth Schedule: lack of plenary power of the District Council to stop land privatisation through sale, transfer, lease, mortgage; supersessionary power of the state legislatures over the laws made by the District Councils; replication of the semi-feudal practices of agriculture in the hill areas; political calculation behind allotment of tribal land to the partition-time refugees

(1947) and the War refugees (1971) from East Pakistan and the revenue interest of the state from the hills by shifting from the House Tax mode to revenue mode. Much, however, depended on the political will of the rulers and the decision makers to protect the tribal lands from being alienated. But the experience from the region was that the state was by and large in censured mood towards the Autonomous District Council and the legislations made by the latter. Thus, some laws passed by the latter became subject to judicial controversy and the judiciary also toeing the treasury view, showed the censured face. There were also predatory roles of the self-motivated and crafty people within the council, who wanted to instrumentalise the political platform of the Autonomous District Council for higher political aspirations. All these made the institutional quality of the Sixth Schedule poor and imperfect.

In Meghalaya, the state-community controversy over land right started in the 1950s, when B.B. Lyngdoh, a public leader, defended people's right in customary law over land and denied state rights. On the other hand, the formal decision to issue mining lease rested with the state government (Karlsson 2011: 213) and the central government had regulatory powers over mines and mineral development in 'public interest'. In the name of 'public interest', an affluent section within the Sixth Schedule areas captured mining that was largely unregulated. The state did not put a cap on mining operations by the mine owners. (Muhkim 2005: 13-14). Dhkar found unregulated rat-hole mining in Meghalaya as a unique case of primitive accumulation that was started with grant of sanads to the Khasi chiefs, who appropriated huge mineral resources in these hills (Dhakar 1994: 84). In the Khasi Hills, Ri-Kynti land is a customary type of self-acquired property based on agreement of a lease with the Jait representatives, who are considered as landlords (Misra 1990: 58-59). In the Garos Hills, all lands are A'khing (clan) lands and only 4.08 per cent being under permanent cultivation, which indicates the narrow size of the land market. But in the Khasi areas, large scale lease markets operate. Way back in 1976-77, the World Agricultural Census, estimated the total leased area in the state at 22,930 hectares, 57.04 per cent being wholly leased and the rest being partly leased holdings (Das 2005: 125-136).

All these developments in the hills marked the continuation of the practice of accumulation and dispossession of the communal land resources. Several factors stood in the way which included the supersessioanry power of the state-made law over customary law and district council law in respect of land, eminent domain of the state, public interest clause and urgency clause in law, etc. The customary laws were branded as institutionally imperfect which failed to cope up with the changing context. The economic argument against the customary laws was that these were market imperfect which debarred market transaction of the land resources in the hills. Absence of legal person in the customary laws made the transaction process difficult in the market economy. The institutionalisation of land rights under the market economy basically facilitates the private and corporate interest. This let loose the rift between the community and the state over the land rights.

Conclusion

The institutional mode of accumulation and dispossession opened up a major conflict between the positive law and natural law in respect of communal land. The colonial jurisprudence tended to deny the community as a person and the community-ownership of land as imperfect with a view to converting communal land to private ownership through two jurisprudential instruments of *res nullius* and *lex loci*. Individual rights in this case, became derivative rights while the state became the ultimate owner of land. The post-colonial Northeast India carried forward the colonial institutional legacy through different land revenue and land reform acts. The central message of all the land revenue acts was state's ownership of land with derivative rights of individuals. This opened up a new conflict between the state process and the community process on the question of land. This conflict became more pronounced in the Sixth Schedule Areas of Northeast India. The Sixth Schedule intended to protect communal land from being alienated, but became the conflictual instituition in practice. Beyond the classical state-community conflict over land, there were remarkable trends of privatisation of communal lands in the Sixth Scheduled areas. Thus, although the Sixth Schedule intended to protect the customary ownership of tribal land from being alienated, it is from the Sixth Scheduled areas of Meghalaya that maximum land alienation has taken place over time. The Sixth Schedule could not stop mining operations and commercial cropping and land privatisation in Meghalaya.

Similarly, the district council in Manipur could not resist mining operations by private companies, commercial cropping by private individuals and land alienation to the non-tribal farmers. In Tripura, tribal lands were allotted to the non-tribal farmers, who came as refugees. Land transfer to non-tribals was not as significant in Mizoram as the New Land Use Policy that vested land ownership in the government. The Village Councils were authorised to manage land within their territorial jurisdictions for the period of 3 years since the interception of the Policy. After the lapse of 3 (three) years, the regular land registration and record of rights would be made only for those persons, who successfully developed such lands. A good performance evaluation of land development could qualify durable allotment of land, failing which the same would be handed over to another family. This left diehard risk to the capital-starved new allottees, who would also fail in good performance and lose their allotment. This system allowed the process of dispossession through the institutional route in Mizoram. In Nagaland, the community process in land was recognised although by the Nagaland Land (Requisition and Acquisition) Act 1965, land could be acquired for certain public purposes, which the village authority could not resist. The Act of 1970, recognised the individual right to transfer *jhum* land only within the village and community boundaries. This Act recognised both the customary land rights and the authority of government over land. It criminalised removal of forest produce from *jhum* land. Thus, the community process in the land issues remained vague in Nagaland till the institutional measures of switching over to terracing, money inducement and technical assistance, irrigation projects and community development project, seed farming, etc. led to privatisation of communal land resources.

The customary laws relating to communal land, thus, became weak enough to defend the same against the onslaught of the formal laws and powerful state institutions. In the Sixth Scheduled areas, the customary laws faced double subordination to the district council and the state laws. Finally, therefore, the state through the institutional mode became the most powerful accumulator and rent seeker from the communal land.

REFERENCES

Agarwal, A.K. (1986). Changing Picture of Agrarian Relations in Arunachal Pradesh in Atul Goswami edited, *Land Reforms and Peasant Movement: A Study of Northeast India*. New Delhi: Omsons Publications.

Agarwal, A.K. (1990). Towards Land Reforms in Arunachal Pradesh in Malabika Dasgupta edited, *Impact of Land Reforms in Northeast India*. New Delhi: Omsons Publications.

Alemchiba, M. (1970). *A Brief History of Nagaland*. Kohima: Naga Institute of Culture.

Alesina, Alberto (1997). *The Political Economy of High and Low Growth*. Washington DC: Annual World Bank Conference on Development Economics.

Ao, Temsula (2010). *Land, Ethics and Economic Management Among Ao Nagas*. Vol. 1. Calcutta: Northeast Researches, Institute of Northeast India Studies.

Arambam, Lokendra (1986). Manipur: A Ritual Theatre State. Pasight: Proceedings of Northeast India History Association.

Aron, Jenine (2000). Growth and Institutions: A Review of Evidence, World Bank Research Observer, 15 (1).

Baden Powell, B.H. (1882). *Land System in British India*. Vol. 1. London: Oxford.

Baden Powell, B.H. (1892). *Land System in British India*. London: Oxford University Press.

Banerjee, Malay (2005). Gumti Hydel Project and the Displaced Persons of the Area. Proceeding of NEIHA, Vol. I, No. XV.

Bareh, Hamlet (1985). *History and Culture of the Khasi People*. Guwahati: Spectrum Publications.

Barpujari, S.K. (1994). Raja Purandar Sing's Management of Salt Wells in Naga Hills in J.B. Bhattacharjee edited, *Studies in the Economic History of Northeast India*. New Delhi: Har Anand Publications.

Baruah, Jeuti (2001). *Customary Laws of the Chkhesangs of Nagaland with Special Reference to Their Land Holding System*. Guwahati: Law Research Institute Eastern Region, Guwahati High Court.

Baruah, Jeuti (2007). *Customary Laws of the Dimasas of North Cachar Hills in Assam with Special Reference to Their Land Holding System*. Guwahati: Law Research Institute, Eastern Region, Guwahati High Court.

Baruah, Jeuti (2007). *Customary Laws of the Karbis of Karbi Anglong in Assam with Special Reference to Their Land Holding System*. Guwahati: Law Research Institute, Eastern Region, Guwahati High Court.

Baruah, Jeuti (2007). *Customary Laws of the Lais of Mizoram with Special Reference to Their Land Holding System*. Guwahati: Law Research Institute, Eastern Region, Guwahati High Court.

Baruah, Jeuti (2007). *Customary Laws of the Tangkhul Nagas of Manipur with Special Reference to Their Land Holding System*. Guwahati: Law Research Institute, Eastern Region, Guwahati High Court.

Baruah, Jeuti (2007). *Customary Laws of Nishis of Arunachal Pradesh with Special Reference to Their Land Holding System*. Guwahati: Law Research Institute Eastern Region, Guwahati High Court.

Baruah, Jeuti (2007). *Customary Laws of Khamptis of Arunachal Pradesh with Special Reference to Their Land Holding System*. Guwahati: Law Research Institute, Eastern Region, Guwahati High Court.

Baruah, Jeuti (2007). *Customary laws of Mismis of Arunachal Pradesh with Special Reference to Their Land Holding System*. Guwahati: Law Research Institute Eastern Region, Guwahati High Court.

Baruah, Jeuti (2007). *Customary Laws of the Paites of Manipur with Special Reference to Their Land Holding System*. Guwahati: Law Research Institute Eastern Region, Guwahati High Court.

Baruah, Jeuti (2009). *Customary Laws of the Riangs of Tripura with Special Reference to Their Land Holding System*. Guwahati: Law Research Institute, Eastern Region. Guwahati High Court.

Baruah, Jeuti (2011). *Customary Laws of the Chakmas of Mizoram with Special Reference to Their Land Holding System*. Guwahati: Law Research Institute, Eastern Region, Guwahati High Court.

Baruah, Jeuti (2011). *Customary Laws of the Chakhesang Nagas of Nagaland with Special Reference to Their Land Holding System*. Guwahati: Law Research Institute, Eastern Region, Guwahati High Court.

Bathari, Uttam (2009). Land, Laws, Alienation and Conflict: Changing Land Relations Among the Karbis in Karbi Anglong District in Walter Fernandes and Sanjay Barbora edited, *Land, People and Politics: Contest Over Tribal Land in Northeast India*. Guwahati: North Eastern Social Research Centre.

Bezbaruah, Prafulla (1958). History Yells: The Hills and the Plains of Assam are But One in Shri Parag Chaliha edited, *The Outlook of NEFA*. Guwahati: Assam Sahitya Sabha.

Bhattacharjee, J.B. (1978). *The Garos and the English 1765-1847*. New Delhi: Radiant Publishers.

Bhattachariya, Jayanta (1990). Social and Political Institutions of Angami Nagas in Jayanta Sarker and B. Datta Ray edited, *Social and Political Institutions of the Hill People of North-East India*. Calcutta: Anthropological Survey of India.

Bhuyan, B.C. (1990). The District Council in the North East: A Case Study of the Powers and Functions of the Karbi Anglong District Council. *Bulletin of Tribal Research Institituе*. Vol. 1, No. XII. Guwahati: Assam Institute of Research for Tribes and Scheduled Castes.

Bordoloi, B.N. (1990). Tribal Development Plans and Programmes in the Sixth Scheduled Areas of Assam with Special Reference to Land: A Critical Appraisal. Vol. 1, No. VII. *Bulletin of Tribal Research Institituе*. Guwahati: Assam Institute of Research for Tribes and Scheduled Castes.

Cantlie, Sir Keith (2008-2009). *Sir Keith Cantlie's Notes on Khasi Law*. Shillong: Chapala Publishing House.

Chakravarti, Mahadev (2002). Internally Displaced Persons in Tripura-Past and Present in C. Joshua Thomas edited, *Dimension of Displaced People in Northeast India*. New Delhi: Regency Publications.

Chakraborti, Dipannita (2004). *Land Question in Tripura*. New Delhi: Akansha Publishing House.

Chakraborti, S.B. and C. Changsen (2004). Customary Rights and the Question of Land in Arabinda Basu, Biman K. Das Gupta and Jayanta Sarker edited, *Anthropology for North-East India*. Calcutta: Indian National Confederation and Academy of Anthropologists, Indian Anthropological Society and National Museum of Mankind.

Chakravarti, Mahadev (1994). Land in Tripura: The Tenural System and Transfer in J.B. Bhattachariya edited, *Studies in Economic History of Northeast India*. New Delhi: Har Anand Publications.

Chakravarti, Sudeep (2013). Root Cause: Revisiting the Inner Line Laws. *Livemint*.

Chatterjee, N. (2008). *The Earlier Mizo Society*. Aizawl: TRI, Government of Mizoram. (Reprint).

Chatterjee, Suhas (1975). *Mizo Chiefs and the Chiefdoms*. New Delhi: MD Publications.

Chatterjee, Suhas (1994). *Making Mizoram: Role of Lal Denga*. New Delhi: MD Publications.

Chaube, S.K. (1999). *Hill Politics in Northeast India*. (Updated version). London: Sangam Books.

Choudhury, Dipak Kumar (2003). *Tripurar Arhanaitik Itihas* (Unabinsha Satabdir Dwitiardha). Agartala: Bhasa.

Chaudhury, B.B. (2004). Adivasi ain Aranyaka: Reconsidering Some Characterisation of Their Polity and Economy in B.B. Chaudhury and Arun Bandopadhyaya edited, *Tribes, Forests and Social Formation in Indian History*. New Delhi: Manohar.

Das, J.N. (1982). *A Study of the Land System of North Eastern Region*. Vol. I. (Mimeographed). Guwahati: LRI Eastern Region, Guwahati High Court.

Das, J.N. (1984). *A Study of Land System of Tripura*. Guwahati: Law Research Institute, Eastern Region, Guwahati High Court. (Mimeographed).

Das, J.N. 1984. *A Study of the Land System in North Eastern Region*, Vol. IV. *Meghalaya*. Guwahati: Law Research Institute, Guwahati High Court. Mimeographed.

Das, J.N. (1986). *A Study of Land System of Northeast India*, Vol. VI. *Mizoram*. (Mimeographed). Guwahati: Law Research Institute, Guwahati High Court.

Das, J.N. (1989). *Land System of Arunachal Pradesh*. Indian Law Institute and Law Research Institute, Eastern Region, Guwahati High Court. Bombay: N.M. Tripathi Pvt. Ltd.

Das, J.N. (1989). *A Study of Land System in Manipur*. Guwahati: Law Research Institute, Guwahati High Court.

Das, J.N. (1990). *A Study of Land System of Tripura*. Guwahati: Law Research Institute, Eastern Region, Guwahati High Court.

Das, Gurudas. (2005). Land in the Hills of Northeast India: Factor Immobility vs Market-led Growth in Thomas, C. Joshua edited, *Polity and Economy: Agenda for Contemporary Northeast India*. New Delhi: Regency Publications.

Datta, P.S. (1995). Report on Mizoram, Workshop on Land Reforms-Agenda for the North East. Gauhati: Papers on the North Eastern Scenario. Mussoorie. Lal Bahadur Shastri National Academy of Administration. Land Reforms Unit. April, 3-5.

Dhakar, Rita Dorothy (1983). Management of Limestone Quarries in the Khasi Hills Till the Beginning of 1879, Barapani: Proceedings of North Eastern History Association. Fourth Session.

Datta, S. (2002). Internally Displaced Persons in Arunachal Pradesh in C. Jasua Thomas edited, *Dimension of Displaced People in Northeast India*. New Delhi: Regency Publications.

Dutta Ray, B. (1985). An Aspect of North Eastern Frontier Strategy of the Raj: An Overview. Agartala: Proceedings of Northeast India History Association.

Deb, B.J. and Dilip Kumar Lahiri (1982). *Lushai Customs and Ceremonies*. New Delhi: Mittal Publications.

Deb Burma, Sukhendu (2008). Refugee Rehabilitation and Land Alienation in Tripura in Walter Fernandes and Sanjay Barbora edited, *Land, People and Politics: Contest Over Tribal Land in Northeast India*. North Eastern Social Research Centre and International Workgroup for Indigenous Affairs.

Devi, Uma (1966). *Evolution of Economic Thought and Theory*. New Delhi: S. Chand & Co.

Dun, E.W. (1980). *Gazetteer of Manipur*. New Delhi: Vivek Publishing Company. (Reprint).

Dutt, R.P. (1986). *India Today*. Calcutta: Monisha.

Dutta, Narendra Chandra (1968). *Land Problems and Land Reforms in Assam*. New Delhi: S. Chand & Co.

Elwin, Verrier (1964). *A Philosophy for NEFA*. Shillong.

Erbanoris, Jyrwa (1988). Critical Assessment of the Working of the Khasi Hills Autonomous District Council in Meghalaya in M.N. Karna, L.S. Gassah and C.J. Thomas edited, *Power to the People of Meghalaya*. New Delhi: Regency Publications.

Ganguli, J.B. (1989). Problem of Land Alienation in Tripura in B.B. Dutta and M.N. Karna edited, *Land Relations in Northeast India*. New Delhi: People's Publishing House.

Ganguli, J.B. (2008). Impact of Northeast Indian Tribal Values and Culture on the Hill Region's Socio-Economic Development in the Pre-Plan Period in Asok Kumar Ray and S.B. Chakrabarti edited, *Society Politics and Development in Northeast India; Essays in Memory of Dr. Basudeb Datta Ray*. New Delhi: Concept Publishing House.

Gassah, L.S. (1994). Revenue Administration in Jaintia Hills during the British Rule. Shillong: *Journal of Northeast India Council of Social Science Research*, Vol. 18: 2.

Ghosh, B.B. (1986). Pattern of Use and Ownership of Land in Nagaland in Atul Goswami edited, *Land Reforms and Peasant Movement*. New Delhi: Omsons Publications.

Ghuman, Ranjit Singh (2010). South Asia in Transition: Agrarian and Rural Transformation. Chandigarh: *Man and Development*, Vol. XXXII, No. 4.

Guha, Abhijit (2000). Dispersion of Tribals from Their Agricultural Land in West Bengal: A Critique of Biplab Dasgupta's 'Overview of the Tribal Problem in India or a View from Below'. Calcutta: *Journal of Anthropological Society*, Vol. 35, No. 1, March.

Guha, Amalendu (1991). *Medieval and Early Colonial Assam: Society, Polity and Economy*. Calcutta: K.P. Bagchi & Co.

Gurdon, P.R.T. (1975). *The Khasis*. New Delhi: Cosmo Publications (Reprint).

Hansaria, Vijoy (2005). *Justice B.L. Hansaria's Sixth Schedule to the Constitution*. Universal Law Publishing Co. Pvt. Ltd. Second edition.

Heimendorf, C.V.F. (1962). *The Apa Tanis and Their Neighbours: A Primitive Civilisation of the Eastern Himalalyas*. London: Routledge & Kagan Paul.

Heimendorf, C.V.F. (1982). *Highlanders of Arunachal Pradesh*. New Delhi: Vikas Publishing House.

Hemendorf, C.V.F. (1985). *Tribes of India—The Struggle for Survival*. New Delhi: OUP (first Indian impression).

Hidayatullah, M. (1979). *The Anundoram Barooah Law Lectures on the Fifth and Sixth Schedule to the Constitution of India, (Second Series)*. Guwahati: Ashok Publishing House.

Himal (2004), The Dam and the Tribal. Kathmandu. *Himal*, May.

Hodson, T.C. (1989). *The Naga Tribes of Manipur*. Delhi: Low Price Publications.

Hungyo, P. (1989). Land Tenure System in the Hills of Manipur: A Comparative Study of the Tangkhul Naga and the Thadou Kuki in B.B. Dutta and M.N. Karna edited, *Land Relations in Northeast India*. New Delhi: People's Publishing House.

Hunter, W.W. (1990). *A Statistical Account of Assam*. Vol. 2. Delhi: Low Price Publications. (Reprint).

Islam, Sirajul (1979). *The Permanent Settlement in Bengal: A Study of its Operation 1790-1819*. Dhaka: Bangla Academy.

Jain, Pankaj (1991). Mizoram and its Land System with Special Reference to Inheritance Laws in *Selected Readings on North East*,

Mussoorie, Lal Bahadur Shastri National Academy of Administration, Mussouri, May.

Joshi, H.G. (2004). *Meghalaya Past and Present*. New Delhi: Mittal Publications.

Kamei, Gangumei (2009). *Manipur is a Gift of History*. Imphal: Free Press. June 2 and July 6.

Karlsson, Bengt G. (2011). *Unruly Hills, Nature and Nation in India's North East*. New Delhi: Orient Blackswan.

Kipgen, S. and Ch. Priyabrata Singh (eds.) (2009). *Land, Identity and Development. Tribalism and the Tragedy of the Commons: Land, Identity and Development—The Manipur Experience*. New Delhi: Akansha Publishing House.

Krishna Ananth, V. (2011). Land Acquisition Laws and the State in the Neo-Liberal Era: Some Observation on the Constitutional Imperatives, Legislations and Judicial Interventions, Neoliberal State and its Challenges, Seminar Volume, OKD Institute of Social Change and Development, Guwahati, 20-21 December.

Kumar, Avinash (2011). The Battle for Land: Unaddressed Issues. *Economic & Political Weekly*, Vol. XLVI, No. 25, June 18.

Longkumar, Lanusashi and Toshimenla Jamir (2012), *Status of Adivasis/ Indigenous Peoples—Land Series: 6, Nagaland*. Delhi: Aakar Books.

Mahajan, V.S. (1994). *Manmohan's India and Other Current Writings*. New Delhi: Deep & Deep Publications.

Marak, Kshirodi (1998). Critical Assessment of the Garo Hills Autonomous District Council in M.N. Karna, L.S. Gassah and C.J. Thomas edited, *Power to the People of Meghalaya*. New Delhi: Regency Publications.

Mathew, Chungmajai (2007). British Revenue Policy in the Naga Hills District (1887-1947). Kohima: Proceedings of Northeast India History Association.

Marak, Julius L.R. (2000). *Garo Customary Laws and Practices*. New Delhi: Akansha Publishing House.

Mazumdar, D.N. (1987). The Emerging Middle Class Among the Garos in B. Dutta Ray edited. *The Emergence and Role of Middle Class in Northeast India*. New Delhi. People's Publishing House.

Mazumdar, D.N. (1990). The Changing Role of the Nokma in Garo Hills in Jayanta Sarkar and B. Dutta Ray edited, *Social and Political Institutions of the Hill People of Northeast India*. Calcutta: Anthropological Survey of India.

Meghalaya Times (2013). Thursday 24 October.

Misra, Bani Prasanna (1983). Society and Politics in the Hill Areas of

North-East India in B. Datta Ray edited, *The Emergence and Role of Middle Class in North-East India.* New Delhi: Uppal Publishing House.

Misra, Bani Prasanna (1990). Some Reflections on the Agrarian Relations in a Khasi State: A Study of Hima Maharam in Jayanta Sarkar and B. Datta Ray edited, *Social and Political Institutions of the Hill People of Northeast India.* Calcutta: Anthropological Survey of India.

Mittal Publication (1984). *Report on the Administration of Northeast India (1921-22).* New Delhi: Mittal Publication.

Mukhim, Patricia (2013). Other Side of the Inner Line Permit. Shillong: *The Shillong Times,* March 23.

Muhkim, Patricia. (2005). Wanted Strict Regulations on Mining. *Dialogue,* Vol. 7, No. 2, October- December.

Nadkarni, M.V., Syed Ajmal Pasha and L.S. Prabhakar (1989). *The Political Economy of Forest Use and Management.* New Delhi: Sage Publications.

Nayak, Pradeep (2013). Policy Shifts in Land Records Management. *Economic and Political Weekly,* Vol. XLVIII, No. 24, June 15.

Nongbri, Tiplut (1995). Report on Meghalaya, Workshop on Land Reforms–Agenda for the North East. Papers on the North Eastern Scenario. Mussoorie, Lal Bahadur Shastri National Academy of Administration, Land Reforms Unit, April, 3-5.

Pamberton, R. Boileau (1966). *Report on the Eastern Frontier of British India.* Guwahati: Depertment of Historical and Antiquarian Studies in Assam.

Pandey, Vikash N. and Akhileswar Pathak (1995). Sociology of Law: Postscript and Prospects. *Economic and Political Weekly,* August, 5-12, 1995.

Pathy, Jagannath (1987). *Anthropology of Development: Demystifications and Relevance.* New Delhi: Gian Publishing House.

Phira, J.M. (1989). *The Meghalaya Land and Revenue Manual,* Land and Land Revenue Series, 2 Vols. Shillong: Government of Meghalaya.

Ratan Kumar, Kh. (2004). Inner Line Regulation and Manipur, (A Historical Background). Shillong: Proceedings of the Northeast India History Association.

Rathakrishnan, L. and K. Ravi Kumar (2013). Land Acquisition in India: Need for a Paradigm Shift, *Kurukshetra,* Vol. 61, No. 5, March 13, 2013.

Ray, Asok Kumar (1991). *Authority and Legitimacy: A Study of the Thadou*

Kukis in Manipur. New Delhi: Rennaissance Publishing House.

Ray, Asok Kumar (1991). Land and Land Reforms: A Study of the Kukis of Manipur in Malabika Dasgupta edited, *Impact of Land Reforms in Northeast India*. New Delhi: Omsons Publications.

Ray, Asok Kumar (2010). *Whither Northeast India?* New Delhi: Om Publications.

Report of the Group I Consisting of Northeast India and Sikkim. National Conference on Problems of the Scheduled Tribes. New Delhi: Vigyan Bhavan, New Delhi, March 31, 1991.

Robb, Peter (1997). The Colonial State and the Construction of Indian Identity: An Example of the Northeast Frontier in the 1880s. Cambridge University Press: *Modern Asian Studies*, Vol. 31, No. 2.

Rosanga, Orestes (2008). Land Revenue System Under Colonial Rule. Aizawl: Proceedings of Northeast India History Association.

Roy, N.C and P.K. Kuri (1996). The Evolution of Property Rights in Land in Arunachal Pradesh. Shillong: *Journal of the Northeast India Council for Social Science Research*, Vol. 20:2, October.

Roy Burman, B.K. (1987). Society, Ecology and Land Reforms in Tribal India, Paper presented in the 'Seminar on Agrarian Structure, Land Reforms and Agricultural Growth'. Almora: G.B. Pant Institute.

Roy Burman, B.K. (1991). Issues in Land Reforms in Tribal Ares of Northeast India: A Preliminary Approach in Malabika Dasgupta edited, *Impact of Land Reforms in Northeast India*. New Delhi: Omsons Publications.

Roy Burman, B.K. (1994). *Indigenous and Tribal People: Gathering Mist and New Horizon*. New Delhi: Mittal Publications.

Roy Burman, B.K. (1998). RGICS Paper No. 47. New Delhi: Rajiv Gandhi Institute for Contemporary Studies.

Roy Burman, Jagat Jyoti (1990). Impact of Land Reforms in Tripura in Malabika Dasgupta edited, *Land Reforms in Northeast India*. New Delhi, Omsons Publications.

Ruiva, Khasim (1989). Land Ownership and its Problems Among the Tangkhuls in B.B. Dutta and M.N. Karna edited, *Land Relations in Northeast India*. New Delhi: People's Publishing House.

Saikia, K.N. (2003). *The Assam Land and Revenue Regulation 1886*. Guwahati: Lawyers Book Stall (Reprint).

Sampat, Preeti (2013). Limits to Absolute Power: Eminent Domain and the Right to Land in India, *Economic and Political Weekly*, Vol. XLVIII, No. 19, May 11.

Sanga, R. (2012). The Manipur (Village Authority in Hill Areas) Act, 1956, Paper at the Seminar on Tribal Issues in Manipur, TRI Auditorioum, Imphal Organised by the Steering Committee on Mega Manipur Tribal Seminar, December 7-8.

Sangma, M.S. (1987). Land Reform System in Garo Hills: A Historical Note in B.B. Datta and M.N. Karna edited, *Land Relations in Northeast India.* New Delhi People's Publishing House.

Sen, Soumen (1987). Land as Property: Its Significance in the Traditional Society and Polity in Khasi and Jaintia Hills in Dutta, B.B. and M.N. Karna edited, *Land Relations in Northeast India.* New Delhi. People's Publishing House.

Shakespeare, Lt. Col. J. (1912). *The Lushai Kuki Clan.* London: MacMillan & Co.

Sharma, Bhupen (1999). Land Relations and Agricultural Practices Among the Hill Tribes of Northeast India (Draft): A Study sponsored by the Ministry of Rural Areas and Employment. Guwahati: Omeo Kumar Das Institute of Social Change and Development.

Sharma, Manorama (2012). Editorial Board, Interrogating Land Policies and Land Rights in Colonial Assam: The Need of a Gender Critique. In Aspects of Land Policy in Assam: Continuity and Change. Guwahati: Vivekananda Kendra Institute of Culture.

Sharma, R.S. (1976). *Forms of Property in the Early Portion of the Rig Veda: Essays in Honour of Professor S.C. Sarkar.* New Delhi: People's Publishing house.

Singh, B.P. (1987). *The Problem of Change: A Study of Northeast India.* New Delhi: OUP.

Singh, K.S. (ed.) (1995). *People of India: Nagaland,* Vol. XXXIV. Calcutta: Anthropological Survey of India.

Singh, N. Lokendra (2001). Some Aspects of Management of Naga Hills Forest During Colonial Rule and Beyond. Imphal: Proceedings of Northeast India History Association.

Singh, Prakash (1972). *Nagaland.* New Delhi: National Book Trust.

Sinha, G.N. (2006). Prospects of Community Forest Management and Role of Panchayats in Arunachal Pradesh. *Annual Journal of Rural Development.* Vol. 1, June. Itanagar: State Forest Research Institute. SIRD-ARUN.

Thakur, Amarendra Kumar (2003). *Slavery in Arunachal Pradesh.* New Delhi: Mittal Publications.

The Shillong Times (2012). Shillong, October.

The World Bank (2007). *India, Land Policies for Growth and Poverty*

Reduction, Agriculture and Rural Development Sector Unit-South Asia Region. Oxford University Press and The World Bank.

Wahi, Namita (2013). Land Acquisition, Development and the Constitution. *Seminar,* February.

Wallerstein, Immanuel (2010). Land, Space, And People: Constraints of the Capitalist World Economy, Keynote address at the 34th Political Economy of the World-System Conference on "Land Rights in the World-System." Florida Atlantic University, April 22. *American Sociological Association,* Vol. XVIII, No. 1.

Williamson, John (2000), What Should the World Bank Think About the Consensus? Washington DC: *World Bank Research Observer,* Vol. 15 (2), August.

3

The Patterns of Change

The Background

Human beings made changes in land-use depending on the particular stage of economic formation and invention of the forces (means) of production. The early human beings did not know the technology of food production through agriculture and, therefore, they had to depend solely on hunting and gathering (possibly in both the pre-hominid mode of individual gathering and the hominid mode of collective gathering). In the archaic human society, the economic system had strong dependency on nature. The degree of dependency on nature, however, varied from place to place corresponding to the innovations of the means of production at different times. Throughout the Stone Age men lived entirely on the products of chase; they produced no food and the technological level also was too low. People gradually learnt to use stone for fabricating tools and equipment for food procurement. Throughout this age, human beings could make no fundamental change in use of land and natural resources. But with progressive reduction of nature's gift, the absolute dependency on hunting-gathering economy also started to reduce. This led them to vigorously search for alternative sources of food. This happened again at different times in different parts of the world. This marked the beginning of change in the archaic land use and a shift from the procurement to the production economy when mankind learnt to transform the things-in-itself to the things-for-us. In the process, the emerging production economy de-captivated the human beings from absolute dependency on nature and procurement economy. Land was converted to a space for production and agricultural economy emerged as a result produced, in turn, the complex economic and social organisations, social relations and structured institutional frames.

The word agriculture, through furrowing, (tilling), derived from the Sanskrit equivalent verb *'krs'* or the Latin equivalent, *'cultura'*, was a revolutionary innovation of mankind in production economy. This was found first in shifting cultivation economy, started about 9,000 years ago, as the earliest mode of cultivation. This was practised by the highlander Neolithic men. They used bamboo, stone or wooden implements for shifting cultivation. With exposure to more advanced civilisation, their main agricultural pattern died hard but the stone implements used in pre-historic shifting cultivation were replaced by iron tools. This cultivation is still the principal mode of subsistence of the tribal brethren (Sharma 1990: 14, 15- 16).

In the larger parts of Northeast India, the dependency on ecology remained higher than the more advanced parts of India. The high hill dwellers' choice of cultivation went invariably towards shifting cultivation. The 'abundant factor' and favourable fallow cycle made the practice of shifting cultivation more sustainable. Goswami found the practice of shifting cultivation in Northeast India is more primitive than that in Orissa, Andhra and Madhya Pradesh and the historical evolution of shifting cultivation was not uniform in all parts of Northeast India (Goswami: 1994:8). In Meghalaya, for example, hunting-gathering economy was in practice before agriculture was discovered. The Khampti tribe of Arunachal Pradesh, on the other hand, practised settled agriculture. The discovery of iron impacted the two economic formations in Northeast India—hunting-gathering and settled agriculture—in two ways. In Meghalaya, the early iron mining and smelting works manufactured artifacts (Thakur 2013: 19) for hunting-gathering, while iron technology of the Khamptis was used for war weapons and plough agriculture in the Dihing river valleys. Exclusive control over iron under the monastery led to the expansion of the monastic order (Thakur 2013: 21) in the transhumant society. But defence and plough technology did not have a uniform form. Thus, among the Apa Tanis, Akas and the Mijis, plough cultivation was generally unnoticed, while among the Nishis, it is hardly 20 to 25 years old. The ploughs was the outcome of the mixture of indigenous origin and neighbouring exposure. In the Seppa area, indigenous plough technology hardly dates back to 20 to 25 years, which was a result of the neighbourhood impact of Assam. With this agrarian class, the halua (ploughman) developed fast in the area as bonded labourers. In some parts of the West Kameng and Tawang districts, plough technology had an indigenous origin before the establishment of the monastic order. (Thakur 2013: 24-25). In some areas, wooden ploughs (thongpa) were in use.

The practice of *jhum* cultivation symbolised the change from the crude to the enlightened state and replaced hunting-gathering economy. It is important to note that agricultural economy in Northeast India, first developed on the ridges with slash-and-burn method and then came down to the flat valley areas, where the mode matured into wet cultivation. The land system under slash and burn method evolved obviously around communal ownership and continued to remain the main agricultural practice of the hill people (Das 2006: 4913). The ridge-to-valley agricultural economy is extremely critical to understand the land use pattern in Northeast India.

Changing Land-Use Pattern in Northeast India

In Northeast India, the traditional land-use pattern became stereotyped and was a response to the physiographic character of land, where settled cultivation appeared in the valley areas that could produce surplus food and shifting cultivation appeared in the hill areas that could produce non-surplus subsistence food. This stereotype was broken with colonial intervention for the first time. The land use for shifting cultivation never got the appreciation of the colonisers because of its "petty production" nature. Precisely, three factors prompted the colonial (and the post-colonial) states to discard land use for shifting cultivation. These were ecological, economic and strategic. The ecological argument against shifting cultivation led the colonial state to popularise sedentary agriculture in the hills. The official view blamed the shifting cultivation for massive destruction of the forest and ecology. More than 50 years ago, the Food and Agriculture Organisation described shifting cultivation as the greatest obstacle not only to the immediate increase of agricultural production, but also to the conservation of production potential for the future, in the form of soils and forests (FAO 1957).

The economic argument against shifting cultivation was the need for economy of scale from which profit and revenue could be generated. The strategic argument against shifting cultivation was to tie up the shifting cultivators to land. Following the colonial legacy, the Indian state took different policy measures and action plans to evince changes in land use pattern in the hills till the Government of India prepared a "National Land Use Policy Guidelines and Action Points" in 1988, that insisted on earmarking areas according to land use, framing suitable legislation and its sincere enforcement. It also made penal provisions for violating the guidelines. The guidelines were not seriously registered by the state governments to make the desired impact. The Draft National Land Utilisation Policy 2013 of the Department of Land Resources of the Ministry of Rural Development, Government of India, once again floated the guiding principles that made the states custodians of land and required the latter to eliminate unsustainable pattern of land utilisation/land management and to provide the necessary legal and institutional support to facilitate capacity building and participatory, transparent and comprehensive land use pattern. It stated that the existing constitutional provisions and rights, the existing laws and rules, standards, procedures, guidelines and stipulations brought out by various ministries, departments and institutions of the Government of India as applicable to land utilisation policy shall continue to be in force for taking decisions in land matters and land use change. This policy stipulated identification of Land Utilisation Zones, planning and management. It also stipulated Reserve Areas, that included areas within the Land Utilisation Zones that are/will be under pressure of the government to cause significant changes in land use in the zone that should be governed by a set of rules, regulations and procedures. This policy served as a guiding framework for preparation of the respective state land utilisation policies.

The state mode of land utilisation and zonalisation plan could not be reconciled with the traditional tribal land use pattern, associated with the historical process of man's journey from hunting-gathering to food producing economy. While the shifting cultivation was the prime mode of the hill economy, people also had symbiotic relations with forests which had both the use-value and the cultural value. Land-man ratio in the hills being more than comfortable, the shifting cultivators did not face any land scarcity. Historically speaking, shifting cultivation itself made the change in land-use from procurement to production economy on sustained basis. In the tribal societies, changes happened in land use at a still later stage with their interaction with the pilgrims and the traders from the plains. Also there was the great role of more powerful political and administrative penetrations in the tribal societies. Thus, as Guha found, the Tibetan administration had penetrated into certain pockets of Arunachal in the late medieval period and impacted the land-use pattern there. (Guha 1991: 4-5, 6-7). In Tripura, change in land use happened with the infiltration of the Bengali farmers.

The post-colonial Indian state also retained the colonial view that remained thoroughly controversial. One section of agricultural scientists dittoed the government view, while the other section gave a dissenting view. The recent science reviews indicated that the deleterious impacts of shifting cultivation on the environment might have been greatly overestimated. Many of the original comparative research studies were fundamentally flawed in that they relied on spatial analogues (adjacent sites with different cultivation practices) without accounting for farmers' conscious selection of particular sites for certain cultivation practices based on perceptions of soil quality and potential agricultural productivity. Researchers failed to explicitly recognise the fundamental assumption that site differences in ecological processes can only be attributed to differences in cultivation practices, if those sites were identical in terms of soil quality, topography, land-use history, climate and biota before cultivation was initiated. This assumption was also critical in chrono-sequence studies that use a series of spatial analogues to investigate patterns over time such as research on the impact of differences in the fallow period on ecological processes. In summary, and in contrast to many policy-makers, shifting cultivation is now considered a highly ecologically and economically efficient agricultural practice provided that the fallow period is sufficiently long. Nevertheless, there is broad agreement among scientists and policy-makers that the current trend towards reduced fallow periods in lands under shifting cultivation, makes this practice unsustainable, and results in reduced crop yields as well as increased environmental degradation due to soil erosional losses, watershed siltation, and atmospheric pollution (Grogan, Lalnunmawia and Tripathi 2012: 164).

Notwithstanding the dissenting view, the liberal state of India, from the very first Five Year Plan started to discourage shifting cultivation. The economic argument was in favour of production of scale which land-use by shifting cultivation could not attain. The progressive changes brought about in the cropping pattern from food-grain production to commercial production also brought about corresponding changes in the land-use pattern. The policy focus was laid on commercial cropping to generate revenue and marketable surplus. With the advent of the neoliberal market economy, land-use pattern was drastically reversed in favour of commercial use.

Both the liberal and the neoliberal Indian state had a deeper conviction that the land-use pattern needed to respond to the market demand. It further reinforced this view by diverting land use from staple production to commercial cropping and then to industrial and commercial use. The state policy was tuned up accordingly and progressive industrial use of land became the usual practice in the neoliberal state. This completed the process of perennial annihilation of communal land and traditional agricultural practices. The policy of changed land-use is found in the 10th Five Year Plan document on 'Poverty Alleviation in Rural India: Strategies and Programmes' that viewed that further reduction in land ceiling and acquisition of land for distribution to the poor was not a credible policy any more. While the document expressed anxiety over further reduction of land ceiling (Planning Commission: 10th Five Year Plan) the policy patronised a shift towards private sector intervention in land use. This invited crony capitalism in the land sector by progressively annihilating the tribal peasantry. The plan document's argument of fragmentation opened up the classical dichotomy between land fragmentation and class fragmentation. Moreover, the National Agricultural Policy tended to create faster agricultural development, promote value addition, accelerate demand driven agro-business to cater domestic and export market of agricultural products. The policy also focused on lease markets, increasing size of land holding, agri-business and private sector participation in contract farming and agri-business.

The official version of contract farming was stated in the report of the Task Force (constituted by the Ministry of Agriculture) that treated contract farms as companies and recommended that "the contract farming should be made legal; it should have both forward and backward linkages and contract farmers association or cooperatives be formed at the plant level that would improve their bargaining power vis-a-vis the company and promote equality of partnership for ensuring smooth functioning of any contract farming arrangement" (Parliamentary Digest 2003).

Corporate gain apart, the extreme negative externalities included, as Ghosh noted, the labour-dispensing and capital-intensive practice; monoculture and reduction of food and livelihood security; lower paid women workers, child labour and high casualisation of labour (Ghosh 2009).The state-withdrawal from the regulatory role was reflected in one of the propositions of the 10th Plan that intended to "completely free tenancy law of all restrictive conditions"(Planning Commission: 10th Five Year Plan) and the land reform focus in the National Agricultural Policy insisted "on consolidation of holdings all over the country on the pattern of north west India". The market focus and technology loaded approach of the National Agricultural Policy was reflected in the matching approach of land reforms that focused on consolidation of holdings all over the country on the pattern of the north western states, development of lease markets for increasing the size of the holdings and legal provisions for lease of private lands and agri-business. This produced a perennial cleavage between the state and market on the one hand and the community on the other.

In the light of the above macro-scenario, we discuss below the modus operandi of changing land-use in the tribal areas of Northeast India.

Sedentisation of the Hill Agriculture

Sedentisation of hill agriculture evinced visible change in the land use pattern in the hill economy of the North East. The fertile valley lands of the Northeast were the major sources of colonial revenue. These lands were also attractive for cash cropping that could beget huge revenue. The hill lands being non-revenue-yielding, a paltry taxation system, called House Tax, Hoe Tax, etc. was imposed on the shifting cultivators. This taxation did not provide sufficient financial opulence to the colonisers. The incredible forest resources of the region drew their larger attention and they captured the forests, first by plunder and then by enclavisation of the forest areas in the administratively defined 'Reserved Forests' or 'Protected Forests' with a view to extracting sizeable amount of profit- revenue. This enclavisation blocked access and movements of the tribal people in the forests and hedged the operational area of shifting cultivation.

The republican state of India made aggressive attacks on shifting cultivation and the communal land system of the tribes. Shifting cultivation was discouraged not only for its low productivity and non-surplus nature, but also for the undefined rights on land. The former Chief Justice of the Supreme Court, Justice Hidayatullah also discredited *jhum* by saying that "the area is ruined when it is used so by the cutting down of trees and removal of grass" and viewed that "some modification of *jhum* cultivation is necessary so that the land may come under permanent cultivation"(Hidayatullah 1979: 82). Defined the land rights were one of the fundamentals of institutional economics which was required for the twin purpose of collateral for institutional loans and for facilitating land market. The Indian state adopted different policy measures to arrest shifting cultivation and to popularise alternative land use pattern. Under the Five-Year Plans, the state governments of this region adopted various measures to regulate and improve shifting cultivation and to wean the shifting cultivators away from the hoe. The Jhumia Rehabilitation Programme received enormous policy support in Tripura and the regulatory mechanism was tightened to discourage shifting cultivation. Sedentisation involved artificial land terracing, irrigation facilities, watershed management, plough cultivation, mono-crop and intensive agriculture, higher technology and capital input; extension services; and land ownership right from the community to the private individuals.

Sedentisation of agriculture, however, had the perpetual problem in the rugged terrains and it was quite difficult to customise it in the higher mountain slopes. By its nature, sedentary cultivation in the hills could not be as land extensive as the valley cultivation. Notwithstanding this, the policy makers recommended short-term measures that included proper land use planning based on land capability classification; checking soil and fertility loss through mechanical measures of terracing, including, puertorian type of terrace, half-moon terrace, levelling and partial terracing, water disposal system and water harvesting technology; soil management practices, including, cover crops, strip and mixed cropping, relay cropping, green manuring; improved productivity through crop management practices, including, improved variety crops, crop planning, use of manure, chemicals and fertilisers, weed control, water management, plant protection and use of implements. The long term measures included study of rainfall patterns, development of terraces, water conservation, cropping pattern, use of implements, studies on effects of burning and building up-soil fertility. As an alternative system of farming in shifting cultivation land, agri-horti-pissiculture, animal husbandry and poultry farming were contemplated (Borthakur, Awasthi and Gupta 1990: 89-96).

The modus operandi for weaning the people from shifting cultivation varied from state to state. In Tripura, Jhumia Rehabilitation Colonies were set up by the government and the *Jhumias* were given individual plots of settled wet-rice cultivation and were provided with various extension services and input supports. Assam's Jhum Control Scheme was a part of the soil conservation programme. Various restrictions were imposed on *jhuming* in the forests. Under the Taungya system, the services of the *Jhumias* were used for the afforestation programme. This system became a common feature in silviculture in the region, including in Tripura. Assam undertook horticulture on the hills on extensive scale. In the Angami and Chakhesang areas of Nagaland, the hill slopes were terraced for practice of continuous cultivation. Terrace areas were extended by giving subsidies to the farmers and the *Jhumias* were urged to grow commercially valuable and quick-growing species on suitable *jhum* plots. In Meghalaya, cash crops like potato horticulture, and other cash crops like cashew nut, black pepper, cardamom, etc. were grown on the hill terraces of Khasi Hills.

In Manipur, wet-rice cultivation was extended through land reclamation and irrigation facilities in Ukhrul district as a part of the *jhum* control programme. The Soil Conservation Department of Manipur also undertook measures for discouraging shifting cultivation. In Arunachal Pradesh, the *jhum* control scheme rested on introduction of terrace cultivation (Ganguli 1990: 34-35). In Manipur, Roy Burman noted, the Forest Department was forced to modify their plan of plantation of pine on a large scale in the 1970s, when the World Bank plan of replacement of sal in Bastar had to be substantially modified in the late 1970s because of adivasi opposition and the Environment Protection Committees in Arunachal were restricting the extraction of timber by contractors (Roy Burman 2008).

The Government of Mizoram discouraged shifting cultivation from the very First Five Year Plan. The Village Council Act of Mizoram in 1953, endowed the latter, wide-ranging powers for management of land and forest. The Lushai Hills district (Jhuming) Regulation 1954 and the Pawi Lakher Autonomous District Council (Jhum) Regulation 1956, empowered the District Councils to regulate land and forest (except the Reserved forests). Two strategies were adopted for this: giving up *jhum* and use the terrace for cash crop cultivation. Most of the farmers, who gave up *jhuming* had more than four hectares of land and were located in close proximity of large towns. These farmers no longer remained owner-cultivators but became new affluent elites in the Mizo society. They employed hired labour to cultivate their terraced fields, while they themselves had taken other vocations. These entrepreneurial elites were a product of the new agronomy promoted by the state that created class division and social stratification in the hitherto egalitarian land system of the Mizo community. This new class had more than four acres of land each (Das 2006: 4914). This development in Mizoram—though not like the 'reverse tenancy'(by leasing in and leasing out by small to big farmers who dominate the lease market) of Punjab agriculture that created a class of tenant exploiters and exploited owners (Singh 1989: A-86-A92)—resembled the Punjab type in spirit and ideology. This led to incipient class interest within the entrepreneurial elites. Lalnunmawia and Lalzarliana wrote that over the years large areas of *jhum* lands were privatised which gave rise to tenant farming in shifting cultivation areas and absentee land ownership, opening avenues for land conflicts (Lalnunmawia and Lalzarliana 2013: 235). All the major centrally sponsored schemes in Mizoram were aimed at introducing permanent land use. Several models were suggested for rehabilitation of *jhum* land and some permanent land use systems were introduced on an experimental basis. These included Sloping Agricultural Land Technology (SALT); Bamboo-based agro-forestry in the hilly terrain; Enhancement of low land rice cultivation and System of Rice Intensification (SRI) method (Lalnunmawia and Lalzarliana 2013: 109, 111-112, 133-136). Two other scientific models for replacement of shifting cultivation were undertaken: improving shifting cultivation practices on steeply sloped lands and replacing shifting with more continuous cultivation practices (Grogan, Paul et. al. 2012: 169-171).

The Indian Council of Agriculture Research also mystified *jhum* cultivation as bad, irrational, outmoded, non-scientific and non-productive and intended to systematically replace it by alternative land-use. Agronomical practices were developed by the agriculture experts of ICAR. The ICAR prescribed the model of three-tier land-use and agri-horti-silvi pastoral system as the ideal model of land-use in the hills that would cause minimum soil erosion and would provide variety of produce for self-consumption and marketing with horticultural crops grown on the slopes.

Table 3.1: The Three-Tier Model of Land-Use and Conservation of ICAR

Slope	*Approx. % of Total Land Area*	*Land Use*	*Conservation Measures*
Top portion	33	Forestry	
Middle portion	33.5	Horticulture	Half-moon terracing for horticultural plants
Lower portion	33.5	Agriculture	Bench terracing

But this model had serious flaws. It did not look into the village structures and the livelihood systems of the hill dwellers. This skirted the spatial components of social formation and village settlement types. In Nagaland for example, the villages are located on the hill tops; many Karbi and Dimasa families also live on the hill tops, in Arunachal and Mizoram most of the village settlements are on the hill tops. To the highlander communities, the three-tier model could be place-annihilating and ruinous. The technological innovations to control *jhum* were not culture-specific and they cut into the socio-economic lives of the *jhumias*. The three-tier model constructed an official hierarchy in which permanent cultivation was accorded a higher status. The premium was laid on intensive and permanent forms of production, while *jhum* was labelled as derogatory, temporary and non-intensive. Second, *jhum* entailed a communal form of cultivation and ownership of land which, in the official logic, discouraged individual initiative and constrained increase in output and productivity (Das 2006: 4916).

P.S. Ramakrishnan consistently made the case for a more nuanced approach to *jhum* cultivation integrating the elements of *jhum* with the innovations in agro-forestry. In fact, he brought to our notice that in terms of maintaining soil fertility in the humid tropics, there is, as yet, no system that could match *jhum*. The longer view of soils and regeneration was built into the practice of *jhum*. This is not a simplistic argument for retaining *jhum* in its unreconstructed form. *Jhum*, after all, comprises a complex series of systems, rather than a monolithic and uniform method. Much depends on the local ecological and cultural milieu. He found that "the activities of industrial man" were responsible for restricting access to land and destroying the forests. He eschewed the simplistic model of demographic pressure on *jhum* land and factored in the local 'ecological dynamics' and customs in *jhum* cultivation (Rangarajan 1994: 2544-2545). The mechanical solutions of the policy-makers could not succeed, as farmers did not show an interest to the technological and 'big science' approach. Therefore, the very official view that shifting cultivation is responsible for soil erosion and ecological damage, remained thoroughly contested but the "correct approach", to Ramakrishnan, lay "in accepting it not as a necessary evil, but recognising it as a way of life; not condemning as an evil practice, but regarding it as an agricultural practice evolved as a reflex to the physiographic character of land" (Rangarajan 1994: 2544-2545). Subsequently, the ICAR itself recognised its follies in not adopting an anthropocentric approach towards mitigating the problem. It broadly outlined the drawbacks as mentioned under: (1) the new settlements cut into their socio-cultural life abruptly; (2) they were not used to cultivating in terraces/using bullocks/implements (3) they found the production too low in the newly built terraces during first year due to the removal of top soil (4) the production technology for terrace was also not properly developed for the region and (5) extreme dearth of trained and dedicated persons. These high end technologies, according to ICAR, did not prove to be "culture specific" and, hence, failed to attract the *jhumias* as it cut into their socio-cultural life. Thus, technocratic solutions to an artificially conjectured problem did not work. The policy directive, thus, needed rethinking and retribution (Das 2006: 4914).

The official version also grossly ignored the fact that shifting cultivation, produces certain crops that are not produced in the wet-land valley areas but have a wide market in the plains. Roy Burman noted that in 1872, about 400 shifting cultivators migrated to Tripura from Chittagong Hill tract and were considered to be a source of great gain and in 1894, a circular was issued to the Sub Divisional Officers to ensure that such migrants do not face any inconvenience. The state had vital interest in this, as at the end of the third quarter of the last century (the 19th century), export duties on cotton and oilseeds produced in the shifting cultivation were the single most important source of revenue for the state. In 1924-25, approximately 9.55 million hectares were under shifting cultivation which fell in the tribal and hilly areas of the country (Roy Burman 1990: 3). Misra also wrote that the Tripura *Jhumias* produced in the 1930s, about 1,000 tonnes of cleaned cotton and about 1,700 tons of oil seed. The export duties on cotton and oilseeds fetched a sum of about one and a half lakh of rupees out of sixteen lakh of state revenue. In 1918-19 the Dharwar variety of cotton grew well, the experimentation of which was made on the *jhums*. The result of the trial was reported to be good in 1923-24. The *jhum* cotton was sent to the government Economic Botanists at Dhaka, the Central Cotton Committee, Bombay, the Bangla Luxmi Cotton Mills, Messrs. Kettlewell Bullen and Co. and the Dhakeswari Mills. The reports were encouraging (Misra 1990: 59).The shifting cultivation produce could thus have the potential of being the robust base for *in-situ* economic development that the post-independence Indian state ruled out from the very beginning. The post-colonial agricultural economists also echoed the British version of wasteful practice of shifting cultivation. They ignored the fact that, as Sharma noted, "almost all the varieties of cereals and vegetables grown on the *jhum* field are not possible to grow in wet plain lands" (Sharma 1990b: 17). Das viewed that shifting cultivation was disfavoured because this form of agriculture is based on the Asiatic Mode of Production where the concept of surplus and the question of trade in surplus did not arise (Das 2006: 4912).

Land use pattern started to change more abruptly within the growing commercialisation of the Indian economy and eventual acquisition of land. The anti-*jhum* state policies were conceived without a thorough understanding of the anthropology of land and without appreciating the importance of analytical economics. The Indian state, or for that matter the state governments of Northeast India were obsessed by the institutional economics and they conceived land in terms of yielding of commercial crops for profit accumulation. This was not futuristic and soon let loose negative consequences on the economy of shifting cultivation and on the tribal people depended on it.

The Inter-Ministerial Task Force for Rehabilitation of Shifting Cultivation located the problem of shifting cultivation more in shortening the fallow cycle and the associated unsustainable practices in management of shifting cultivation rather than in shifting cultivation itself. Given the demographic pressure on the existing land under shifting cultivation with corresponding decline of productivity and also given the increasing land for urban and industrial use and cash cropping, the village communities were left with little scope to protect this practice. The local institutions were also weakened by the state legislations and neoliberal market policies. The Task Force, therefore, felt the need for (i) scientific fallow cycle management to maintain sustainability of land and ii) crafting of effective local institutions to facilitate such scientific intervention. The recommendations let loose significant ramifications to the shifting cultivators. These included a pilot programme for *jhumia* rehabilitation, rapid regeneration of forest fallows and its sustainable management followed a 'big bang' approach that could also benefit from commoditisation of the shifting cultivation products. Penetration of the market mechanism through 'certification' of organic agriculture from shifting cultivation and growing organic forest fallow products did hit at the core of the staple producing shifting cultivation.

The other two more critical recommendations of the Task Force were: i) a modified credit policy that recognises the communal tenure of land holding and communal production system in equivalent terms to that of private property collateral, that would discourage the active trend of anti-poor privatisation of shifting cultivation areas; and ii) long-term security of land tenure in favour of individual or group households for successful fallow management. This would allow sufficient on-field innovation, technology adoption and follow up by the farmers (GoI 2008). A regional seminar on land use planning at Dimapur, recommended sedentisation of shifting cultivation through various resettlement schemes, cash cropping and market linkaging, land development through terracing and introducing furrow technique. Review of the community rights of the tribal communities and the land tenure systems were the other important recommendations. Concerted efforts of the government and non-government organisations, research and educational institutions were sought for formulation of an integrated programme for control of *jhum* cultivation (Soil and Water Conservation Department 1990).

The government of Assam undertook three major schemes

in different districts of the state to wean people from shifting cultivation. Bordoloi gave a detailed account of these schemes:

i. A Model Villages scheme was untaken in Karbi Anglong District Council in 1964. In each Model Village 50 *Jhumia* families were resettled. Each family was provided with an 'L' pattern well-ventilated and spacious house on a plot of about one bigha and permanent cultivable land of about five bighas. These lands were well irrigated and other infrastructure facilities like road, educational institutions, and drinking water facilities were also provided. The families living in the Model Villages were exempted from House Tax.

   This scheme was not all successful. Many families left those villages and returned to their original abode. Lack of follow-up measures apart, this scheme did not take the social and cultural factors into consideration. Eventually, these houses were used for keeping cattle, pigs, poultry and for storing fuels. Behind these houses, the people constructed traditional houses where they started to live. Many people also left the villages considering these village sites inauspicious and haunted by ghosts and evil spirits. In fact the tribal families in the Model Villages could not adapt paddy cultivation practices by ploughing. These families did not receive credit support from the District Council either (Bordoloi 1990: 36-37; Bordoloi 1986: 129).

ii. The Assam Plantation Crops Development Corporation Ltd. undertook plantation of coffee and rubber in 1975. The Corporation started with nine coffee plantations in the two hill districts of Assam and seven rubber plantations in Karbi Anglong district of Assam. Gradually, more land areas were brought under coffee and rubber plantations. The Corporation claimed high production of coffee and rubber and calculated good income of the families.

   But the main objectives of the Corporation were still

to be achieved. While the beneficiary list for the scheme was finalised, it was yet to receive approval from the government (Bordoloi 1986: 37-38).The roles of the Coffee Board, Tea Board and the Rubber Board in changing land use were more complicated. In the late 1980s, the council encouraged farmers to contract out land to the Coffee Board that consolidated enough land for commercial cultivation. The villagers pooled in the common land and placed it under the managerial supervision of an employee of the Coffee Board (usually a non-tribal). The Board supported the farmers initially. But in the latter part of the 1990s, the prices of coffee fell, and the board withdrew its support to the farmers. There was a similar story with other plantation crops such as rubber and tea (Barbora 2002: 1288).The Coffee Board recognised only individual owners of land holding patta for extending subsidies and loans. This dismissed the communal ownership of land. The emerging Dimasa elites demanded individual patta and started to appropriate community land for personal use. It was reported that 'one Dimasa leader holds 200 acres of land by depriving others of their rights (Fernandes 2008: 60).

Sedentization of agriculture in the Karbi Anglong district led to cultivation of cash crops and horticultural plants, which led to emergence of individual ownership of land. With the growth of population and influx of East Bengal refugees and Nepalese, the tribal people started attaching more importance to the right of individual ownership. They secured individual ownership rights on obtaining annual patta, which could not be transferred, sold, mortgaged, leased, bartered, gifted or otherwise given to the non-tribals without the prior approval of the Executive Committee of the District Council as per the Mikir Hills District (Transfer of Land) Act, 1959. In Karbi Anglong District, the kind of dispossession was unique. While the land for permanent cultivation belonged to the individual families as per the law, the standing crops, plants and fruits were not theirs (Bordoloi 1986: 131).

iii. A Composite Project for weaning *jhum* for settled cultivation was undertaken in the two hill districts under the Fifth Plan. Allotment of reclaimed plots, infrastructure and input facilities for settled cultivation were to be extended to them. An evaluation of the project revealed a total failure picture. The expenditure incurred was wasteful because large intervention was made without pilot testing; the beneficiaries were not consulted before launching the project and were not involved either in the implementation process; the people, who formulated the scheme, had no knowledge about the socio-cultural factors governing the *jhumia* societies; there was no proper land ownership record, no cooperation among the concerned development sectors and the fund utilisation for this project was not properly worked out (Bordoloi 1990: 38-39).

In Nagaland, diffusion of paddy farming brought remarkable change in land use and Terrace Rice Cultivation (TRC) was promoted by the agriculture department to contain *jhum*. The government efforts were complemented by the Baptist Church in Nagaland. Besides in Tuensang district agri-business and commercial farming were promoted (Das 2010:178). Changed cropping pattern reversed the concept of community labour called field companies (consisting of men and women in the same age group) in Nagaland. The revenue base of the government was widened by drawing revenue from the forest and the settled lands. In Nagaland, there are Reserved Forest, Protected Forest and Private forest—the areas of the latter being more than other two types of forests. The NCEAR once recommended government takeover of private managed forests and profit-sharing with the local communities (Singh 1972: 167-174). The entire process was, thus, governmentalsed for agri-business and commercial farming, which dismissed the community process.

In Tripura, Dasgupta found pull and push factors in the transition of traditional shifting cultivation. The pull factors were the government efforts to wean shifting cultivation and to adapt settled cultivation. The 'abundance factor' acted behind adaption of settled cultivation. The ameliorative measures of the government to address temporary insecurity of the farmers were a powerful pull factor.

In 1931, Maharaja Bir Chandra Singh, selected large tracts of land in Kalyanpur for settled plough cultivation. One hundred and ten sq. miles was reserved for plough cultivation for five tribal *jhumias*. These reserved were increased to 1950 sq. miles in 1943. Sale, gift, transfer and lease of these lands were not allowed. The Jhumia resettlement scheme in 1953-54, also acted as a pull factor. In the 7th Plan, animal husbandry, horticulture and pissiculture were added in the *Jhumia* resettlement scheme. A land purchase scheme was also introduced. Rubber plantation was a pull factor (Dasgupta 2005: 97-98, 105-107). The push factors were forest reservation that disallowed *jhum* cultivation; population increase; refugee settlement, etc. Refugee settlement led to de-reservation of the tribal reserves. The economic consequences were poverty, landlessness and alienation; the social ramifications were tribal-non-tribal conflict. A cultural crisis arose because of exposure of the tribal people to Bengali culture. Land became saleable while the better jobs lost out to the non-tribal people. Dasgupta also saw class formation among the Mogs in course of their transformation from *jhum* to peasant cultivation within the broad contours of the capitalist mode of production promoted by the economic policies of the government. Emergence of tribal elites and eventual patron-client relationship led to a vertically differentiated society. She applied multiple criteria, based on the degree of possession of the means of production, level of household income, and exploitation through hiring of labour. Leasing out of land, moneylending and trading led to class categorisation and division in the Mog tribe ((Dasgupta 2005: 108-127). Transition from shifting to permanent cultivation created new forms of relationship within one's own community threatening its egalitarian structure. One section still pursued shifting cultivation and could not acquire enough assets to procure land. The other section owned permanent fields but did not forsake their shifting rights. As shifting cycle decreased, the former group faced dire poverty (Chakraborty 2004: 62).

NLUP–The Flagship Programme in Mizoram

Government of Mizoram undertook several policy initiatives to encourage particular land-use practices and to improve shifting cultivation practices on steep slopes by promoting alternative cultivation practices. The New Land Use Policy in Mizoram is a culmination of all the institutional measures to wean the practice of shifting cultivation. The Fifth Plan gave major focus on promoting permanent cultivation and minimising shifting cultivation (Government of Mizoram 1989: 223-226). In 1984, the idea of a New Land Use Policy was conceived and the first land use policy was initiated as far back as in 1985-91, that introduced the *jhum* control programme on a modest scale. In 1993-1998, this project was developed into a large scale project. Major switchover from *jhum* cultivation invited hazards. The shortcomings of the policy were brought out by a study made by MSSRF, a Chennai based organisation. This policy was later replaced by Mizoram Intodelhna Programme (MIP) in 2002—a financial assistance programme for the poor rural farmers. Both these programmes could not make any major breakthrough. The New Land Use Policy (NLUP) became a flagship programme under the nodal agency of the Department of Agriculture, Government of Mizoram. In the implementation of the programme, the state government identified as many as eight departments, including, Agriculture, Horticulture, Sericulture, Fishery, Soil Conservation, Animal Husbandry, Forest and Industry Development. The implementation of the policy started on January 1, 2011, with the major objective of transforming the economy of Mizoram by progressively switching over from the practice of shifting cultivation to wet rice cultivation and other livelihood opportunities, improvement of income for urban and rural poor through sustainable farming, non-farming, micro-enterprises, including, promotion and modernisation of small-scale and cottage industries for a more sustainable land use. This programme would ensure farmers' access to irrigation facilities, input support, crop diversification, commercial agriculture, disposal of market surplus and would also provide non-farm income opportunities. A package, including rural infrastructure development (minor irrigation, water harvesting system, rural electrification), transport and communication (road network and agri-link road, telecommunication facilities in rural areas), quality seed and tissue culture laboratory, horticultural processing units, rural warehouse, power requirements for NLUP through PPP mode and banking facilities were required for the programme. Biodiversity and environment protection were the long-term objectives of the project. The rural land use plan prepared under the NLUP, would substantiate the long-term objectives. Under the rural land use plan, 60 percent of land was earmarked for rain forest; 10 percent for development of catchment areas into thick rain forest; 10 percent for village community timber/fuel/wood forest; 5 percent for habitation, roads and industries and only 15 percent land use for cultivation were envisaged under the NLUP. The NLUP also provided for 2 ha. per beneficiary family (Government of Mizoram, Comprehensive Project under New Land Use Policy for sustained economic development and upliftment of the poor in Mizoram, (Mimeographed); Nlup.mizoram.gov.in/page/concise/concise-summary-of-nlup.html).

The Criticalities

J.N. Das's study of land system in Mizoram in 1986, found no regular exploitative tenancy system and so, tenancy reform stage did not arrive in Mizoram so far as agricultural land was concerned (although urban tenancy prevailed in town areas from the British time) (Das 1986: 219). Till the 1980s, land discourse in Mizoram was centred on customary law and the community process in land matters. The NLUP approach undermined both the customary law and the community process in shifting cultivation that ensured food security to the poor tribal communities in the otherwise food-deficit state of Mizoram. It was admitted by the government that Mizoram is still not self-sufficient in rice production although paddy continued to remain the chief food crop and the staple food of the Mizos. It occupies almost 50 percent of the total cropped area and more than 88 percent of the total area is under food grains (Government of Mizoram, Comprehensive project under New Land Use Policy for sustained economic development and upliftment of the poor in Mizoram, (Mimeographed); Nlup.mizoram.gov.in/page/concise/concise-summary-of-nlup.html). Three major criticalities appeared: (i) changing focus of land reforms; (ii) changes in cropping pattern and (iii) the prospect of new crops in the export market.

While in Mizoram, the community ownership of land underwent a major change in response to the changes in land use pattern and cropping pattern under the pressure of adoption of sedentary cultivation, this led to growing privatization of land and emergence of big landholders. A paradigm shift was made in the NLUP document, which stated that the customary community ownership is now undergoing certain modifications to meet the need in the face of changing land use opportunities. It also stated that terrace and valley lands are considered as private lands with permanent, heritable and transferable rights through the Land Settlement Certificate, although these lands are not mortgageable as collateral. The document admitted that private rights on land have emerged leading to the concentration of better lands in the hands of the few affluent persons within the communities, disturbing the egalitarian character of tribal society. As a consequence, tenancy arrangements are also becoming more common usually in respect of terrace and valley lands, although at present they probably represent less than 10 per cent of the land area. All tenants are governed by customary practices and work on crop sharing basis of 33 to 50 per cent of the production. Most of such tenants come from neighbouring Assam.

This marked a shift from the communitarian mode to private

rights mode of agrarian relations in Mizoram. Moreover, under NLUP, the land reforms needed to see that (i) customary tribal land holding system be linked with sustainable development, although more than 99 per cent of land in Mizoram is yet to be surveyed and records are still to be prepared; (ii) land settlement be made; (iii) new land holding system and new ownership pattern be introduced along with land and water management system; (iv) new tenancy laws be formulated and enacted; (v) for restoration of ecological balance, hill top area, higher elevation, etc. be given priority for forest reserve and (vi) water harvesting system be taken up to improve surface and groundwater management, water recharging system and moisture control of soil.

Change in the cropping pattern towards commercial plantation of agro-horticultural produces (passion fruit, grape, orange, aloe vera, banana, chaw chaw, arecanut, tung-oil, etc) and the market focus of the agro-based industries put a big question mark on *in situ* production and availability of staple food-grains although food security and poverty eradication are shown in the anticipated socio-economic benefit list of the project. Commercial focus of horticultural products, therefore, might lead not only to non-availability of the staple food-grains but also might be strategically undesirable, specially, in this state, where food supply from outside the state is very often delayed or discontinued due to natural hazards like landslides and communication blocks. There is the possibility of crop failure causing loss of labour, seed input and capital investment.

The market challenges of the horticultural crops are also to be seriously registered. These challenges might come from the other fruit bowls of the country like Himachal Pradesh, Maharashtra and Uttarakhand because agricultural marketing in Mizoram, as the Document admitted, is one of the weakest links in the agricultural economy of the region that is largely unorganised and is dominated by private traders and middlemen. The Comprehensive Project Document started with a high pitch export promotion policy in pursuance of the EXIM policy of the Government of India under the trade liberalisation regime but conceived the export only within the border trade framework (Indo-Myanmar and Indo-Bangla). According to the Concise Summary of New Land Use Policy, prepared by the NLUP Implementation board, 2013, the NLUP Marketing Cell, aimed at creating District and State Level wholesale markets, proposed and concretised the plan for a state-wide Internet NLUP pathway and warehouse construction through the PPP mode. But as the export markets are dominated by metropolitan capital and more powerful players, the state market of Mizoram would find it difficult to break into the export market of its own without the backing of the Indian state or without the backing of big export houses. But the bigger market challenges might come from the Regional Trading Agreements (RTAs). There are not less than 200 RTAs, notified under the GATT and WTO. In this larger spectrum, the economic rationality of the neoliberal economy conceived the regions as natural economic zones engulfing more than one nation-state spaces where fielding the horticultural trade basket of Mizoram might involve every fear of losing out in the larger market.

The other component of the NLUP plan is self-employment and income generation through petty trade (non-farm). As per the NLUP, petty trade would include carpentry and wood processing, blacksmithy, rice hulling, noodles making, petty trade and handloom. The two sectors—timber and handloom—have faced major policy challenges in India today. These challenges should have been taken into consideration before planning for petty trade under the NLUP. Secondly, pushing out the people from land dependency towards self-employment is a neoliberal method of delinking people from land. The government views were that reduced land-productivity, excessive fragmentation of land made land redistribution non-viable. In the neoliberal frame, the sprawling land market throughout the country for land speculation annihilates the community land. This is made by the state in exercise of its power of eminent domain. Thirdly, in the market economy regime, the skill-level for the products became mandatory. A skill gap study of the Northeast conducted by the National Skill

Development Corporation (www.nsdcindia.org/pdf/n)showed that despite Mizoram having different degrees of market potential for export of horticultural products in Europe, America and Asia, the state has gaps in different kinds of skills necessary for exportable production. Fourthly, the changed land use from shifting to sedentary and permanent land use systems left three significant ramifications. a) Sedantisation of agriculture encouraged penetration of private property regime and market economy to create a vertical division in the society and b) change in the cropping pattern from subsistence to commercial/cash crops would polarise the community. The cash crop cultivation followed a typical beneficiary approach. The third ramification was more critical. The NLUP made provisions for revertible allotment of lands through Land Settlement Certificate (LSC) in case of discontinuation of the activities for which land was allotted to a beneficiary. The reverted land could be re-allotted to other reliable farmers. The incipient social contract ethos in such land grants not only made the land grant a subject of contract but also created a *flexi-clientele* class in the Mizo society. Introduction of wet-rice cultivation transformed the economy from producing subsistence food to producing rice for marketable surplus. Thus, both the changes in the land use pattern (from shifting to sedentary) and the changes in cropping pattern had equal and opposite reactions in the hitherto communitarian land relations of the Mizo community.

More significant changes took place in the concept of labour when these twin change—one in land use and the other in cropping pattern—took place in the state. The tribal concept of community labour is based on mutuality and cooperation. It is an extended form of social exchange, rather than a mercenary *quid pro quo* for selling labour. The somatic attachment of the community with land acts both as motive and as emotive factors. On the other hand, the farm labour, when hired against money payment loses all stakes over land. In the era of globalisation, all the schemes of the government focused on privatisation of land resources and on progressive penetration of the post-Fordist mode in land economy in the tribal societies of Northeast

India. The process of privatisation, however, remained not only restricted to the non-tribals in tribal areas, but also happened within the tribe itself, and as a result, a section of people emerged from within the tribal societies, who could accumulate huge land for private gain. This section became extremely critical as they progressively abandoned their community bond once built around the communal land system. The post-Fordist economy converted the lands as the sites for capital investment and labour flow was directed to commercial production of scale for market transaction without catering to the subsistence need of the tribal community. The major wave of cash crop cultivation in Mizoram discarded the local crop varieties and considered these as uneconomic and undesirable in the market. In the mid-tropical zone of Mizoram, coffee, betel nut, palm oil and in Champhai area, grapes and tea started to be grown, where shifting cultivation was earlier in practice. It is to be noted in this connection that 'the horticulture scheme could not attract much attention of the Mizos till the 1960s and the hill men were more interested in piggery and poultry farms than on the fruit-bearing plants' (Government of Mizoram 1989: 120). The traditional institutions that could regulate shifting cultivation land and could keep fallow management at the desired level also became weak with the rise of tenant farming in shifting cultivation areas in Mizoram (Lalnunmawia and Lalzarliana 2013: 235).

Within the neoliberal frame, intervention of new techniques and extension services for exportable varieties of fruits, including the exotic and passion fruits, geared up the changes in land-use pattern to make the products more commercially viable. This scenario opened the gate for investment flow from both the public and the private sectors through the public-private partnership (PPP) route. The horticultural enterprises in Mizoram went towards full-fledged commercial activities which led to growth of wholesale and retail niche markets, contract farming, processing and value addition of the products, adoption of export-fit food crop, vegetable and fruit crops, ornamental flowers, medicinal plants, rubber, tea and coffee, teak and NTFP. The Department of Horticulture and the

Department of Agriculture in the state played the major roles in evincing commercialisation of agricultural production and market economy. Contract Farming, which came up in a big way in the WTO regime, was introduced in Mizoram. AFPL established a contract farming base for Stevia in Mizoram covering about 200 acres of land through the Mizoram Stevia Growers Association. This contract farming agreement is facilitated by the Department of Horticulture, Government of Mizoram. The power equation among the local elites, policy makers, programmatic intervention and the market forces became significant in this connection. It was reported in a local daily that Mizoram also planned large-scale rubber cultivation on 50,000 ha. of land in the next twenty years starting with 2,500 ha. a year. The Soil and Water Conservation Department planted six rubber nurseries from 2010 under the NLUP (Newslink. 2013). The landed elites in Mizoram emerged through the LHC (Land Holding Certificate) route, not through the jotdari route as in Bengal or Zamindari route as in Tripura or the farm route as in the Green Revolution areas of Punjab and Haryana.

The Extended Debate

Our critique on land-use in the tribal areas of Northeast India in general, and Mizoram in, particular, is made in the light of the current macro-economic scenario. In the tribal economy, land has two uses: economic use and social use. Both the uses constituted each other and formed the core of tribal ontology. Therefore, when we critique the land use policy in particular, reference of the Mizo society, we need to focus on both the uses of land and the implication of the contemporary process of delinking the two. The process started in the colonial times and came down in history to the neoliberal era. This scrambled the meaning of land space in the tribal societies and converted the land space only as an economic reality as in institutional economics. Roy Burman critiqued the initiatives taken by the Northeast Council for appraisal of the legal systems in the different states on land and land-based resources. The Council tended to augment the legal positivistic orientation, notwithstanding legal pluralism in dealing with inheritance, succession, torts and minor crimes in tribal societies. This, he found, would be a source of trouble in future. He also critiqued the recommendations of the National Committee on Development of Backward Areas' of 1981 for individualisation of communal ownership in the Northeast for the sake of 'progress' and viewed that the development programmes short circuited the community, that only the powerful individuals within the community could do with the support of bureaucracy. This created neo-feudal rights (Roy Burman 1988: 693-697).

Shankar Raman has shown that the *jhum* landscape,, regenerating fallows and forests is a better form of land use and forest cover than monoculture oil palm plantations that cause permanent deforestation, a fact, that the India State of Forest Report 2011 (ISFR) notes to explain declines in Mizoram's forest cover. Although *jhum* is a regenerative system of organic farming, Mizoram, the first Indian State to enact legislation to promote organic farming, is now pushing hard to eradicate it under its New Land Use Policy (NLUP).

Regenerating fields and forests in the *jhum* landscape provide resources for many years. The farmer obtains firewood, charcoal, wild vegetables and fruits, wood and bamboo for house construction and other home needs.

Yet, government policy tilts firmly against *jhum*. The State's NLUP deploys over Rs. 2,800 crore over a five-year period "to put an end to wasteful shifting cultivation" and to replace it with "permanent and stable trades." Under this policy, the State provides Rs. 1,00,000 in a year directly to households, aiming to shift beneficiaries into alternative occupations like horticulture, livestock-rearing, or settled cultivation. Though the policy has created opportunities for families seeking to diversify or enhance income, NLUP's primary objective to eradicate "wasteful" shifting cultivation remained unchanged which appears misdirected.

Even before NLUP was implemented, despite decades of extensive shifting cultivation, over 90 per cent of Mizoram's land area was under forest cover, much of it bamboo forests resulting from *jhum*. Recent declines in forest cover have occurred at a period when area under *jhum* cultivation has actually declined, while area under settled cultivation has increased, suggesting that the land use policy has been counterproductive to forests (Shankar Raman 2014).

Industrial Use of Land

In the post-independence time, India has followed a development policy based on public sector investment, heavy industries, mega dams and large-scale infrastructure. All these required acquisition of land. Incidentally, all the major natural resource endowments of the country are located in the tribal areas. The state acquired that land for extraction of resources by the instrument of 'eminent domain'. Northeast India became a major target of land acquisition and became a major supplier of raw materials for industrial production elsewhere. This region did not get the benefit neither *in situ* or *ex-situ*, of industrial development and became victim of regional imbalance in terms of economic growth and employment opportunities. Most of such resources, so acquired, were used for public sector and a large quantum of the resources including coal, limestone, uranium etc.were sold abroad. In the post-liberal era, the policy shift towards private and corporate economy, made India surrender its public sector ethos. Michael Levien stated that within the context of the political economy the Indian state has moved towards increasing commodification of land. He referred to the 1994 Rehabilitation Policy draft by the Ministry of Rural Development that stated that on account of liberalisation "it is expected that there will be large-scale investment, both on account of internal generation of capital and increased inflow of foreign investment, thereby creating enhanced demand for land to be provided within a shorter time span in an increasingly competitive market-ruled economic structure". "The private companies, thus, look to the State to acquire land for them through the PPP mode" (Levien 2011: 66-71).This made a major shift in the approach of land reform. The approach shift was made by removing government protection to agricultural land and opening trajectory for industrial or commercial use of land through the mutuality of law, state and neoliberal capital. This trivialised the agricultural use of land and de-linked land from its subsistence use.

Two significant sectors of Northeast India, the mineral and the water sectors became subject to widespread privatisation through corporate intervention and through foreign direct investment in recent times. The process of giving away these resources was further facilitated by the Northeast Industrial Policy and the corresponding industrial policies of the states. These policies exposed serious dependency syndromes both at the policy level and at the operational level under the neoliberal frame. The investor-friendly industrial policies of the North Eastern states provided large subsidy packages to the foreign direct investors and the corporate cronies. The major subsidies were extended on land, water and mineral resources with a view to attracting FDI and corporate investment.

Guided by this vision, the corporate cronies of the Indian state, captured land for FDI or corporate investment. In Indian context, the lands, such captured, received legal recognition by the SEZ Act, EPZ Act, etc. Public purpose in the SEZ Act came to include real estate development, leisure and entertainment, and a vaguely defined social infrastructure. Public purpose, thus, converged with private interest that eventually dispossessed the communal land. The SEZ, EPZ, etc. formed enclosures within the territorial boundaries of the state. Lands were acquired by the state for the investors for building infrastructure for power industries, real estate, IT, Export Processing Zone, Special Economic Zone, etc. In Northeast India, the FDI-led industries, power and irrigation projects intended to attract maximum FDI although the percentage of FDI in the whole region remained abysmally low compared to other parts of the country. But investment drive made the state governments to venture land reforms in such a way as to satisfy the requirements and conditionalities of the investors. These went, of course, in the name of development although there was very little *in-situ* gain for the local communities from these development projects. At the same time, these industries came to heavily depend on the local resource bases—be it mineral, forest, water or land resources.

Md. Asif wrote that the types of industries set up in Manipur included market-based food processing or cement industries, depending exclusively on local resources and hydel power projects—exclusively depending on the local water resources. With the expansion of transport infrastructure, the sequence of resource exploitation would proceed further into the less accessible areas of the North East. Tripura also has cheap availability of energy from gas-based power generation (Asif 1999: 52). Arunachal's water resources were opened to the foreign investors for hydro-electricity projects. The policies and institutions of the state were reformulated in response to that.

The State Scenarios

Meghalaya

W.W. Hunter found coal mines in eleven places of the Khasi Hills: By-rang, cherra, Lait-ryng-ieu, Mao-long, Mao-stoh, Mao-sin-ram, Mao-don, Mao-nai-chhora, Mao-beh-lyrkar, Shella and Thanjinath. In Jaitia Hills coal mines were found in five places: Am-wi, La-ka-dong, Nar-pu, Sah-ting-gah and Sher-mang. The (British) government held perpetual lease of Cherra Punji mines from the chief or *Siyem* of Cherra. In 1844, government transferred its right to work in the mines to private company (Hunter 1999: 232-233). The practice of leasing out land for mining started from that time. The *Siyems*, who were the custodians of the community land turned out to be the owners of the same and captured the mining fields for profitable industrial use of land. They also started to lease out land to the community people and allowed them to pursue mining activities. The local tribe by customary law came to enjoy the right to land and mine and sale any mineral within the limits of landed property on obtaining permission from the *Nokma* or village chief, who would collect royalty from the people for giving such permission. Due to limited extent of exposed coal, only narrow strips of 10-20 metres in width across the hill slopes were allotted to individuals for mining operations. This led to the growth of about 2500 small unorganised mining units in Meghalaya employing roughly 40,000 persons per day, mostly from Nepal, Bangladesh, Assam, Bihar and West Bengal" (De Chaudhury 1999: 97). In this way, the system of permission to the community members to carry on mining operation was replaced by hired labour from other parts of the country.

Table 3.2: Mineral Wealth in the Hills of the North Eastern States

State	*Important Minerals*
Arunachal Pradesh	Petroleum (Ningru and Dum Duma), limestone (Lohit), dolomite (Kameng), graphite (Lohit, Sabansiri), cooer ore, gold and pyrites.
Assam	Coal (United Mikirs, N.C. Hills, Sibsagar, Lakhimpur), petroleum and natural gas (Digboy, Lakhimpur, Sibsagar), Limestone (Lakhimpur, United Mikirs, N.C. Hills, Karbi angling, Nango and Sibsagar), magnetite, quartzite, kaolin, sillimanite.
Manipur	Asbestos, chromite, copper ore, coal, iron ore, lignite, limestone, nickel ore and petroleum.
Meghalaya	Cement-grade limestone (East Khasi Hills, West Garo Hills, Jayantia Hills), flux and chemical-grade limestone (Khasi and Jayantia hills), sillimanite (Sonapahar, West Khasi hills), coal (Mikir Hills, Khasi Hills, Garo Hills and Jayantia Hills), uranium.
Mizoram	Lignite, sandstone and pyrites.
Nagaland	Coal (Nizira coalfield, Mon district), limestone (Phek), nickeliferous chromite (Tuensang).
Tripura	Oil and natural gas, glass sand, plastic clay, shale and sand.

Source: Centre for Science and Environment, *State of India's Environment: A Citizen's Report* 6, 2008.

Meghalaya came under the Coal Mines Nationalisation Act 1973, in the year 1976, when the demand for Meghalaya coal suddenly jumped with expansion of export as well as domestic consumption although coal mining in the state, however, remained an unorganised activity. (De Chaudhury 1999: 94).

Later on, appropriate modification of the Meghalaya Land Transfer Act, 1971, was made to accommodate private investment by non-tribal subjects. Suitable investment-friendly Industrial Policy was also formulated to that effect (Karlsson 2005: 175). The Uranium and limestone mining by Lafarge, a transnational company, was possible in Meghalaya, by easing the Land Transfer Act, which amounted to accumulation by dispossession. The anti-Lafarge group in Meghalaya made multiple charges against Lafarge: that it was not an industrial establishment but an extractive undertaking; land was acquired by Lafarge through non-transparent *benami* transaction; Lafarge obtained environment clearance without proper assessment for mining lease; it violated the Land Transfer Act and bypassed the normal process of land acquisition; no proper lease document was issued to Lafarge; and that Lafarge had illegally encroached on the land of about forty persons (Karlsson 2011: 176,190-234). In many cases, the forest department issued unauthorised certificates for mining operation. In Shella village, for example, the Divisional Forest Officer, Khasi Hills Division of the forest department, issued a certificate declaring that that the lands in this village were barren wastelands. The official was accused of handing over the certificate direct to Lafarge without observing the rules and without observing the proper procedures. The Shella Action Committee, an association of land owners in the area, made a complaint to the ministry of environment and forests, when the ministry deputed its own officers to make a spot inspection at Shella village. It was found that these lands were actually agricultural and crop production lands and forest lands. The ministry ordered closure of all non-forest activities in and around Shella village (Lyngdoh 2010).

Similar charges were made against other companies by the Meghalaya-based media, including Shillong Times (2010) and Meghalaya Times (2010) against M/s Seven City Developers Private Limited for illegal acquisition of around 5300 acres in

Umshopai village, Jirang, in Ri Bhoi district and for obtaining NOC from the land owners for registration of the land without the approval of the state government. NOC was issued to companies including Lafarge Umium Mining Pvt. Ltd. for limestone mining from forest areas.

Box 3.2: Lost Treasure

Meghalaya is home to one of the longest cave systems in the sub-continent. The Meghalaya Adventure Association, which maps ancient and unique caves, has identified 970 caves in the state. The list includes Krem Kotasi-Unlawn in Lumsnong in the Jaintia Hills District. This is the longest natural cave system in India. The breath-taking caves also have a river and an 11 metre high waterfall.

Rampant limestone quarrying has destroyed this natural treasure. Most of the caves are already obliterated; one cave system—the Krem Puja at Nongtrai village near Cherapunji—has been destroyed by Lafarge, a French company mining limestone to feed its cement plant at Bangladesh.

Extract from: *Meghalaya's Lost Treasure, State of India's Environment, A Citizen's Report-6*, 2008. Centre for Science and Environment, New Delhi.

The Shillong Times reported that the current Draft Mining Policy of Meghalaya seeks to come up with the rules and regulations aimed at scientific and sustainable mining of the state minerals; minimise adverse effect on the environment and ecology; generate employment and develop and exploit mineral resources taking into account the 'interest' of the state. The term 'exploit' raised suspicion of having a colonial perspective of exploitation and was "deliberately used to pave the way for the eventual takeover of Meghalaya's mineral resources by the prospective multinationals" (*The Shillong Times*, 2010). Secondly the mining activities in Meghalaya in the "interest of the state" have to be understood in the larger context of neoliberalism in which 'state interest' became identified with private interest of the corporate agencies, who are non-futuristic in their activities. This makes the claim of scientific and sustainable mining an oxymoron. The Meghalaya Mines and Mineral Policy, 2012, became market-oriented although it stated that the policy objectives would be in consonance with such laws and practices, as are specifically stipulated in the Sixth Schedule and the Meghalaya Land Transfer Act 1971. But the District Council has no enough power to perform its protective role. This policy also required the state government to strictly monitor the transfer/lease of land to the need-based and actual requirement to avoid alienation of tribal land. But the 'Border area priority clause' and 'special incentives' to the enterprises in these areas (10 km towards the state from the international border) in the Industrial Policy of the state made the community land vulnerable. The mining lease holders made mega-profit from mineral extraction on small mining, without defining the smallness, which led to emergence of black capitalism in Meghalaya.

Manipur

The Draft Industrial Policy of Manipur 2011, also made investment friendly environment and infrastructure development for encouraging FDI and corporate investment from outside the State. Land subsidies as per the policy, include: micro and small enterprise 25 per cent; micro small enterprise for EOU and units owned and managed by the weaker section 30%; Large and Medium Units (as per definition) 15 per cent; The cost of land development would be recovered from the industrial unit in fifteen equal annual installments. The government will constitute a Committee for allotment of land for industrial units and frame allotment rules which shall be notified. Besides, power subsidy would be given to the eligible units on power tariff for a period of 5 (five) years at the rates fixed by the government from time to time from the date of commercial production subject to the ceiling given below: Ceiling of subsidy per annum: upto 1.0 MW 30 per cent Rs. 10 lakh and above 1.0 MW 25 per cent Rs. 25 Lakh.

The hill districts of Manipur are rich in mineral resources. There are chromite, limestone, serpentinite and oil deposits in Ukhrul, Tamenglong and Chandel districts and in Jiribam area.

The mineral deposits became the attraction of the private companies. A number of Bhubaneswar-based companies flocked to Ukhrul for chromite and limestone mining. These private companies, through the PPP mode entered the communal land resources in Ukhrul. Leasing out land to the private companies became a public issue in the state of Manipur. In Ukhrul district, the government has leased out communal land of four tribal villages including Shiroi, Shingchagamnao, Lunghar and Nampisha to the Bhubaneswar-based private mining companies for chromite and limestone mining through Public-Private-Partnership mode. M/s. Rourkela Minerals and Ores, Odisha, got the lease of 85 ha. of land in the year 2007 for 20 years in Shingchangamnao village for chromite mining; M/s. Orissa Industries Ltd. Bhubaneswar got the lease of 132.78 ha. of land in the year 2011 for 20 years in Shiroi village for chromite mining; M/s. Sarvesh Refractory Pvt. Ltd., Odisha, got the lease of 132. 781 ha. of land in the year 2012 for 20 years

Table 3.3: Mining Companies in Ukhrul (Manipur)

Name of the Company	*Land Area Leased*	*Year of Lease*	*Lease Period*	*Village*	*Purpose*
M/s Rourkela Minerals and Ores, Orissa	85 ha.	2007	20 yrs.	Shinghan gamnao	Chromite mining
M/s Orissa Industries Ltd., BBSR	132.78 ha.	2011	20 yrs.	Shiroi	Chromite miming
M/s Sarvesh Refractory Pvt. Ltd. Orissa	132.781 ha.	2012	20 yrs.	Lunghar	Chromite mining
M/s Anand Exports, BBSR	0.51 ha.	2012	20 yrs.	Nampisha	Chromite mining
M/s Super Ores & Minerals Pvt. Ltd.	2 sq.km. each village	2012	20 yrs.	Phungyr & Hundung	Limestone mining

Source: Dominic Leo, Reassembling the Notion of Land: From the Lived Experience of the Paomei Naga Tribe of Manipur, *Journal of Tribal Intellectual Collection: India*, Vol. 1, No. 4, June 2013, www.daltri.journals.org/JTICI/article4.html.

in Lunghar village for chromite mining and M/s. Anand Exports, Bhubaneswar, got the lease of 0. 51 ha of land in the year 2012, for 20 years at Nampisha village for chromite mining. Besides, M/s. Super Ores & Minerals Pvt. Ltd. got the lease of 2 sq. kms of land each in Phungyr and Hundung villages in the year 2012 for 20 years for limestone mining. Thus, a total land area of 351. 7 ha. has been leased out to the private companies. In Phungyr and Hundung villages, a land area of four sq. kms. was leased out through the PPP mode.

Box 3.2: Oil Drilling in Manipur

The Ministry of Petroleum and Natural Gas, GoI had granted a license to a Netherland-based company called 'Jubilant Oil and Gas Private Limited (JOGPL) for exploration and drilling works in two oil blocks in Manipur in Jiribam (Imphal East), Tamenglong and Churachandpur districts of Manipur. The total area granted is nearly 4000 sq. kms. It is estimated that Manipur has nearly 5 trillion cubic feet of oil. Jubilant Energy plans to drill from 30 oil wells in Manipur. SENES India did the Environmental and Social Impact Assessment Study in consultation with JOGPL representatives.

The land-use and land-cover of the study area was interpreted from the satellite data, top-sheet of the area, and subsequently by ground trot during reconnaissance surveys. The survey data showed that the majority of the land area comprised reserved forest (9.76 per cent); unclassified forest (73.33 per cent); and wildlife sanctuary (11.70 per cent). The water bodies including rivers comprised 1.97 per cent and the village settlements in the study area comprised 1.63 per cent of the total area. The socio-economic study was made in the villages in and around the proposed drill sites (2.0 kms of each drill sites). These villages were, Aina, Dailon, Parbung, Parvachawm, Santing, Kamkeilon, Sipuikon/Tipaimukh, Damdei, Tinsuong, Lungthulien, Sartuinek, Patpuihmun, Kangreng, Savaipaih, Leijangphai, Bukpi and Lower Kharkhuplien—almost all were scheduled tribe villages.

The company was conferred the full ownership of all oil resources in Manipur and the innocent villagers were persuaded to sign NOC for seismic surveys. They were not informed about the terms and conditions in the contract and license agreements between the Government of India, Government of Manipur and the company. The state also remained silent in the matter and its role was to facilitate the company to exploit the resources of the tribal communities. This amounted to outright sale of community resources to a for-profit private company. The activists considered such an agreement as a ploy for grabbing of community land through deception and manipulation. This hid the fact that the lands were mostly agricultural lands of the tribal people. The impact study on Topography and Drainage saw topography as a space without the social content. Deceitful silence on the part of the state, lack of transparency and accountability in the deal amounted virtually to primitive accumulation and violation of the Rights of Indigenous People.

The water resources of Manipur were let out for dam construction. The Tipaimukh dam project in Barak Valley, located at the tri-juncture of Assam, Manipur and Mizoram, has affected the land resources of the Hmar and the Zaliangrong Nagas most. The dam is expected to produce 150 MW hydel power but it would oust as many as 1,310 families of 31 villages from their lands, submerge 12,286 ha. of forest and 2,703 ha. of cultivable lands, endangering the thinning forests and rare orchids found in the region. A study made by NCAS in 1999, reported that it would submerge 286.20 sq.kms of land area, rendering 40,000 people landless; cultivable land of 27247 hectares will be lost; eight villages in Barak valley and ninety villages in Tamenglong district of Manipur will be under water (National Centre for Advocacy Studies 1999; Sutradhar 2002: 32). The devastating effect of the dam on the Zaliangrong tribes has been recorded by Manirul Hassan (Hassan 2002: 293-294) which has threatened not only the communal land but also the loss of culture of the tribal people.

Box 3.3: Dam and Displacement

The Khuga Dam Multipurpose Project is located near Mata village in south Churachandpur, Manipur. The ethnic groups belong to the Chin-Kuki group including Thangkhal, Vaipeh, Zou, Guite, Thadou, Paite, Haokip, Simte, etc. The project was started in 1983 and was finally inaugurated in 2010. This project submerged many villages including M. Tanglian, Khenglang, Panglian, Sehken, Zoumun, Ngawiphai, Mata Mualtam, Mualnum, Sumchinvum, Zezau, Buelian, Geljang, Thianglam and Lamjang and displaced about 3000 tribal people. Some tribal people in these villages worked as tenant farmers and some worked as wage labour in Churachanpur town. Most of the lands were under wet-cultivation and a very small portion was under *jhum* cultivation.The wet-field areas were most affected by the dam project.

Mr. Ngultinkhup Vaiphei narrated his dreadful experience when his village Buellian was acquired by the Khuga dam authorities. He was one of many who obtained patta for two acres of land. This land is under the dam water now. "We could never think that our land would be acquired by the state. Because, how they could take our land on which we are living from our forefather's time? It is recognised by our customary law and now it is recognised by the Land Reforms Act. The state collects revenue for the land which means, the state recognised our land rights through grant of patta. One day, all the villagers were given a sudden notice to vacate the land and homes. We did not understand who gave the notice and language of the notice. There was nobody to discuss. We felt helpless out of fear. Sometimes, some people would come and write on paper. (may be journalists or surveyors). They said that we would get money if we leave the village. Some of us were very angry and protested. But we were evicted one by one till the whole village was vacated. We therefore could not unite in defence of our rights. Money given was not sufficient for our food, shelter and clothes. We made some arrangement with the village authority of New Mata village from whom I and some of the displaced persons bought a very small plot of land. The compensation money was not sufficient to buy the land. I added the meagre household assets to meet the price of a 30′x20′ ft. plot that was much smaller than the one where I lived. But I could not buy agricultural land. Our families started to depend on charcoal making and firewood collection. We sell the charcoal to the households in Churachandpur town and to the Mahajans who dictate the price. To add to family income I am slicing bamboo for making baskets that I will sell in the market."

Like Ngultinkhup, many fellow villagers lost their land and had to live in cramped and crowded huts. They became daily labourers or vegetable sellers in Churachandpur town. Many families were also lost and their whereabouts were unknown.

Arunachal Pradesh: The Future Powerhouse of India

The biodiversity rich and quiet mountains of Arunachal were embraced by the major river systems like Sabansiri, Kameng, Manas, Dibang, Lohit, Jiadhal, Ranganadi, Purthimari and Pagladiya. In 2001, the Central Electricity Authority made a preliminary ranking study of hydropower potential of various river basins in the country. In this study, the Brahmaputra basin received highest marks and 168 projects with a total installed capacity of 63,328 MW were identified.

Table 3.4: Hydropower Potential Assessed and Developed in NER

States	*Potential Assessed (MW)*	*Potential Developed (MW)*
Arunachal	50328	281
Assam	674	250
Manipur	1784	105
Meghalaya	2394	185
Mizoram	2196	000
Nagaland	1574	91
Tripura	21	15
Sikkim	4286	84
NER	63257	1011

Source: http://North East.nic.in/Power.htm

The tag of being the country's 'future powerhouse' was proactively used for the region since the Northeast Business Summit in Mumbai in July, 2002. The Hydro power Initiative launched by the Ministry of Power in 2003, also had a major focus on the North East. The 'Pasighat Proclamation on Power'-2007, at NEC's Sectoral Summit on the Power Sector identified the region's hydropower potential as one of the priority areas that could contribute to the country's energy security. The large hydropower projects in the Northeast was primarily a process driven by the Central Government till the gradual liberalisation of hydropower policies allowed the state to invite the private players (Vagholikar and Das 2010: 3-4). The Report of the Inter-Ministerial Group on NE Hydro 2010 assessed about 63,257 MW hydroelectric power potential in the North East-43 per cent of the total hydropower potential of the country. Arunachal's contribution, as assessed was highest in the region-50,328 MW and thus Arunachal Pradesh became the major hydropower player in the North Eastern region.

According to one estimate, in a ten-year period, Arunachal Pradesh proposes to have hydropower capacity, which will be only a little less than the total hydro power capacity added in the whole country. Therefore, Baruah wrote, "the primary implication for Northeast India seems quite clear: the region is entering the era of late capitalism in a familiar role—as supplier of key natural resources to fuel the economic engines of economic dynamism elsewhere. But the people of the region will have to bear the disproportionate burden of the cost and the risks of large dams in the Himalayan Rivers"(Baruah 2012: 84-85).

The hydroelectric power policy of Arunachal Government finds high potential from harnessing the water resources of five major river basins and much smaller river system in the state. If the available potential could be harnessed, the state would be floating in "Hydro Dollars" as the Arab Countries that are floating in "Petro Dollars"(Baruah 2012: 84-85). The state government has liberalised the hydro power policy and has opened its door for investigation, DPR preparation and subsequent implementation of the hydro power projects. Accordingly, CPSUs like the NEEPCO Ltd., NHPC Ltd., NTPC (Hydro) Ltd., and central government organisations, like the CWC and the Brahmaputra Board have been allowed to undertake investigation works at various sites. The government has also invited Private Sector participation (both Indian and Foreign) in the development of hydroelectric/gas based projects in the State. These companies would have the option to execute such projects on Build, Own and Operate (BOO) or Build, Own and Transfer (BOT). In both the cases, the cost of the project would have to be matched by the Private Sector Company.

Land for the project would be acquired by the state government and be given on lease to the private party on premium and ground rent bases; the company can offer equity to the Government of Arunachal Pradesh in lieu of the payment of the cost of the land; the land required for the works will be assessed by the developer and be transferred by the state government to the developer on lease basis against payment of land revenue as per approved government rate; the period of lease will be determined as per requirement from time to time; the state government shall acquire land for the developer under the Land Acquisition Act, 1894, at the expense of the developer- such private lands within the State of Arunachal Pradesh, as per requirement of the developer for the project. Rehabilitation & Resettlement of the PAFs shall be executed by the state government as per the approved rehabilitation and re-settlement plan financed by the developer, keeping in view the latest guidelines of the Government of India. But there is no full guarantee of R&R to the PAFs. Thus, a circular issued by NEEPCO stated that the gates of Rangamati diversion dam may require opening from time to time. The Corporation will not take any responsibility for any loss of life of human, pet animals and property damage. With lives, farming and grazing on riverine island, livelihood will also come under threat (Government of Arunachal Pradesh 2013). Water sector privatisation for power generation and land acquisition in the state have largely followed the process of primitive accumulation.

The hydro-dollar craze in Arunachal Pradesh caused popular discontent and provoked civil society/media activism. The issue of displacement of Idu people due to the Talon/ Debang Multipurpose Project was reported in *India Together*, February 17, 2008. It mentioned a memorandum submitted to the Chairman of the State Pollution Control Board expressing worries on construction of Talon/Debang Multipurpose Project, that would completely displace the Idu people, who are dependent on the river as a source of livelihood. Predatory nature of big dams, involved huge social cost on the local communities, who were forcefully evicted from their homelands and the natural resources on which their livelihood depended. There are reports that women of the affected communities were rendered destitute by the project and were forced into prostitution (Gohain 2008: 19-21). Similarly, the Siang dam submerged more than fifty villages in Upper, East and West Sinag districts and affected the Adi tribe and the Lower Sabansiri dam affected 250 families on the river banks belonging to Galo and Mishing tribes. As there are no cadastral records, the state government had no authority to take a decision against the claims of ownership by the affected tribes. But the stealth and secrecy in the process of granting MoA and illegitimate transactions between the government and the companies, led to trading of communal lands. Liberalisation led to an open door policy towards the FDI and private investors. The latter were provided subsidies and incentives of different types, whereas a clause in the MoA absolved either party of responsibility for the damage caused in case of earthquakes or landslides, although Arunachal falls in the high seismic and land slide zone.

Another serious problem is the upstream and downstream impacts on the villages around. An internal memo of the Ministry of Home Affairs warned of a new 'Red Terror Corridor' along the Assam-Arunachal border (Baruah 2012: 85-87). The documents of these projects stated that only a small number of people would be affected but the report ignored the high number of affected people in the downstream areas of the dam and its surroundings. The government side argued that the hydro-electricity projects in the Northeast are benign and have submerged relatively a small number of projects compared to those in other parts of the country. But what is small to the state is not at all small for a tribe, whose total population is still less than one thousand and who are likely to be annihilated as a result of the project. Thus, though it looks small, the number of population is big in local perception.

And yet the Government of Arunachal Pradesh invited private investor companies and entered into nearly 200 hydro-power project MoU with them. The dam-affected people, civil society groups and the media became vocal against this act, which has taken place without any consultative process. A large

Box 3.4: Small is Big

"The small displacement argument to sell these projects as being benign needs to be confronted. The entire population of the Idu Mismi tribe is around 9,500 and at least 17 large hydel projects have been planned in our home, the Dibang Valley in Arunachal Pradesh. As per this faulty argument, little social impact will be indicated even if our entire population is supposedly displaced!"

"We have been given constitutional and legal protection, particularly with respect to our land rights and restricted entry of outsiders. The projects are going to require both skilled and unskilled labour which Arunachal Pradesh cannot provide. Seventeen large projects in Dibang valley will bring in outside labour, upwards of 150,000 people, for a long period, as these are long gestation projects. We are concerned about demographic change and other socio-cultural impasse associated with this, as the Idu Musmis are only 95,000 in number. The development projects are in glaring contradiction to the constitutional and legal protection we have been given".

Dr. Mite Lingi, Chairman of the Idu Indigenous Peoples' Forum, www.aranyak

number of projects got environment clearance which was grossly erroneous, having incorrect data, unverified and superfluous statements and casual approach. (www.aranyak.org). A public hearing revealed that twelve villages and their lands would be submerged, while EIA identified only two villages, displacing 38 families. The EIA of the Siyom project did not allow the option of not giving their lands in the first place. The people only had the choice of the type of compensation. The EIA report stated that 83 per cent of the project affected families and their homesteads and/or agricultural lands would be submerged by the project. But the Resettlement and Rehabilitation (R&R) package in the EIA report did not include compensation for loss of *jhum* land and reduced access of forest land. In the existing planning and decision-making process, the social and ecological impacts were not assessed for decision-making either. The mega project of dam affected the *jhum* dependent livelihoods of the communities and the agro-biodiversity supported by *jhum* cultivation (Menon 2008: 131, 133).

Small population and large dams invited multiple conflicts in the state: between the tribal communities and the state; the community and the private companies and intra-community conflicts. These conflicts show the complexity of local politics of hydro-power development.

Box 3.5: Hydropower Woes

A people's forum in Arunachal stated that "since our state is hilly, there is very little land where permanent cultivation is possible.Virtually all our available arable lands will be submerged by the 2700 MW Lower Sinag Project in the affected area in the Siang Valley. The magnitude of impact has to be understood keeping in this context in mind. It is misleading to argue that the land being lost is a small percentage of the total area of the district or state and wrongly assume that the project is benign.

Azing Pertin of the Siang Peoples' Forum in Arunachal www.aranyak.org

The Arunachal scenario needs to be reviewed in consonance with the Draft National Water Policy offering subsidies and incentives to the private companies that led towards a pareto-optimal market economy. The amorphous benefit sharing is a gentrified version of primitive accumulation. Moreover, water pricing and progressive commercialisation of water result in change of flow of water, limit the community access to water resources and the land rights of owners and users. Judy Whitehead found resemblance of dam displacement with Marx's vivid descriptions of the enclosure movement in England in the late 18th century and found that both are examples of primitive accumulation and an integral part of the deepening commoditisation of environment. Viewed from this angle, the disjuncture between positive appraisals of dams as increasing wealth through raising the forces of production in agriculture and displacement of people fits into a familiar neoliberal jigsaw, what Marx described as entanglement of all peoples in the net of the world market (Whitehead 2003: 4225-4226, 4227). Thus, just as the colonials created the category of wasteland as *terra nullius* that is to be colonised, neoliberalism created the category of waste-water to be privatised.

Boz 3.6: Vijoy Taram, Convener, of the Forum for Siang Dialogue

"These dams cannot be imposed on us, our traditional Kebang (Council of Adi Tribal Elders) decides on all issues of community land and water rights". "Nobody asked the Kebang's opinion before launching these projects". "With three per cent of land fit for agriculture, Arunachal is India's most sparsely cultivated state: of the few patches of fertile alluvial fields, the most prized are the lower banks of Siang where 51:51 square kms. will be drowned by the Lower Siang Project". "Loss of plain lands to dam project will leave nothing for farmers. Land use restriction will apply in the catchment areas of the reservoir, posing livelihood challenges and putting more pressure on the remaining forests".

In May 2013, the Government of Arunachal Pradesh allotted the 3750 MW Upper Siang Stage II Project to the NHPC and NEEPCO for an upfront payment of Rs. 225 crore. This project will bring at least 10,000 labourers from outside. This would have a disaster impact on Idu Mismi Cultural identity and language that has been identified by UNESCO as part of its indigenous language programme.

"Another disaster in the making", *Tehelka*, Vol. 10, Issue 28, July 13, 2013.

Assam and Nagaland

In Karbi Anglong, the Jamuna Irrigation Project irrigated only 2500 acres of cultivable land, displacing many tribal and non-tribal families and destroyed cultivation lands. Many families were affected similarly by other smaller irrigation projects in Karbi Anglong district (Bordoloi 1986: 143-144, 146). Mining for Assam's 'black gold', coal has taken a heavy toll. North Eastern Coalfield Limited has started coal extraction in Patkai Hills, devastating the forest covers, groundwater and paddy field around Patkai. In Tirup and Tikok, too, large-scale coal mining has contaminated several rivers. In 1996, the Assam Government allowed rock traders to blast in the Chandradinga Hills which is a reserved forest covering 284 ha., to supply rocks to Bangladesh. Blasting was allowed in five ha. of land. There are eight major and twelve small stone quarries along the foothills of Karbi Anglong and Golaghat districts, some of which have been leased out to big extraction companies illegally. The quarries have caused massive siltation and clogging in the downstream. Illegal grant of lease for small mines was made through criminal nexus (CSE: 225, 222). All these activities became different modes of primitive accumulation.

Bordoloi has shown the magnitude of displacement of the tribal people due to industrial projects in Assam. He showed that Dhansiri Irrigation Project acquired an area of 1,184 bighas of land belonging to 1,001 tribal families in 65 villages. This data was obtained from the Special Land Acquisition Officer Udalguri till 1982. A comparative data collected by Bordoloi showed that 34,886 acres of land were acquired for the project from the three villages namely, Tambolbari, Bania para and Routa pahar. About 24,470 acres of land were under periodic patta and the rest were under annual patta(Bordoloi 1991: 264-266).This was another development analogous to the "riparian doctrine".

Under the Vision of Nagaland 2020, massive development projects have been undertaken by the state. This has converted many traditional Naga villages into Model Villages, such as Tourist destination and Green villages. Twelve potential industrial zones have been identified for setting up industrial units and lands have been acquired for the same. About 746 acres of land have been acquired for Cheithu Airport in Kohima district. Almost 70 per cent of the total land belongs to the community of Chiechama village and the remaining 30 per cent belongs to private individuals. The Deputy Commissioner's office complex at Chmukedima with a total area of 64.30 acres was acquired by the government (Longkumar and Jamir 2012: 48-49).

The Industrial Policy of Nagaland 2000 (revised in 2004) has the mission to facilitate rapid and sustained industrial development in the state through enhanced investment and employment for the people. In the backdrop of liberalisation and privatisation, the state of Nagaland threw open its doors

Box 3.7: Brick Capitalism in Tripura

Balicherra is an ADC village in North Tripura. The majority of the people belong to the Halam tribe followed by Khoira, Tripuri, Riang and the Minority Groups. In this village all the farmers are Ryotwari farmers having land records as Ryotwari owners. There are 34 ryotwari farmers who cultivate horticulture and rubber. Basides there are 273 Khas farmers who got Forest Patta under the JFM scheme. They are engaged in fishery, horticulture and paddy cultivation.

A recent development in Balicherra village is that a brick field industry is set up inside the village. The owner of the brick field is an outsider non-tribal from Dharmanagar who has made an informal agreement with Ryotwari Patta owner of this village to acquire land for the brick field and to cut the earth by bulldozer and carry the earth truck loaded to the brick field about one kilometre away in the same village. A total area of land acquired for the brick field is about 1.25 to 1.50 ha of Ryotwari land. The brick field owner has brought labourers from Ranchi who reside in the labour barrack inside the same brick field. The institution of Kalim (traditional chief) has lost its traditional power once Ryotwari patta was given to the villagers under the Tripura Land Reforms Act 1960. Therefore he has lost control over the land use pattern in the village.

This is only a beginning and the villagers now apprehend that more patta lands might be given to the non-tribals through informal agreements for industrial purposes and more such brick fields would come up in different other villages in time to come to change the land use pattern on a large scale.

to foreign investors, having far-reaching consequences on the people's rights over land resources. Hydel power generation in Nagaland became the target of many agencies and corporations including the multinationals. 75 MW Doyang Hydel Electric Project and 24 MW Thermal Power Station at Chumukdima took away a large percentage of land from the local community. The Doyang Hydel Project commissioned in 2000, by the government of Nagaland in collaboration with NEEPCO, covers a catchment area of 260,600 ha. which falls entirely within the community lands. Twenty-two villages fell within the perimeter of the immediate catchment area, with eleven villages most seriously affected. Considerable areas of fertile agricultural land

and pristine forests were submerged. Out of the total catchment area of Doyang Hydel Electric Project, forest accounts for 521.20 ha., terrace field, 125.42 ha. and area under *jhum* cultivation accounts for 1,673.81 hectares. The mode of land acquisition for the Doyang Hydel Electric Project ignored the traditional village authority. Clause 1.5 of the 1992 MoU states "the government of Nagaland accepts the position that NEEPCO will not be burdened with any additional costs to the project for economic rehabilitation of the affected owners". The villagers were lured with a better life and future but the harsh reality is that many villagers have lost their best cultivable land, their orchids and forests (Longkumar and Jamir 2012: 51-52).

Private coal mining is in practice in many parts of Nagaland. These mines are located in private lands which are beyond governmental regulation. Most of these mines are rat-hole mines, carried out in the *jhum* land and are contracted out for mining. Within the stipulated lease period, the contractors and the agencies try to maximise profit from mining operation. The mine waste is dumped on agricultural land exposing the sulphurous coal dust and creating both health and environmental hazards in the area. These wastes are being carried downstream by the rain water destroying the entire environment in the slopes and aquatic life in the rivers. This has led to concentration of large areas of land in the hands of the few rich and affluent people. They acquired large tracts of land from both individuals and communities, while some lands were leased for a specific period of years (Longkumar and Jamir 2012: 53-56). Militarisation in the state captured land through a real process of primitive accumulation. Between 1955-1964, 190 villages were burnt down to ashes in the Sema region; 60 out of 64 villages in Chakesang region were razed to the ground and in the Ao region, 49 villages out of the total 56, were burnt totally. To prevent roadside ambush by the Naga insurgents, regular clearance of the jungle of considerable distance was made mandatory in many strategic places, which the local villagers within their village territory had to clear without compensation. Besides, illegal migrants, particularly, in the foothills and in the

Nagaland-Assam border resorted to land grabbing. On the Dimapur-Kohima highway roadsides, many settlements of outsiders have sprung up, who carry on many petty businesses there. (Longkumar and Jamir 2012: 56-59)

A brief of the industrial policies in the Northeast reflects how the states acquired land for FDI or corporate investment fix. Otherisation of the tribal people of Northeast India in the state projects of development was the result of an all-encompassing and ungoverned accumulation of land based resources and eventual annihilation of the community space. All the rhetoric of 'development' in the state industrial policies were visualised only through the lens of foreign and/or corporate capital investment in the land sector and lands were acquired through the instrument of eminent domain. A modernist development paradigm, as the industrial policies envisaged for the respective states, targeted the resource rich tribal areas in Northeast India. Historically, there were two trends: first, capital transformed some pre-modern societies into modern through the linear path and second, capital annihilated some pre-modern societies through accumulation by dispossession. The tribal societies of Northeast India exhibited the second trend.

Table 3.4: Sequential Exhaustion of Forest Cover in Northeast India (in sq. kms.)

State	*1993 Assessment*			*1995 Assessment*		
	Dense Forest	*Open Forest*	*Total Forest*	*Dense Forest*	*Open Forest*	*Total Forest*
Arunachal	54510	14151	68661	54176	14445	68621
Assam	15998	8510	24508	15694	8367	24061
Manipur	5307	12314	17621	5318	12240	17558
Meghalaya	3305	12464	15769	4045	11669	15714
Mizoram	4238	14459	18697	4281	14295	18576
Nagaland	3487	10861	14348	3487	10804	14291
Tripura	1819	3719	5538	1819	3719	5538
Total	88664	76478	165142	88820	75539	164359

Source: Mohammed Asif, Development Initiative and Concomitant Issues of Displacement and Improvement in Northeastern States, in Kailash S. Agarwal edited, *Dynamics of Identity and Inter-group Relations*, IIAS, Shimla, 1999, p. 51.

The forest-based industries and enterprises in the Northeast became over-taxing and hard pressing to the natural resource bases. Asif has found Sequential Exhaustion of natural resources in Northeast India in the existing paradigm of development.

According to the Citizen's Report 6 on the 'State of Indian Environment' of the Centre of Science and Environment New Delhi, the seven states of Northeast India contribute just above five per cent to the total value of minerals produced in India. Of this, the major share comes from Assam and Meghalaya, contributing above four per cent and one percent respectively. Though the share of the Northeast in the production of metallic and non-metallic minerals in the country is negligible, the environmental and social impacts of the same are very high (CSE 2008: 220).

Changing Cropping Pattern in Northeast India

Tropical land products were necessary to meet the metropolitan needs and the cropping pattern shifted accordingly from the securing local need to meeting the needs in the metropolis. This was the beginning of delinking crop from the community. The market-oriented cropping pattern required new skill and capital that the subsistence farmers in the hills did not possess. The drive came from external entrepreneurs, who trained the tribal farmers to cultivate export crops. In the Garo Hills, during the colonial time, Mr. Williamson, a member of the Agricultural and Horticultural Society, procured seeds of some good variety of cotton and distributed them among the Garos. Similar interventions of potato, tea, coffee, lac, economic variety of timber, Spanish chestnut, mango, lichis, cinchona, orange, peach, jack trees, Guinea grass cultivation, were made. Most of the plantations failed except lac and its cultivation was pulled up to scale so that lac finally became an export item. Therefore, although different types of crops like cotton, pepper, vegetable marrows, baigun, termeric, pulses, Indian corn were cultivated side by side with rice cultivation, the colonial efforts to introduce the better variety did not succeed (Bhattacharjee 1978: 204-206). Mr. David Scott, introduced commercial plantation, improved breed of cattle, initiated potato and vegetable cultivation in the Khasi Hills and found potentials for horticultural crops like opium, wheat, potato, turnip, betel-roots, buck-wheat, maize, barley, etc. in Khasi Hills (White 1988: 7).

In the post-independence period, the trend of change in the cropping pattern started in the 1960s, with the Green Revolution in Punjab and Haryana. A market-oriented cropping pattern was sounded for the first time in the National Food Congress in 1970, that resolved that the present system of farming being subsistence farming, did not permit an efficient agriculture and any national and scientific system of agriculture would necessitate considerable change in the system of farming and land use. The cropping pattern also needs to be changed and every farmer should produce only the most efficient crop in the region. The original industry has to be "market-oriented" (FFHC and Ministry of Agriculture, 1970). On liberalisation of the economy, private sector investment was highly encouraged. The 9th Plan harnessed corporate investment in agriculture and the 10th Plan harnessed coexistence of semi- feudal agriculture with corporate and commercial farming wherein the large farmers leased in lands from the small and marginal farmers. The 10th Plan document expressed anxiety over land distribution and further reduction of land ceiling. The 11th Plan document again focused on market driven agriculture (Planning Commission 9th and 10th Plan; Vol II and 11th Plan, Vol. III).

The policy shift towards private sector intervention and commercial farming created another area of serious contention. The contours of National Agricultural Policy recognised growth of agriculture with distributive equity, but tended to promote value addition and agro-business. As a result, the tribal people not only lost subsistence cropping but also their non-farm employment scenario did not show signs of hope. In the context of globalisation, the agricultural policy sought to attain demand driven growth to cater to the external market and to maximise benefits from exports of agricultural products. Export promotion, consequent upon dismantling the Quantitative Restrictions on imports as per WTO agreement and dismantling restrictions on movement of agricultural commodities throughout the country, became two other contentious policy issues. Whereas, the policy recommended stepping up of public investment in addressing regional imbalance, it encouraged acceleration of supportive infrastructure for agriculture and rural development particularly rural connectivity through the private sector investment. The private sector was also encouraged in agricultural research, HRD, post-harvest management and marketing. The interests of the state and the market might well collide here. Besides, collaboration between producer cooperatives and corporate sector for promoting agro-processing industry were also encouraged. The institutional restructuring under the National Agricultural Policy focused on development of lease markets for increasing size of land holding, giving lands on lease for cultivation, agri-business and on private sector participation through contract farming (10th Plan, Vol. II). This marked another tragedy of the communal land by giving wider space to contract or corporate farming for high value crops. The Task Force for contract farming recommended that "the contract farming should be made legal; it should have both forward and backward linkages and contract farmers association or cooperatives be formed at the plant level that would improve their bargaining power vis-a-vis the company and promote equality of partnership for ensuring smooth functioning of any contract farming arrangement" (Parliament Digest, 2003).

But the principal crises let loose by contract farming were: land privatisation, transfer of production decision to corporate purchaser and its hegemony in investment in agriculture, credit and input and vulnerability of the contract farmer and overall food and livelihood insecurity. The focus on non-food crops, the refusal right of a company to pick up contracted produce, liability of the growers for defaults of commitments, sub-contracting out procurement of the company to the large growers, preference for large growers, high capitalisation and annihilation of the small farmers were the extreme criticalities of contract farming (Gopalkrishnan and Sreenivasa 2009: 52-

54). The role of the state in contract farming became either intermediary, promotional or facilitative and had to abdicate the regulatory role. Contract farming is also not free from input price volatility, market risk and price crash of export crops like cotton, pepper, rubber, etc. The contract farming in Kuppam disengaged the farmers from the production process, precision farming was labour displacing, and grading and standardization process of products was stringent. The government assisted export houses and processing units with public finance ignored the regulations (Dash 2004: 55). Contract farming flouted the tenancy laws. One of the propositions of the 10th Plan to "completely free tenancy law of all restrictive conditions" (Planning Commission, 10th Plan, Vol. II) and land reform focus in the National Agricultural Policy "on consolidation of holdings all over the country on the pattern of north west India" could well be contextualised here.

After the 1980s, the cropping pattern changed and included new oilseed crops like sunflower, groundnut, castor, linseed. During 2001-02, the Government of India launched the centrally-sponsored scheme on Technology Mission for integrated development of horticulture that focused on area coverage, quality production and on creation of post-harvest facilities in the region. Meghalaya occupied 9.5 thousand hectare in pineapple, followed by 8.2 thousand hectares in citrus and 6.2 thousand hectares in banana cultivation. Assam had maximum area under vegetable and fruit cultivation of 331.4 and 118.5 thousand hectares respectively. Mizoram had the lowest area of vegetable cultivation of 1.7 thousand hectares and Sikkim occupied the lowest area of 9. 5 thousand hectares in fruit cultivation (Hatai 2012: 19-20). Marketing of agricultural products needed non-food grain production. The North Eastern Regional Agricultural Marketing Corporation Ltd. (NERAMAC) was created for promotion of agricultural marketing in the Northeast that built tie-up arrangements with the National Horticultural Mission and the National Food Security Mission for procurement and supply. In collaboration with the Ministry of Food Processing Industries, Ministry of

Development of NER, NEC, American Soya bean Association, Indian Institute of Packaging, etc. it has conducted a number of programmes, seminars, workshops, training on agricultural marketing, creating awareness, capacity building, investors' meets, etc. Under the PPP mode, it has set up vermin-compost plant utilising agro-horticultural waste in Guwahati. Food processing industries have been set up at Nalkata, Agartala and Byrnihat. Credit agencies, including commercial bank branches in the North Eastern region, NABARD's SHG-Bank linkage programme, MFIs and NGOs for lending have been harnessed. Adoption of farm technology for substantially raising the farm productivity and output was once more emphasised during the Twelfth Plan (Patel 2012: 22). Under the growth euphoria of the post-liberal economy, the NE Vision 2020, targeted increase in present cultivable area by reducing *Jhuming*; improving productivity of fruits and establishing fruit processing industries; *Jhum* cultivation for cash crops and horticulture, etc. The NE Vision 2020, ascribed low agricultural productivity to community ownership and absence of individual right. The short term vision was to move farmers from subsistence cultivation to cash crop-oriented production.

The NEPED project for raising cash crop and horticulture in Nagaland was claimed to be a replicable model (Patel 2012: 23). In the meantime, many tribes of the Northeast, including, the Dimasas, Khasis, Garos, Mizos and Tangkhuls have turned to commercial crops with the hope of earning a quick buck. While some Dimasa villages succeeded in growing orange without changing their land ownership pattern, the Coffee Board and the Rubber Board gave loans and subsidies only to individuals and heads of families understood as men. This has changed the power structure in the West Garo Hills resulting in class formation and elite monopoly of land for commercial plantation. This trivialises the communal ownership that is recognised in the Sixth Schedule.In Tripura, Das found, orange cultivation on *jhum* field gave rise to permanent individual rights in orange plantation plots which ripened into ownership (Das 1984: 150-152, 156, 157). The True Potato Seed (TPS)

Technology for Production of Table Potato and Production of Certified Vegetable Seeds were initiated by the Government of Tripura under the Rastriya Krishi Vikas Yojna (RKVY) in 2007-08. Forty-one projects under Stream I of RKVY were undertaken during the first three years across all segments of agriculture and allied sectors, viz. Agriculture, Horticulture, Animal Resource Development, Fisheries, TTAADC and Tripura Cooperative Milk Producers' Union Ltd. (Sharma 2012: 26). In Jampui Hills, the Orange Growers Cooperative societies in Tlasih and Bhagmun villages, got the ryotwari status. In additional four villages, namely, Paschim Hmunpui, Purba Hmunpui, Behliang Chiip and Banglabari, the cooperative societies were also granted Ryotwari status. Besides, individual families were allotted lands by government under the Rules of Allotment framed under TLR & LR Act 1960. In Bhagmun village, there are 44 individual household, who got an allotment order for a total area of 270.60 acres. In Tallish village 33 allotters have got allotment order for a total area of 217.10 acres. These 33 households possess land as members of the cooperative society. In Bagman village, an additional 33 families got land allotment as members of cooperative society (Das 1990: 139-140). Orange plantation was initiated in Tamei (Tamenglong district) in Manipur by the Department of Horticulture and Soil Conservation. The official argument being that, rodents destroy paddy cultivation. Orange cultivation in this situation might be the way for enhancing income of the farmers. The National Research Centre for Citrus at Nagpur has sent the orange saplings for Manipur (*Sangai Express* 2013: July 25). The plantation of tropical orange seedlings from Nagpur might also bring about hazards in the crops. Such change in cropping pattern made a shift from production of staple towards cash crop.

The trend of change in the traditional cropping pattern was partly reflected in the Report of the National Committee on the Development of Backward Areas on Development of North Eastern Region of November, 1981, that had the following recommendations for control of shifting cultivation: detailed survey to identify the specific problems of various agro-climatic situations and the ethnic groups; selection of crops and varieties to suit different farming systems based on the needs of farmers; identified crops should have an assured market and should fulfil specific needs such as fodder, etc; development of different types of farming systems suited to irrigate and rain fed situation coupled with efficient management of soil and water; proper use of the biomass and recycling of wastes in the various farming systems; studies on development of suitable irrigation system for hill slopes with scientific water management; participatory research and extension involving farmers to bring about community empowerment by considering a number of socio-economic issues in order to achieve success. The market focus of the changing cropping pattern led the Nagaland Parliamentary Secretary for Agriculture, Dr. Benjongliba Ayer to underscore the need for Nagaland state to adopt and practise precision farming in order to achieve sustainable agriculture. He said, "We should now start treating agriculture as a business by focusing on integrated food production, processing, storage and manufacturing by value addition chains" (*The Sentinel* 2013: October 20).

Denial of re-distribution, waiving ceiling laws, corporate and MNC intervention in the crop and seed market, globalization of agriculture under the WTO regime, etc. ended the food security commitment of the developmental state and eliminated productive energy of the subsistence tribal farmers. The neoliberal economic policies stood for property rights that resulted in land 'enclosure'. These enclosures received incentives for investment fixing for specific commercial cropping. Changing cropping pattern also demanded changes in cropping policy and land policy. In a workshop on Farmers' Rights held in Shillong, it was stated that the marginal farmers in the Himalayan region lack market opportunities. Moreover, coping with market fluctuation in the WTO regime is a seemingly emerging crisis in the farm sector. The Bretton Woods Institutions recommended large-scale corporate agriculture as the way forward against small-scale peasant agriculture that hindered capitalist development. But cash crops and crop diversification in the WTO regime reduced people's purchasing power. In Northeast India, this demands serious critical investigation. The North Eastern crisis might, in these circumstances, be located within a contradictory policy triangle of 'growth mediated food security', the 'support led food security' and public distribution system. The role of private capital being what it is, investment in the commercial agriculture and commercial plantation require reversal of the land tenure system and the slash-and-burn cultivation system (Ray 2007: 237-238). The risks are more than one and include de-peasantisation, de-agrarianisation, decline in productivity, lack of employment and increasing external dependency for food security. Besides, commercial cropping is loan-driven, which has another set of risks following lack of market, fall in market price, crop failure and market failure.

The DONER Ministry and the World Bank undertook a joint study on 'Natural Resources, Water, Environment Nexus for Development and Growth of Northeast India'. The Executive Summary of the Strategy Paper stated that the objective of the study was to develop a vision for the development and management of water and related natural resources and environmental issues in the Northeast for sustainable and equitable growth. The Strategy Paper focused on water and forest resources in the region and laid down the institutional framework that would deal with their management. Accordingly, the new River Basin Management Institute would work across the Northeast and to which decision-making power would be devolved with strong participation of the states. There was volatile resistance of as many as 20 civil society groups against the World Bank-DONER meeting on this paper on natural resource development at Guwahati on November 11-12, 2005 (Ray 2007: 240).

Horticulture in Northeast India

In India, the Prime Minister's Action Plan for Northeast India created export infrastructure under the Assistance to States for

Development of Infrastructure and Other Activities Scheme. This included, among other things, transport assistance for export of horticultural products from the region under the Export Development Fund. Four agricultural zones were established in the region, including Tripura, for pineapple, Sikkim for floriculture, orchid and cherry pepper and ginger, Assam for fresh and processed ginger. Recently, Dabur Food Ltd. has undertaken marketing of pineapples from Nagaland and Exotic Juice Ltd. is promoting passion fruit. Besides, in the seven states of the North East, Community Information Centres have been established in 79 districts covering 487 blocks.

All these were expected to convert the disadvantaged region of Northeast India into main suppliers of primary commodities. But the real scenario is that the primary suppliers have less say in the price policy, as buyers of the finished products were from the private companies. In this scenario, the suppliers are to invariably suffer loss. The income loss of the primary suppliers is likely to give rise to major impoverishment and pauperisation (Ray 2007: 231-232). Emphasis on non-food agriculture towards cash crop and horticulture, promoted market economy in the hills of North East. The NEDFi brought out the following table for the targeted area and production of fruits and vegetables in Northeast India (NEDFi 2006: 13).

Table 3.6: Targeted Area and Production of Fruits and Vegetable in Northeast States (2009-10)

Area (in 000HA), Productivity (in 000′ MT), Productivity (in MT/HA)

	Fruits			*Vegetable*		
	Area	*Production*	*Productivity*	*Area*	*Production*	*Productivity*
Arunachal	52.00	260.00	5.0	26.00	182.00	7.0
Assam	138.50	1800.50	13.0	296.75	3857.75	13.0
Manipur	32.62	228.34	7.0	15.90	159.00	10.0
Meghalaya	30.00	300.00	10.0	44.62	446.20	10.0
Mizoram	23.75	166.25	7.0	10.20	102.00	10.0
Nagaland	31.25	406.25	13.0	32.87	394.44	12.0
Sikkim	35.37	141.48	4.0	21.30	170.40	8.0
Tripura	35.37	565.92	16.0	39.12	469.44	12.0
NER	**358.86**	**3868.74**	**10.78**	**486.76**	**5781.23**	**11.88**

It was brought out that the average area of crop diversification and commercialisation are yet to emerge in the economy of scale, except in certain plantations including (tea), spices (ginger, large cardamom) and tuber potato crops. Three plantation crops, that is, tea, coffee and rubber cover an area of 3.33 lakh ha.; Rubber, with an area coverage of about 45 thousand ha., and coffee, about 10 thousand ha. are recent introductions as a result of efforts of the respective Commodity Boards. Small-scale cultivation of tea in Assam, spreading over 40 thousand hectares, is a new innovation integrating small land holders in the tea production system. Rubber, with area coverage of over 25 thousand ha., is already a source of revenue of the state economy of Tripura (NEDFi 2006: 13).

Table 3.7: Changes in Agricultural Pattern from Foodgrains to Horticulture

Items	*Foodgrains*		*Fruits*		*Vegetables*	
Year	*1990-91*	*2003-04*	*1990-91*	*2003-04*	*1990-91*	*2003-04*
NER	71.8	64.41	3.76	4.78	6.12	8.14
India	68.82	65.94	1.55	2.14	3.01	3.29

A centrally sponsored Technology Mission for Integrated Development of Horticulture was launched during the 9th Plan aiming at convergence and synergy among numerous ongoing government programmes through horizontal and vertical integration of these programmes that could ensure adequate, appropriate, timely and concurrent attention to all the links in the production, post-harvest and consumption chain. The Small Farmers' Agribusiness Consortium (SFAC) was involved in the scheme. The Technology Mission, through its four Mini Missions addressed all the aspects of horticulture development with an end-to-end approach. Mini Mission-I involving research was coordinated and implemented by the ICAR. Mini Mission-II covering production and productivity improvement activities was coordinated by the Department of Agriculture & Cooperation and implemented by the Agricultural/ Horticultural Departments of the states. Mini Mission III involving post-harvest management and marketing of exports was coordinated by the National Horticultural Board and Mini Mission IV involving processing was coordinated and implemented by the Ministry of Food Processing Industries. The state level SFACs were also consulted in most of the implementing states for monitoring and implementing the programme at the grassroots level (NEDFi 2006: 13,14,15). At one breath, the NEDFi Database presented the land reform agenda as congenial for crop diversification and commercial agriculture. It discarded the traditional community ownership of land prevailing in the tribal areas of the Northeast region and upheld the argument in favour of private land for all practical purposes. It was mentioned that better productivity and better economic returns from the privately owned land provide incentives for crop diversification and commercial agriculture and that the prevailing land tenure systems in the hill districts and absence of legalised ownership rights have hampered the flow of bank credit to this sector (NEDFi 2006: 15).

The Small Farmers' Agri-Business Consortium located at Delhi, has made its way into the North Eastern states through the Technology Mission for Integrated Development of Horticulture. A feasibility study for setting up Nine Collection and Procurement Centres of Agro-horticulture commodities in nine places of Northeast India was conducted by OKD Institute, Guwahati. The places under study were Diphu, Haflong and Krishnai in Assam; Bomdila and Roing in Arunachal Pradesh; Churchandpur in Manipur; Vairangte in Mizoram and Nongpo and Phulbari in Meghalaya. Four Mini Missions of horticulture were introduced under the Horticultural Mission (HTM) in Northeast India that allocated funds for implementation. Despite some achievements in bringing additional hectares of land under different horticultural crops, and markets and other infrastructures established for that, the evidences from the study show that only ginger and to some extent pineapple could reach the markets outside the region. There was little evidence that products like oranges, apples, passion fruits and kiwis from this region could find space in the markets outside the region.

There were certain constraints including insufficient production to logistics and high costs involved to place the products in the markets. Moreover, these products really had surpluses in and around the proposed procurement centres and there were wastages (OKDISCD 2008).

The risk analyses findings were similar in all the places. The analyses revealed certain serious concerns in the horticultural sector in the region. It was found that in the post Horticulture Technology Mission period, there was significant decline in the production of both fruits and vegetables in the region. The decline in production of fruits was primarily caused by decline in productivity, though there was expansion of areas under cultivation. The decline in the production of vegetables was caused by both area and productivity decline. There was, however, variation across the states. The areas under fruits did, however, rise during the post-HTM period in the states of Arunachal, Manipur, Nagaland and Tripura but these did show decline in acreage in Assam, Meghalaya and Mizoram. Acreage under vegetables had shown a significant decline in Assam, Arunachal, Mizoram and Nagaland and productivity of vegetables in Assam, Arunachal, Meghalaya, Mizoram and Nagaland during the post-HTM period. The analyses brought out that the trend of area and productivity changes in the region was not encouraging. The question raised in this connection was, does poor market access play a distinctive role for the farmers? (OKDISCD 2008).

The market-linked agriculture followed a chain market where the petty farmers lost hold over the price mechanism of the Mandi owners and wholesale dealers. This increased the possibility of the petty farmers to leave their lands barren. Export-oriented and market-based approach was promoted, in addition to horticulture, in the bamboo sector in the North East. The bamboo products became the market good. The Bamboo Policy of Arunachal Pradesh, Assam Bamboo and Cane Policy, Manipur Bamboo Policy, Bamboo Policy of Mizoram, Bamboo Policy of Government of Nagaland and State Bamboo Policy of Tripura—all followed the export-oriented and market-based approach (NEDFi 2009: 20-22, 54-55, 11-12, 68-69, 100-104). The same approach was adopted in case of some medicinal and aromatic plants which was reflected in the Annual Report of NEDFi in 2008. As market economy is born with market risk, the market-linked products *ipso facto* could not avoid those. The farmers, who worked in the farm sector, were, therefore, to face the perpetual security threat and social-economic and ecological adversities in the market-driven cash crop production. Bamboo and cane being forest products over which the community has the first usufruct right, were brought within the fold of the market economy.

Table 3.8: Area Under Senile Orchids Rejuvenation (*in ha*)

State	*Area*
Arunachal Pradesh	1000
Assam	600
Manipur	650
Meghalaya	——
Mizoram	880
Nagaland	700
Tripura	675

Source: Annual Report 2011-12, Horticultural Mission for Northeast and Himalayan States, Department of Agriculture and Cooperation, Ministry of Agriculture, GoI, New Delhi.

Table 3.9: Land Area Under Horticultural Cultivation (*in ha*)

State	*Fruits*	*Vegetables*	*Flowers*	*Spices*	*Aromatic*
Arunachal Pradesh	2890	264	185	911	79
Assam	5200	500	——	2238	——
Manipur	2860	1505	505	280	——
Meghalaya	1910	1353	281	428	——
Mizoram	1425	2270	275	100	20
Nagaland	3278	1313	870	1300	100
Tripura	1394	2920	221	742	——

Source: Annual Report 2011-12, Horticultural Mission for Northeast and Himalayan States, Department of Agriculture and Cooperation, Ministry of Agriculture, GoI, New Delhi.

Table 3.10: Area Under Protected Cultivation (*sq. kms*)

State	*Green House*	*Shed Net*
Arunachal Pradesh	58000	——
Assam	2000	——
Manipur	99600	75300
Meghalalya	79700	25000
Mizoram	70000	15000
Nagaland	75000	20000
Tripura	——	——

Source: Annual Report 2011-12, Horticultural Mission for Northeast and Himalayan States, Department of Agriculture and Cooperation, Ministry of Agriculture, GoI, New Delhi.

This scenario is comparable to a study by K.K. Sen, et al. in Pranmati Watershed in the Indian Himalayas. The study findings were very similar to those of Northeast India: increased expansion of agriculture on community forests; increased area under cash crop; increased mean manure input in agricultural land use and decreased fodder output from crops. The study found that local forest management institutions were not adequately empowered to respond to the growing economic aspirations of people. In the late 19th century, land rights were granted to farmers on cultivated terraced slopes, whereas all uncultivated lands were registered as government reserve and protected forests. Local people were allowed to use non-timber forest resources, but the government decided on the level of use. In the 1930s, 18.5 percent of the forest area was classified as Village Panchayat (community forests), and the power to regulate the use of resources was transferred to Van Panchayat (forest councils). The Councils needed government approval for commercial extraction of non-timber forest resources. Agriculture and commercial timber extraction were banned on all forested lands. Such institutions were reversed and the changes caused complete abandonment or long-term fallowing, increased the use of chemical fertilisers and plantation of fodder trees on farmland for livestock feed. All these implied loss of forest biodiversity and ecosystem in the fragile Himalayan landscape (Sen, Semwal, Rana, Nautiyal, Maikhuri, Rao and Saxena 2002: 56-62).

Institutional finance to the farmers became critical in the changing paradigm towards commercial agriculture. During the 1990s, public sector banks shed a large number of small borrower accounts and threw the small farmers out of the banking system. Development of agriculture looked for the conventional economic returns to justify bank investment. The concept of social banking was abandoned and the credit policy was designed to persuade banks to finance the new range of projects. For financial inclusion, the term agriculture was extended so as to include the allied sectors. It was felt that raising income level would not only involve higher agricultural growth but also raising the production level of products like milk, meat, poultry, vegetables and fruits. The need for value addition, storage, transportation, processing and marketing became important. Emphasis was laid on capital formation in agriculture. The crop cultivation to horticulture etc. required more investment in building marketing infrastructure, introduction of bio-technology and other innovations in agriculture through R&D, loan portfolios of banks and other rural lending institutions. The RBI, accordingly, advised the banks to use sources of NGOs/SHGs/, MFIs and CSOs as intermediaries in providing financial and banking services. These could act as business facilitators or as business correspondents and the commercial banks were not required to obtain RBI's prior approval for using these intermediaries as business facilitators.

According to the 'India Vision 2020', tapping the full potential of Indian agriculture to meet the rising domestic demand and to take advantage of the liberalisation of international trade would require, first and foremost, the recognition of the vital role that agriculture could continue to play in national development. The other necessary conditions were: greater public investment in research; expansion and development of rural infrastructure, including, roads, storage capacity and organised markets; improved farmer education;

effective involvement of the private sector to provide technology; investment and organisational expertise for commercialisation and modification of land regulations to achieve greater production efficiency. A suitable land use pattern based on the principle that each region focusing on crops best suited to their agro-climatic characteristics, soil types and water resources needed be devised. Strong measures were needed to address the problem of land degradation that affects an estimated 45 per cent of total land area. India's objective for 2020, the Vision stated, must not only be to produce the food its population requires but also to fully exploit the comparative advantages it possesses—agro-climatic variety, irrigation, scientific capabilities and low labour cost—to become a low cost, high profit producer for the world market. The second generation reforms in agriculture envisaged creation of more jobs in the agricultural sector, exploitation of on-farm and off-farm employment potential, raised incomes of farmers and rural labour and a boost to demand for industrial products and services. These required substantial increase in public investment in irrigation; watershed development; rural infrastructure; drinking water; housing and sanitation to raise productivity of Indian agriculture, boost export as per the WTO Rules and help rural prosperity and poverty reduction in India. A document of the World Bank stressed the need for economic governance, rule of law and efficiency of land markets as ownership disputes, longer time to settle disputes, obsolete tenancy and rent control laws obstruct business development. Improving access to finance for business was another field of institutional reforms in this connection. The institutional reforms, or for that matter, governance reform programmes were made by the states in this line in order to create congenial investment climate and to attract FDI and corporate investment.

Rubber in Tripura: Boon or Bane!

Rubber cultivation was promoted by the colonials in view of the wide demand of rubber in European countries, England, Ceylon, Straight Settlements, Canada, Australia, Commonwealth, France and in USA. The colonials first introduced rubber cultivation in the southern states of Kerala, Tamil Nadu and Karnataka in 1902. The Robber Act was passed in 1947. The Rubber Board, created under this act, was engaged in rubber cultivation in the country as a profitable cash crop. Viswanathan and Sivakoti found, at the national level, that Northeast India currently accounts for the second largest area under rubber cultivation. And among the seven states of the North Eastern region, Tripura accounts for the highest share in area (56 per cent) followed by Assam (26 per cent), Meghalaya (9 per cent) and the rest (9 per cent) by the four states viz. Nagaland, Manipur, Mizoram and Arunachal Pradesh. The states of Tripura, Assam and Meghalaya account for 91 per cent of the total rubber plantation area and produce 96 per cent of the rubber in the region (Viswanathan and Shivakoti 2007: 118).

The rubber crop stepped into Tripura in 1963, through the Forest Department as an experimental measure for soil conservation. Later on, the Rubber Board started its activities in a one-man office in 1967 that was upgraded as the regional office in 1979 for extensive rubber plantation in the state. Tripura Forest Development Plantation Corporation Ltd. (TFDPC) was established in 1976, for further expansion of rubber cultivation. Tripura Rehabilitation Plantation Corporation Ltd. (TRPC Ltd.) was established in 1983, for rehabilitation of the *Jhumias*. Commercial value apart, rubber-based welfare programmes in Tripura centred on rehabilitation of the *Jhumias* as the Rubber Board and the government set to work together for rehabilitation through a variety of programmes. Besides, the Rubber Board, other agencies including TFDPC Ltd., TRPC Ltd., NEC, the State Government and Tripura Tribal Area Autonomous District Council started working together towards the goal of *Jhumia* rehabilitation. Group Plantation and Block Plantation Schemes were undertaken in Tripura and the Rubber Board kept promoting rubber from village to village. Community development in the state was geared towards rubber cultivation (Raghavan 2009: 90-96)

Gupta estimated that, about 64 percent of the total rubber

plantations in Northeast India are located in Tripura. The commercial success of rubber in Tripura led to the creation of the Tripura Forest Development and Plantation Corporation (TFDPC) in 1976, to establish large-scale rubber plantations through its 44 centers. The Tripura Rehabilitation Plantation Corporation (TRPC) was set up in 1984 to oversee the settlement of *Jhumias* on rubber plantations. Rubber cultivation required the *Jhumia* families to work on a cooperative basis. It provided paid employment opportunities to all members of a *Jhumia* colony. Rubber production provided the highest net production income ratio as compared to other plantation crops. It also provided additional income through sale of by-products and after the latex production ceases, rubber trees were used for timber and firewood. The rubber-based TRPC schemes had the features, such as, meeting initial plantation creation costs, granting permission to practise homing within plantation plots for an initial two years with additional income support through wages for weeding the jhoom crops, providing training in rubber plantation techniques, involving the *Jhumias* in decision-making through their participation on the Beneficiaries Committee, granting ownership rights over 1.5 ha of land between 500-600 rubber trees, and providing community facilities inside the plantation centres. These ensured further economic and cultural protection to the *Jhumias* and helped gradual transformation of their economy from shifting to settled cultivation. Since 1984, the TRPC settled about 580 *Jhumia* families on about 2608 hectares of rubber plantations. Out of all the families settled through these schemes, almost 90 per cent families had completely given up homing. Orange cultivation in the Jampui Hills in North Tripura, is reported to have improved the orange growing *Jhumias* and as a policy measure, the orange growers were eligible to acquire permanent rights over land. About 60 per cent of all orange growing families have completely given up *jhuming* (Gupta 2000: 622-623).But the multiple land ownership systems in the tribal communities in Tripura were found unsuitable for the state and corporate initiatives of rubber cultivation. In order to overcome complications of land ownership, the Tribal Welfare Programme provided development assistance to individual cultivators and encouraged them to take up rubber plantation as well as other horticultural and forest plantation. Under the Block Plantation Scheme, a compact land was identified for rubber cultivation, where the scheduled caste and scheduled tribe families had ownership of land. Implementation of the Block Plantation Scheme followed a family-oriented approach rather than individual beneficiary-oriented approach. Group approach was followed where Rubber Producer Societies were promoted for processing work.

The institutional support extended by the Rubber Board included R&D, Finance and farm inputs, HRD, quality up-gradation and marketing support. Marketing support was extended through the license system regulated by the Board. There were about 119 licensed rubber dealers in Tripura, followed by 24 dealers in Assam, and 15 dealers in Meghalaya. There were also numerous private rubber dealers at the village level who acted as middlemen between rubber growers and the dealers/traders at sub-district or district levels. Being the sole promoting agency for expansion of rubber cultivation, the Rubber Board itself became very active in the market through the numerous rubber producers/growers societies and rubber marketing societies. The existing land pattern shows that rubber occupies the dominant position in Tripura followed by Meghalaya. Involvement of family labour became significant in rubber plantation.

Table 3.11: Changes in Cropping Pattern in ADC Villages in North Tripura

Kathuasara ADC village, North Tripura	Before 40 years *jhum* cultivation (paddy vegetable, forest produce and oil seeds) (mainly subsistence)	After 40 years teak forestry by the forest department in the 1970s on 300-350 ha; betel nut on 150 ha; fishery 10 ha; paan leaf 5 ha; banana 2 ha; rubber 30. Rice 3-4 ha. (Mainly commercial)

Noagang ADC village, North Tripura	*Jhum* cultivation (paddy, betel nut and forest produce) (mainly subsistence)	After 40 years rubber, horticulture, banana, orange, pineapple, betel nut. Bamboo (Under JFM) . (Mainly commercial)
Balicherra ADC village, North Tripura	*Jhum* cultivation (paddy, betel nut and forest produce) (mainly subsistence)	Rubber, horticulture, fishery, paddy (paddy cultivation reduced). (mainly commercial)

Box 3.8: Land Use Pattern and Cropping Pattern in Noagang ADC Village

Noagang was established as an ADC village in 1999 which falls in the Panisagar RD Block of North Tripura. About 95 per cent people in this village are tribal people, mostly belonging to the Halam tribe. The total cultivable land of this village is 28 ha. out of which 24 ha. of land is under cultivation. The total tilla land in this village is 1514 ha.; mono-cropped area is 7.24 ha.; double cropped land is 16.19 ha.; khas land is 2 ha. and fallow khas land is 1.48 ha. The National Highway 44 connecting Assam and Agartala passes through this village.

Ever since ADC was introduced in this village, both the traditional cropping pattern and land use pattern have undergone major changes. Paddy production from the *jhum* field has drastically declined. Rubber and tea plantation has captured significant areas of land under cultivation. The situation in 2012-2013, is that 72 ha. of land has come under rubber and tea plantation and 50 ha. of land has come under horticultural gardening. In contrast, land under paddy cultivation has reduced significantly to 5 ha. in this village. Rubber, horticulture, spice and bamboo are promoted in Mission Mode in the state.* The JAICA project, a bilateral project of Japan and the forest department of Tripura is promoting bamboo, yongchuk, gondogi, fishery, crop nursery and plantation among the targeted families possessing individual patta land.

Under the Forest Rights Act, the tribals get patta land for the JFM programme which created conflict within the members of the JFM committees. This land is now being transferred by sale. As per the act, such lands are inheritable but not transferable. So sale of patta land so made cannot be registered. The Kalim Kabur (the headman) of the village remains the only witness in case of sale and a copy of the sale agreement is maintained by him.

In this village 5 hactare of land (3-4 Kani) has been acquired on which a government polytechnic is being constructed. A mission compound has been constructed on 40 kani (about 6 ha.) and a Presbyterian Church building has been constructed on 2 kani of land. Besides, 3.5 kani of land has been acquired for construction of a market place. A total of 12 ha. of land has been acquired for all these purposes.

Noagang ADC Village, at a Glance. Annual Financial Report 2012-13 and Budget for 2013-14 Financial Year (in Bengali).

The Rubber Integrated Farm Livelihood System was claimed to be a sustainable system and also claimed to have avoided market dependency for purchase of items. Considering the small and marginal land holding and shifting cultivation as major hurdles—property rights to rubber small holders; efficient and transparent rubber marketing system; financial and R&D support; plant protection, crop processing and product development; marketing, price control, value addition and ancillary by-products were found critical (Viswanathan and Shivakoti 2007: 131-132). Private titles to land to rubber producers and growers could act as collateral and, thus, the Rubber Integrated Farm Livelihood System led the shifting cultivators towards the nascent market economy in the hills of Tripura. The tribal communal land rights were engineered in Tripura extensively through the Rubber Producers' Societies and Rubber Growers' Societies that emerged as the umbrella organisations (which are also the other name of SHGs). Such developments in the state of Tripura finally headed towards integration of rubber production with the global market economy through the route of private companies like Tripura Latex Co. Pvt. Ltd. (which is to set up a Centrifugal Factory at Rangmala in West Tripura); S. Manimalayar Rubber (P) Ltd. as a trading company floated by the Rubber Board and other rubber producers' companies (Raghavan 2009: 96-97). Rubber plantation was taken up by the government and the private individuals on a large scale and the lands were mortgaged to the corporation and the beneficiaries were not motivated to take care of the land (Dasgupta 1990: 311).Rubber plantation ousted other plantations, particularly, the cultivation of staple. This led to a mad rush for cash income, whereas, the lands of the tribes, so privatised and mortgaged, went out of the people's control.

Rubber plantation in Tripura that started as a part of the afforestation programme in 1963 with public sector investment was gradually shifted to the private sector. The intervention of the World Bank in 1993 and entry of market economy in the rubber plantation economy stymied the welfare approach of the state and made the weaker section of the tribals vulnerable to market price fluctuations. Wage differences between skilled

Box 3.9: Forest Department Acquired Tribal Land

In the 1970s the forest department of Tripura planted teak trees in Kathuasara where only 17 Halam families lived. These villagers objected to it as they practised *jhum* cultivation for subsistence. Acquisition of land for teak plantation threatened their livelihood. The village elders of Kathuasara in protest argued with the forest department on "Who came first "in the forest areas. Notwithstanding the protest, the forest department acquired about 300-350 hectares of land with the backing of state power and planted 20-25 thousand teak on it. The area of land acquired for plantation was significant in a village area of 5.5 sq. miles. The 17 families of Kathuasara and 13-14 families of Charaibari ST Para were pushed inside the hills. Many families fled to Ichabil Tea estate, Karimgunj Bill and Ramkrishnanagar (Karimgunj) in Assam. They decided to resist the forest department if they were further pushed back. Some of the families had to flee had Ryotwari Patta in their names. They came back to their old abode with the hope of getting their patta back. In the Tehsil records of Charaibari and Kameswar, Ryotwari records and a few Allottee records were still available, said Jaylal Manik of Kathuasara ADC village. But only 2 or 3 families got back their land patta and the rest did not. This annihilated the subsistence farmers of the Halam community in Kathusara. They lost their lands perennially and became lumpen.

and unskilled labour and private rubber plantation in forest areas added more criticalities to the rubber economy. On the other hand, price boom in rubber market increased the land price leading to the practice of leasing out of land of the tribal owners to non-tribals at a premium, particularly, in South Tripura district (Biswas 2006).

The drastic change in the cropping pattern and the land-use pattern of the tribal population of Tripura brought about by extensive rubber cultivation affected the hitherto existing communal land holding system. More intervention of the Rubber Board in the 1980s, corresponded to the ever growing industrial demand for natural rubber in the state. The political economy of rubber cultivation in the state was governed by the fact that the traditional robber growing regions had "already reached the extensive margin" and hence, this made it "imperative to go in for area expansion in the NER" (Viswanathan and Shivakoti 2007: 118). It invited the private rubber dealers and the middleman, who appropriated an excessive amount of money to the deprivation of the rubber producers. Commodity fetishism in rubber led to a mad rush of people to take up rubber cultivation for money income that finally crystallised in a folk saying on the lips of the community people that the Rongmala (land of colour) has transformed into Rammala (land of money) while the rubber tappers are thrown into abject poverty, poor living conditions and food insecurity.

Box 3.10: Whose Forest! Whose Rights!

Tripura, once rich in forest resources, has lost it due to anthropogenic disturbances. Several factors have caused such disturbances:

(a) The JFM was started in Tripura from 1990. The JFM Committees were formed for protection and regeneration of forests. But the JFM approach created conflict of the rights among the tribal people. The major problems of the JFM approach were: loss of customary rights of the people; impositional and non-consensual nature of the JFM approach; failure to recognise needs of local people and exclusion of the shifting cultivators and pastoralists from the definition of indigenous in the Forest Rights Act. As a result the local people became labour on their own land. JFM privileged some people from within the community who got a greater share from the forest proceeds though their relations with the forest department was contractual.

(b) In Tripura JFM was promoted on patta land, whereas rubber cultivation was Promoted through rubber cooperatives. In some area it was share-based and in some other area it was wage-based. The wage-based cultivation reduced the tribal people to labour. On the other hand, the JAICA project, a bilateral project of Japan and the forest department in Tripura, promoted nursery and plantation and did not include the tribal farmers most of who did not possess patta.

(c) The horticultural programme was taken up in mission mode in Tripura. Under the mini mission 2 in Tripura significant area expansion programme was taken up. Mini mission 4 focused on enterprise development on food processing which was not very rewarding to the tribal people as they did not know fruit processing and lacked market support. They fell into the traps of the Mahajans who procured the horticultural products at an extremely low price. For example, for one sori of banana, the Mahajans gave Rs. 40-50 to the farmers, whereas the end price per sori of banana was Rs. 150-200. Thus the tribal people did not get the right price.

Athrmura in Khwai district and Longtunai Hills in Dhalai district are abodes of the Riang tribe. The Tripura government is planning to declare Atharmura and Longtunai Hills as an Elephant Reserve. Four sanctuaries and two national parks, established in the state, displaced a large number of Riangs from their own abode.

The cropping pattern also changed in the hills of Manipur. In many hill areas of Manipur like Ukhrul and Mao areas, cash crop and horticulture have captured huge areas of community land, the products of which are not consumed *in situ*. Many people in the hill areas have taken recourse to cash crop and horticulture despite market risks and market failures. Contract farming has started in its crude form in Kharam Pallen, a village located in Saitu-Ghamphazol Block of Senapati District in Manipur.

Box 3.11: Contract Farming in Manipur!

Village Kharam Pallen is located in Saitu-Ghamphazol Block of Senapati District in Manipur. This village is inhabited by the Kharam tribe.

Over the last 4-5 years, contract farming of ginger has been forced into this village. Two crop investors (Mahajans) from the valley areas invested money as a loan to the tribal farmers to cultivate ginger and made an informal contract with them on a yearly basis. Throughout the production cycle the land remains tied up with ginger cultivation. The investors buy back the whole product and dictate the wholesale price over which the tribal cultivators have no say. While bying back, the loan money is adjusted with the crop price. After adjustment, the tribal farmers get very low net wholesale price compared to the labour they give. The ginger growers are small growers based on family labour. The gap between procurement price and sale price is as high as Rs. 1000 per qtl: Rs. 8000 per qtl. Informal contract farming has robbed the farmers of the crop decision and created an interlocking arrangement of investment, credit input, land, and the product of the land during the contract period. As there is no warehouse, the farmers let the crop remain under the soil. This causes huge crop damages by earth insects. The investors abdicate all sorts of market risks as well as risk due to crop damage. They also give distorted information of market price. This system made the tribal farmers quasi-bonded labourers on their own land and the investors became the de facto owners of communal land for the lock-in period of ginger cultivation.

There is a dominant elite version of cropping pattern and land use in the hills of Manipur. Below an elite vision of cropping pattern and land use in Zogam, is presented.

Box 3.12: Elite Vision of Cropping Pattern and Land Use in the Zogam: The Trend

There is a move towards creation of Zogam, the territorial boundary of which covers the states of Manipur, Mizoram and Myanmar. The blue print of economic development of Zogam emphasises the primary sectors while focus has been given on:

(i) The mining sector and mining research on oil and natural earth production for national development.

(ii) Tea and coffee plantation (cash crop) over thousands of acres of land for export with the hope that tea could earn "multi-million dollars" in less than ten years' time while coffee could be a major source of foreign income in the near future.

(iii) A company from France in collaboration with some businessmen in Myanmar has set up a vine plantation and a wine factory in the Shan state of Myanmar which can also be developed in Zogam the climate of which is not much different from that of the Shan state.

(iv) Agar wood could be another billion dollar project in Zogam. The Zawthan plantation, a natural grown tree in Zogam, which is used for family consumption, is a good source of income and may fulfil the millionaire's dream of the tribal people.

(v) Mulberry, pineapple, mango, orange, lemon, plums, banana, fig tree and sugarcane are expected to have better trade prospects through processing and bottling.

(Source: Rev. Dr. Gin Khan Khual, Development Challenges and Opportunities of the Zomi, Souvenir, The Third World Zomi Convention, Churachandpur, Manipur, India, 2013).

The market focus of the elite vision in Zogam and the blue-print for economic development did not look into the larger context of marketing of agro-products under the WTO regime. The WTO Rules on sanitary and phyto-sanitary measures made it difficult exporting domestic agricultural produce to the developed country markets. Standards became important factors in global trade. The developing countries also faced the challenge of labour standard. From the social policy angle, the commercial farm products need protection of the state from the global market. The Zogam blue-print does not address the larger issues at the global level. At the same time, the entire blue-print of economic development goes towards incipient privatisation of land resources, contrary to the communal land system of the tribes.

Box 3.13: Notes from the Field: Nagaland

A micro-level field study in four villages, namely Lothur, Salomi, Anatongre and Phelungre in Pungro sub-division in Kiphire district in Nagaland, found emergence of commercial cropping and wealth accumulation by private individuals.

Lothur village is inhabited by the *Yimchunger* tribe. The villagers mainly practise shifting cultivation and produce maize, gini peas for subsistence use. In this village commercial production of maize has started over the past few years. This caused a rich-poor divide in land holding pattern. Intra-tribal sale of land has raised land price per kheti (approximately 200 sft. where one tin of paddy containing about 15 kgs is grown). Per kheti land price ranges between Rs. 40,000 to Rs. 60,000. Anatongre village is inhabited by the Tikhir tribe. Land ownership here is of two types: community land and individual land. They cultivate maize, naga beans/naga dal and rice for subsistence use. Recently, commercial production of maize has started in this village. This has caused a rich-poor divide in land holding. A similar trend is found in Phelungre village, inhabited by the Sangtam tribe. In this village commercial production of maize, bananas and mangos has started which has caused a rich-poor divide. In Salomi village inhabited by the same tribe, timber has become the major export item. Usually people sell timber grown in their private land. Illegal extraction from reserve forests is also in practice with the mediation of the local power elites, local middlemen, timber merchants and the outside agents.

In these villages wealth is measured in terms of the number of mithone or buffalo one could possess. Thus a person possessing the animal wealth, can establish a new village with some families from the parent village, where he becomes the headman. The boundary of such villages is measured by visual distance. In the absence of proper records, he could visualise as much land as his village boundary as possible. These wealthy families later increased their land holding by intra-tribe sale which often led to inter -tribal and inter-village conflicts.

The Garos of Meghalaya under the Sixth Schedule have experienced a changeover to commercial crops, individual ownership against the women's ownership, and class formation. Many Garos of the East Garo Hills have taken up rubber cultivation showing signs of formation of class and patriarchy. The Rubber Board and other financial bodies insisted on individual pattas as preconditions for loans and subsidies. Patta owners were usually understood as males. This scotched the community process envisaged in the Sixth Schedule. Roy

Burman commenting on the Bordoloi Committee Report made a distinction between the community process and the state process with their clearly delineated spheres and without impinging on one another. But, while the Sixth Schedule accommodated the community process, the institutions themselves became subordinate to state control and the members of the District Council tended to draw their legitimacy mainly from the state process rather than from the community process (Roy Burman 1997: 22). Similar trend of erosion of community process has been observed after the enactment of the Chotanagpur Tenancy Act of 1908 (Upadhyaya 2005: 4436-7).

Conclusion

Changes in the land use pattern and cropping pattern in the hills of Northeast India went with growing privatisation of communal land resources and aggrandisement of the same for capital fixation. Both industrial use of communal land and commercial cropping economy in the hills became capital intensive that the petty producers in the hills were unable to mobilise. The subsistence land use pattern and absence of written record of right, scoped the investors—both big and small—first to aggrandise communal land by primitive means and then with the state patronage for capital fixation. But while they did it, they also required definite legal titles over the land which the community did not have. The state, in support of the investors, assumed the surrogate role and used the eminent domain for acquisition of communal lands in favour of the investors. This threw the communal land to *res nullius* status that created the alibi to vacate the community from the land. The next step was to accord a definite title to those investors mainly through lease title till the community members were completely uprooted and annihilated from their abode and their livelihood resources. The lease mode of land privatisation, privileged the investors for temporal fixation of capital to earn a quick buck, particularly, in the neoliberal era. On the other hand, the changes in cropping and land-use pattern towards commercial economy proved perilous to the ordinary tribal population in this region while the self-aggrandising individuals either through primitive accumulation or through accumulation by dispossession amassed huge land resources in their hands and indulged in land speculation in terms of sale-purchase-lease-mortgage. Northeast India is not a manufacturing region. Here industrial use of land amounted to extraction and commoditisation of the land-based resources, including, the forest and mineral resources. Industrial use, therefore, did not accord any major *in situ* benefit to the tribal people in the real sense of the term. The state became a big patron of horticultural plantation which was taken up on mission mode. In Tripura, the *Jhumias* were settled on rubber cultivation but the neoliberal market economy stymied the welfare approach of the state and made rubber cultivation absolutely market-oriented. Some villages in north Tripura were to be declared as an elephant reserve. In Manipur, while cash cropping destroyed the food security and livelihood system of the tribals, an elite vision in the hills welcomed commercial cropping, individual land rights and mining wealth extraction in the hills. In Mizoram, the New Land Use Policy made drastic reversal of the mode of production in the hills and in Arunachal Pradesh, the water resources were given to the foreign investors and the corporate companies for earning hydro-dollars. These developments have perennially dispossessed the tribal communities, annihilated them from the land-based resources and threw them into the peril.

REFERENCES

Asif, Mohammed (1999). Development Initiative and Concomitant Issues of Displacement and Improvement in Northeastern States, in Kailash S. Agarwal edited, *Dynamics of Identity and Inter-group Relations*. Shimla: Indian Institute of Advanced Study.

Barbora, Sanjoy (2002). Ethnic Politics and Land Use Genesis of Conflicts in India's North-East, *Economic and Political Weekly*, March, 13.

Bhattacharjee, J.B. (1978). *The Garos and the English-1765-1874*. New Delhi: Radiant Publishers.

Baruah, Sanjib (2012). Hydropower, Mega Dams and the Politics of Risk, *Seminar* 640, December.

Behera M.C. and Jamuer Basar (eds.) *Interventions and Tribal Development—Challenges Before Tribes of India in the Era of Globalisation*. New Delhi: Serial Publications.

Biswas, Indraneel (2006). A Status Report on Rubber Plantation in Tripura, *Mission Technical Bulletin*.

Bordoloi, B.N. (1986). *Alieanation of Tribal Land and Indebtedness*. Guwahati: Tribal Research Institute.

Bordoloi, B.N. (1986). Problem of Transfer and Alienation of Tribal Land in the Karbi Anglong District of Assam with Special Reference to the Karbis, in B.N. Bordoloi, *Alieanation of Tribal Land and Indebtedness*. Guwahati: Tribal Research Instiutute.

Bordoloi, B.N. (1990). Tribal Development Plans and Programmes in the Sixth Scheduled Areas of Assam with Special Reference to Land: A Critical Approach. *Bulletin of Assam Institute of Research for Tribes and Scheduled Castes*. Vol. 1, No. VII. Guwahati.

Bordoloi, B.N. (1991). *Transition and Alienation of Tribal Land in Assam with Special Reference to Karbis of Karbi Anglong District*. Guwahati: Western Book Depot.

Borthakur, D.N., R.P. Awasthi and R.N. Gupta (1990). Alternative System of Farming in Increasing Productivity in Jhum Land, in D.N. Mazumdar edited, *Shifting Cultivation in Northeast India*. New Delhi: Omsons Publications.

Chakraborty, Dipannita (2004). *Land Question in Tripura*. New Delhi: Akansha Publishing House.

Chakraborty, Gorky and Asok Kumar Ray (2009). Contextualising Space in India's Northeast vis-à-vis South Asia: The Realities and Imaginaries. Proceedings of the International Conference on Region Formation in Contemporary South Asia, The University of Delhi, 25-27 November.

Choudhury, Pratap Chandra (1987). *The History of Civilization of the People of Assam to the Twelfth Century*. New Delhi: Spectrum Publications.

Centre for Science and Environment (CSE) (2008). State of India's Environment: A Citizen's Report-6, New Delhi.

Das, J.N. (1984). A Study of Land System of Northeast India.Vol. III. Tripura (Mimeographed). Guwahati: LRI Eastern Region. Guwahati High Court.

Das, J.N. (1986). A Study of Land System of Northeast India Vol: VI. Mizoram (Mimeographed). Guwahati: LRI Eastern Region,

Guwahati High Court.

Das, Debajyoti (2006). Demystifying the Myth of Shifting Cultivation Agronomy in the North-East. *Economic & Political Weekly*, November 25.

Das, Debojyoti (2010). Communities, Conservation and Challenge of Participation: An Ethnographic Detour of Conservation Programme and the Fate of Jhumias in Naga Villages in Maguni Charan Behera edited. *Interventions and Tribal Development: Challenges Before Tribes in India in An Era of Globalization*. Delhi: Serials Publications.

Das, J.N. (1990). *A Study of the Land System in Tripura*. Guwahati: Law Research Institute, Guwahati High Court.

Dasgupta, Malabika (1990). Rehabilitating Jhumias on Rubber Plantation in D.N. Mazumdar edited, *Shifting Cultivation in Northeast India*. New Delhi: Omsons Publications.

Dasgupta, Malabika (2005). *Transition in the Economy of the Tribals*. New Delhi: Inter India Publications.

Dash, Minati (2004). Political Economy of Contract Farming, *Mainstream*. December 25.

De Chaudhury, S. (1999). A Perspective of Coal Mining, in V.S. Mahajan, S.K. Agnihotri and R.P. Athparia edited, *Energy and Energy Resource Management*. New Delhi: Deep & Deep Publications Pvt. Ltd.

DONER Ministry and the World Bank (2006). New Delhi: Executive Summary of the Strategy Paper on the 'Study on Natural Resources, Water, Environment Nexus for Development and Growth of Northeast India' June 28.

Fernandes, Walter (2008). Globalization, Land Laws and Land Reforms in R.S. Despandey edited, *Contract Farming and Tenancy Reforms—Entangled without Tether*. Mussoorie: Centre for Rural Studies, Lal Bahadur Shastri Academy of Administration.

Ganguli, J.B. (1991). Socio-Economic Problems of Transition from Shifting Cultivation to Sedentary Cultivation in North-East India in D.N. Mazumdar, edited, *Shifting Cultivaion in Northeast India*. New Delhi: Omsons Publications.

Ganguli, Jalad Baran (2006). *Economic History of Northeast India*. New Delhi: Akansha Publishing House.

Ghosh, Jayati (2009) in NSA Policy Brief No. 348. New Delhi: All India Kisan Sabha Proposals on Minimum Support Prices, 7th March.

Gohain, Hiren (2008). Big Dams, Big Floods: On Predatory Development. *Economic and Political Weekly*, Vol. XLIII, No. 30.

July 26.

Gopalkrishnan, Shankar and Priya Sreenivasa (2009). Corporate Retail: Dangerous Implications for Indian Economy. *Economic and Political Weekly*, August 8.

Government of Arunachal Pradesh (2013). Hydro electric Power Policy, http://www.arunachalhydro.org.in/pdf/State%20Mega%20 Hydro.pdf; Tehelka, Vol. 10, Issue 28, July 13.

Government of India (2008). Ministry of Environment and Forest. Report of the Inter-Ministerial National Task Force on Rehabilitation of Shifting Cultivation Areas.

Government of Mizoram (1989). *Mizoram District Gazetteer*.

Government of Mizoram Comprehensive Project under New Land Use Policy for Sustained Economic Development and Upliftment of the Poor in Mizoram, (Mimeographed).

Grogan, Paul, F. Lalnunmawia, S.K. Tripathi (2012). Shifting Cultivation in Steeply Sloped Regions: A Review of Management Options and Research Priorities for Mizoram State, Northeast India, Agroforest Syst (2012) DOI 10.1007/s10457-011-9469-1, Received: 1 March 2011/Accepted: 30 December 2011/Published online: 15 January 2012, Springer Science+Business Media B.V. 2012.

Guha, Amalendu (1991). *Medieval and Early Colonial Assam: Society, Polity and Economy*. Calcutta: K.P. Bagchi & Co.

Gupta, A.K. (2000). Shifting Cultivation and Conservation of Biological Diversity in Tripura, Northeast India, *Human Ecology*, Vol. 28, No. 4 (Dec.).

Habib, Irfan (2010). Note Towards a Marxist Perception of Indian History, *The Marxist*, XXVI, 4, October–December.

Harvey, David (1990). *The Condition of Postmodernity: An Enquiry into the Origin of Cultural Change*. Oxford: Blackwell Publishing.

Hassan, Manirul (2002). State, Development and Population Displacement in Northeast India, in C. Joshua Thomas edited, *Dimension of Displaced People in Northeast India*. New Delhi: Regency Publications.

Hatai, Laxmi Dhar (2012). Revitalising of Hill Agriculture in North-East: An Overview. *Kurukshtra, A Journal on Rural Development*. New Delhi: Ministry of Rural Development, November.

Hidayatullah, M. (1979). *The Fifth and the Sixth Schedule to the Constitution of India. The Anundoram Barooah Law Lecture (Second Series)*. New Delhi: Ashok Publishing House.

Hunter, W.W. (1990). *A Statistical Account of Assam*, Vol. 2. Delhi: Low

Price Publications.

Johnson, David (2003). Articulating the Global and the Local: Land reforms in Post-Apartheid South Africa in Suman Gupta et.al. edited, *India in the Age of Globalisation—Contemporary Discourses and Texts*. New Delhi: Nehru Memorial Museum and Library.

FFHC and Ministry of Agriculture (1970). National Food Congress. New Delhi: GoI.

Karlsson, Bengt G. (2011). *Unruly Hills, Nature and Nation in India's North East*. New Delhi: Orient BlackSwan.

Lalnunmawia, F. and C. Lalzarliana (2013). *Land Use System in Mizoram*. New Delhi: Akansha Publishing House.

Levien, Michael (2011). Rationalising Dispossession: The Land Acquisition and Resettlement Bills. *Economic & Political Weekly*, Vol. XLVI, No. 11, March 12.

Longkumar, Lanusashi and Toshimenla Jamir (2012). *Status of Adivasis/ Indigenous Peoples Land Series: 6, Nagaland*. Delhi: Aakar Books.

Lyngdoh, G.W. (2010). The Giant's Gigantic Blunder, http:// www.meghalayatimes.info/index.php May 17.

Menon, Manju (2008). Land Alienation due to Large Hydro-Power Projects in Arunachal Pradesh in Walter Fernandes and Sanjay Barbora edited, *Land, People and Politics: Contest Over Tribal Land in Northeast India*. North Eastern Social Research Centre and International Workgroup for Indigenous Affairs.

Misra, Bani Prasanna (1990). A Positive Approach to the Problem of Shifting Cultivation in D.N. Mazumdar edited, *Shifting Cultivation in Northeast India*. New Delhi: Omsons Publications.

Nathan, Dev (2005). Hill Economies of the North-eastern Region, Emerging Challenges and Opportunities, *Economic and Political Economy*, June 18.

National Centre for Advocacy Studies (1999). Pune: Info Pack. January 3, April.

NEDFi Database Quarterly (2006). *Quarterly Journal of North Eastern States Economy*. Shillong: (Horticulture), Vol. 5, Issue 1, January.

NEDFi (2008). *Quarterly Journal of North Eastern State's Economy* (MAP). Vol. 9, Issue-I.

NEDFi (2009). *Quarterly Journal of North Eastern State's Economy*. Shillong: (Bamboo). Vol. 6, Issue-I, II, III, January.

Newslink, Aizawl, (2013). Mizoram Plans Large-scale Rubber Cultivation, September.

Nlup.mizoram.gov.in/page/concise/concise-summary-of-nlup.html.

OKDISCD (2008). Guwahati: Detailed Project Report on Setting Up

Procurement Centre for Horticultural products in Diphu, Haflong and Krishnai in Assam; Bomdila and Roing in Arunachal Pradesh; Churchandpur in Manipur; Vairangte in Mizoram and Nongpo and Phulbari in Meghalaya. (Mimeographed).

Patel, Amrit (2012). Harnessing Agricultural Potential in North Eastern Region. *Kurukshtra, A Journal of Rural Development*. New Delhi: Ministry of Agriculture. November.

Parliament Digest (2003). New Delhi: NCAS. Winter.

Planning Commission. *9th and 10th Five Year Plan*, Vol. 2: Poverty Alleviation in Rural India- Strategies and Programmes. *11th Five Year Plan*, Vol. III. New Delhi: Government of India.

Qadri, Fozil Ahmed, ed. *Society and Economy in Northeast India*. New Delhi: Regency Publications.

Raghavan, K.K. (2009). Rubber for Tribal Development in Tripura in Gautam Kumar Bera edited, *Tribal Development in Tripura*. New Delhi: EHB Publications.

Rangarajan, Mahesh (1994) Review of P.S.Ramakrishnan, (1993). Shifting Agriculture and Sustainable Development: An Interdisciplinary Study from North-Eastern India. *Economic and Political Weekly*, Vol. 29, No. 39, September 24.

Ray, Asok Kumar (2007). *Revisiting Northeast India in the Era of Globalisation*. New Delhi: Om Publications.

Ray, Asok Kumar. (2011). Challenges of Welfare State Under Neo-liberalism. Seminar on "Neoliberal State and its Challenges, Omeo Kumar Das Institute for Social Change and Development Guwahati, 20-21 December.

Roy Burman, B.K. (1990). An Overview of Shifting Cultivation in India in D.N. Mazumdar edited, *Shifting Cultivaion in Northeast India*. New Delhi: Omson Publications.

Roy Burman, B.K. (1997). Sixth Schedule of the Constitution in L.S. Gassah edited, *Autonomous District Council*. New Delhi: Omsons Publications.

Roy Burman, B.K. (1988). Problems and Prospects of Tribal Development in North-East India. *Economic and Political Weekly*. Vol. 24, No. 13, April 1.

Roy Burman, B.K. (2008). Ambiguities, Incongruities, Inadequacies in Scheduled Tribes and Other Technical Forest Dwellers (Recognition of Forest Rights) Act 2006, A Case For Constructive Engagement. *Mainstream*, Vol. XLVI, No. 15. 29 March.

Sangai Express (2013). Imphal: "Kikhonbou Encourages Orange

Planters". July 25.

Sangma, Milton S. (1991). Crafts and Technology of Garos, in Jayprakash Singh and Gautam Sengupta edited, *Archaeology of Northeast India*. New Delhi: Har Anand Publications.

Sen, K.K., R.L. Semwal, U. Rana, S. Nautiyal, R.K. Maikhuri, K.S. Rao and K.G. Saxena (2002). Patterns and Implications of Land Use/ Cover Change: A Case Study in Pranmati Watershed (Garhwal Himalaya, India) *Mountain Research and Development*, Vol. 22, No. 1, February.

Sengupta, Mayuri (2013). Shifting Cultivation and the Riang Tribe of Tripura. *Economic and Political Weekly*, Vol. XLVIII, No. 40, October 5.

Shankar Raman, T.R. (2014). Mizoram: Bamboozled by Land Use Policy, *The Hindu*, 14th May. (Summarised)

Sharma, Brij Bihari and M.K. Dhaka (2012). True Potato seed (TPS): A Revolution in Potato Cultivation in North Eastern States of India. *Kurukshtra: A Journal of Rural Development*. New Delhi: Ministry of Agriculture.

Sharma, Tarun C. (1990a). The Pre-Historic Background of Shifting Cultivation in D.N. Mazumdar, edited, *Shifting Cultivation in Northeast India*. New Delhi: Omsons Publications.

Sharma Thakur, G.C. (1994): Tribal Elements in Assamese Culture. *Bulletin of Assam Institute of Research for Tribals and Scheduled Castes*. Vol. 1, No. IX. Guwahati: Assam Institute of Research for Tribals and Scheduled Castes.

Singh, I. (1989). Reverse Tenancy in Punjab Agriculture: Impact of Technological Change, *Economic and Political Weekly*, 24 (25), June 24.

Singh, Prakash (1972). *Nagaland*. New Delhi: National Book Trust.

Soil and Water Conservation Department (State Land Use Board), Nagaland (1990). Proceedings of the North Eastern Regional Seminar on 'Land-Use Planning and Watershed Management for Control of Shifting Cultivation'. Dimapur, 8-9 March.

Sutradhar, Abhijit (2002). Anti Dam Movement in Northeast India: Protests and Reactions Over Tipaimukh Dam (Manipur), *Journal of Political Studies*. Vol. 5. Department of Political Science, North Bengal University, March 11.

Thakur, Amarendra Kr. (2013). Iron and Social Change in Pre-Coloinal Northeast India, *Social Change and Development*, Journal of OKDISCD, Guwahti, Vol. X, No. 1, January.

The Sentinel (2013). Guwahati: 20 October.

The Meghalaya Times, September 22, 2011.

The Shillong Times (2010). Shillong: 'Minding the Mines of the State'.

The Shillong Times, October 27, 2011.

Tribal Research Institute (TRI), Government of Mizoram. (1982). *Know Your Own Land*, (Mizoram: Series IV). Calcutta: Firma KLM Private Limited.

Upadhyaya, Karol (2005). Community Rights in Land in Jharkhand. *Economic and Political Weekly*. October 8.

Vagholikar, Neeraj and Partha J. Das. (2010) Damming Northeast India: Juggernaut of Hydropower Projects Threatens Social and Environmental Security of Region. http://chimalaya.files.wordpress.com/2010/12/damming-North East-india-final.pdf.

Viswanathan, P.K. and Ganesh P. Shivakoti (2007). Conceptualising Sustainable Farm-Livelihood System in the Era of Globalisation: A Study of Rubber Integrated Farm Livelihood system in Northeast India, *Social Change and Development*. Guwahati: OKD Institute of Social Change and Development, Vol. 5.

Whitehead, Judy (2003). Space, Place and Primitive Accumulation in Narmada Valley and Beyond, *Economic and Political Weekly*, October 4.

White, Major Adam (1988). *A Memoir of Late David Scott, Esq*. Compiled by S.K. Bhuyan. Guwahati: Department of Historical and Antiquarian Studies in Assam.

World Bank (2006). *Inclusive Growth and Service Delivery: Building on Global Success—World Bank Development Policy Review*. Delhi: Macmillan India Limited.

www.nsdcindia.org/pdf/n.

4

Land and Identity

Land, right, identity and class became a critical quadrangle in the journey of mankind from the early society to the contemporary one under neoliberalism. And as capital continued to annihilate space, social relations within the space and social control over the land use, this quadrangle became really deceptive to the relational character of communal land and built the core of distraught identity of the tribal communities. The tribal community in this situation could survive only on involuntarily allowing misappropriation of their natural resources, labour time and on paying absolute rent to the class having defining and enforceable property rights with the backing of the state support. In this order, natural resources received a fetish character and became subject to either primitive accumulation or accumulation by dispossession. Absolute rent and exploitation of surplus labour became the common modes of accumulation. In these circumstances, kinship groups and local institutional networks disappeared; the socio-economic support systems of the community collapsed; the producers and consumers were delinked from land and the cultural markers of the community were erased.

Historically, radical imposition of abstract space on diverse local place-based histories happened with the Enlightenment and with the rise of capitalism. Imposition of abstract space brought with it new institutions that trivialised the social and economic dynamics of local space which came to be conceived of as homogeneous, isometric and infinitely extended entity. Its primary property was metrically determinable pure extension. It provided a geometric template of nature within which Western science flourished and provided a grid upon which the earth's resources were mapped. We can here make a distinction between abstract space (devoid of content, objective, distance) and place (subjective, familial here-and-now and local) following Descartes that matter and space were the same thing and that space was a pure extension. In this early modern paradigm shift, there was little place for space as a valid concept in its own right. As a result, place was disempowered and all power now resided in space, devoid of content (Whitehead 2003: 4229-4230).

In the processes of primitive accumulation, the "concepts of abstract space are often forcibly imposed on local places, resulting in a radical reconfiguration of class and gender relations. Primitive accumulation involves a rearrangement of space, since it constitutes 'an annihilation of pre-existing property' and of customary ways relating to landscapes and water-scapes. It is usually accompanied by an erasure, or at least, a denigration of pre-existing ways of relating to such resources, which are often defined as nomadic, unsettled, uncivilised, etc". "The concept of abstract space enables developers to maintain a highly objectified and external relation to the landscape, which becomes emptied of people, history, entitlements, myth and magic. It is replaced by a quantifiable area consisting of commodifiable resources which collides, rather than interconnects with existing senses of place, history, and the environment" (Whitehead 2003: 4229-4230).

This distinction is critical for Northeast India. The valley agriculture in this region, its settled and surplus yielding features, stationary habitation patterns and concentrated manpower made a robust case for a more organised economic system that produced two classes: a land-owning class and a class to provide physical labour. Besides, the service class was also patronised by the existing dynastic power through land grants, like the Bhuyans in Assam who, as Guha said, helped the weak kings from frequent Bhot and Bodo Cachari invasions' (Guha 1991: 41), or the service class in Manipur that received 'talablouba' patta from the king. The other patronised class consisted of the court mandarins and the court mendicants, who provided intellectual and divine props to the rulers of this region. Larger areas of land were given to them free of rent. The tenants-cultivators had to pay rent and the slaves and forced labour (forced labour is called Lalup in Manipur) were used for personal services to the rulers. In this proto-feudal three-class set up in the valley areas of this region, there was a conscious effort for extension of space as far as practicable which often touched upon the contours of tribal lands. Spatial extension was responsible for the emergence of the category of 'Zamindari Garos' or for the Jaintia kings to extend their kingdom to the Jaintia Hills or for the Zamindar of Chakla Rosanabad to extend rule to Hill Tiperrah or for extension of suzerainty over the hill people in Manipur to establish lord-subordinate or patron-client relationships. The concepts of *lex loci rei sitae, res nullius* and *terra nullius* were the jurisprudential instruments of place annihilation of the tribal people by the state.

Given the *intelligible differentia* in land-based identity between the plains and the hills, we look into how the four factors—Land, Right, Labour and Class problematised the identity question and broke the primordial construction of identity of the hill tribes crystallised around the philistine land institutions in Northeast India. Contrary to James Scott's thesis of "*state evasion*", the identity construction of the pre-state tribes of Northeast India was a response to the development of the productive forces and production relations. Thus when the road construction was started by the British as a part of the war preparations for the First Anglo-Burmese War (1824-26), the tributary relations of the Kukis and the Nagas with the Raja of Manipur turned into non-tributary relations making a departure thereby from tributary to labour relations when the Raja and the local chiefs acted as labour agents for supply of local tribal labour for colonial road construction (Hasnu 2005). It is also important to note in this connection that the small act of the colonials uprooted the tribes from their pristine state and shook their land-based ontology. The mode of production remaining at the centre, the troubled identity of the tribes of Northeast India can be understood as partly institution-driven and partly elite-mediated. Below we discuss the two at some length.

Institution-Driven Identity

The pristine communal land ownership system was egalitarian, convivial and collectivist, while the colonial legal institutions produced the concept of possessive individualism by annihilating the communal land system. It was thus primarily responsible for the distraught identity of the tribes. Roy Burman noted that the "early slash and burn agriculturist societies were marked by more stable convivial-ingratiating mode of livelihood; the settled agriculturists were having convivial-custodial mode of livelihood; the peasants involved in market economy moved towards convivial predatory mode of livelihood; the colonial industrial societies generated predatory septral mode of livelihood and today when existence of life on the planet has become problematic, the highly industrialised societies are pushing ahead a predatory demiurgic schizophrenic mode of livelihood with a tendency to bring the whole of humanity within its ambit" (Roy Burman 1994: 11). He further noted that "the tribal people primarily perceive itself as tied together by moral bond having its root in ontology and not in history as in the case of the state. While tribe has in its core an existential quality of extension of self to the surroundings, a specific tribe is a structure with the existential quality of life as the lidger and slices of history as the coating" (Roy Burman 1995: 4). Roy Burman's 'moral bond' and Weber's '*Ethnische Gemainschaften*' suggesting blood ties and emotional attachment inside a certain group, formed the essentialist version of identity formation in the traditional tribal societies. We can conveniently add on here the "Landscape" approach of social anthropology that includes the physical elements, living elements, abstract elements and the human element which are the outcomes of conscious transformative activities. These elements interact in spatially and temporally specific ways, generating sets of material outcome that are contingent upon the prevailing set of social relations within which cultural forms are constructed (Lodhi 2007: 1439).

An essentialist-normative formulation of identity is seen as a social (human) process that gives a sense of bond, togetherness, reciprocity, community and so on in the course of its existence and in the course of its taking part in changing the reality (nature). This at the same time unleashes an enormous amount of symbolic values that eventually come to exist on its own right. Such identity formation is therefore essentially a product of the endo-biotic and somatic attachments of the human communities to land space and to the totality of the ecology. Besides production of the means of livelihood, the endo-biotic and somatic attachments also produce land as a space for reproduction of culture, belief system and multiple social institutions to build the robust foundation of identity. These are self-evident and remain beyond discourse and subjective interpretations. Land-culture connectivity in the tribal society is also manifested in the agrarian calendar, fertility cult, tree worship, sowing and harvest festivals, cultural performances, popular lores and even in the romantic chores. Apart from the free ride on the natural resources, they propitiate their gods and goddesses when selecting the sites for cultivation and habitation. They "exhibit their strong social solidarity, cooperation and fraternity in such participation"(Ayer and Bhave 1995). What distinguished the indigenous tribal people from other people is, Laldena wrote, "their emotional attachment to the land where they live". "Land contains their history and sense of identity and it ensures their economic viability as an independent people". He quoted Julian Burger to illustrate the point. "The earth is the foundation of indigenous people. It is the seat of spirituality, the foundation from which our cultures and languages flourish. The earth is our historian, the keeper of events and the bones of our forefathers. Earth provides us food, medicine, shelter and clothing. It is the source of our independence; it is our mother. We do not dominate her, we must harmonise with her". Laldena further wrote, "for the indigenous people, their oral history is more important than anything else. Go to Tipaimukh, you will come across many standing tombs of our forefathers on the way. Those are the living witnesses of our ownership of land. They are our documents". (Laldena 2013: 89). Therefore, both the emotive and cognitive aspects constituted the anthropology of land and eventually contributed to the identity formation of the tribal people.

Intervention of institutional economics broke this matrix. Preponderance of institutional economics trivialised the anthropological roots of land and following growth-fundamentalism, the state and market forces together evinced drastic changes in the land use pattern and cropping pattern in the tribal societies. In this way the somatic bond and economic life of the tribal people were broken. The somatic proximity and emotional bond of the collectivised tribal communities and experiential knowledge of the tribal communities were also broken along with this. With the change in the mode of production and with the involuntary integration of the tribal communities in the state and market economy, the cultural essentialism of the tribal identity began to get eroded. The state's argument for evincing the new institutional order in the tribal societies was based on its pejorative image about the latter as backward, incapable and imperfect. The market economy added on to this image of the tribal societies.

The first institutional interface of the tribes happened with the more organised valley civilisation and then with the colonial state when the latter ruthlessly let loose the process of primitive accumulation of the land-based resources in the tribal areas. The tribal communities rose to rebellions that were crushed by brutal force. Then the colonials took full control of the tribal chiefs and headmen and brought them to structured subordination. This was followed by large-scale re-structuration of the clan villages. Structured subordination emphasised the shift from *clan to territory* and corresponding shift of allegiance of the people from *clan to territory* that resulted in annihilation of the historicity of community identity and the beginning of territorial identity. The territorial villages were administratively defined that became the captive spaces of the tribal communities. The identity scramble as a result was obvious as many of the traditional practices of land allocation and distribution by the chiefs or headmen to the community members came to be finally governed by the colonial administrative law. The House Tax system was introduced in these villages and the chiefs were made responsible for collection of House Tax for onward deposition to the British treasury. Through the chiefs, the British could accumulate huge wealth from land, forest and mineral resources. The most critical institution-driven identity change was invited by the colonial concept of private property which was deeply embedded in the positivistic-jurisprudential path-model. The predatory principles of positivistic-jurisprudence of the colonial state worked against the plural customs governing communal lands, dismissed the essentialism of primordial identity and imposed the hegemonic colonial policies, legislations and acts on them. The colonial state viewed the tribal people as marauding 'barbarian'; savage and warlike; pagan and primitive. Therefore all the adjectives—'Barbarians', savage, pagan and primitive—remained always antithetical to colonial state projects. These adjectives also formed the core of the colonial racist policies and institutions. Guided by the predatory racist policies and institutions, the colonial state reconstructed its relations with the tribal world. Based on the racist policies two missions emerged: the 'Civilising Mission' of the colonial church and the 'War Mission' for empire building through primitive accumulation. Wherever the first mission failed, the second mission was resorted to ward them off by war and plunder. Thus *Sword* and *Sermon* were institutionalised in the colonial dealings with the tribal people and in the capture of their land resources. The homogenised positive law of the colonial state facilitated the process further.

The homogenised jurisprudential principles were carried forward to the post-colonial state and as a part of the state-building project, the state took a pejorative view of the customary laws of the tribal communities. While the Indian state was preoccupied with the post-colonial reconstruction project, the development paradigm was institutionalised by governmental intervention. This let loose similar ramifications on the tribal land system as under the colonial era. The institutional response of the Indian state towards the tribes was both hot and cold. In Assam, the East India Company replaced the system of 'Khel' as it restricted government's cash income. The revenue sources of the "Khels" were basically in terms of goods and services (Sharmah and Dutta 2013: 80). In the hill districts of Assam, the Autonomous District Council was created that gave a berth to legal pluralism which included the customary rights of the tribals on land and forest and a laissez faire stand of the state for administration of the tribal people. But it at the same time, inverted the right perception of the tribes, who came under the Autonomous District Council, about communal land and the customary land rights became merely the *derivative* rights.

The Draft National Tribal Policy of the Ministry of Tribal Affairs, in recognition of the normative aspect of tribal land, acknowledged that the tribal communities' entire way of life is woven around harmony with and preservation of nature. There is a very strong symbiotic relationship between the STs and the forests and they have been at the forefront of the conservation regime. Due to faulty processes of declaring reserved forests in the past, the rights of the tribals over their traditional land holdings in the forests were gradually extinguished. Insecurity of tenure and fear of eviction from these lands led the tribal communities to feel emotionally as well as physically alienated from forests and forest lands. The Draft policy also stated that ownership of land signifies livelihood, culture and identity in a tribal economy. On the other hand, the resource drive of the Indian state regularly superseded her laissez faire stand and capture of communal land continued in the pretext of land acquisition in public purpose. To the state, land resource was significant only for economic growth, while to the tribal community land resource was essential both for subsistence and for their ontological survival. This duality built the dual perception of land-use between the state and the tribal community. On the other hand, growth fundamentalism and land acquisition by the state went parallel and subsequently the political economy imperative of land-use superseded the normative anthropology of land-use and in this process, the protectionist policy of the state and the land-community symbiosis became fraught with peril and annihilation. The communal land within the state process finally became the conquered space for resource mobilisation.

Obliteration of the plural meanings of land hit at the core of land-based identity of the tribal people. The Draft Report of the Committee on State Agrarian Relations and Unfinished Task of Land Reforms, Ministry of Rural Development, Government of India, once more acknowledged the cultural and historic plurality of the community land. This report also acknowledged the critical gaps in knowledge and understanding of the complexities of social institutions of the tribes in the North Eastern region. The report stated that the different areas have their own systems of governance including the Autonomous District Councils and Autonomous Regional Councils, which are endowed with rule-making powers and implementation. These systems have, however, strengthened the district level institutions at the expense of the Village Councils, which could be dissolved by the former. The people inhabiting the tribal areas had fierce pride in their community and had jealous possessiveness of their traditional institutions. Interventions from the Central or the State Governments without understanding the local institutions, social fabric and the will of the people created disenchantment, anger and rebellion. It was necessary to seal such critical gaps through sustained research and interventions reflecting the felt need and differentiated solutions. But the message of this report like many others of the same sort, remained only in words, not in deeds and the state intervention in the communal land continued unabated.

The perceptual hiatus on land between the traditional and the non-traditional societies is historic-epistemological. Broadly, there are two major perceptions related to land: i) land is individual property that is transferable; ii) the community has the stewardship of land, the real value of which can never be expressed in terms of market. This made the fundamental difference between traditional and market economies on land and the difference in perceptions of land. (Chakraborty 2012) The colonial construction of land was based on the centre-periphery notion, whereas, the tribal construct of land was based essentially on the communitarian ethos. The changed land-use pattern and the eventual land relation and identity obliterated the distinctiveness of the tribes by dismissing their Jurally fragmented practices of land use. This detached the somatic proximity of the people to land and their social place was reconfigured as a space for capital investment and eventual commercialisation.

Land-based identity of the tribal communities of the Northeast, therefore, stood as a critique of modernist accumulation of communal land under market economy, and so, provided a strong alibi to zealously guard their communal land institutions, their relational nature and the host of social functions associated with land and forest. Both the productive and reproductive functions of land were significant for the completeness of identity formation in the tribal societies. Forests, for example, provided them the sources of legends, folklores, usages; music, colour, weaving, shelter, utensils, weapons; rituals, ceremonies, signals, prosperity and calamity predictions (Sangpliang 2010: 35-36, 45-60). The cognitive and perceptual aspects of land in the traditional tribal society made the fundamental difference of land as understood in the institutional economics and much of the perceptual gap was responsible for the troubled identity of the tribal communities of Northeast India. Privatisation of land created a cosmology that hindered endogenous growth of culture; blocked its creative and re-creative functions, robbed of culture as the collective endowments of the community and transformed the processual aspect of culture towards an imitative world.

Table 4.1: Perception Gap on Land

Traditional Perception	*Modernist Perception*
Land right is customarily acquired	Land rights are legally acquired
Land is not as such alienable	Land is subject to alienation and appropriation
Largely community ownership	Land is privately owned
Individual ownership is subsumed in community ownership	Individual right is the basis of development and economic growth
Place value (culture, ecology, habitat, social relation, emotion)	Space value (annihilation of culture, ecology, social relations, emotions)
Land gives identity to the ethnic groups	Land is a cosmopolitan, melting pot of identity
Community is the person	Community is not a legal person
Land for subsistence product	Land for surplus product
Land is non-revenue yielding	Land is revenue yielding
Land is product yielding and identity creating	Both product and revenue yielding
Oral/customary basis of land	Legal tenure/record of rights
Symbol of community solidarity	Symbol of power, wealth and status
Processual aspect of labour	Institutional aspect of labour
Community labour	Hired or tenant labour
Land for subsistence use	Land is to earn rent, interest and profit
Natural regeneration/no capital input, folk technology	Value addition/technology and capital intensity
Jural fragmentation of land use	Uni-jural structural model of land use
Convivial labour relation	Contractual labour relations
Labour as social investment	Labour as economic investment
Land and labour are ontological	Land and labour are reified
Integrated with society	Separated from society

Land-based collective identity developed from the organic unity of man and land first, and from the constituent concepts of production, reproduction and tradition making (centred on land) then. Associating the problem of identity with the production process (which follows reproduction and tradition making), Lokendrajit singled out that man's product acquired an existence independent of the creator and started having a life of its own in a time axis; secondly, man's participation in the production process is a mode of changing himself, nature and the society; thirdly, the development in the world of products generates surplus energy in the society. A society that fails to create its own world of products is penetrated by an external world of products along with accompanying institutions (colonisation). Failure to counter these forces may freeze the society at a receiving end to a passive medium—a phenomenon crucial to understand identity crisis; fourthly, the super structural institutions cannot be used as a category to describe the identity of a society. Their true character is revealed while tracing the morphogenesis of a society and fifthly, the process of production and reproduction is directly linked with the process of tradition making. A synthesis of production and reproduction in the human mode of existence is what makes tradition possible. Tradition here is development of man's creation in time, the world of his products using successive generations in a process of incarnation. It is the active process of decoding the message in the world of products by successive generations when it is their turn in time. This is critical in identifying the problem of identity and its crisis (Lokendrajit 1988: 226-228).

Datta found that the practice of *jhum* (with all its socio-economic nuances) and the inter personal relations in the societies practising *jhum* are inter-related. The traditional spirit of egalitarian adjustments in the predominantly Indo-Mongoloid *jhumia* societies of the Northeast must have been determined by the compulsions of the *jhum* economy (Dutta 1992: 38-39). Kamei, in this connection, has noted that a tribal community enjoys the prerogative over sharing of the common resources. These are the hills, lands and forests. Membership of a person in a tribal community through blood relations and kinship entitles him to get access to the resources of the community. His membership of a clan is an important status or criteria for getting access to the resources of the village. It is in this context that ethnicity, identity and land ownership are inextricably interlinked in the tribal society (Kamei 2009: 102-103). Shimray wrote that the Naga concept of land includes village land, territory, forests, economy and culture. At the same time, they are the objects which they possess and control that are inherited and immutable. Nagas have their own way of understanding land and its implications. Such implications manifest through their daily activities and livelihood. Moreover, land is the basic foundation of the Naga social, cultural and economic systems. Within the given village territory and its ecosystem, the values, the beliefs and cultural practices are regulated by traditional social institutions. Land and forests provide security and a sense of belongingness. Naga historical tradition is strongly linked with the land they live on. Land is more than just a habitat or a political boundary; it is the basis of their identity (Shimray 2009: 247).

The cumulative outcome of land-based identity is the source of both pride and prejudice of the tribal communities of Northeast India. These two outcomes had two ramifications: while they acted as a binding force, they also otherised one tribe against the other. Otherisation often led to inter-tribe conflict and identity scramble. The inter-tribal conflict was often manifested in land boundary disputes between the tribes, who have lived in "accidental proximity" with each other. Boundary, as an institution of the state was responsible for scrambled identity of the borderlanders of Assam-Nagaland, Manipur-Nagaland, Tripura-Bangladesh, Assam-Meghalaya, Meghalaya-Sylhet and so on. Much of these conflicts emerged because of territorialisation of the ethnic spaces and institutionalisation of the cartographic boundaries by the colonial and the post-colonial states.

The post-independence institutional accumulation process started with land reform programmes of the states that were at the core of the troubled identity of the ethnic groups. In Northeast India, the homogeneous land reform agenda of the state governments and individuation of land rights challenged the historical presence of the communal equalitarian land system in the hills. The land reform programme denied usufructuary rights of the community members and the custodial right of the clan or the headman over the communal land. In Manipur, for example, the Land Revenue and Land Reforms Act was passed in 1960, that excluded the Hill areas from its purview. The Act was extended to the Hill areas first by an amendment in 1975. The extension of the Act in the hill areas was again an act of spatial extension of the Land Revenue Act that created identity tension of the tribes. They feared the hegemony of the valley economy of which the land revenue and land reforms act was a part. The hill people were apprehensive of losing their identity resulting from settlement of the plain people on the hill lands. In Tripura, the tribal identity was worse scrambled, when the state patronised the refugees from Bangladesh to settle on tribal land and engaged them in wet-rice cultivation for revenue generation. This rendered the tribal people landless and led to the growth in the number of tribal agricultural labourers in Tripura. The host of legislative and policy measures from the colonial to post-colonial times for revenue generation and for establishing absolute property rights in land resulted in gross misappropriation of the hill resources leading to massive annihilation of the community ownership of land. Both the colonial and post-colonial forest administration restricted the access of the local communities to land and shifted the regulatory power to the state agencies. By the strength of the eminent domain, the state took control and ownership of all land-based resources. The new institutional measure for recording of land rights was introduced, which divorced the community, whose land rights were not recorded.

The process of institutional accumulation of resources hit at the core of the land-based identity of the tribes and this accumulation was extended further into the hills. In Nagaland, establishing the right over salt wells by the East India Company, imposition of house tax on some chiefs, the series of punitive expeditions, erection of boundary pillars and permanent embankment, revenue triangular masonry pillars, proclamation of the Inner Line Regulation, transfer of Naga territories to Assam, tea plantation, control of tax-revenue and trade, Jhum Regulation, and plantation economy, broke the traditional ties between the original settlers of Assam and Nagaland. This was done by application of certain sections of the Assam Land Regulation 1886, in the Naga Hills. The land-based identity of the Nagas became subject to colonial recognition, like the Lushai, Khasi and the Garo chiefs. The Baliapara Frontier Jhum Land Regulation 1947 made a difference by acknowledging customary land right to the tribes that included individual ownership. But this recognition was conditional and individual ownership of land was eventually established within the main framework of communal possession. The communal land was brought under a controlled legal regime subject to acquisition for public purposes. The trivialisation of customary rights had a strong bearing on the identity of the communities. The Arunachal Pradesh (Land Settlement and Records) Act-2000, governmentalised rights over land and individual rights could be accrued only within the governmentalized frame. Mizoram introduced the Patta System, replaced shifting cultivation (as per NLUP) and undertook different institutional measures to change cropping and land use pattern. This destroyed the essentialism of the land-based identity of the Mizo society. The institution of District Council transferred the decision-making power of the tribes on land to the Council and broke the corporate life of the tribal communities to scramble their identity. As production relations had to do with institutional innovation and as both had a bearing on the identity formation process, the predatory production relations and the equally predatory institutions deformed their identity. This had exactly happened with the tribal people in Northeast India. In Tripura, the shift from the tributary mode to the taxation mode led to the growth of wage labour. In Mizoram, the growth economics of the state converted the poor people to wage labour. In Nagaland, the customs of communal labour by the 'field companies' died out when the government took institutional measures to replace *jhum* cultivation by terrace cultivation.

A big blow to tribal identity came from the other angle of an exogenous paradigm of development and the related institutions. The policy makers and planners found the Northeast region a food deficit region with lower productivity of land from shifting cultivation. Efforts were made to replace the non-surplus yielding shifting cultivation by the land reforms programme and to institutionalise sedentary cultivation. This reform became highly contentious and created a serious development dilemma. The basic contradiction was between the hard core institutional economics of the Indian state and the moral economics of the tribal communities. Land in institutional economics came to be perceived as a revenue yielding entity where both production and productivity occupied the central stage, whereas the same in moral economics was perceived as a place for subsistence production and social reproduction. Roy Burman noted that access to land and land-based production and transaction among peasants and tribals were tied up with diverse historic-ecological contexts. The societal obligations stood as counterparts of rights at different levels much of which was stuck in the feudal and semi-feudal political economy. Though the freedom struggle demands were met by abolition of feudal and semi-feudal impositions, the perspective statement about land reform programmes remained silent about the strategy of transformation of pre-feudal, feudal and semi-feudal obligations into communitarian obligations based on the principle of socialist humanism (Roy Burman 1991: 18-19).

The most critical dilution happened when the fate of the tribal communities was tagged with the historic trajectory of private property under British colonialism that introduced the Permanent Settlement of Bengal 1793. This was extended in the post-independence property rights regime. "Interestingly, the power of eminent domain gained constitutional primacy over the right to property in India at the behest of land reforms for redistributive justice"(Sampat 2013: 41). In post-colonial India, this negotiation did not die out. At the country level, there were serious judicial involvements on the issue of property rights till the same was displaced from Part III of the Constitution and was diverted to non-fundamental rights. The Green Revolution model of the 1960s, transgressed from institutional to technological factors that led to rapid expansion of tube-well irrigation in the Green Revolution belt. It simultaneously caused an identity shift of the peasantry to wage-labour, in which the growth objective trivialised the benefit and equity objectives. The tenancy model on the other hand, envisaged a peasant society, an experimentation on which was done in Kerala through the Kerala Land Reforms Act of 1963 and in West Bengal through the 'Operation Burga' in the 1970s (Ray 2004). The capitalist model in Punjab and Haryana well superseded the peasant society by "post-peasant" society and changed the concept of labour upon which a peasant society was based. This model established distinct economic categories and structured classifications in the rural society (Ray 2004), opposed to the tenancy model. The welfare state of India was, thus, tossing between the two contradictory ideological frames of peasant economy vis-à-vis farm economy and re-distributive economy vis-à-vis capitalist economy, while the land system in the hills of Northeast India was sandwiched between the two.

In the hill areas of Northeast India on the other hand, the peasantry shift of the Punjab type did not happen. The planners and policy makers had an empirico-positivistic orientation about land reforms. This orientation made them introspect into the broader spectrum of economic democracy and to brand-categorise the metropolitan land owning system, and hence, the land reform programme. The land reform programme, was later imposed on the tribal land system, the complicated nature of which never fitted with the formal land reform programme. The crisis was both institutional and identity-related. The land reform and revenue administration of the states of the North Eastern region miserably failed to see the land system of the tribe as a historico-ontological product, a marker of common identity and community consciousness. These trivialised the complementarity between the 'economic' and the 'social' in the tribal society and caused serious ideological and epistemological dissonance between the so-called "little tradition" of the tribes and the "great tradition" of the Indian state. In the hills of Northeast India, the land system that is primarily based on customary laws—saw the land reforms programme and individual titles with a great deal of suspicion. The ideological conflict around the two institutions—tribal and state—therefore lay in, what Roy Barman said, "the distinction between the title to land, particularly, in the Western sense of the term and the actual user of the land. Here one often comes across the conflict between statutory title to land and traditional land use pattern. The state may lay claim to areas on land which are 'unused' or 'vacant' but, in fact, the right to use these lands under the traditional system may be well defined and accepted. In numerous instances, this failure to distinguish between statutory and traditional titles has resulted in a shortfall in lands said to be available for a project" (Roy Barman 1991: 20). He then raised the questions on nature of use. "Is the land use permanent or shifting? What is the status of the person using the land? In many instances, where only one crop is cultivated, land is used successively. That is, it produces a crop in one season, and in the off-season it is used by graziers. Specific social arrangements may permit and support concurrent use of land, another having the right to the trees on the land." "With regard to land held and used in common, other inquiries are required to determine who has the right to use it, how it is used, whether the use is seasonal, who controls use and whether any fees are charged for use. An analysis of land pattern must also examine tree cultivation patterns, attitude towards tree, the effect of planting trees on land ownership, titles, species preferences and cultural practices with regard to trees" (Roy Burman 1991: 20-21). The major changes in the land use pattern in the tribal areas of the hill region were greatly influenced by a mix of the state policy of the Tribal Panchshil, allowing the tribal people to live according to their genus on the one hand and gross accumulation of communal land resources for 'public purposes' on the other. The liberal paradigm of development demanded revenue generation and settled cultivation as an ideal practice. This, in turn, required proper land record and more importantly a legal person for ownership and use of land. Community was not considered as a person as per the legal definition of ownership. In the traditional land ownership system of Northeast India, the issue of 'legal person' came in a big way with the extension of the state land revenue and land reform acts in the tribal areas. The nature of the practice of shifting cultivation being what it is, the issue of 'legal person' often confounded the communal perception on land. The government tended to control shifting cultivation by alternative use of land for agro-forestry; horticulture and commercial cropping that could yield both surplus and rent. The institutional alternatives left erosive ramifications on the essentialism of the tribal collective identity. The *jhumia* colonisation scheme in Tripura, for example, introduced private ownership of land with heritable and transferable right and money economy that lured the traders and the moneylenders. This led to mortgage of their land, which their passed on to the hands of the non-tribals. Even within the tribal communities, there emerged a tendency of land concentration in fewer hands (Saha 1987: 24) who managed to become 'legal persons' while the rest of the community people survived with community perception about land use.

Thus tribal identity faced a two-way pressure from the external forces as well as from the internal forces. The *jhumia* colonisation scheme also entailed an unfavourable change in the occupational structure and in the concept of labour under the private ownership of land in the colonies. Introduction of private ownership of land led to usury and debt. What is most derogatory is the loss of social security the community enjoyed under the communal ownership of land. The state-sponsored programme of *jhumia* rehabilitation often tended to miss the point that the community construct of land is distinct from the state construct and the communal identity is distinct from the state-constructed identity. The tribal identity is formed around the immediate environment and land on which they heavily depend. Conversion of community land converted the organic part of the social economy and upset the tribal culture and its sacrosanctity. The semantic transformation of land, thus, brought about by institutional economics also caused somatic detachment of the tribal community from land. The harvest festivals like Kawnpui and Fano Dawi (a festival held to ensure lucky in hunting in the new year to ensure good crops), Chapacharkut (*jhum* harvest feast) and Pawl Kut (thanks-giving) among the Lushais, for example, gave way in course of the changing land use pattern. Reconstruction of space for commercial use was reductionist in nature that gave space to the crafty players both outside and within the community. Moreover, community orientation of land to family orientation, as the NLUP in Mizoram insisted, added further criticality to the communal land-related identity of the tribe.

Change in land use pattern of the tribals in the post-liberal phase, affected the land-man relations and led to an encounter with the commercial use of land. Such an identity encounter was not merely ethno-political, it was an encounter against the larger forces of the accumulators. Dasgupta has found that the Dumbur Hydro-electric project deprived the settled tribal farmers of their lands who fell back on *jhuming*. Commercial cropping replaced subsistence cropping and the more prosperous families emerged as de facto owners of land to grow commercial crops. There emerged two sets of labour among the *jhumias*—those, who depend on their own or family labour for *jhum* and those who hired labour against payment of cash or kind. Hired labour was a result of product mix. Hired labour replaced the reciprocity of labour and growing monetisation of the *jhum* economy gave birth to absentee landlordism. These developments led to the demise of exchange of labour and demise of the *Kar worship,* when a group of villagers used to assert their joint right over a specific area of land, where they would *jhum* in a particular year. Market behaviour and kinship behaviour became incompatible (Dasgupta 2004: 236-40).

Development-induced displacement was rationalised by the state through a number of factors including economic reconstruction, resource nationalism, eminent domain, public interest, rehabilitation schemes, land grants and model villages. Literature is not paltry that all these did violence to justice to the tribal communities and to their identity. The model village scheme in Tripura became a big flop and the rehabilitation schemes faced a similar fate. The tribal people faced the brunt of development by losing lands, home and livelihood. They also lost the age-old community bond and the organic unity of the community.

Som made a study on the Riang tribes in north Tripura. Plantation villages were classified into three sets: Traditional Village Set (TV Set) located at a distance from rubber plantation centres; Settled Village Set (SV Set) located at the fringe of the rubber plantation centres and Forest Village Set (FV Set) set up under the Soil Conservation (Forestry) Scheme. In the three village sets changes in occupational structure and organisation of labour were different. While in the TV Set *jhuming* continued as the mainstay of the majority, in the SV Set, the basic economic structure revolved around agricultural work supplemented by industrial work; there was occupation mix and a complicated division of labour. In the FV Set, the basic economic structure revolved around industrial work supplemented by agricultural work. In the TV Set, organisation of labour remained traditional while it was marginally affected in the FV Set. In the FV Set it was significantly affected (Som 1991: 115, 116- 124). Space re-engineering of the Riang villages through artifactual classification by set led to serious dislocation of community from land, change in occupational structure within the same geographical space and eventual identity scramble.

Sengupta found major changes in the Riang tribe in terms of shift from labour of household kin to hired labour, who also worked in *jhum* cultivated areas. Due to scarcity of land the area of *jhum* cultivation began to be taken on rent from other tribes. This altered the traditional communal ownership of land and agricultural produce and forced many Riangs to work under other tribals. This widened the intra-tribal social differentiation and altered the political power in the region. As a part of the resettlement process, the tribals were given lands for permanent settlement. In South district, a large number of Riangs became settled cultivators, who eventually became the affluent class and also took other employment opportunities. They started the practice of hiring the Riang labourers to cultivate on their fields. This led to class division and social stratification in the once egalitarian society. She wrote that initially plain lands were given to the Riangs for settlement. However, with the increase of refugees and reduced availability of land the *Jhumias* were resettled in the flat hills. With the help of the Rehabilitation and Plantation Corporation and the Tribal Welfare Development Board, the government resettled some of the *Jhumia* families, giving them household and business opportunities in rubber plantations (Sengupta 2003: 63). *Jhum* cultivation to settled cultivation and subsistence economy to commercial cultivation in Tripura caused a serious scramble of identity. The process of primitive accumulation and accumulation by dispossession divided the community in a class line by erasing all the markers of community identity. The macro-economic integration process really disintegrated and deconstructed the community, its population composition, its land resources and its communal forms of labour and brought the community within the framework of a regimented class society.

The growth focus of institutional economics both in the liberal and in the neoliberal frames of development also destroyed the myth and the belief system of the tribal people. In Arunachal Pradesh, the Talon/Debang Multipurpose Project did greatly affect the Idu community's traditions, customs, faith and belief that were greatly attached to the river Talon/Debang. The construction of the dam heralded the end of their culture and tradition as *India Together* reported on February 17, 2008:

> The river Talon/Debang is sacred to us, as is the river Ganga to the Hindus...... We believe that after the death the lgu-myi (First Order Priest) Sineru carries forward our soul through the river. The hills, the rivers and the mountains are deeply embedded in our ethos. It is the life force of our community. Destruction of these will be a threat to the community itself. Development at the cost of culture is not acceptable to us.

Box 4.1: Interaction with Lizum Nochi, an activist

The Debang Multipurpose Dam Project displaced only a few families but the land area under the project was quite big. The proposed dam has every risk of downstream effect in Roing. The local people did not know about the MoUs between the private companies and the government. The private companies made upfront money payment to the government. The government also did not let the people know about this deal. The people were informed about the government deals with private companies through the NGOs. The project affected shifting cultivation land, wet-rice cultivation fields, forest produce and land-base identity of the people. Nochi further said, 'the Idu people still believe in their forest-based identity; they talk to every creature of nature, every tree of nature. If you cut the trees, it hits at the very soul of the people'. (An interaction with Lijum Nochi by the authors in Tripura University on January 9, 2015.)

Box 4.2: The Tipaimukh Dam and the Zaliangrong Community

The Zaliangrong people who live in these areas, live in a well-knit web of community life. Their ancestral emotional bonds to their land, the mother earth, constitute their cultural and psychological frame that cannot be compromised or negotiated. The dam on the Ahu (Barak) waterfalls, the biggest and the most beautiful natural gift in Manipur, will destroy an important aspect of their heritage—the innumerable lores and legends which are an inalienable part of their bank of memories inherited through centuries. The high water mark of the dam will also destroy five most important lakes located just above the Ahu water falls where the magical sword of Jodonang, the national hero of the Nagas, is believed to be hidden. All these priceless and inalienable parts of their cultural heritage cannot be left to the mindless destruction by the dam project authorities.

(Source: Manirul Hassan, State, Development and Population Displacement in Northeast India, in C. Jasua Thomas edited, *Dimension of Displaced People in Northeast India*. New Delhi, Regency Publications, 2002).

Referring to the Garo Hills, Karlsson noted that on privatisation of land, other aspects of their social life were affected. This posed a threat to the family system, created a new landholding section of people, reversed the gender dimension of *jhum* cultivation; converted the female land ownership system towards male ownership, the matrilineage and matrilocal systems and declined female labour input (Karlsson 2011: 14). The state-sponsored change in the land use pattern towards individuation and its eventual impact on the erstwhile land relations and collective identity became more pronounced. In the context of the market economy, the choice of cropping pattern has changed towards cash crop. The Shivaraman Committee recommended gradual introduction of settled cultivation and the NEC has expedited this process through various alternative schemes (Datta 1992: 43). The joint effort of the North Eastern Council and the state governments to stop shifting and adopt settled cultivation and state acquisition of land as per respective land laws, over which no individual or joint ownership rights exist in the settlement records (Ganguli 2004: 112,116, 117), added to the criticalities and further problematised the communal land-based identity of the tribes. But 'the state's argument of higher land erosion due to shifting cultivation in the Northeast remained without any proof' (Datta 1992: 42).

Such a state of affairs invited two criticalities: one is, Northeast India being predominantly an ethnic region raised the question as to who owns the land resources—the ethnic community or the state? The conflict between the state region and ethnic region, and between state right and the community right surfaced at the dawn of colonisation itself and this conflict died hard in the post-colonial times. By virtue of the forest laws, government could convert the community land (wasteland, as in Assam) into government property and could enclave those areas as Reserved or Protected areas for commercial use. In Assam, Handique noted, the concept of 'Block' was introduced by the Forest Department under which certain tracts of the forest reserve were allotted to the contractors for exploitation (Handique 2004: 115). The reserved forests became the de-communitised zones. The policy creation of the reserve enclaves of forest let loose the community-enclave tension first and community-state tension later. This created considerable tension between the tribal identity as a social construct and that as a state construct. The official epistemology of land reforms and the processual epistemology of the tribal communities could never be reconciled in the true sense of the term.

Roy Burman noted that "Land reforms as presumably conceptualised by international agencies like the FAO and as spelt out in the national programme in India, are heavily biased in favour of settled agriculturists"(Roy Burman 1991: 17-18) congenial to the market economy. Settled agriculture also bred the vicious land-power nexus and class differentiation. He reminded us that in most of the hills of Northeast India, dependence on forest products was much more than in the central tribal belt and drew our attention to the fact that "access to land for land-based production and transactions among the peasants and tribals is tied up with diverse systems of the moral economy in diverse historic-ecological contexts. There are societal obligations as counterparts of the rights at different levels" (Roy Burman 1991: 18). The trade-off between empirico-positivistic orientation (tied up with legal positivism) and historic-comparative method (tied up with legal pluralism) (Roy Burman 1991: 18) had a strong bearing both on land use pattern and on land relations and identity in the hills of Northeast India. Although many international agencies like the Ford Foundation and the World Bank talked about social capital as the software part of development', the tougher conditionalities of property right and Rule of Law in the neoliberal era came to protect the property right of the investors and their cronies to destroy the land-based identity of the tribal people. These international agencies adopted a sanitised participatory approach to development to mystify the ordinary people about the predatory nature of this approach.

The growing crisis arising out of commercial and corporate use of land struck at the archaic land relations and folk profession of the tribal people. Growing land displacement and eventual pauperisation of the tribal people as a result of land grabbing and failure to cope with the market economy led to many negative consequences on the tribes and all of them faced the common consequences both in the Fifth and the Sixth scheduled areas of the country. The Report of the Working Group on land relations for formulation of the Eleventh Five Year Plan found several reasons for alienation: i) Sale and transfer of land by tribals to other tribals and non-tribals; ii) Indebtedness; iii) Forcible eviction/unauthorized occupation by non-tribals or by public authorities; iv) Conversion of communal ownership to individual ownership; v) Increasing urbanisation; vi) Treating the tribal community as encroachers; vii) Government land allotted to tribals under various schemes without substantive possession; viii) Environment-disturbing developments close to tribal habitats, forcing the tribals to move out, though there is no formal transfer and acquisition of land. The Eleventh Plan Document (Vol: 3) also echoed the same problems in the tribal society and admitted the fact that community ownership continues to be the dominant mode in tribal societies and takes precedence over individual ownership (Report of the Working Group on Land Relations. 2006. Planning Commission).

The pertinent question that can be raised here is against whom the state applies the power of eminent domain and whose lands are acquisitioned with more ease? The review of the literature reveals that it is mainly the marginal communities like the tribes, whose resources were dispossessed and it is the unwritten nature of the customary land system that privileged the process of dispossession. The unwritten natuure of customary law conveniently turned the community land into *terra nullius* which was then easily acquired by the state or grabbed by the corporate cronies without facing any legal litigation. The simple logic of accumulation by dispossession was that the more the land system is uninstitutionalised, the easier is the task of accumulation. Sampat, thus, aptly noted that "the extent and range of the exercise of eminent domain has historically largely depended on whom it is directed towards—the more economically, socially and politically the targets, the easier to acquire their land and resources" (Sampat

2013: 41). Updation of land records, as per the Eleventh Plan Document, is nothing new. Record of right is a state agenda of land privatisation. This goes against the essentials of community

Box 4.3: Changing Trends in Rights Perception and Identity

Individual Rights on Communal Land

In some Kuki villages in Churachandpur the chiefs became private land owners and many elites established new villages to avail themselves of the various government schemes. On introduction of MGMNREGA many such new villages came up that were registered under the law of the land. Many of these villages did not have physical existence or did not have villagers. The purpose of establishing such villages was to derive the benefits from the government schemes. These people used their cultivable land and forest areas as collateral for government loans. Private purchase became the usual practice which was eventually recognised by government through grant of patta. In this process many women also managed to get land registered in their own names.

Non-Resident Chiefs (NRC)

Emergence of 'absentee chiefs' or the 'non-resident chiefs' (NRC) is a new phenomenon among the Kukis in Manipur. These chiefs reside in the urban locations which has created a communication gap between the villagers and the chiefs. Most of the time these chiefs revert money from various development schemes meant for the village to their personal benefit. They ignore the welfare of the villagers while they settle in faraway places in the city with all sorts of city comforts. These chiefs cannot be removed as they became chiefs by inheritance as per the customary laws.

Payment of Tributes

In the post-independence period, many villagers stopped paying customary tributaries to the Kuki chiefs. The chiefs also abdicated their custodial right over forest and village land and started selling the forest trees and the culturable land for money income. In some villages, the chiefs allowed the households of other villages to cultivate land within their village against receipt of annual tax. In this process, many Nepali cultivators penetrated into the cultivable lands of the Kukis at the foothills.

land as a social arrangement and breaks the land-based identity of the tribal people. Several critical questions can again be raised: whose lands the RoR will record? Who form the community? What is their identity and in whose name would the community lands be recorded? The larger possibility as per the rules of RoR is that the old colonial jurisprudence of *res nullius* would be progressively invoked to annihilate the beneficiaries of the communal ownership of land. Therefore, the institutional innovations in the contemporary context are highly likely to throw the rank and file of the tribal communities of Northeast India out of their land and identity to a community-less, lumpen state.

The positivist- naturalist trade-off on land rights considered the communal land as a mere concession-subject to be removed and annihilated at any convenient point of space and time by the state. The power of eminent domain remained in the hands of the state and the state, therefore, enjoyed considerable advantage for deliberate removal and annihilation of communal right in the pretext of 'public interest'. In this trade-off, a section of the tribal communities—relatively educated and enlightened—sided with the state. This section constituted the elites of the tribal communities. They surrendered the traditional value attached to community land, while at the same time, retained the customary right as an ideological instrument in the otherwise ideology-less situation.

Elite-Mediated Identity

Guha found emergence of a small stratum of middle class people of local origin which were not in existence there earlier. Formation of Jaintia Darbar in 1900, the Khasi National Darbar in 1923 and the Khasi States Federation in 1934 were marked by a conflict between the *Siyems* and those, who grabbed communal land on the one hand and the commoners on the other. In Mizoram and in other hills, communal ownership over land progressively gave way to the rise of private property. Some sixty hereditary chiefs, deemed as owners of the soil, ruled over the people and the district magistrate ruled over them. The formation of an educated, Christian elite helped the process (Guha 1988: 322). Even under the terms of the Nine Point Agreement (known as the Hyderi Agreement) with the NNC, the NNC was made responsible for the imposition, collection and expenditure of land revenue, House Tax and other taxes as might be imposed by it (Guha 1988: 326) though this was something ridiculous on the part of the state.

Elite-mediated ethnic identity marked the departure from the primordial essentialism based on land-community-kin convergence. It became more a part of 'Self-Categorisation' of identity distinct from historico-anthropologically evolved collective consciousness and identity. The identity reconstruction like this, became manipulative, subjective and community-neutral. Elite-mediated identity emerged in the tribal society first in the colonial context, in which, the concept of ethnicity got significantly disembedded from its original social and cultural milieu. The elites reproduced a kind of ethnic image against the primordial essentialism and acted instrumental to colonial capture of the community resources. The instrumental nature of the elite mediated ethnic identity, at that stage, fulfilled the material and political interests of the colonisers, who pejorised historic-anthropological construct of ethnicity through racialisation of the tribal communities. Ethnic identity, in this sense, became essentially a colonial fiction away from the anthropological reality. Elite-mediation in identity formation emerged first from the primordial institutions of chieftainships that romanticised their mythical status and, under the British protection, built a new patron-client relationship with the members of the community. The Khasi *Siyems*, Mizo and Kuki chiefs, to mention a few, fell in this category. They worked in favour of the colonial accumulators, who could in turn, successfully win over the traditional power elites in two ways: (a) by allowing prescriptive rights to them against certain assigned duties that were not there in the tradition. In order to entrench the accumulated wealth of the colonials from the wrath of the community people, the British also allowed them to exercise their traditional authoritative powers towards the community people. This helped the colonials to rule the community and exploit the communal resources with less administrative cost. (b) In case of any recalcitrance on the part of these chiefs, the institutional power was let loose against them. By these two instruments, the British could evince a new cropping pattern and new land-use pattern that could yield profit-revenue. These elite-chiefs were also allowed to lease-out mining activities as in the Khasi Hills to the outsiders, from which the colonials could also amass a substantial volume of profit-revenue. In this way, the Khasi *Siyems* of Meghalaya and the Lushai-Kuki-Zomi chiefs of Manipur and Mizoram could amass a huge amount of personal wealth, so much so, that their personal sophistication and life-style could contest any affluent Westerner.

The spectator posture of the rank and file of the community at this point of time, also facilitated the process of accumulation of communal resources without much popular resistance. It was through these elite-chief-colonial nexus that 'occupancy' of land was transformed into 'ownership'; ceased to be a 'sacred' entity and became a commodity. In the Khasi and Jaintia Hills the position of the chiefs was legalised as landlords. In Garo Hills, the Nokmas were virtually made the proprietors of their respective domains by demarcating the boundaries and by offering them the documents of possession. In the Lushai Hills, the same was achieved by offering boundary paper (Ramrilekhas).

With the growth of trade in horticultural goods and minerals, the concept of private property in land had already crept in and the *Siyems, Dolois, Wahadadars* and other dignitaries became the biggest landlords in the Khasi Hills. The Khasi state virtually was an estate that did not deter the landlords to levy rent upon tenants or extract crop share from them. Collection of market levies from the traders was another source of their earning which increased manifold after the British suzerainty over the Khasi Hills (Misra 1983: 18-19). The Khasi *Siyems* with the backing of the colonial power started to claim the status of Zamindars in the communal lands (*Ri Raid*) and to issue formal lease deeds to their own people on strict conditionality bases. Misra has mentioned an example of such lease deed forms in Balat and Ranikor in a Khasi state.

Box 4.4: Lease Form Issued by the *Siyem*

The land————— leased out for cultivation in Lawmyrlaw is the Re Kynti of three clans (1)Kharthongni Ryia (2) Bangto and (3) Paliar and situated in Nongla within Hima Maharam.

We, the main representatives and administrators of the three clans who are the owners of the Re Kur Re Kynti Lawanyriau in Nongnah within Hima Maharam give this in writing to you U ka———— ———————— of ———— crops in the plots named ——— ——— about ——— by——— in area within the Re Kur Re Kynti of our three clans and that this portion of the land so leased out has been shown to you. You will cultivate this land according to the terms and conditions given below:-

The lease will be valid for one crop season only.

You will not cultivate more land than what is given to you.

You will pay without fail during harvest the rent upon this land at the rate of one-fifth of the produce or according to the changes made from time to time.

If you cut the forest and do not sow without any valid reason then you must pay compensation for the damage to the forest caused by you.

You are not allowed to sublet the land without first obtaining the permission from us, the landlords.

If you do not take due care and abandon this land, it will be taken back from you.

You are not permitted to put fire in this land.

You are not allowed to construct houses except field sheds.

You will obey correctly all the terms and conditions.

Dated Domoskhai Signature

The ———19..

On behalf of the three clans of Nongna 1 U ka———— of ——— take this plot of land on lease for cultivating————— from you, the landlords, according to the terms and conditions above. I promise to obey all these and if I violate any you, the landlords, will take back the land immediately from me.

Dated Domoskhai

The ———19......

Signature of leasee

Witness (1)

(2)

(Source: Misra 1979, p. 891)

Box 4.5: Form of the Office of the *Siyem* of Maharam)

Patta No——————— of 1968——————— dated Mawkyrwat the ——————————— 1968.

To

U/Ka————— village——————— Maharam Siyemship.

This lease (patta) is given to you by me so that you may cultivate the paddy field in the area called——————within the Reid Balat and Ranigor, the dimension of the land being ————————*kiar* as per the boundaries shown below:-
North————— East————— South———— West—————

You will observe the following terms and conditions:-

(1) You must renew this patta and pay duely the lease money (*bai patta*) before 31 March of every year.
(2) That you will not sell, mortgage or transfer the land in any manner without the knowledge and sanction of the *Siyem*.
(3) That you will have no claim upon this land given on lease to you if you leave Hima Maharam or give up possession for three years or if you do not pay regularly the khajana (*bai khajana*)
(4) If you violate any of the conditions of the patta the Siyem will take away your rights.

Signed

Siyem of Maharam *Siyemship*

I agree to abide by the terms and conditions made above in full faith and knowledge without being compelled by anyone.

Leasee

(Source: Misra 1979, p. 892)

Through these instruments, the *Siyems* in the Khasi Hills did institutionalise the practice of primitive accumulation through leasing out lands against monetary gains. In this process, they changed their identity as 'pseudo zamindars', broke the relational character of *Siyemship* organisation and turned the latter to contractual relations. The people, who took the land lease, also accepted them as landlords and as per the lease deed, build a rent paying relation. A bigger blow to identity came when the *Siyems*, who leased out the land, still claimed to be the administrators of the respective clans.

The lease patta was issued on *Raid* land (community land). The leasee got cropping and cultivation rights over the plot of land on which they were not allowed to construct houses. For them, the *Siyems*, not the state, became the right giving authorities over which the *Siyems* established their rights through primitive accumulation. The *Siyems* also started to indiscriminately leaser-out *Ri Raid* land to both Khasis and non-Khasis for cultivation. Under these circumstances, people from outside the *Raid* could also grab land by means of patta. Ironically, those who lost land, were the people from the *Raid* whereas, those who profited were from the towns. In the Garo villages, a class of landed gentry, mainly absentee landlords in nature, emerged.

Referring to the Lushais, Das wrote that the British government considered the chiefs to be their friends, whose assistance was necessary for peaceful governance of the territories of the Lushai hills. He followed N.E. Parry, who said that it is desirable that in the governance of his village, a chief should not be interfered with and that his orders should not be upset unless glaring injustice was manifest. The rules for the administration of the Lushai Hills and the instructions for the Assistants to the Superintendent of the Lushai Hills contained in the printed file of standing orders are still in force. Parry also stated that unless the authority of the chiefs was maintained, it would be practically impossible to run the district administration with less expense and with less staff. Rule by the chief, as the indigenous form of government, had grown with the people and suited their needs, and the chiefs were looked upon with respect. It was desirable, therefore, that "in the management of the village, a chief should be given as free a hand as possible"(Das 1990: 12,13).

Colonial education and evangelisation opened up new opportunities to the emerging Naga elites for different professions. This not only caused a shift in their lifestyle but also caused a shift in the agricultural practices. The economic development within the Naga society "expanded social division of labour and served to modify the tribal organisation of settled agricultural villages". Moreover, many war returnees, who served the Allied Forces during the First World War came home with "enough money to become petty landlords". All these led to emergence of an elite class in Naga society. The British administration introduced a hierarchy-based on their bureaucratic organisation. (Sanyu 1988: 439-440).

In Manipur, Col. J. Shakespeare was appointed as the Political Agent in 1906-07. He made demarcation of tribal land and issued paper similar to Ramrileika, to the different chiefs and headmen of the tribes. This paper was given to the Kuki tribes to settle them in strategic locations so that the latter could act as buffer against the recalcitrant Naga and the Lushai tribes, who were carrying out sporadic violence on the borderlines of the British territories. This paper was based on a geographical marker of certain land sphere. Though it was not 'patta' it was as good as the 'patta' system. This arrangement of land grant strengthened chiefs' right over land and his political hold over the community that were not there in their original social and political formations. The British, in this way, regularised and incorporated the tribal chieftains in the colonial administrative system and such incorporation became a unique mode of primitive accumulation and accumulation by dispossession. Through the chiefs, the colonials collected House Tax from the tribal households without enroaching on the powers of the chiefs. In the colonial administrative interest their customary laws were remade and reinforced. The chiefs and their lineage eventually got the opportunity to usurp the community resources and to concentrate land in their hands with British patronage. Although they continued to practise shifting cultivation, they used to allot the best part of the land to their councillors and the other parts to the people. It is from this stock of the chiefs that the first generation elites emerged from the Kuki and Lushai chiefs, Khasi Syems, Jaintia and Cachar rulers and so on.

The Chin Hills Regulation 1886, empowered the Superintendent to appoint and remove the headmen, define the limits of their jurisdiction and declare what clan, or village, or both would be subject to him. Though the Superintendent was guided by the customary laws in making a declaration to this effect, in actual practice, the colonial process prevailed over the customary process. Thus, any act of defiance on the part of the community was branded as an act of barbarism, excessive or unusual and liable to punishment. This was akin to the old Anglo-Saxon jurisprudential practice. The Regulation constituted a Sessions division and a District court for criminal, civil, revenue and general purposes, with the Superintendent as the sessions judge. This act also disallowed formation of any new village without the consent of the Superintendent. The Chin Lushai Conference of 1892, resolved to bring the whole tract of Chin-Lushai Hills under one administrative head, subordinate to the Chief Commissioner of Assam. These patronised the chieftains/headmen to assert their influence in the decision-making system of the state. A section of them—relatively educated and enlightened—emerged as new elites in the fields of politics and theology. Another section, seceded from their own community, became urban elites and internalised the Western values. In the post-colonial Indian state, things did not change much and these elites reappeared as the "enlightened others" from within their own communities. Therefore, the process of identity dilution stated in the colonial period, continued in the post-colonial period.

In the spree of encouraging plantation, wide-ranging changes were observed among the Tangkhul Nagas inhabiting the remote hills of Manipur. Land, that was traditionally classified into five different categories, started losing the community connotation as more and more community land began to be usurped by the emerging elites to further their effort of increasing the area under plantation. So, cash crops such as potato, maize, soyabean, millets, sesame, groundnuts, plums, pears, oranges, pineapples, bananas, along with a variety of vegetables gained acreage, causing eventual transfer of community land (Chakraborty 2010: 10). The tribal elites played the trump card of tradition to usurp community land either by erecting fences or by other forms of upgradation that could create an ambience of a permanent structure or by improvements made on land. These elites usurped community resources also by selective interpretation of customary law in their personal favour. Therefore, the erstwhile temporary users, on assuming elite status, became the de facto landowners. They did not cultivate themselves but leased-out land to others for cash cropping. They also started to collect land tax from the leasee cultivators. Collection of absolute rent from leased out lands became a new mode of primitive accumulation. Today, this has become a general practice in many areas of the hills like Churachandpur, Ukhrul, Hundung, Phungyar in Manipur, and in different hill areas of Meghalaya and Mizoram.

Saxena stated that in the 1980s, there were efforts to prepare land records in Meghalaya as absence of the same led to concentration of land in the hands of a few elites. This effort of the government faced mass resistance. The small holders suspected that the state would impose land tax once land rights were recorded. The elites were able to whip up tribal sentiments against the government. Though it was clarified that it had no intention to impose land tax on the surveyed land, people were reluctant to allow government to enter and disrupt their community cohesiveness. The poor were not organised. They were tied up in social relations to the elites of their own clan, and to them, the tribal land owners were greater benefactors than the remote, heartless and corrupt government. Even when the survey would have benefited the poor, they chose to support the clan leaders in opposing preparation of land records (Saxena

2005: 314). Concentration of land in fewer hands and the problem of rising landlessness among the tribal society, therefore, became an alarming problem in the society of highlanders. These changes along with the penetration of the market economy helped the tribal elites to graduate from the rudimentary 'class-in-itself' stage to the 'class-for-itself' stage. These untribal features corrupted the tribal elites of the hills within a short period, which had wide-ranging ramifications for the community as a whole. So penetration of market forces, monetisation of the economy and increase in cash income led to investments in land (Chakraborty 2010: 8) And, yet, these elites continued to ride on the identity consciousness of the tribal community to gain wealth, power and influence.

It is to be noted that identity conflicts in the liberal frame first started against the dominant maze of the nation-state. In the North East, ethno-nationalism emerged with different hues and colours and also mobilised trans-national communities, both for resource raising and for widening their constituency among the ethnic brethren, well beyond the border of the Indian state. This was a classic manifestation to modernity-tradition conflict or core-periphery conflict. But the classic scramble took place when land began to be grabbed by the people of the same community. This scenario, within the tribal societies, was an *'emic'* phenomenon rather than an *'etic'* phenomenon. This created division in the primordial and collective allegiance of the communities to land while the elite concentration of land converged with the state agenda of land privatisation.

Primordialism was used by two sections of tribal elites in two ways. The traditional elites, with the blessings of the colonial power, got a defined *locus standi* on land through various instruments offered by the colonial and post-colonial state and by virtue of these, they tended to maintain their status quo and reacted vehemently to the land reform agenda of the state on the apprehension of losing their land rights. On the other hand, the modern elites, who received education and were more enlightened compared to the traditionalists, built their fates through non-land routes, while at the same time they did not surrender the primordial trump card. This section stood at a different court and reconstituted the land-based identity, unlike the traditionalists, subtly but perceptibly, through mobilising the community in favour of land privatisation. They threw the community into a state of mystification with very simplistic and uncontested historical narratives of land ownership systems, while they themselves created some kind of "nexo-feudal" (Roy Burman 1990: 48) arrangement with the state. This section of elites is visible, for example, among certain sections of the tribes of Manipur, whose personal affluence evokes jealousy. While they kept the community under mystification, extreme subjectivity of this elite class made them engaged in mobilisation of the community for the hedonistic ends in which ethnic identity alone became the focal point, not the class identity that had already emerged. The self-actualisation drive of the ethnic elites managed to emerge also in the political landscape in the Northeast and eventually they came to possess large areas of lands and to convert those into elite enclaves. They made their routes easy to enter and regulate the domestic land market. The elite enclaves, thus made, converted the lived space of the community people to a gentrified space with impersonal relations. The commercial highways, ecologically rich areas, prospective business niches in the hills were of greater attractions to these elites than the remote distant, out-of-the-way places. The gentrified spaces were a unique combination of ecology and economy. The emerging land market in the hill areas, hitherto unknown, allured the elites to capture land. These elites re-articulated land-based identity politics and behind the mask of primordiality, they made such politics a means to fulfil their private agenda. They themselves created economic inequality within the community by wrongful and primitive means of accumulation of land resources and by changing the land-use pattern. Although, technological intervention and modernisation of the productive forces were parts of the convergence programme of the Indian state, these were not well-received concepts in the shifting cultivation economy in Northeast India. Modernisation and technology entered in the hills through the elite route and the elites were highly incentivised for that. Certain contingent factors contributed to elite-mediated identity articulation. These included (i) the Bordoloi Committee's recommendations that the tribals should be vested with powers on land, forest, agriculture, local laws and village and town management; (ii) para 3 of the Sixth Schedule to the Constitution which has provision for allotment, occupation, or use or setting apart of land; (iii) the constitutional provisions of protective discrimination in favour of the scheduled tribes; (iv) the tribal panchshil and not the least, (v) the issue of Bengali infiltration—both the 'surplus Bhadraloks' (gentry) including the clerks, doctors, teachers, and lawyers during the British times and the refugee Bengalis in the post-partition era. The crafty instrumental elites made the best of all or any one of these contingent factors and in this endeavour they were emotionally backed by the rank and file of the tribal community. In this way they were able to reduce the state-community or intra-community conflict over land privatisation by foregrounding and sensitising any of the above factors as critical political issues. The spectator posture of the dispossessed class failed to countervail the emerging trend of the elite's capture of land.

Identity politics quickly resorted to culture as the rallying point of the community and, hence, the course of their movement changed along the culture line deliberately bypassing the issue of privatisation of tribal land. The metaphor of cultural identity, thus, once more mystified the rank and file of the tribal community and diverted them from the unfavourable consequences of wrongful dispossession of the communal resources either by the state or by the corporate bodies or by the elite entrepreneurs. Conway wrote, "the kind of focus on identity, demands identity formation as a contradictory and conflictual social process that forms the basis of any politics, including, the politics of social movements. Identity formation is conceived here as a cultural process having to do with everyday practices that construct people's lived experience, practices that construct identities, procedure, meaning and make sense of the world"(Conway 2007: 25).

The elite-mediated identity in Northeast India made a distinction between the category of primordial-essentialism on the one hand and the category of situational and strategic adjustment on the other. These categories had two contradictory ideological orientations—'*epimethean*' (valuing the past, docile) orientation and '*promethean*' (futuristic changes) orientation. While the first category conceived identity as a product of collective consciousness, belongingness and experiential continuity with the past, the second category conceived identity for the pursuit of personal aggrandisement. Both these categories were subsumed into landed class from within this community either through sale, transfer or lease or through their smarter roles in the unorganised land markets in the tribal and hill areas. This *novo rich* captured the public discourse on land reforms in the hills. They toed with the primitive accumulation path for wealth, affluence and power, and diverted the land privatisation issue towards territorial movement in the hill areas. These movements also in some cases took a militant path for self-determination, secession and even for trans-territorial unification. Such developments completed the process of a scramble of identity initiated by accumulation and dispossession and consequent destruction of the somatic identity of the tribal community. Movements for autonomy and self-determination acted as *momentum catharsis* to the anxieties of the otherwise land-dispossessed poor tribal community. These movements were of an extremely microscopic nature, whereas, land privatisation became a more universal phenomenon in the hills of the Northeast than a particular problem of a single tribe. While the autonomy/sovereignty movements got popularity due to the general problem of regional imbalance in regional economic development, the elite-mediated movements held only the state responsible for resource capture and people's dispossession. In this connection, Karlsson wrote that "people in the Northeast commonly assert that they are being robbed of their natural resources. The oil resources of Assam are commonly used as an example, pointing to the fact that most of the revenue generated are appropriated by Delhi, while only a fraction remains in the state. And this is also claimed for most of the other natural resources in the region, that the entire economic chain is controlled by 'outsiders' and that the profits generated are being rippled off by them. The Indian state is identified as the main instrument in perpetrating the exploitative resources" (Karlsson 2011: 50). He further noted that most of the insurgent groups active in Northeast India make this condition the very *raison de'etre* stating their objective as the liberation of their people/nation from the tyranny or exploitative nature of Indian rule. The majority of the organisations describe their cause as a national one establishing territorial sovereignty for their particular ethnic constituency, be it Nagalim for the Nagas, Bodoland for the Bodos, or Ahom for the people of Assam. Territorial claims often overlap and this has interestingly become a source of inter-ethnic violence and, in some cases, 'ethnic cleansing'. Some organizations seek national liberation within India, with some kind of autonomy arrangements, whereas, others strive for complete independence" (Karlsson 2011: 50-51). At the regional scale, therefore, land became a source of a particular kind of rent-seeking which is of political significance. Absence of a common cause in all these ethnic movements nuclearised the movement and nuclearisation became the usual route of elite articulation of tribal identity in the region. On the other hand, the 'Universal' nature of land privatisation in the hills in the seven states of Northeast India could, alternatively, provide the ideological rallying point for a pan-tribal resistance movement. This did not happen. The elites of the region scotched this possibility by mobilising their own nuclear community around land grabbing and diverted the momentum towards territorial movements {in the same way as the radical left in Bihar diverted their discourse from land reform to politics of backwardness to render land struggle less attractive (Thakkar 2013: 19-20)}.

The elite-mediated identity opened up a critical niche on the Manipur Land Revenue and Land Reforms Act-1960. Within the modernist frame, the elite discourse was bifurcated. One section of the elites opposed the land reform measures under the Manipur Land Revenue and Land Reforms Act, on the ground that this act would put a ceiling on land holding and bring all lands in the hills on record by cadastrally surveying the land. The scope for primitive accumulation of the unrecorded land, communal land was wide open to the elites. Their opposition was not essentially an expression of primordial rejection of the state law but was a calculated and strategic move for primitive accumulation and essentially was an act of *mis-ordered concupiscence*. This section took the position that the Sixth Schedule would act as a shield against state acquisition and would resist land alienation. To countervail the discourse, another section pleaded for extension of the Act in the hill areas of Manipur with the hope of getting ensured and defined property rights title that could act as collateral for bank loans, other kinds of institutional finance and would also open the scope for land speculation sale/purchase, lease, mortgage. The political and social movements led by these two elite groups on the single issue of land reforms in the state of Manipur, therefore, produced two different elite narratives. These groups were reified by the protective role of the Sixth Schedule while both the Sixth Schedule and the Manipur Land Revenue and Land Records Act, as state institutions, had the monopolising power, supersessionary power and the power of eminent domain.

In Mizoram, on the other hand, some elements of primordial essentialism were reflected in the text of the Mizo Peace Accord of 1986 that categorically mentioned that "notwithstanding anything contained in the Constitution, no act of Parliament in respect of religious or social practice of the Mizos, Mizo customary law and procedure, administration of civil and criminal justice, involving decisions according to Mizo customary law and ownership and transfer of land, shall apply to the state of Mizoram unless the legislative assembly of Mizoram by a resolution so decided..." (Lalnithanga 1997: 63-67). In Nagaland, the point 9 of the Hyderi Agreement with NNC in 1947, stated that no alienation of land with all its resources in the Naga Hills could be made except with the consent of the

NNC. While the spirit of the Mizo Accord was to protect the communal land, the state package of land revenue and land reforms made provisions for private ownership of community land. Besides, the subsequent history produced a different narrative when the post-accord elite generation became instrumental in opening up the economy to the global market forces notwithstanding the clause of the Accord. The protective cover on tribal land in Nagaland was often unveiled by state accumulation of community land in public interest and later the private companies got state approval for mining operation's and for enclavisation of communal space by construction of SEZ at the foot hills of Nagaland (Dimapur). The law of the land also kept an 'exception' clause for transfer of *jhum* land outside the village or community with the permission of the Deputy Commissioner. In Nagaland, land gift by the village council to the government also had dispossessing content. These arrangements became self-deceptive and troubled the identity consciousness of the tribal people.

The Tripura Land Revenue and Land Reforms Act 1960 was amended in 1975 enabling the tribes to sell their lands only to the members of their community. It was soon found that this was only an eyewash as very few tribals were in a position to buy such lands. Land changed hands covertly through the administrative manipulation that dispossessed several non-tribals, who had developed the land with hard work. Thus, those who depended on land found it improper, the way land was being taken away from the actual tiller. After the formation of the Tripura Tribal Area Autonomous District Council (TTAADC), those non-tribals, who previously resided in these blocks but were dispossesed of their lands viewed it as a "diabolical scheme sponsored by the lackeys of imperialists. They thought it to be a narrow, selfish interest of the ruling class of exploiters in the tribal society" (Chakravarti 2004: 125). In addition to this, government restriction on shifting cultivation in certain areas and capture of 'Jangal abadi' by the settled cultivators, dispossessed the tribal people, who turned into labourers on their own land. The coveted moves of the non-tribals coaxed the tribals to mortgage their lands to the settlers on the plea of putting such lands for proper use. These mortgagees did not return the lands even after expiry of the mortgage period. It became more contentious in the neoliberal era as the state acquired vast tracts of lands for development and infrastructure projects and transferred the land to the private and corporate cronies and contractors. In this situation, the neo-elites, who took leadership in the land centric movement had also successfully located themselves in the affluent metropolis and with their monetary and political power, acquired land from their traditional areas. In this process, they had virtually staged an exit from their own societies. These lumpenised, de-territorialised tribal elites had captured the public domain, the political space and the policy-making space, where they had re-articulated the land privatisation issue as territorial identity issue.

These developments added new dimensions to the production-relation debate in Northeast India. It can be noted in this connection that the post-colonial and post-liberal land acquisition did not lead to accumulation of capital enough to pioneer an industrial economy in the North East. Northeast India, being a resource rich but capital starved region, did not witness indigenous capital formation and *in situ* development either. The cravings of the emerging elites for ruthless accumulation of land could not build a robust capital base for promoting the home market for manufactured goods and for service industry. The region still has high order dependency on externally manufactured goods and services. This scenario did not lead to "proletarisation" of the tribal people "so much as their pauperisation", as Patnaik would say (Patnaik 1990: 3). While organised land grabbing became a general phenomenon in the tribal societies of the North East, the elites of the region failed to rally people on class lines on a regional scale. This scenario also dethroned the economic debate on land privatisation in the public domain. In this scenario, the land-based identity was once more diverted in spite of the fact that the Naga-Kuki and Kuki-Paite conflicts in Manipur in the 1990s,

Karbi-Kuki conflict (2003), Hmar-Dimasa conflict (2004) and ethnic tension among the Khasi, Jaintia and Garo, Karbi-Kuki conflict in Assam (2003) had deep connection with land. Infiltration threatened the communal land system. Introduction of plough cultivation, encroachment of migrants on tribal land and capture of land by the state or corporates changed the ethnic composition. The boundary alteration and land transfer added to the troubled identity of the tribes. Contest over land resources that is why, became the pivot of inter-tribal, intra-tribal and tribal-non-tribal conflicts. In Manipur, the Kuki-Naga clash started over the resource mobilisation on Moreh border trade between the NSCN and the Kuki National Army. Oinam noted that Moreh was the finance nerve of militant groups of Nagas and Kukis. There were three immediate reasons behind the clash: control and occupation of resources on the border town; tax on Kuki residents in Naga territory by the Naga militants and refusal of the Kukis to pay double tax and refusal to renew land agreements with the Kukis residing in Naga areas (Oinam 2003: 20-21). In Meghalaya, the militant groups acquired "a major portion of their finance by taxing the extraction of natural resources, specially the coal trade, and, earlier, from business in timber. During the height of the coal season, from November to April, when there is less rain and roads and coal pits are dried up, the militants are busy collecting money by erecting road blocks, where every truck has to pay a certain sum to be allowed to pass or by demanding shares of money collected at the official district council gates" (Karlsson 2011: 57). In the Dimasa society, there were intra-tribal skirmishes around the issue of land. Borbora presented the case of land transfer in a Dimasa village called Gunjung. A member of the Daolagpu clan, a permanent business man from Haflong whose family originally hailed from Gunjung, could manage to get the right to infidel patta on land used by the villagers for *jhum*, grazing and collection of forest products. He obtained permanent ownership right over roughly 700 acres of such land for tea plantation in collusion with the headman of Gunjung. The deal was that the villagers would reap the benefit. This happened in

1993 and as of now, there is enough tension within the community (Barbora 2012: 1288).

The Dimasas had an encounter with the Hmars in 2003 that received varied explanations ranging from the land-related grievances to the extremity of the militant groups. The Damasas viewed the presence of Hmars in their lands growing exponentially in the past few decades. Their revolutionary migration and intent on grabbing Dimasa lands was perceived to have a long-term effect on the indigenous Damasas (Asikis 2011: 183). The Hmars were found to encroach on the land and cut timber in the forests of NC Hills. Their inclusion in the NC Hills voter list complicated the situation. A more reasoned factor responsible for this conflict is the business and literary skill of the Hmars that made them competitors in the Dimasa land and in grabbing the region's resources at the cost of the Dimasas (Asikis 2011: 184-186). On the other hand, the political movement of the Missing Students' Organisation for the Sixth Schedule status was based on the perception that the latter could give legislative, administrative and judicial powers over a number of policy areas, including land regulation, natural resource management, customary law and taxation (Asikis 2011: 127).

With the changes of land use and cropping pattern evinced by the elites in league with the state, the social composition of the people also changed. In Mizoram, for example, the land holding certificate (LHC) issued by the District Council, amounted to privatisation of land by the LHC holders, who used the same for obtaining concessional land and subsidies from financial institutions and government to convert community lands to private orchards. Capturing such benefits by the LHC elites, bred inequality and caused marginalisation of the poor tribal brethren. The most critical threat came from one section of the tribal society itself. What Lalnunmawia and Lalzarliana found in Mizoram was similar in all the tribal areas of the North East. Landlessness, social insecurity caused by plantation and cash crops, eclipse of traditional community institutions, reduced land space for subsistence crops, progressive pauperisation and migration were common in all the states (Lalnunmawia and Lalzarliana 2103: 34) With their movement background, the elite community failed to resist privatisation of land and accumulation by dispossession.

In the post-liberal frame in particular, where spatial barriers have diminished, the power elites have shifted their allegiance towards external corporate investors and drew their sensitivity to the spatially differentiated qualities in the geographical space of Northeast India. These elites by their command and power over land spaces, took different policy measures to make the respective states in the region more attractive to the highly mobile metropolitan capital. These power elites could, as Harvey said, "implement strategies of local labour control, of skill enhancement, of infrastructural provision, of tax regulation, of state policy and so on, in order to attract development within their particular space" (Harvey 1990: 295). In this way, they went towards the horrendous path of a de-controlled and de-regulatory regime to make the region a preferred destination of corporate investment and FDI. The other section of local elites got engaged in the brisk business of sale-purchase-lease-mortgage and speculation of land and kept alive the continuity of primitive accumulation.

The ideological encounter of the region's elites against resource privatisation was both of a civic-republican nature and of a political nature. Rooted in the meta-narrative of 'dispossession' and trans-historic annihilation of the relational character of land, the ideological encounter was launched by the elites on two principles—normative and instrumental—by the two corresponding communities—Zealots and the Herodians. The Zealot communities went along the normative principle and their encounter was restorative-conservateural in nature. They waged a civic-republican encounter against state usurpation of communal land that robbed them of their usufruct right, reciprocity between community and ecology, and converted "Place" into "Space" (*terra nullius*). These provided normative energy to Zealot activism in the region. Their ideological contests against state usurpation were common in

Assam, Manipur and in Tripura. In all the three states, the Land Revenue and Land Records Acts were not well-received by the Zealot communities. They tended to zealously guard the customary land rights against capture and dispossession by the state and led a series of Zealot movements in the region.

The Herodian role, on the other hand, was instrumental. The Herodian 'actor heroes' in all the hills of Assam, Manipur, Tripura and in Nagaland, Mizoram and Meghalaya capitalised the potent community solidarity in the territorial autonomy movement and reversed land privatisation discourse to territorial discourse by using their class privilege. Reification of community land remaining a common factor between the two—the consciousness on land on the part of the Zealots and Herodian was polarised. Reified consciousness privileged the Herodian, while the same destroyed the community. This led to a type of class formation in tribal society and the *novo rich'* lifestyle soon came to contest the Westerners. This also increased the Pareto Optimal behaviour of the latter that gradually distanced the people from obtaining social optima from communal land. This scenario provoked different reactions from different sections of population. To a section, it served as an emotional springboard for larger territorial politics (e.g. Meghalaya) in order to get a berth in the power structure while to the other section it was a movement space against the mis-ordered homogenisation of the land revenue act (e.g. Manipur) in the hills. To the third section, land revenue administration was an opportunity for accumulation of more land (Manipur) who flagged the issue in their movement for an allocative political demand for the Sixth Schedule and yet to the fourth section, land revenue administration was geared towards "crofts" leading to a minifundio economy (average 7 acres for agricultural, horticultural and allied activities as per the NLUP land administration in Mizoram) (Comprehensive project under the New Land Use Policy: 2009) against the dooms of the once communal land system there.

The modus operandi of land concentration by the Herodian actor heroes followed a two-class mode with two modes of exploitation. One mode was employment of hired labour that, though did not produce the classical class model, started to work in the flexible and unorganised labour market regime as contract workers. The hired labour were paid less than the total value they produced. In the second mode, the class-model being landlord and tenant, the latter was exploited in the form of absolute rent. Thus, "to be in harmony with the labour theory of value, the differential rent was considered to be a transfer value" (Baruah 2012: 85). This way, in the hills of Northeast India, land was fetishised and land lease started to be widely practised on which both these class-modes came to operate for flexible accumulation. One can, thus, well come across a Garo or a Naga owning a thousand acres of land as absentee landlords, realising rent from land, sharecropping and land mortgages. A similar trend is observed among the Karbis also, in which the enterprising individuals came together to form committees and then with the blessings of official agencies secured land deeds either from the headman or from the Autonomous District Council. The results of these activities today are that 'an influential, educated and well-connected Dimasa individual owns over 700 acres of land that used to be used for *jhum* cultivation, grazing livestock and collection of firewood in Gujung village on grant of permanent ownership by the village headman in the name of tea plantation'. Similar situations have also been observed among the Akas of West Kameng district and Angamis in Nagaland in recent studies (Barbora 2012: 1288).

The unorganised land market in the tribal areas and the slackened role of the *State-Rei-Publicae* in the land market, privileged the Herodians actor heroes to capture lands, who adopted at least four visible modes of accumulation, including hired labour, tenant labour, sale-transfer-mortgage and speculation with communal land. Other institutional routes of accumulation by dispossession in the tribal societies included *Xukti Bandhak, Khoi bandhak, Mena, Adhi,* etc. besides sale-mortgage-lease-gift-will. In spite of all the efforts of accumulation, the Herodians failed to build up a Punjab-type latifundio economy, in which the large farmers cultivated their owned land as well as lands transferred from the poor to the rich through sale or lease (Rudra et al. 1990: 21) to become an agrarian capitalist class. This class, in the North East, remained captive of the sullied mode of accumulation that allowed them only to survive with comfort and luxury, not to become the 'transition agents' in the tribal societies.

A section of them chose to align with the foreign direct investors and corporate bodies to play a surrogate role. Land acquisition being at the centre of neoliberalism, this section cashed in on it in a big way. They sat on the saddle of the customary rules but eventually vitiated those by wrongful interpretation of those. This caused the real secession of the tribal new elites from the customary land-based milieu. Therefore, communal lands in the highland traditional societies of Northeast India no longer remained communal and came under both external and internal threats. They toed with pro-market policies of the global political economy, pleaded for a homogenised and uniform individual property law that could conveniently handle acquisition and appropriation. They facilitated the inflated land markets in the hill areas with corresponding dispossession of the community right and preferred to catch up with the trends of market economy rather than losing it out. Baruah stated, "There is surely an element of fantasy in Mizoram Chief Minister Zoramthanga's promise that a new World Bank financed road would be 'smooth and sleek like a snake'. A policy document of the Arunachal Pradesh government has a similar note of fantasy when it proclaims that the state could be floating on 'hydro-dollars'" (Baruah 2012:83). The pro-FDI stand of this section of people in Northeast India facilitated the neoliberal market function that in the hills, caused trans-generational annihilation of communal resources including water, minerals and forests resources. Another section of them were, "the tribal civil and armed activists, who are exploiting the hill areas. For example, chromite mining in Ukhrul is done right under the nose of NSCN-IM. UNC is the one, who gave permission for oil exploration to Jubilant Energy in Tamenglong" (*Sangai Express*, June 25, 2013).

The New Labour Identity

In the pre-capitalistic tribal society the concept of land and labour differed diametrically from that in the institutional economics. In the tribal society, neither land nor labour was viewed as a factor of production entailing factor price. Both were integrated with the communal system of economy and the society to build a symbiosis. Land in the tribal society had a twin function: economic (production) function and the social-reproduction function. In its economic function, land was open to the community usufructs—subject to 'reversion and re-allotment' and not a space for absolute rights (Hertskovits 1952: 324-325) and a privatised space. In its social function, land transformed the abstract *space* to *place* for reproduction of culture and community consciousness, relational and comunicative place and of an integrated ecology. The somatic attachment of people to land produced the legend, usage and the communicative language. In its social function, labour in the tribal society was more a social obligation, reciprocity and exchange and a collective consciousness than a mercenary *quid pro quo* for selling the labour time. The importance of social matrix of land and labour in the pre-capitalistic tribal community, for these reasons, went well beyond the exercise of rights of a *conative* order towards greater community obligation of a *cognitive* order embracing the normative, cultural and behavioural codes so that their institutions could run well. Within the social matrix, property right over land therefore did not go beyond the custodial right of the tribal chiefs and the headmen. The anthropological understanding of property rights among the aboriginals therefore was essentially communal. Pathy in this connection noted, "The common ties of blood, language, customs, etc. appeared not as the consequence but as the precondition of the joint (temporary) appropriation and use of the soil. The individuals being powerless, the social organisation contains and represses its members in a dictatorial way. In essence, the communal character appears as a negative unity in relation to the outside world. The community as a whole controls the means of production, while each kin-based production unit owns tools and products" (Pathy 1987: 158).

The most universal feature of labour in the preliterate societies is labour cooperation in which both family and community act as cooperative institutions. Labour cooperation is required both for survival and for gratification of values (Herskovits 1952: 110). In a pecuniary society on the other hand, there is a labour market and a monetary unit of measurement of labour. Although in the many preliterate societies, slavery and dynastic political control exploited the workers, these did not have a representative character. Social sanction had a great role in case of negligence of cooperative labour. In the preliterate societies, labour was not merely a response to reward but to the social, ties to the entrepreneur. The social factors caught up and enmeshed the economic factors in a wider net (Herskovits 1952: 117, 119). In the preliterate society, though the primary motive for work was subsistence, the whole of economic life was not driven by this alone. The force of tradition, appreciation of work, desire for emulation and group approval functioned in shaping the economic activities (Herskovits 1952: 120).

The preliterate society also differs from the pecuniary society in terms of division of labour. In the former, division of labour is made according to specialisation of producing a commodity or categories of commodities, not the part thereof, contrary to the pecuniary society, where division of labour is according to specialisation of producing a very small part of a commodity (Herskovits 1952: 125).

The concept of sex division of labour in the pre-literate society did not follow the conventional economic theory. In the food gathering economy, women provided more labour and, thus, they enjoyed higher status, whereas in agricultural economy, men enjoyed a the higher status although women's work participation was equally high. In the economy of shifting cultivation however, there is man-woman labour inter-dependency. The *differentia specifica* of community labour is its social construction contrary to its market construction. The tribal community and the market economy, therefore, looked at labour from two opposite economic and ideological angles. In the tribal society, labour was organically linked with the larger social organisation and with the process of production function and reproduction functions of the community. In such organisation, community ownership went simultaneously with community labour participation, responsibility sharing and harmonisation of interests. Labour was also a social obligation of mutual help, reciprocity and of community integration. The non-conflictual and unpaid nature of labour relations helped both in integration maximisation and in loyalty maximisation to the community.

Table 5.3: Concept and Ideology of Labour

Preliterate Society	*Pecuniary Society*
Homo societus	Homo economicus
Focus on community	Focus on individuals
Economic functions are relational	Economic relations are personal
Labour is socially constructed	Pecuniary society has a labour market
Labour has no monetary unit of measurement	Labour has a monetary unit of measurement
Labour is a response to social obligation	Labour is a response to mercenary reward
Labour is embedded in social reproduction	Labour is subject to factor price
Social sanction against the lazy	Legal sanction against the lazy
Labour as a community asset	Labour as a class
Reward to labour is cognition and prestige	Reward to labour in terms of wages and incentives.
Division of labour according to specialisation, producing a commodity, not the part thereof	Division of labour is according to specialisation, producing a very small part of a commodity

The concept of labour as a class has crept into the tribal society with land privatisation and changes in the land use and the cropping pattern first within the colonial state mode and then in the post-colonial state mode. While the subsistence economic mode produced labour as an interchangeable service to the community and individual service being subsumed within that, the surplus economy produced labour as a factor of production, (conceived within a class frame). The tribe and the state, therefore, looked at labour from two opposite economic and ideological angles. In the tribal society, labour is organically linked with the larger social organisation and with their taking part in the process of production and reproduction functions of land. In such organisation, community ownership goes simultaneously with community labour participation, responsibility sharing and harmonisation of interests. Labour is also a social obligation of mutual help, reciprocity and of community integration. The non-conflictual nature of land and labour relations helps in integration maximisation and loyalty maximisation to the community. On the other hand, the state looks at labour as an entity disembedded from the community and from its cultural milieu. While retaining its relational character of land with the forces of production, in the state's view, labour is the 'sale of labour' power of a worker, independent of his will. This amounted to reification of labour which de-communitised the concept of labour and brought it to the premise of a kind of production relation, habitually producing conflict and antagonism. Therefore, in the Khasi Hills, as Hunter wrote, agricultural day labour (both men and women) appeared under the colonial rule and with the establishment of Shillong in 1864 onward, the demand for wage labour markedly increased (Hunter 1990: 227). Privatisation of tribal land led to re-restructuration of community labour relations in the privatised farms that restructured their primordial identity. There also emerged, subtly but perceptibly, an army of labour reserve consisting of those who were dispossessed of the communal land. The ramifications of this scenario was obvious. De-communitised labour entered in wage-labour relations in the private farms where no durable engagements were found. The involuntary entry of the subsistence agriculturists into the surplus-yielding farm relations robbed them of their true identity.

In the Northeast, Biswas has noted, the defining character of the relationship between land and labour is its embeddedness in a marked social boundary. This social boundary is often transgressed by the market forces and is subverted in the universalising flow of capital that converts labour into a saleable commodity. The state and market jointly act as an adversary to the presumed social boundaries of the communities (Biswas 2009: 48-49). The official view of the state stresses the need for scientific and modern technological intervention for weaning the farmers from shifting cultivation. This has been largely responsible for breaking down the embeddedness of labour. It has not only expedited dispossession of tribal land but also has dismantled the very concept of labour on which tribal value-based identity once rested. During the 19th century, as Guha wrote, after the dispension of the Chinese labour in the tea gardens in 1843, the local people remained practically the sole source of labour and the most important source of (labour) recruitment was the Kachari tribe of Darrang district (Guha 1988: 15). During the First World War, a large number of Kuki tribes men were recruited from Manipur for shipment to Europe to work as labour there.

In Mizoram, for example, most of the farmers are subsistence farmers; technology and high external inputs were 'inappropriate and unacceptable' to them. But technology and input intervention by the state became necessary for enhancing land productivity. Hence, the state drive for abolition of *jhum* cultivation. In Arunachal Pradesh, Roy noted that change over from "Dao-hoe technology to tractor thresher technology" was a part of the *jhum*-discarding programme although a very narrow section of the tribal society adopted it (Roy 1994: 54). Ray made a study on women's labour in informal cross border trade (ICBT) at Zokhawthar border of Mizoram-Myanmar. These women are dismembered from the land economy and took part in ICBT leading to large-scale feminisation of poverty (Ray 2015). In Tripura, lack of alternative employment led many shifting cultivators to take up the job of rubber tappers against a flat daily rate of Rs. 150. They lived in abject poverty with poor housing and sanitation provisions. (Bhowmick and Chauhan 2013: 33).

Instead of acting as positive externalities, these led to social division of labour between the more affluent class, who, under the *jhum* rehabilitation programme, once received land for wet-rice cultivation. This deprived the disadvantaged section of the community from their usufruct right to land. This resulted in break of organisation of labour woven in the traditional productive forces. In Khampti areas, Roy noted that large land holding tribal peasantry engaged even migrated labour work for cultivation of vegetables for sale in the market at higher price (Roy 1994: 63).

The rehabilitation colonies under the *jhumia* rehabilitation programme in Tripura, broke the very corporate life of the tribes and their collective identity. There was also revealing occupational changes among the tribal cultivators. Chakraborti noted that the percentage of the tribal population engaged in agriculture was 85.60 percent in 1961; their number increased in 2001. But their percentage slid down to 41.62 percent. Agricultural labour among the indigenous tribes was only 5.04 percent in 1961, that rose as high as to 36.22 percent in 2001. Percentage of tribals in other services rose from 2.57 percent in 1961 to 20 percent in 2001. The decline in percentage share of cultivators and the corresponding rise in agricultural labour in the tribal society pointed to a basic change in the occupational pattern of the tribal society(Chakraborti 2011: 48-49). Along with changes in the occupational pattern, they were alienated from their corporate living and collective identity and became de-communitised and lumpen. Many of the community practices waned along with the change in the traditional economic practices. The Rengma Nagas, for example, practised communal labour for weeding and harvests. They had field companies of young boys and girls, who had songs and chants as the companies were ready to work in the field. There were the *Ngada* ceremony to celebrate crop and harvest; Genna for felling jungle for shifting cultivation; *Zu Kuli* to get rid of the evils of the previous years; *Ndu* prayer for strong arms (for agricultural works), rain making ceremony; hunting rituals and the folktales on finding of rice and magic rice. All those went to the background in course of time. Das found that the system of reciprocity existed among the Nishis and Apa Tanis. The labour gang of the Apa Tani boys and girls was known as Patang and that of the Nishis was known as *Dorum Rey*. These institutions served as the labour pool on the principle of reciprocity of labour. But emergence of wage labour transcended the general principle of reciprocity (Mills 1980: 75-76, 80, 95, 175, 271: Das 1993: 117-118)

All these identity markers have lost their value as a result of introduction of *jhum* replacing method of cultivation. The Thadou-Kuki custom of Kilhalho or field puja performed after fields have been cut and burnt (for *jhum* cultivation) and their Kut festival, a harvest-time rendezvous, got lost due to large-scale infiltration of Nepali farmers in the agricultural field of the tribe, particularly in the Sadar Hills in Senapati district of North Manipur. This brought about major changes in the concept of community labour of the Kukis. The age-old system of Parati, the institution of division and reciprocity of labour (both women Parati and men Parati) in the Khasi community during the agricultural season side by side with non-Khasi agricultural labours (Dwivedi and Sahay 2013) have lost owing to the shift of institutional control from the community to the Autonomous District Council. The Wangala festival of the Garos was to advance the growth of swidden crops and to create the conditions for reaping and consuming, harvesting and thanksgiving for the rice grains that the Swiddens could yield. This is now being performed out-of-village contexts in the secular public sphere with state patronage. The "Hundred Drums Wangala" festival has emerged at the initiative of local historians and folklorists which has got media coverage and internet access by the educated elite. It also became a symbol of agro-political identity. From the early 1990s onwards, Bangladeshi Agro has also organised Wangala dance festivals in the "Garo belt". Wangala dance is performed in the Republic Day parade to show the allegiance of the Garo people towards the Indian state. This has given the dance a multiple meaning (Maaker 2013: 221–239).

In supersession of the subsistence economy in the hills, the classical growth paradigm in developing countries like India came to be based on the presupposition that modern economy would expand by breaking up traditional (pre-capitalist) economies and by transferring both economic resources and labourers from the traditional to the modern economy. In the context of the tribal economy in Northeast India, on the other hand, convergence of ethnicity in the evolutionary framework of a modern capitalist society did not take place. Our experience is that capitalist economy expanded by exploitation of resources from this region, not by transforming the labourers to a higher mode of production. Resource privatisation alienated the community from its economic and cultural engagements with land and as a result, a lumpen 'surplus' labour force emerged from the dispossessed tribals. This surplus labour force was not absorbed in the modern sector due largely to the absence of *in-situ* industrialisation, lack of employable skill and labour mobility in the *ex-situ* labour market. Gross informalisation of labour and high immobility of tribal labour added to this problem.

In Northeast India, the surplus labour force of the tribes largely remained stationary and immobile. This impelled them to fall back on their economy as wage workers on highly exploitative terms, thus, once more scrambling the community identity. Although some glimpses of communal labour were still persistent in larger parts of the Northeast both as a continuation of the pristine agricultural practices and as a continuation of the traditional cultural practice, these survived in a morbid condition till the post-colonial and post-liberal regimes completely broke the continuity and showcased these as the treasures of antiquity. The ramification was large scale lumpenisation of the community. It is, therefore, not uncommon to find Mizo manual labourers working under BRTF as muster roll workers or under the PWD contractors. They work for 8-9 hours a day at abysmally low wages (Laitanga 1982: 22). In East Lungdar village, the workers are engaged in the unorganised sectors of mining, quarry, construction, storage and transportation (Rosangluaia 2004: 16-17). Shift from inter-dependency of labour to wage labour became a growing phenomenon in the tribal societies of Northeast India. In the era of heightened global competition, large enterprises made mega-profits from the existing surplus labour pools at minimal labour cost while the labour force was uprooted from the community milieu.

There is also a great role of the capitalist enclosures in identity fragmentation in the tribal societies. Enclosures are historically and theoretically linked to the division between commodity production and reproduction of labour. Angelis wrote that capitalism separated the producers from the means of production. The Bloody Legislation against the expropriated aimed at criminalising and repressing popular behaviour induced by the expropriation of land (vagrancy, begging, theft). This was an act of "primitive accumulation by separating the producers from the means of production. (Angelis 2001: 5, 17). This trend in different parts of Northeast India was explained in a set of three articles (Basu et. al 2004). The motive forces behind this trend were increasing privatisation and enclavisation of land either through commoditisation or through commercialisation of land space. Chakraborti found penetration of the commodity market, monetisation and commercialisation of produce, new techno-economic inputs and the resultant magnitude of labour and investment in the hill societies. Ganguli found growing commercialisation and monetisation of hill economies, and change in shifting cultivation mode to peasant mode of production. Peasantisation of the tribal society made it more stratified. Some households became the owners of land and practised wet rice cultivation both with family labour and/ or employing labour on payment of wage in cash or kind. The marginalised group, somehow, survived with slash and burn cultivation in the dwindling areas of degraded forest patches outside the reserved or otherwise closed forest areas (enclosures). Many poor families supplemented their income by working as wage labourers on public works of government, in forests, under the forest department and even on the farms of fellow villages. Das Gupta found that the prosperous *jhumias* in Tripura, grow commercial crops along with paddy for self-consumption where a new set of labour relations has emerged; while the landless *jhumias* carry on *jhum* with reciprocal labour, some land owning *jhumias* do *jhuming* with hired labour on wage payment in cash and kind or combination of both. Hired labour is also used by the landed *jhumias* for commercial cropping who, she termed as 'absentee *jhumias*'—the prosperous tribal and occasionally the non-tribals living in the vicinity of areas suitable for *jhuming* use these lands for shifting cultivation. Hired labour is the result of product-mix of *jhuming* in favour of commercial crops which is market dependent. This gradually gave way to market behavior, which is incompatible with kinship behaviour.

The neo-classical economics and the emerging market forces in this way annihilated the very concept of community labour in the hill areas. De-coupling peasants from land became the condition of development of the labour market and consolidation of the capitalist production relations. A micro level study made by the Tribal Research Institution, Mizoram, in Durtlang village in 1981 is indicative of this trend. Due to proximity of this village to the state capital Aizawl, there has been frequent immigration of the households from other villages. It was found during the survey that out of a sample of eight households, seven had recently immigrated into Durtlang. Out of the seven, three came from Muthi and one each from Naosel, Aizawl, Luangmual and Phullen. In spite of the rapid social change, the original tribal propensity to migrate from village to village continues to be a distinctive feature of their lifestyle. Owing to the fast growth of population and the improvement of general standard of life, a serious problem is posed to the newcomers in regard to the acquisition of adequate *jhum* land for their sustenance. Such holdings being quite inadequate for their needs, they were forced to acquire some land outside the village, often at a fairly long distance. This preventd them for maintaining a desirable standard of living and many of the newcomers undertook work on a daily labour basis. The prevailing rate of daily labour in the village was rRs. 7 only. Similar incidents of daily labour were found in Sihpir village. These labourers were unskilled and were temporarily employed in various works like tilling and weeding *jhum* and garden, daily labour, manual workforce, etc. the daily rate being Rs. 7/-, 8/- and 10/- only. The usual working hours was 8 hours (from 8 am to 4 pm). Some people in Lungdai village worked as daily labour to supplement their family income. The daily rate of unskilled labour was Rs. 6 to 7 while that of skilled labour was between Rs. 20 to 25 five only. A similar trend was found in Meghalaya, where the landless people cultivate the land of the land owning families as daily wage-based labourers, the rate of daily wage being abysmally low: Rs. 15 for adult males for working both inside and outside the village. The adult female labour gets Rs. 8 and the child labour gets Rs. 4. Some people also go out of the village to the neighbouring areas to hire themselves as labourers. In other areas, the wage rate for the landless cultivators is still low (Laitanga 1981: 8-9, 41, 68; Dutta 1987: 84, 88). Lack of employment opportunities in Champhai district of Mizoram, a sizeable section of tribal youth has taken up the job of porters, who carry the tradable goods from Zokhawmawii (Tedim district in Chin state of Myanmar) to Zokhawthar Land Customs Station through the border bridge over Tiao river (Chakraborty and Ray 2015).

In Kharam Pallen village, under the Saitu-Ghamphazol Block of Senapati District in Manipur, contract farming of ginger has changed the occupational pattern of the tribal people. Contact farming employed the tribal cultivators on an informal contract basis. They encouraged the tribal farmers to use more land and labour for raising the contract crop. The ginger growers are small growers based on family labour, who became quasi-bonded labourers on their own land and the investors became the de facto owners of the communal land for the lock-in period of cultivation of ginger. Such labour being totally unorganised, it created a vertical division in the erstwhile communitarian society; ceased to be any more a part of the community and became victims of market economy. Induction of wage-based hired labour or rent-based tenant farmer in contract farming scrambled the ethnic labour system in the tribal society (Ray 2013).

In Northeast India, there is a trend of rise in unpaid labour. In NER contribution of agriculture to Net State Domestic Product indicates a decline in Assam, Manipur and Meghalaya, but is more consistent compared to the rest of the North Eastern states except Arunachal Pradesh. In terms of employment share, 90 per cent rural women of Arunachal Pradesh and Nagaland are still engaged in agriculture, whereas Meghalaya shows a consistent decline in participation rates in the agricultural sector for both the sexes. However, an increased participation in the workforce does not necessarily reflect better living or working conditions for tribal women because they tend to fall under the unpaid labour force. Thus, despite their high participation rates in the labour and workforce, the percentage of women in paid labour or employed in professional/technical/managerial occupations in tribal-dominated states is very discouraging (Borah 2012). There are also cases, when private property seeped into the agrarian practice in certain tribes, who depended on unpaid labour of the wives and children. In two separate studies, Das and Roy noted the agrarian practice of the Khamptis in Lohit district in Arunachal Pradesh once needed more number of family members, who could work in the field and the richness of a person depended on the number of able-bodied members of the family; more number of wives and children to work together in the fields (Das 1993: 117-118; Roy 1994: 58). These wives and children gave unpaid labour to the family.

With the change in land ownership, land-use and cropping patterns, the concept of labour started to shift from serving the community to serving the individual, who could privatise land and whose economic activities in this way turned hedonistic. And labour in the hills being totally unorganised, it created a vertical division in the erstwhile communitarian society; ceased to be any more a part of the community and became victims of market economy. Induction of wage-based hired labour or rent-based tenant farmer in tribal society scrambled the ethnic identity. In the privatised and new property regime, labour was used for utility maximisation of the propertied class to the eclipse of social functions of community labour.

In Arunachal Pradesh, land use pattern changed when the state government gave top priority to increase the farmers' income and emphasised all income-generating activities including, cash crop, floriculture, fruit culture, fish and pig rearing, agro-processing and so on, along with all other activities. They were considered necessary for the purpose. While it was assumed that better management of land through agro-forestry and horticultural plantation in the hills could address the problem of shifting cultivation, involvement of private sector, financial institutions and incentivisation of farmers could not provide financial opulence to the farmers. Private sector intervention destructed the primordial land-labour bond and identity. On the other side, there are cases when private property seeped into the agrarian practice in certain tribes. Das and Roy's study among the Khamptis of Arunachal Pradesh, was indicative of the fact that gender relations was not only a family relation but also a production relation in a given state of the development of the productive forces. Such agrarian practices in course of time, led to larger accumulation of land resources in the hands of the rich farmers of the Khampti tribe.

The riparian doctrine, to Asif, influenced the policy makers to give primacy to quantitative economics and importance to the produce in the market rather than to other social considerations. This state of affairs stressed the tribal communities, to whom the notion of free market and inter-group competition were unknown. They, therefore, found it difficult to adapt to the new situation. The massive open cast mining and subsequent installation of thermal units contemplated in the North East, for example, posed a threat of displacement to the tribal people (Asif 1999: 54). And along with physical displacement, they also suffered cultural and identity displacement. The lores and festivals which were "very much inter-linked with mode of production" (Misra 1983: 27), were put to disuse and were thrown to the oblivion that eventually annihilated the identity of the tribes. That is why we now see that many tribal festivals of Northeast India received a fetish character, which is projected in the visual media of the country.

Modernity with all its institutional forms became problematic in the tribal societies as it first superseded and then annihilated the previous ones. It introduced multiple modes of production, including, sedentary agriculture, three-tier model, plantation (including horticulture and cash crops), farm mode, agro-industrial, industrial and market modes and not the least, the private mode of production. These deconstructed and reconstructed the identities of the tribal communities in Northeast India. Moreover, in the era of globalisation, the twin process of space-time annihilation and space-time compression disembedded the tribal communities from their milieu society. The institutional package of globalisation hard-hit the core of the cognitive aspects of tribal identity in the Northeast region of India. Shift of the place value of land to the space value also caused a parallel shift of land as a symbol of community to a symbol of wealth, power and status. Over-accumulation of land resources plunged a section of the tribal society into leading a life of conspicuous consumption, exposing the 'Veblen Effect' on them. These developments in the contemporary tribal societies of Northeast India created a challenge to the social theory of tribal identity.

Finally, land in the neoliberal market economy replaced the fixed, self, referential and inward-looking place-myth with market place that became wider, cut across the jealously guarded cultural boundaries and the socially-constructed geography of difference. The rational choice model of the neo-liberal economy hedged the non-market cultural aspects of social intercourse. Re-spatialisation of land dismantled the social boundary and the markers of identity, made these fragile, more fraught and obviously artificial. While breaking the image of cultural space, the neoliberal market economy also invited the doom of tribal identity with banalities and distractions of the lived space. In this way, the inner core of tribal culture was bemused and was relegated to the backyard of the dominant discourse of the market economy.

The opposition between space and place in present-day neoliberal capitalism involves reordering of spatial relationships to bring geography within the web of a world market that draws a parallel between scientific and managerial concepts of abstract, manipulable space and the process of primitive accumulation, delinking the people from history, art, archaeology, culture— in short, *place*. This is based on hedonism, which along with primitive accumulation, also annihilates the community and its identity. Therefore, primitive accumulation, accumulation by dispossession, abstract space, jurisprudential principle of *terra nullius* and hedonistic land grabbing forcibly reconstruct the identity through large-scale reification of the community and fetishisation of community lands in the hills of Northeast India.

The political economy of emerging capitalism moulded the erstwhile community relations that diluted their pristine identity. Converting place into space through submergence and enclosure and according *terra nullius* status to these undermined social and material relations within place. When place is annihilated, the community loses its production function, social reproduction function, negotiating power, collective imagination and so on. Reorganisation and reconfiguration of space in the political economy frame produce different kinds of activities and create different categories of land-based activities that are fundamentally different from the pristine functions of land. This marks the threshold of the conflict between community process around land and the neoliberal process around the same in the tribal societies of Northeast India.

Conclusion

Land-based identity of the tribal people is an anthropological construct, a response to the development of the productive forces and a product of the endo-biotic and somatic attachments of the human communities to ecology. Besides, producing means of livelihood, such attachments also produce land as a space for reproduction of culture and institutions to build the robust foundation of identity. Such construction suffered from its re-configuration as a result of forcible imposition of abstract space on the local place, which produced new institutions to break the egalitarian ethos of communal land. Such institutions were market-driven against which the land-based identity of the tribes stood as a critique. The cognitive differences between the traditionalist and the modernist scrambled the social construct of tribal identity. The scramble was further confounded by the post-colonial and the post-liberal institutions. This finally led to class cleavage within the tribal societies.

Elite constriction of identity was based on the distinction between primordial essentialism on the one hand and situational/strategic adjustment on the other with two contradictory ideological orientations, which also produced class cleavage in the tribal societies between the Zealot community and the Herodian community.

Lastly, the ideology of communal labour had much to do with land-based identity of the tribes. The communitarian ethos of labour was destroyed with privatisation of communal land, commercial cropping and with industrial use of land. The concept of wage labour crept into the tribal societies, where communal labour was increasingly fetishised under market economy. This scenario gave rise to daily-rated labour, master roll labour, unpaid labour and feminisation of labour in different hill areas of the region. This destroyed labour as a socially embedded concept, broke the corporate living of the tribal communities, their cultural practices and marked the threshold of the conflict between community process and the neoliberal process around land in Northeast India.

REFERENCES

Angelis, Massimo De (2001). Marx and Primitive Accumulation: The Continuous Character of Capital's "Enclosures" The Miror Image of Alternatives. *The Commoner*, No. 2. September 2001.

Asif, Mohammed (1999). Development Initiative and Concomitant Issues of Displacement and Improvement in Northeastern States, in Kailash S. Agarwal edited, *Dynamics of Identity and Inter-group Relations*. Simla: Indian Institute of Advanced Study.

Asikis, Paha (2011). *Ethnic Mobilisation and Violence in Northeast India*. New Delhi: Routledge.

Ayer, K. Gopal and S.V. Bhave (1995). Report on Tripura, Workshop on Land Reforms—Agenda for the North East, Gauhati. Papers on the North Eastern Scenario. Mussourie: Land Reforms Unit, Lal Bahadur Shastri National Academy of Administration, Mussourie, April, 3-5.

Barbora, Sanjoy (2012). Ethnic Politics and Land Use: Genesis of Conflicts in India's North-East, *Economic and Political Weekly*, Vol. 37, No. 13. March 30.

Baruah, Sanjib (2012). Hydropower, Mega Dams and the Politics of Risk, *Seminar* 640, December.

Basu, Arabinda and Chakraborti S.B. (ed.) (2004). *Science of Man*. Anthropological Society of India, Calcutta.

Basu, Biman, K. Das Gupta and Jayanta Sarker (eds.) (2004) *Anthropology for North-East India*. Calcutta: Indian National Confederation and Academy of Anthropologists, Indian Anthropological Society and National Museum of Mankind.

Bhaumick, Indraneel and Chauan, Pradip (2013). An Enquiry into Enmployment Status, Income and Assets of Rubber Tappers working in the Large Estates of Tripura. Noida: *Labour and Development*, Vol. 20, No. 2. December.

Biswas, Prasenjit (2009). Land and Inter-Ethnic Conflict in India's North-East: Middle Ground in a State of Exception, in Ch. Priyo Ranjan Singh edited, *Tribalism and the Tragedy of the Commons: Land, Identity and Development–The Manipur Experience*. New Delhi: Akansha Publishing House.

Borah, Bornali (2012). Patterns of Employment Among Tribal Women in the North Eastern Region of India. Proceedings of the National Seminar on Labour Market and Issues of Adivasis in India. January 22-23, 2015. National Institute of Rural Development and Panchayati Raj, Rajendranagar, Hyderabad.

Chakraborty, Gorky (2010). Encountering Globalisation in the Hill Areas of North East India, *Occasional Paper 23*. IDSK, Kolkata.

Chakraborty, Gorky (2012). Roots abnd Ramifications of a Colonial 'Construct': The Wastelands in Assam. *Occasional Paper 39*. IDSK, Kolkata.

Chakraborty, Gorky and Asok Ray (2015). *The Look East Policy from Peoples' Perspective: A Study on Mizoram*. Kolkata: IDSK, mimeo.

Chakravarti, Dipannita (2004). *Land Question in Tripura*. New Delhi: Akansha Publishing House.

Chakraborti, Dipannita (2011). A Glimpse into the Occupational Pattern of Tripura During the Post-Independence Period. Silchar: *Social Scanner*. Vol. 2-3. July.

Conway, Janet M. (2007). *Identity, Place and Knowledge—Social Movements, Contesting Globalisation*. Delhi: Aakar Books.

Das, J.N. (1990). A Study of Land System in Mizoram. LRI, Eastern Region. Guwahati: Guwahati High Court. (Mimeograph).

Das, Gurudas (1993). Tribal Formation and Economic Base in Arunachal. Shillong: Proceedings of Northeast India History Association.

Dasgupta, Malabika (2004). Change in the Land and Labour Relations in Jhuming in Tripura, in Arabinda Basu, Biman K. Dasgupta and Jayanta Sarkar edited, *Anthropology in Northeast India- A Reader*. Calcutta: Indian National Confederation and Academy of Anthropologists; Indian Anthropological Society and National Museum of Mankind.

Datta, P.S. (1992). *India's North East: A Study in Transition*. New Delhi: Har Anand Publications.

Dutta, B.B. (1987). Land Relations in Khasi Hills- A Study, in B.B. Dutta and M.N. Karna edited, *Land Relations in Northeast India*. New Delhi: People's Publishing House.

Dwivedi, Sanjoy and Vijoy Sahay (2013). Parati System of the Khasis: An Insight into the Institutionalised System of Division of Labour. International Conference of the International Union of Anthropological and Ethnological Sciences. Manchester: UK, 5th-10th August.

Ganguli, J.B. (2004). The Economics of Transition from Shifting to Settled Cultivation in Northeast India, in Arabinda Basu, Biman K. Dasgupta and Jayanta Sarkar edited, *Anthropology in Northeast India: A Reader*. Calcutta: Indian National Confederation and Academy of Anthropologists; Indian Anthropological Society and National Museum of Mankind.

Government of India (2006). Report of the Working Group on Land Relations for formulation of 11th Five Year Plan, July 31.

Government of Mizoram (2009). Comprehensive Project Under New Land Use Policy (NLUP) for Sustained Economic Development and the Uplift of the Poor of Mizoram. Aizawl. Mimeographed.

Guha, Amalendu (1988 Reprint). *Planter Raj to Swaraj: Freedom Struggle and Electoral Politics in Assam 1826-1947.* Delhi: People's Publishing House.

Guha, Amalendu (1991). *Medieval and Early Colonial Assam—Society, Polity and Economy.* Calcutta: K.P. Bagchi & Co.

Handique, Rajib (2004). *British Forest Policy in Assam.* New Delhi. Concept Publishing Co.

Harvey, David (1990). *The Postmodern Condition.* Cambridge & Oxford: Blackwell Publishing.

Hasnu, Santosh Rex (2005). Colonial Road Construction in North-East India c. 1824-1891. www.nehrumeuseum/nic.in/en/new/425, 20th april2005html.

Hassan, Manirul (2002). State, Development and Population Displacement in Northeast India, in C. Jasua Thomas edited. *Dimension of Displaced People in Northeast India.* New Delhi: Regency Publications.

Herskovits, Melville J. (1852). *Economic Anthropology: A Study in Comparative Economics*, New York: Alfred A. Knopf.

Hunter, W.W. (1990). *A Statistical Account of Assam*, Vol. 2. Delhi: Low Price Publications (Reprint).

Kamei, Gangumei (2009). Ethnicity, Identity and Land in Tribal Manipur in Ch. Priyo Ranjan Singh, edited, *Tribalism and the Tragedy of the Commons: Land, Identity and Development: The Manipur Experience.* New Delhi: Akansha Publishing House.

Karlssons, Bengt G. (2011). *Unruly Hills, Nature and Nation in India's North East.* New Delhi: Orient BlackSwan.

Laitanga, C. (compiled and edited) (1982). *Know Your Own Land (Mizoram, Series IV).* Calcutta: Firma KLM on Behalf of Tribal Research Insitute, Aizawl.

Lalnunmawia, F. and C. Lalzarliana (2103). *Land Use System in Mizoram.* New Delhi: Akansha Publishing House.

Lalnithanga, P. (1997). *State of Our Union Mizoram.* New Delhi: Publications Division, Ministry of Information and Broadcasting, Government of India.

Lodhi, A.H. Akram (2007). Land Market and Neo-liberal enclosures: An Agrarian Political Economy Perspective. *Third World Quarterly*, Vol. 28, No. 8. Routledge.

Lokendrajit, Soyam (1988). Identity and Crisis of Identity, in Naorem Sanajaoba edited, *Manipur Past and Present (The Heritage and Ordeals of a Civilisation), Vol. 1, History, Polity and Law.* New Delhi: Mittal Publications.

Maaker, Erik de (2013). Performing the Garo Nation? Garo Wangala

Dancing Between Faith and Folklore. *Asian Ethnology*, Vol. 72, No. 2.

Laldena (2013). Historical Perspective of the Process of Marginalisation: A Study of Hill People's Experience in Manipur in Vungzamawi, K. et al. edited, *Prism of the Zomi People*. Imphal: Zomi Human Rights Foundation.

Mills, J.P. (1980). *The Rengma Nagas*. Guwahati: Spectrum Publications (Reprint).

Misra, Bani Prasanna (1979). Agrarian Relations in a Khasi State. *Economic and Political Weekly*, Vol. 14. No. 20. May 19.

Misra, Bani Prasanna (1983). Society and Politics in the Hill Areas of North-East India in B. Datta Ray edited, *The Emergence and Role of Middle Class in North-East India*. New Delhi: Uppal Publishing House.

Oinam, Bhagat (2003). Pattern of Ethnic Conflict in the North East: A Study of Manipur. *Economic and Political Weekly*, Vol. 24.

Pathy, Jagannath. (1987). *Anthropology of Development Demystification and Relevance*. New Delhi: Gyan Publishing House.

Patnaik, Utsa (ed.) (1990). *Agrarian Relation and Accumulation: A Mode of Production Debate in India*. New Delhi: Oxford University Press.

Planning Commission. *The Eleventh Plan Document*, (Vol: III). New Delhi: Planning Commission.

Ray, Asok Kumar (2013). Fieldwork in Manipur During February.

Ray, Asok Kumar (2004). Emerging Concerns of Rural Sociology, Annual Conference of Indian Sociological Society. Gorakhpur University, December 27-29.

Ray, Asok Kumar (2015). Women in Informal Sector Economy: An Empirical Study on Mizoram-Myanmar Cross Border Trade, Proceedings of the 17th Annual Conference of North Eastern Economic Association, Itanagar, October 30 -31.

Rosangluaia, R.S. (2004). *Know Your Own Land (Mizoram, Series V)*. Aizawl: Tribal Research Institute.

Roy, Himansu (1994). Agriculture in Tribal Society (A Case Study of Lohit District in Arunachal Pradesh. *Indian Anthropologist*, 24 (2).

Roy Burman, B.K. (1990). Some Views on Land Use and Allied Topics, in P.C. Barua edited, *Development Planning of Northeast India*. Guwahati: North Eastern Institute of Bank Management.

Roy Burman, B.K. (1991). Issues in Land Reforms in Tribal Areas of Northeast India: A Preliminary Appraisal, in Malabika Dasgupta edited, *Impact of Land Reforms in Northeast India*. New Delhi: Omsons Publications.

Roy Burman, B.K. (1994) SustainableDevelopment: Ecological and Socio-Cultural Dimensions: Keynote Address at *National* Seminar on Sustainable Development, February 23-25, 1994. Chandigarh: Department of Sociology, Punjab University.

Roy Burman, B.K. (1995). 'Indigenous' and 'Tribal' Peoples and the UN and International Agencies, Emerging Reality About Tribal Social Category. RGICS Paper No. 27. Rajiv Gandhi Institute for Contemporary Studies.

Rudra, Ashok, A. Majid and B.D. Talib (1990). Big farmers of Punjab, in Utsa Patnaik edited, *Agrarian Relations and Accumulation: The Mode of Production Debate in India.* Published for Sameeksha Trust. New Delhi: OUP.

Saha, Niranjan (1987). Land Systems and Agricultural Development in the Hills of North East, in B.B. Dutta and M.N. Karna edited, *Land Relations in Northeast India.* New Delhi: People's Publishing House.

Sangai Express (2013). e-paper. Imphal: June 25.

Sampat, Preeti (2013). Limits of Absolute Power, Eminent Domain and the Right to Land in India, *Economic and Political Weekly*, Vol. XLVIII, No. 19, May 11.

Sangpliang, Rekha M. (2010). *Forest in the Life of the Khasis.* New Delhi: Concept Publishing Company.

Sanyu Visitor, Emergence of Middle Class in Nagaland. Proceedings of Northeast India History Association, Ninth Session (1988). (Kohima).

Saxena, N.C. (2005). Updating Land Records: Is Computerisation Sufficient? *Economic and Political Weekly*, January.

Sengupta, Mayura (2003). Shifting Cultivation and the Riang Tribe of Tripura. *Economic and Political Weekly*, Vol. XLVIII, No. 40, October 5.

Sarmah, Bhupen and Binayak Dutta (2013). *History of Judiciary in Assam: Law, Law Courts and Lawyers.* Guwahati: DVS Publishers.

Shimray, U.A. (2009). Land Ownership System of the Naga Community: Uniqueness in Tradition, in Ch. Priyo Ranjan Singh Edited, *Tribalism and the Tragedy of the Commons: Land, Identity and Development—The Manipur Experience.* New Delhi: Akansha Publishing House.

Som, Tapan Kumar (1991). Land Utilisation and Changing Economy in the Context of Rubber Plantation Industry: A Sociological Study in the North Tripura District, in Malabika Dasgupta edited, *Impact of Land Reforms in Northeast India.* New Delhi: Omsons Publications.

Thakur, Manish (2013). Land Question in Bihar: Madhubani as a Metaphor. *Economic and Political Weekly*, Vol. XLVIII, No. 19, May 11.

Whitehead, Judy (2003). Space, Place and Primitive Accumulation in Narmada Valley and Beyond. *Economic and Political Weekly*, October 4.

5

Whither Communal Land!

With the changes in the mode of production, all the pristine land-based social relations underwent corresponding changes. The process of changes in the mode of production started with the historical decline of the primordial economy and the advent of institutional economy in the hills that replaced the *tributary mode* by the typical *rent-revenue* mode of accumulation. But land *rent* or *revenue* was insignificant from the hill lands. The forests resources in the hills became the major attraction for *revenue* generation.

The situation changed when the communal land space was factored in the critical paradigms of modernity and development evinced first by the colonials. The micro-geographical spaces of the tribal habitats and the natural resources lying therein had enormous consumptive-utilitarian values to the colonial state. These led the latter to go for rapid enclavisation of community space through marking the native reserves like Forest Reserves, Inner Line, Scheduled Districts, Excluded and Partially Excluded Areas and so on, where the colonial rules were applied differently although their sovereign jurisdiction extended over those areas for larger resource augmentation. They, therefore, made a master plan in these areas for resource augmentation through primitive accumulation, positive jurisprudence, revenue administration and through institutional economics. The colonial rulers produced new "boundaries and hierarchies, zones and enclaves" as the physical spaces embedded in local resource use regimes became incorporated into global resource use regimes. This involved radical subversion of existing social, political and economic networks and property regimes (Baruah 2008: 16). The importance of such spatial and ecological order was quickly woven into the larger colonial economy and the wealthy spatial enclaves in the hills became the profitable zones to be plundered and exploited by the colonial forces. Such reconfigured space now came to reregulate the populations and their movements within these, increased state control over land, dismissed community access and sharpened the state-community rift.

These measures, taken together, led to disjunction of communal space from the people. The pejorative connotation of the Inner Line Regulation was criminalisation of the so-called "trespassers". It is interesting to know that Inner Line was not a stationary concept. It kept extending towards different hills as and when required. The Inner Line system was also a mechanism of colonial evasion of tribal recalcitrance at the frontier on the one hand and a mechanism of capture of the land spaces of many tribes for strategic purposes and resource augmentation on the other. The twin process of 'evasion' and 'capture' correspondingly structured and re-structured the communal space and the tribal ontology associated with this. The colonial rule also intended to introduce the British system of assessment, registration of the ownership of land (R.P. Dutt 2008: 227-228) from which the tribal communities were not free. The colonial rulers impugned the practice of shifting cultivation for not being congenial to "improvement", productivity, commercial profit and innovations. Shifting cultivation was considered as a lazy and impoverished practice on the parts of the tribal communities. Hence, such a practice needed to be replaced. The colonials introduced Hill House Tax, Dao Tax, Hoe Tax, etc. in the hills as land tax was not possible to extract due to prevalence of shifting cultivation. Such taxes, however, did not give any financial opulence to the colonisers. The purpose of such taxation was more strategic than economic.

In the next part, we will see the role of colonial anthropology in accumulation of resources from the tribal areas and then look into the problem of accumulation and dispossession in the larger angle of political economy.

Colonial Anthropology, Race Theory and Accumulation

The colonials needed to align tradition with modernity for capture of natural wealth endowments in the tribal areas in Northeast India. Knowledge about the pre-colonial tribal economy became necessary in order to locate the resources of the region as well as to fold the tribal economic resources within the colonial economy. This anthropological knowledge came down from the colonials themselves to the tribal societies. The colonial administrators and the missionaries, who came with them, used this anthropological knowledge for governing the natives and to remove the superstitions and ignorance of the local customs of the tribes. They blamed the ethnic spaces of Northeast India for blocking market access and resource access that the colonisers cherished. Those spaces needed to be accessed by the powers of "sword and sermon". This made the colonials look beyond the highbrow mathematical model of economics towards an anthropological model in the tribal areas of Northeast India. Anthropology was dominated by the metaphorical race theory that provided a *grand alibi* for capture of communal land resources in the hills. The process, so stated, finally resulted in annihilation of both the communal land and the community. The colonial state process in this region was juxtaposed with the anthropological approach. In this connection, Lewis viewed that recording of the differences between the Western and non-Western culture would support continued differences which gave the colonials the right to exploit the people (Lewis 1973: 584).

The state geared up the governing mechanism of land, wrested the customary rights on communal land of the racially inferior tribes and introduced positivist concept of rights. This created great divide in the rights perception between the tribal communities and the colonial state. The British resorted to Darwin's evolutionary schem, in which the Whites placed themselves at the most advanced stage of civilisation and the tribal people were despised as laggards and heathens, who deserved to be ruled and whose resources deserved to be appropriated by the former for more "rational use". This stock of people was despised for being 'racially and intellectually incapable' to manage their own resources and for failure to catch up with the level of modern Western civilisation. This perception of the colonisers ran through the times and made them set the anthropological model that initiated an irrevocable process of annihilation of the communal resources. In this way, colonial anthropology, race theory and accumulation became mutually constitutive for imperial augmentation in the hills of Northeast India. Roy Burman following Godalier, explained the scenario. "Since the nineteenth century, the word 'tribe' became synonymous with the 'primitive'. In this historical ethnocentric approach, the industrial or post- industrial West is at one polar end of human social formations and those at the other polar end or close to it constitutes the primitive social formation, the laggards in the evolutionary schema of social organisation, the most backward segment of humanity" (Roy Burman 1995: 1). Given this antithesis, the colonial conquest followed a longitudinal white-native and/or modernity-pre-modernity divide which was eventually crystallised in theory and ideology. The antithesis between modernisation theory of sociology and pre-modernisation theory of anthropology created a temporal division between the two disciplines although both the theorisations happened within the same spatio-temporal reality in which colonial mode of production operated. This division made the modernisation theory a subject of the 'enlightened present' of the colonisers and anthropology a subject of the 'unkempt past' of the tribal communities. The colonial modernity nurtured this antithesis, which gave a reasoned *alibi* for resource augmentation, accumulation, resource capture and and finally for rule. While both the colonial modernity and the tribal un-modernity rode on the same spatio-temporal saddle, the former always took the front seat.

'Race theory' and anthropology became complementary to each other and built the meta-narrative of colonial accumulation. Resource grabbing and privatisation of land space; growth fundamentalism and extended production; trade and revenue maximisation; administrative interventions; changes in cropping and land use pattern; extension of the power state and, not the least, theological intervention constructed the fundamentals of such meta-narrative. Both race theory and anthropology placed the tribal communities in the *past* of time based on Darwin's evolutionary schema that justified annihilation of communal land space with the march of colonisation, representing the enlightened present. The race theory and the enlightenment project were purposively harboured to customise the process of primitive accumulation and accumulation by dispossession. This let loose a contradiction between the rational choice of methodological individualism and the convivial socio-economic relations of the tribal community. This *past-present* classification of time constructed the '*inferior* of the tribes' and made the latter a major subject of the 'race discourse' led by the evolutionary-biological school and manned by J.S. Mill, Risley, Henry Maine and Baden Powell. They racialised the natives as well as 'racialised the space' (space Darwinism) suitable only for grabbing and primitive accumulation. The post-Industrial Revolution and its hard rationality of science were constructed on these lines. J.S. Mill's propagation of the providential nature of the *Pax Britannica* went parallel to his great adoration of the race theory, phrenology and phylogenetics. Mill castigated the socio-economic institutions of the so-called racially inferior colonised tribes as imperfect, incapable and ineffective. He established on the other hand, the ascendancy of the socio-economic institutions of the colonisers, deeming them as perfect, efficient and effective. He then attributed this difference to the racial differences.

Risley's anthropometric approach established the thesis of capability deficit of the land and forest dependent tribal communities and on the basis of this, he built a rationale for 'White Man's Rule' and took a hedonist position for resource capture and wealth accumulation. Race theory and capitalist expansion hence, went together to form an ideology of colonial land accumulation first and the colonial rule later. [On the other hand, Elwin viewed the virtues of primitiveness such as self-reliant, community work, spirit of cooperation, artistic creativeness, honesty, truthfulness, hospitality. The primitive people were crafty products of the self-seeking, individualistic, industrial civilisation (Guha 1999: 284)].

Understanding of the non-European communities was the primary task of the colonial anthropologists for the purpose of augmentation and conquest. Much of the ethnographic information about the tribal society was gathered by the vindictive colonial agents like the merchants, missionaries and administrators. The anthropologists, trained in race theory, provided powerful intellectual support to them. The post-1857 rebellion impelled the colonial administration to halt Lord Dalhousie's aggressive policy of absorption of land as it earned a lot of ill-will. In its place, policies of indirect rule were adopted to accommodate and appropriate tribal land and to complete the project of colonial conquest. Therefore, "after 1857, anthropology supplanted history as the principal colonial modality of knowledge and rule. Rule through anthropological knowledge, not just its political economy, was important for keeping India under British rule"(Bordoloi 2014: 48).

Anthropological polarisation between the White and the Black received official patronage and served the colonial capital and colonial rule in multiple ways. Although anthropology was resorted to in pursuance of the administrative goals and so, larger institutional arrangements were made both in India and abroad for training the ICS probationers and civil servants (Mathur 1989: 65), their orientation was basically racist that was instrumental in resource capture in the tribal areas. This provoked the colonials to send a series of expeditions to different parts of the region at different points of time, when the tribes rose to rebel against resource capture. The colonisation process in the Northeast region was gradual, depending on the strategic importance, availability of resource endowments and market potential of the raw materials available therein. The spatial spread of capital and market in the hill areas mystified the consciousness of the tribal communities as well, whereas in the doxic path of capitalist accumulation, the imperialists themselves surrendered their rational thinking to brutalise their mode of accumulation. The colonial understanding on land resources was built around individual acquisitiveness, accumulation, self-agrandisement and commoditisation. For this, they resorted to the Roman jurisprudential principle of *terra nullius,* meaning land "not owned" by anyone, and such a *terra nullius* principle became an ideal principle for space grabbing in the tribal areas. This jurisprudential principle also gave them *carte blanche* over the communal resources lying in the tribal areas.

The self-aggrandisement drive of the colonisers led them to introduce the principles of justice and injustice, rights and duties, institutions and administration around the concept of private property. While doing so, the former maintained a conspicuous class distance from the tribes and simultaneously continued to strengthen their own solidarity and cohesiveness for resource capture from the tribal areas. The mutual constitutivity of economics of grabbing and race theory facilitated the process of privatisation of communal land although racial inferiority and backwardness of the tribal community had no socio-historical evidence. But this became an essential condition for growth of the European capital. Immigrating from Europe, the colonial rulers justified resource capture with the combination of white ethnogenesis and primitive accumulation/accumulation by dispossession. Later on, they politically and administratively subjugated the tribal people and propagated this act as, what Pathy (Pathy 1987: 2-3) called, "White Man's Burden".

By projecting the so-called capability deficit of the tribes in resource handling, the colonials popularised the practice of commercial plantation for which communal lands were captured by force, fraud and deceit. The tribal people were imparted new skills in commercial plantation that destroyed their indigenous practices of shifting cultivation and the extant land use pattern. Guided by the anthropological account of the land-use pattern in the hills as the marker of backwardness, the mid-19th century forest officers and botanists were up to deconstruct the practice of shifting cultivation for introducing commercial crops in the hills. It is to be noted that all the actions of the East India Company were calculated on the bases of profit and mercantile interest, raw material exploitation for British industries and marketing of the manufactured goods. In the Naga Hills, nothing of the sort was available at that point of time and, thus, Lord Dalhousie found little interest in possession of the Naga Hills (Progs of NEIHA 1987: 380-381). On the other hand, Assam's silk potential came to the notice of the colonials and the demand of silk being what it was for the British export merchandise, Mr. David Scott, the Agent to the Governor General on the Northeast Frontier and Commissioner of Northeast Rangpur, became a great champion of free trade and played the role of a benevolent despot. He "introduced the mulberry plant, with a view for its increase; and brought workmen from Rungpore, who taught the *natives* an improved mode of preparing and spinning the moongah silk, a staple commodity of the country. He laboured to improve the breed of cattle and distribute potatoes and other useful vegetables among the *natives.* The prisoners in jail were taught various useful occupations and an agricultural farm was established" (White 1988: 7).

The Khasi Hills similarly had the possibility of improving and extending its agricultural and horticultural produce and Scott found the potential for better quality and higher quantity of opium production at a cheaper rate there. Other crops, including wheat, potatoes, turnips, betel-roots, buckwheat, maize, barley etc. also had potential in the Khasi Hills. Besides, the mineral properties of the Khasi Hills, including, limestone, coal, iron, slate and grey sandstone were found abundantly. For the resources to develop fully, the British used force to silence the local movement, invaded the people of this area and proved their strength to the Khasis. They were severely punished till they quietly submitted to the British control (Pamberton 1991: 263-264). Racialisation of the plebeian voice against resource exploitation and forceful suppression of the same featured the process of primitive accumulation at this point of time. Both, during the rule of the East India Company as well as during the British rule, all expeditions sent to different parts of the hills in Northeast India had the ultimate design of amassing colonial wealth from the hills. Mr. Scott's knowledge of jungle warfare was unquestionable. His armed revenge to the tribes like the Garos and the Khasis, into whose lands the British intruded, was well recorded (White 1988: 9,10). The philanthropic David Scott, who once gave a glowing tribute about the civilised nature of the Khasi *Pnars*, "had no compunction to turn a somersault and called them wild and bloodthirsty *savages*, whose thirst for vengeance could be quenched only by blood of their opponents when the Khasi *Pnars* rose to rebellion to drive out the British" (Rymbai 1993: 84). But what was a *savage* and *racist* act in the eyes of the British, was an expression of the plebeian voice from the standpoint of the Khasis.

The *terra nullius* treatment of communal land space caused cultural reductionism of the lived space of the so-called 'racially inferior' tribes and, it at the same time, provided an apology for the civilising mission in which *terra nullius* as a jurisprudential approach subtly intruded in the cultural arena of the tribal people. Trans-meaning of *terra nullius* further rationalised colonial capture of land-based resources and showed the world that such capture was necessary to enlighten them, improve their fate by commercial agriculture and to elevate them to higher stage of civilisation, following Rostow's logic. This rationale of the providential *Pax Brittannica* was carried forward to all the tribal areas, where capital investment on *terra nullius* was made. Race prejudice and the providential *Pax Britannica* went parallel till the race theory became the state doctrine of the colonial rulers. David Scott, in the hills of Northeast India, became the actor hero to push the doctrine deeper in the tribal societies. He had two faces. One face expressed his great attachment to the natives and with his philanthropological mind, he seldom admitted in a diplomatic way, the moral superiority of the Europeans and instanced the honesty of the native servants (White 1988: 6), (although bribery and corruption in their worst and oppressive forms were universal among the native functionaries as well under the colonial rule). The other face of David Scott was his deep-rooted racial hatred, racial prejudice and despotism. Thus, he was in the habit of distributing the New Testament in the Assamese language to the *natives* and found the Garrow and the Cassyah in a *"rude state of civilisation"* (White 1988: 7). While he was a captive of racial prejudice, Mr. Scott's trust and faith towards the native servants was not more than just a deployment of a social strategy to run the British administration *within* the broad racial framework. It was a soft method of British public administration with community approval that Scott had followed in the hills. This social strategy was ultimately linked to a complex process of revenue-profit generation from the resource-rich tribal areas. Therefore, given the choice between large-scale accumulation of resources and petty corruption of the native servants, the British public administration preferred the latter rather than the former. The process of crude and rational accumulation was subsequently butteressed by a more polite approach mix of eduction, theology and ideology.

In the hills of Northeast India, it was the colonial intention to link Western education with evangelism to enlighten the tribes and hence, to seek a social base for its expansion in the hills. A truer proof of this is obtained from Eric Stroke, who was quoted by Prabhat Kumar Mukhopadhyaya. He wrote, "Hitherto British manufacturers had only a limited market in India because of the poverty of the people and their unformed taste. Education and Christianity would remove these obstacles. In this way, the noblest species of conquest, the spread of true religion and knowledge, would not forfeit its earthly rewards; for whatever our principle and our language are introduced, our commerce follow" (Mukhopadhyaya 1972: 354). It is pitiable that some of the Indian leaders, including ironically, Rammohan Roy, shared the views of the early missionaries and upheld the theory of divine providence of the *Pax Britannica*. (Hussain 1983: 42)]. At the ideological level, therefore, sword, sermon, education and colonial merchandise became a mutually exclusive quadrangle to 'uplift the tribal people' of Northeast India. In the mainland, on the other hand, there were two distinct trends: one was towards materialism and the other was towards resurgence of Hinduism with assimilation of Western culture, but with greater resistance against Christianity (Thomas 1969: 247). Christianity in India appeared in two ways. One, as an intellectual movement for mystification of mass consciousness about colonialism and the other as an administrative policy which preferred to choose the individual line of proselytisation of the 'racially inferior'. Both these movements, however, operated on the same wave length of colonialism. In the tribal societies of Northeast India, there was no difference in the basic approach. Roy noted , " following the administration and army and all these connoted came the 'messengers of Christ'... They penetrated deep into many of these communities... these missionaries, some of them very well meaning and pious souls, determined to save these communities of people from over-lasting domination, as they saw it, were all of people from the great establishment of the foreign rulers, and ... their mission was directed towards upholding and strengthening that establishment" (Roy 1972: 19).

In the North East, Christianity came as an administrative policy backed by state patronage and institutional force. The teachings of the Gospel became one of the most important modes of resource capture. State patronage was at the back of the missionaries. [The first subsidy was given to the Garo Mission in 1929. (Downs 1983: 73), official support was provided by the Political Agent of Manipur to Rev. Pettigrew with an amount of Rs. 895 out of the total expenditure of Rs. 4619 on education for the year 1896-97, for construction of a new school building in Ukhrul (Administrative Report of Manipur. 1896-97 and 1898-99) and financial grants were made to the Welsh Presbyterian Church in the Khasi and Jaintia Hills (Rymbai 1993: 82)]. The ecclesiastical interventions trivialised the communal land space and turned the Khasi and Jaintia Hills as their preserve by large-scale accumulation of communal lands.

Heathenisation of the tribal communities denied *lex loci* status to communal land of the tribal people. Huge land areas were captured for building colonial infrastructure for administration, army cantonments, urban infrastucture, commercial hubs, educational and health institutions and for ecclesiastical establishments. This is how the so-called European areas in Shillong emerged that eventually became a contested space of the community until the entire community was baptised and was passed over to Christianity. The mission took advantage of the superstition of 'haunt of spirit' to obtain land at a cheap price in all hill areas of the Northeast (Misra 1983: 20). Moreover, in an agreement between David Scott and Chera *Siyems* in 1829, it was stated that the latter voluntarily ceded land to the east of Cherapunjee to the British for construction of a sanatorium. This land was insufficient. The succeeding *Siyem* readily ceded more territory to the south east, for the sanatorium (Syiemlieh 1983: 118). But what was *voluntary* was in fact not voluntary and what was *readily* was not readily in deed. In fact, they did it either under constant threat and surveillance of the British or for obtaining some concrete benefits and services from the colonials.

The promoted land spaces of the colonisers sheltered the lumpen incomers; racialised the space and made an enclave for the upper class people, churches and the businessmen. This scrambled the demographics by exclusionary zoning of the local inhabitants. This was followed by conversion of the *Gemeinschaft* to the *Gesselschaft* with the jurisprudential instrument of *terra nullius* and in the process of the civilising mission, the communal space became the privatised space of the 3-Cs (Capital, Colonisers and Church). The principle of *terra nullius,* thus, eventually became integrated with the world system of colonisation, the Judeo-Christian roots of which could be found in Bauman's "genealogy of *ex nihilo* philosophy in which *ex nihilo* was used to defend monotheism of the centre against polytheism of the periphery as Rome became Christianised, and this became the groundwork for *terra nullius* narratives during colonial conquests by later Christian monarchs. From this perspective, *terra nullius* faithfully re-enacted the Euro-Christian dogma of creation: something providential arising from nothing (*ex nihilo*). It was only a short and convenient step to inscribe ownerlessness on emptiness (*terra nullius*)—a void awaiting the dominion of monotheists and their laws" (Geisler 2012: 18). The colonisers instrumentalised monotheism along with the *ex nihilo* principles in the hills of Northeast India. This justified the capture of the land space of the tribals as ex nihilo, ownerless, and empty. The very consciousness of the tribal people was theologically mystified as "born sinners", who were frightened of the horrifying myths of the 'flesh-hungry maggots and the hell-fire. They could be saved from the flesh-hungry maggots only when they could embrace Christianity. In this way, the monotheist dogma won over the consciousness of the tribal people, who in turn, surrendered the mundane land questions in favour of spiritual pursuit.

While the colonials were primarily interested in extraction of raw materials to feed in the home economy, the missionaries were busy civilising the heathens with a futuristic vision. These two movements were parallel and were constitutive of each other and so, colonisers through the missionary path sought their moral legitimacy to rule and accumulate the communal resources, just as the monotheist Christian monarch did in Rome. And as *Sword and Sermon* went together, David Scott was of the opinion that labours of the missionaries should be combined with instruction of agriculture and mechanical arts with a view to raising these rude people in the scale of society (White 1988: 7-8). The Nagas were described as Naked Nagas and savage people in primitive anthropology to construct their backwardness and the missionaries invested enough zeal to make them civilised. In fact, the early anthropologists in the 'land of the heathens' in Northeast India, also loved to snap masculine and feminine photographs in exposed order to take pride of their tenacity in *anthropological fieldwork* and to show to the world, the reasons for 'racial otherisation' of the indigenous tribes. At the same time, as we have seen, they combined the mission work with commercial plantation and finally with the land administration. In the Naga Hills, the missionaries taught the people Christianity and the art of cultivating tea simultaneously (Elwin 1969: 96, 100, 515, 517.) This annihilated the customary land ownership, material culture and the extant productive forces of the tribal people. Mr. Scott also proposed an irrigation system to make the land permanently fertile with reduced labour of the people, who practised jhoom cultivation. He said, by cutting the sides of the hill into steps, the soil would be rendered flat, and the loss consequently avoided, while, by having a command of water, (it is not proposed to raise the water artificially, but merely to dam up the rivulets and turn the stream where it may be required), good crops would be ensured independently of the vicissitudes of seasons"(White 1988: 80). He made plans for horticulture and some fruit trees including mangoes, peaches, the China fruits, pears, etc. Horticultural plantation de-constructed the erstwhile agricultural practices and the related social relations of the tribal people and re-constructed their relations for integration into the market economy. This is how through the route of race theory, capital, colonisers and mission intruded into the communal land system in Northeast India.

The colonial economic institutions branded the tribal institutions as irrational, inefficient (following Aristotle's dictum that rationality is unknown to the slaves) and market imperfect. To set matters right, the colonial land administration was invigorated. Being anxious for revenue and in order to ascertain the exact resources of the country, Mr. Scott obtained the survey of land from the government. The survey work was entirely performed by the native surveyors while the European surveyors marked out the given tract and surveyed the boundary (White 1988: 8). Land administration was *ipso facto* tagged with the British Common Law that trivialised the customary land ownership of the tribal people. Race and Christianity served as twin Ideological State Apparatus to dispossess the tribal people and the 19th century missionaries took the *doctrine of conversion* just as the colonial empire took the missions as partners to promote commerce and civilisation. The race theory built the foundation of natural inequality and rationalised all conflicts emanating from private accumulation and eventual inequality as part of the universal struggle of individualistic aggrandisements. Any act of dissent was criminalised and institutional force was set in motoin to tame it. This state of affairs mystified the tribal consciousness in two ways: (i) by theological mystification that insulated the colonial design of accumulation and (b) by preaching the doctrine of conversion.

A large number of anthropological and ethnographic research studies in Northeast India made by the Indian scholars reproduced the colonial version of lack of 'fit' of the tribal institutions with the colonial ones that had already penetrated in the region. Striking a 'fit' was difficult and it was difficult because anthropology was catalytic to the first interface between the pre-capitalist formations in the region and the emerging capitalist/colonial relations in the tribal societies. This invited the inevitable trade-off between institutional economics and communal economics. The first trade-off centred round the concept of right in which anthropology of right and political economy of right clashed headlong and land became a warring space for the colonial state and the community institutions. The colonial construction of land right followed the Anglo-Saxon version of private ownership, inheritance and sale right and the ascendancy of the positive over the customary laws. Elwin wrote, on establishing the ascendancy of the positive law of the colonials, some of the old British officers also pleaded for granting greater proprietary or ownership right over land to the tribals in NEFA (Elwin.1964: 72). This was also a strategic, not a normative gesture on the part of the colonials. The latter knew well that hardly any substantial revenue could be derived from the hill agriculture. They targeted the forest and the mineral resources of the hills over which they tended to establish monopoly right.

Enclavisation of space was extremely exploitative that made the *gemeinschaft* subservient to privately owned lands and, thus, the colonials broke, as Polanyi would say, the "embeddedness of society and economy"(Humphreys, 1969: 166-167, 174) of the tribal societies. Very conveniently, therefore, the colonials could erase the land-community symbiosis, annihilate the subsistence economy, destroy the concept of community labour and its ontological essence. In this way, it also broke the inter-dependence of the tribal people on geography, culture, society and economy. Resource grabbing strategy also mystified the extant ecological practices and beliefs, misinterpreted the customary ownership and pictured a predatory image of the forest and the human beings living therein. Wrong notions were imparted to the students about the sacred groves in Khasi society, that there is no sacredness in them. These groves were revered only because the Khasis were animists (Dutta and Karna 1987: 2). The colonials despised "the Khasis' regard for the sacred groves and prohibited forests, sacred pools and rivers as relics of the pagan superstition of benighted people, who believed that gods or evil spirits had their abode there" (Rymbai 1993: 85). "The early converts began to fell trees stealthily in the sacred forests or to fish surreptitiously in the sacred pools. As there was no visitation of the evil spirits on them, they began to believe more and more in the words of the missionaries and felt more encouraged to indulge in desecration of those sacred places. ... With the converts destroying the forests, the sepoys and government started leasing out the forests and pools to people. The early 19th century missionaries sowed the seed of contempt for sacred forests, protected forests, sacred pools and rivers that germinated in revenue creation and profiteering by the timber merchants (Rymbai 1993: 86, 87, 88).

Similar wrong imaging of the forests was made by describing forests as jungles, where no civilised being could dare to tread. Whereas the same forests were the space for the idyllic practice of hunting and for extraction of huge profit-revenue. Elwin wrote, the luxuriant practice of 'official hunting' was prevalent in NEFA (Elwin 1964: 72) David Scott in Assam was fond of hunting and shooting and used to attend the call of his youthful friends to join them in a tiger boat hunt or other animating sports (White 1988: 25). The forests, which were initially considered obstacles to empire building, came to be gradually exploited for imperial ends by the British colonial administration (Handique 2012: 122). The colonial anthropologists, on the one hand, intended to keep the tribes as museum specimens, while on the other hand, supported the act of resource aggrandisement from there. Elwin contested the museum specimen concept and defended only a policy of 'temporary isolation' with a sane desire to protect them from the landlords and Zamindars, moneylenders and merchants. But things did not happen as desired. The people of NEFA, he wrote, did not live like the Noble Savage but had to face poverty, disease, anxiety, cruelty and exploitation of the landlords and Zamindars, moneylenders and merchants (Elwin 1964: 46-47). He had a protectionist, not an isolationist viewpoint in respect of the tribes. On the other hand, the idea of assimilation created another path dependency on a formal framework that dispossessed the poor tribes and pauperised them progressively on the social scene.

Anthropology shifted from race to culture. Functionalism and culture (Bronislaw Malinowski, and Melville J. Herskovits) made the critical shift (although the posthumous publication of Malinowski's field diaries in some parts revealed a racist and abusive attitude towards the 'natives'). (*International Encyclopedia of the Social and Behavioural Sciences*: 2704). While the race theory was foundational to the European imperialism, functionalism intended to give a sanitized stability to it. Herskovits's anthropological approach to economics was premised on the unity of process and institutions; non-economic aspects and social expediency of property rights; its intangible meaning and legal, sociological and ethical concepts of property. He viewed property as a social institution and gave a cross-cultural perspective of property rights (Hertkovits 1952: 313-321). Karl Polanyi also saw the role of the non-economic factor (culture) in driving the economic activities that positivism and scientism of modern economics ignored (Humphreys 1969: 66-67, 74).

The cultural paradigm broke the conventional White-Native antithesis to become a relational paradigm. The political economy reason for factoring in culture was to make the latter instrumental again in accumulation. Following the Malinowskian tradition, the anthropological fieldworks focused on single tribes and on a historicised functionalism, suitable for indirect rule of the tribes. Indirect rule apparently strengthened traditional rulers of the tribes though, it is through them that the process of resource accumulation continued unabated. Cultural anthropology, thus, displayed the power relationship between the colonisers and the colonised communities and cultural approach became helpful in minimising disruption by enabling the "community people to keep some of their socio-cultural institutions while the administrators collected taxes, commercial companies expanded their networks, and missionaries could seek for converts without too much fear for their skins" (Maini 2000:162). Through the cultural route, the colonials propagated the Anglo-Saxon world vision of an ideal peak of civilisation and human development and acquainted the colonial administrators with diversity of customs in different segments of the population. The myth of the 'noble and contented 'savage' was spread all over the colonised world. There was also stress on their moral inferiority which helped to maintain the *status quo* of land colonisation. This was the time when colonialism was expanding (Pathy 1987: 3). Colonialism was, thus, not an economic doctrine alone but a racial doctrine of resource capture and rule as well. The power of the *Sword and Sermon* made the tribal people surrender their lands and forest resources to the colonial rulers as well as made them theologically surrender themselves to the evangelical missionaries and in the Weberian way, accumulation of wealth was juxtaposed with an act of *'moral calling'* for the sake of uplifting the savages till the Bible went into the hands of the tribal people and land into the hands of the colonisers. The community also self-imposed the *Doctrine of Degeneration* that reified the community consciousness.

The abundance of natural resources in the hills and presence of a stronghold of Hinduism in the valley areas of the region, impelled the colonial missionaries to make a longitudinal evangelical planning. Thus, the Diocese of Kohima alone could have 30 parishes and mission centres covering a total land area of 16, 487 sq. kms by an 1989 estimate (Syemlieh 1990). The early missionaries in Northeast India occupied good land for establishment of churches, schools, health centres and residential houses of the missionaries. In Tripura, there was a great tug of war between the New Zealand Baptist Mission Society, the Tripura Darbar and the Revenue and Political Department of Tripura over grants of land to the Mission Society. While the church authorities made several requests for land acquisition on a Municipality site on philanthropic and religious grounds, the Diwan of Tripura Darbar viewed that the site was within the Taluk that was non-transferable without expressed sanction of the Maharaja. He viewed that the transfer of land was made to the missionaries by a jotedar without expressed sanction of the Maharaja (Chakravorti 1989: 236-237). It was not unusual, therefore, for the native people, with whom the missionaries came in first contact, to suspect the white-faced missionaries resembling the colonial rulers, as the 'agents of the Company'. The cultural focus of the colonial anthropologists, thus, became extremely challenging. They not only made the tribes laboratory specimens but also exaggerated the segmentary and pluralistic foci of the colonised societies to convey disunity among the people. These served the colonials to implement their policies (Pathy 1987: 3) of capture of land and setting one tribe against the other.

Two points are critical in this connection: (i) the colonial theoretical equation of culture with religion and (ii) the real role of culture in the mode of production. Let us take the first point: in any society, including the tribal society, intellectual and spiritual vacuum and the crisis of the world view takes place only when there is a substantive change in the mode of production. But it is an accepted fact that in the North East, there was no substantive change in the mode of production in the tribal societies under colonialism. There was no dynamic force within the tribal societies either to supersede the extant world view of the tribes. Explanation of social change in terms of religious change, thus, does not *per se* provide a scientific explanation. This Feurbackian notion is both false and a-historic. Religion is based largely on tradition and is characterised by relative permanency, while culture is subject to constant change. Religion and culture are, thus, two separate phenomena and deserve separate treatment. (Ray 1992: 54-55) Engels noted, "great historical turning points have been *accompanied* by religious changes only so far as the three world religions which have existed upto the present Buddhism, Christianity and Islam are concerned (Engels 1972: 355) and in no case were such turning points preceded by religious changes. And if Max Weber, the German sociologist, endeavoured to conceptually link the 'Protestant Ethics' with the emergence of the 'Spirit of Capitalism' it was similarly a-historic and the truth was put upside down. Secondly, identification of religion with culture remains an accepted reality as long as things were conceived religiously, spiritually and metaphysically by the colonials.

On the other hand, Marx understood culture not in abstraction but as innovation and progress of the material means of production to change the reality—'from thing in itself to thing for us'. The cultural practices reduced dependency of human beings on ecology. This also correspondingly diminished the essentialism and exclusivism of ecological anthropology in course of changing the reality. Thus, for example, in Arunachal Pradesh, the early use of the wooden plough in certain places was replaced by the iron plough commensurating the innovations of iron ore and smelting technology. The Marxist view on the non-economic forces was also different from those of Herskovits and Polanyi. He equated the *non-economic* forces with force, fraud, plunder, capture—in short, primitive accumulation contrary to Herskovits' thesis of the non-economic life of the primitive people as a countervail to modern capitalistic economy in terms of money, market, trade, etc.

Political Economy Regimes

Anthropology, in course of time, gave way to political economy that could strongly institutionalise the private property regime in the tribal societies, through creating more structured governing mechanisms and state intervention so that the resources from the hills could be drained out for building blocks of the empire. It is for this reason that from the metaphorical realm of racial anthropology, the land privatisation project shifted to political economy that introduced the metropolitan model of land administration in communal land system record of private rights to own, control and use land. The colonial political economy frame and its administrative model exerted powerful influence on the processual aspect of communal land economy, destructed the fundamentals of land-based ontology of the tribal people, destructed the static, pre-given subsistence use of land and forest and the holism of the primordial social and economic institutions. Ruling was never the end function of the British. It was consequential upon folding in the incredible natural resources from the tribal region.

The Chin Lushai Conference held at Fort William in 1892 viewed that the "boundaries of the new administration should be, generally speaking, the boundaries of the tract occupied by the savages newly brought under British control" (Chin Lushai Conference 1982). It is from here that the colonial political economy process became active in annihilation of the communal land space. While both racial anthropology and revenue administration operated in the combined interest of usurpation and annihilation, revenue interest from land needed a stronger institutional framework. The colonials calculated the factor endowments of land, forest and mineral resources and the revenue potential from these and brought those under their legal and institutional frameworks. The broader institutional frame of land administration was homogeneous and its rational-legal nature challenged the relational aspect of communal land. Land, henceforward, came to be a strictly administratively defined and an institutionally regulated resource. A clear, legal and secure document in favour of legal persons became the requirement for ownership of land, capital investment, institutional credit, sale, purchase and mortgage and land administration became a system for managing such private rights holders. The profit motive from land was at the centre of revenue administration which claimed to have resolved the so-called 'chaotic nature' of communal land resources. The land relations in the pre-modern communities in the hills were diverse that could not be dealt with separately with efficiency. Therefore, the colonial land administration was homogenised. The main body of revenue administration and the land laws superseded the customary laws of the tribal societies and subjected tribal lands to the British laws, British land administration and to British possession. The stationary character of land deserved a separate and special administrative-legal framework than the products of land like timber and minerals. The economic importance of landed property being central to the colonials, the latter sought to annihilate the communal land right by positive law. New definition to ownership, possession and use of land was given that led to class formation of two types: between the colonials (patrician) class and the tribes and the affluent and the poor tribes. Both these classes attained overwhelming importance under colonialism.

The primary colonisation of land took place in the historical settlement of the tribal communities on the *terra cognita*. Primary colonisation was governed by the principle of *primacy* of occupation which gave only *usufruct* rights to the community members. This gave them the natural title to land space that in course of time became the historical title. The space of the primary settlers became the lived place of the community with both *conative* and *cognitive* functions. Abundance factor of land and the communitarian ethos of the communal land system made the primary land-colonisation non-adversarial and convivial. It is for this reason that the shifting cultivators in the hills emerged as a uni-class community. Under the colonial rule, the customary rights were recognised only as *derivative* rights under a complex and conflicting policy, legal, and institutional framework like the *Ramrileikha* to the Lushai chiefs, settlement rights to the Kuki chiefs and so on. They envisioned their own future through rent-seeking only within such land spaces as allotted by their colonial masters. Such institutional arrangements squeezed, both the "operational area" and the "social space" of the tribal people.

On the other hand, the colonials extended the structured revenue administration both for accumulation and for making it a symbol of the colonial sovereignty. It turned the community land space as the 'governed space' of the colonisers, distinct from the natural space of the tribal communities. Land administration had formally three distinct interests: to bring the communal under the territorial state, accumulate the raw materials from tribal areas for industrial supply in the metropolis and to drew maximum profit-revenue from the land resources located therein. These formed the bases of the top-down land-forest administration in the hill areas. The land administration, started by the East India Company, had a combined responsibility of civil administration and commerce (Grant of Diwani 1765). Later on, these were separated and the former was entrusted to a separate bureaucratic class (The Regulation Act of 1873). In the hills, the revenue administration became more elaborate in the forest sector as it was the main source of profit-revenue.

The crises and sufferings caused by the revenue administration were felt in Assam, as Guha wrote, when the colonial land administration replaced the service for kind payment of revenue. The land revenue collected through local currency was remitted to Calcutta for recoinage, which did not flow back, resulting in acute money shortage. The wet-rice cultivation infrastructure constructed and maintained at public cost was discontinued during 1825-40, to the detriment of agricultural production. The public works policy became adversarial. The surplus revenue above the establishment cost was remitted out of the province, that led to usury practices by the non-indigenous trading community. Prices also fell and the revenue defaulter's stock of paddy was auctioned at abysmally low rate. Cash shortage led to collection of gold, ivory, mooga silk, manjit cotton cloth, etc. against revenue that were put on sale to the traders. This made the defaulters flee from their homesteads to squat on the remote wastelands or they sold themselves as slaves. In this situation, David Scott's sericulture project that claimed to have export potential, revenue and prosperity of the country (Guha 1991: 142-45, 147), was dismissed in favour of Jenkins' plan for the Europeans to hold large land areas either on long-term lease or with free-hold right that could pave the path of colonial capitalism. Jenkins also encouraged monetisation of the revenue system and created absolute property rights in land. His idea was to attract the European planters and displace the local ryots through discriminatory land revenue policy (Guha 1991: 148-149, 154). Therefore, the period from the Treaty of Yandabo (1826) to the formation of the province of Assam (1874), Assam witnessed a close connection between wasteland administration and tea industry, enactment of different legal measures, revenue laws and regulations (Gangopadhyaya 1990: 3) that could establish monopoly control over the waste lands. Driven by revenue interest, many planters encroached upon the *jhum* lands by declaring such lands as wasteland. The communal allocation of land as a social arrangement came into conflict with state allocation of land as a legal-administrative arrangement. The purposive aspect of social allocation of land resources was promotion and protection of the communitarian value in the tribal society. The administrative laws of the state, on the other hand, had the purposive aspect of annihilation of the communal resources. The substantive law of the colonial state, therefore, never registered and recognised the processual aspects of the customary laws governing the land ownership system of the tribal communities with sufficient seriousness. The colonials adopted the policies of 'Exclusion' and 'Partially Exclusion' for administration of the tribal areas and later, "Exchusion" was institutionalised in the Sixth Schedule in the post-colonial Indian Constitution. But these provisions of the Constitution were engineered so much as to give precedence to the substantive law of the state over the processual aspects of the customary land laws of the tribal communities in this region.

The colonial land tenure system in the hills differed from

the Brahmaputra valley on three important counts: (i) absence of land record and tenural mode; (ii) marginal nature of land administration and (iii) forest as the major source of profit/ revenue. These built the colonial rationale for rights-denial to the tribal communities. The British clubbed together all the resource endowments in the hills in the jurisprudential package of *res nullius* that denied any right of the tribal people over these. However, as cadastral survey on the hill terrains was not possible, the British introduced a mini-mode of taxation like house tax, hoe tax, dao tax, etc. At the same time, they continued their efforts to introduce the improved method of cultivation, from where surplus could be generated. In Manipur, during the First World War, the British first took steps for improved method of cultivation and two farmers from the valley were sent to Gauhati and Dacca to learn the improved method. A small group of tribal people was sent to Europe to examine the probability of terrace cultivation on the hill slopes. These steps, however, remained ineffective. Land revenue being only 50 per cent of the total revenue of the state, the British administrators commercialised agriculture and the land under rice cultivation, increased from 26, 500 hectares in 1891 to 75, 370 hectares in 1941. The forest resources of this region suffered the consequences of mindless and ruthless logging and lumbering business. The indigenous modes of forest replenishment and afforestation were eroded following displacement of the tribal people. This opened the path of absolute monopoly of the state (Khouthonjam and Thangam 2011: 118, 111) that led to annihilation of community space.

On the other hand, the institution of chieftainship systems was incorporated within the imperial administration for not only collecting hill house tax but also for governing the community through the chieftains at less administrative expense. The teleological bias of the imperial bureaucracy and its immensely increased power soon destroyed the fragile hill economy and exposed the serious contradiction between imperial accumulation and tribal dispossession; dismissed the transitional path-model (of Riggs) and marked the threshold of potent plebeian discontent against the aggressive, utilitarian and self-aggrandising colonisation. The administrative mode of dispossession, therefore, came into the tribal world not only with a "congenital blood stain on one cheek", but with blood and dirt "dripping from head to foot, from every pore" (Fowkes 1990: 637). Owing to historical reasons, in the tribal societies of Northeast India, the Western type of capitalist development did not happen. A realistic transition required higher level of technological innovation and the consequent changes in the productive forces; market; capital, including human capital, social infrastructure and state patronage—a thoroughly capitalist path- the incipient transition philosophy of which lay in narcissism and hedonism, opposed to the communal character of land. In the specific context of the hill economy in Northeast India, none of the above factors was present. Therefore, the assumptions that colonial land administration and its instruments of resource accumulation would just operate by the *administrative* mode, remained historically wrong. The biased homogeneity of the imperial land administration in the hills hit at the core of the communal land system; hedged the possibility of transition; trivialised the golden canons of anthropology of economics and let loose the dislocating consequences in the tribal societies. Imperial jurisprudence reversed the rights perception on land-forest symbiosis in the tribal communities and separated forest administration from the land revenue administration. This separation affected the shifting cultivation, hunting-gathering economy and the social fabric of the tribes and threw them to the ever-losing end of the game. In administrative terms, this was a contradiction between the Western modes of organisation and the indigenous modes of organisation. But in *historical* terms, these modes produced an irreconcilable conflict between the accumulators and the dispossessed, manifested in a 'modern-pre-modern trade-off. Thus, destruction and annihilation narratives featured the late 19th century colonisation in the hills of Northeast India. This scenario demystified the path dependency on an administrative model on communal land.

The British people gave the chiefs some *derivative* rights just for strategic administration so as to avoid any popular resistance against grabbing and to (ii) accumulate resources with proper social approval. The chiefs had also to support the colonial administrators in collection of House Tax, implementation of the Settlement Rules, land classification and allotment rules, regulation of *Jhum* Land, etc. They underwent 'Structured Subordination' and private property began to creep in through the route of 'Structured Subordination'. The hitherto convivial labour relations also took the turn towards contractual relations. In course of time, the process of internal colonisation was expedited by the chiefs using their political authority. In Meghalaya, the *Ri Kynti* land was the customary privilege of the Bakhraw clan like the Khor kongar and Nongkhaw. Gradually, other clans also started to follow the same practice by planting orchards, constructing ponds and buildings on *Re Raid* and by claiming private possession of it. That is how the *Ri-Kynti* of the present day came into existence. With the increase of population, *Ri-Kynti* land multiplied now with different names and different places. The *Siyems* began to realise the profit by issuing patta on *Ri Raid* land which originally belonged to the *Ki Khun Ki hajar* (sons of the soil). (Lyngdoh 1992:48-49). This resulted in drastic reduction in the proportion of *Re Raid* lands, as Misra wrote, to as less as 10 per cent of the total landmass. The *Siyems* also started to lease out *Ri Raid* land. They became oppressive and drove out the people from *Re Raid* if the latter undermined his authority. In this process, the areas of Ranikor-Langshnon-Munnai Balat in Hima Maharam were transformed into *Ri Kynti* of the *Jait* system. (Misra 1979: 889-890). The Kuki and Zomi chiefs of Manipur also adopted the practice of sale of communal land to the outside agencies; the Lushai chiefs of Mizoram amassed huge landed wealth by privatisation of communal lands. They transformed the custodial rights into private right and fetishised communal land to grab it. The vicious pentagon of *sale-purchase-lease-rent-mortgage* was routinised in the tribal economic practices.

In this process, the chiefs/headmen ceased to be any longer

a critique of external colonisation of communal land and the *'promethean'* authorities made the traditional authority structure as the *cultural symbol* to defend their hedonist act. This state of things led to the emergence of the *nouveau riche* that signaled a crisis of the traditional *'epimethean'* authority. The existential realities of land privatisation in the hill economy in Northeast India, came to bear enormous testimony of similar non-economic forces of primitive accumulation to the dismissal of the autarkical demands of the hill people signalling the civilisational disaster of them.

The colonial land/forest administration rationalised institutional force as *non sequitur* that had a great role in eventual annihilation of the corporate place of the tribal people in Northeast India. This they did in connivance with the chiefs and headmen. This, destroyed the non-hierarchical acephalous tribal societies. In Northeast India, neither the 'civilising' mission of the colonisers nor the land/forest administration were intended to pull up the communities to a truly and genuine modernised and ("refracted") society, as they could be a potential threat to the colonial accumulators.

Under the neoliberal regime, there was stronger state-market punctuation. This punctuation worked in two ways: First, land aggrandisement was made through enclosure. Neoliberal enclosure in Northeast India intervened in agrarian restructuring in order to enhance relative surplus value and in doing so, it led to capitalistic accumulation (Lodhi 2007: 1439). The extreme market focus of land use pattern and cropping pattern made the corresponding restructuration of the land administration and land use that opened the flood gate for foreign and private capital investment. This reversed the state mode of land administration and brought the market-mode of land deregulation in place. In the market-mode, the rationale for resource nationalism gave way to the neoliberal economy in which the state became the surrogate to the foreign investors to allow unbridled *sale-purchase-lease-mortgage* of tribal lands, financial and other subsidies to them in land and water resources of this region. These practices gained momentum and perpetuated the idyllic process of accumulation and dispossession of the communal resources.

Second, there was high patronage to the foreign direct investors and corporate cronies for *industrial use* of land as a development *mantra* of the new millennium. Therefore, the industrial policy of the Northeast region and the state policies of the states of Northeast India tried to make the region and the states the ideal destination of FDI fixation for industrial use of land. This is something unique in the case of Northeast India which has never grown as a manufacturing region. The land administration in the region was geared up accordingly that exposed the gap between the *technique-oriented* PODSCORB (planning, organizing, directing, staffing, coordinating, reporting and budgeting) land administration of neoliberal order and the *culture-oriented* land use practices of the tribal societies. Land revenue administration had still a bigger structural issue to encounter. This issue was once raised by Dutt, who said that the economic system is determined by the interaction of productive forces and production relations. Economic administration, which is a part of the system and has a machinery of its own, namely the bureaucracy, helps in smooth functioning of the system. He found the control system that devised the economic administration in the post-independence period earned both public discredit and annoyance of the organised private sector. The latter demanded dismantling of the control system. This prevented the planned economy from determing the process of development resulting in market take-over with all its bias for those, who could make themselves felt in the market. So, he found that economic administration in the first two decades of the post-independence era blocked transition to a new economic system and economic administration adjusted with it to indulge in primary accumulation guided by the 'first person ethics (Dutt 1996: 598-599) which led to perennial annihilation of the communal resources.

In the neoliberal era, this tradition was not surrendered. In performing the surrogate role, the Indian state started land acquisition for FDI and corporate investment under the assumption of self-driven nature of the market economy. The resource rich tribal areas of Northeast India were not free from land hunger of the foreign direct investors and the corporate bodies and from folding the communal land resources into the market economy. This demanded new institutional restructuring in the natural resource dependent region of Northeast India and all the states became busy in preparing the industrial policies to offer as many subsidies as possible. The model of development economics of the World Bank considered the traditional institutions of land and forest governance largely weak and inefficient, responsible for erosion of resources and conflict within the communities. In the resource rich region of Northeast India, therefore—following the canons of the metropolitan development economics—there was a felt need for institutional restructuring and institutional strengthening for a resource intensive growth strategy, including land mapping, demarcation, tenural rights of land and forest. The Indian state and following it, the state governments of Northeast India, ventured towards institutional restructuring in land economics and New Public Management of land. They also formulated and adopted investor-friendly policies and took proactive legislations to make the North Eastern states, the ideal destination for FDI and corporate investment. Some of the exemplary acts made by the states on market-led agriculture in Northeast India are:

a) The Mizoram State Agricultural Produce Marketing (Regulation) Act 1996, allowed setting up of Competitive Markets by private persons, farmers and consumers. Under Section 8 of the act, for every notified market area, there shall be one principal market yard and one or more sub-market yards. The major features of the act are: direct sale/procurement from the farmers field; institutional support to contract farming through i. registration of sponsoring company, ii. recording of Contract Farming agreement, iii. time-bound dispute resolution mechanism and iv. indemnity to farmers land, promotion of PPP financing, construction, operation and management of agricultural markets; Market fee/tax, (u/s 21, the market committee shall levy and collect market fee in respect of agricultural produce bought or sold in the market area); Single Point levy in the entire process of marketing; Fee on Direct Marketing, Contract Farming, Processing Exports Licensing (U/S 38, any person, who desires to operate in the market area shall apply to the market committee for grant of license). Besides, agricultural produce marketing, the number of pass holders (without heritable and transferable rights) far outweighed the number of settlement holders holding land under permanent cultivation, which restricted the size of the land market. It is only in case of the non-farm lands, i.e. trade and house sites that the numbers of settlement holders were much greater than pass holders that indicated a fast growing urban land market.

b) The Nagaland Agricultural Produce Marketing (Development and Regulation) Act- 2005 introduced contract farming in Nagaland and created a class of contract farming producers. Under this act, individual agriculturists or associations of agriculturists or a village council or a similar body in whom the ownership or control of agricultural lands vests temporarily or permanently, who, by written agreement, agrees to sell his/its agricultural produce to a contract farming sponsor. This act introduced direct marketing" of the agricultural produces by the producers and buyers to and from, the entrepreneurs, company or dealers and producers, without processing the transactions through normal market regulatory systems and export of agricultural produce to outside India and import of the same from outside India.

c) The Meghalaya Agricultural Produce Market Act, 1980, allowed setting up of Competitive Markets by private persons, farmers and consumers. The main features of the act are: provision for direct sale/procurement from the farmers field, institutional support to contract farming through registration of sponsoring company, recording of Contract Farming agreement, time-bound dispute resolution mechanism and indemnity to farmers land. Promotion of PPP in financing, construction, operation and management of agricultural markets; market fee/tax to be levied and collected by market committee on the agricultural produce bought or sold in the market area; Single Point levy in the entire process of marketing, fee on direct marketing, contract farming, processing and export and grant of license to operate in the market area by the market committee.

d) In Arunachal Pradesh, Water Resource Management Authority Bill was passed. This act laid down that from the date of commencement of this Act, no person shall use any water source without obtaining the Entitlement from the respective River Basin Agency. The Authority shall determine the distribution of Entitlements for various Categories of Use and the equitable distribution of Entitlements of water within each Category of Use. It introduced a water tariff system and Water Users' Associations for water management. The Water Resource Management Authority in Arunachal Pradesh in this way, wrested the community right over water, fetishised the water resources by introducing water tariff system and water charge. For industrial use of water, the Authority was given power to review and clear water resource projects at the sub-basin and river basin level. The authority was empowered to form a new category of Water User Association to annihilate the community stake in water use, established a regulatory system for water resources of the state and established a system of enforcement, monitoring and measurement of the Entitlements for the use of water. Finally, the authority patronised the private sector in the water sector. Parallel to this, the ridiculous component of this

> act is the higher rate of water charges (one and a half times of the normal rates of water charges fixed under clause(d) of Section 11 of this Act) chargeable from a person, having more than two children, to get entitlement of water for the purpose of agriculture under this Act provided that, a person having more than two children on the date of commencement of this Act, shall not be required to pay the higher charges so long as the number of children he had on the date of commencement does not increase.

The land reforms policies in the neoliberal frame made a switchover from the redistributive policies and from being a project of de-colonisation towards more nuanced policies for commercial plantation and industrial use of land in favour of market economy. This left enormous scope to exploit the tribal peasantry and to appropriate their land resources. This exposed the robust link between neoliberal land reforms policies and the growing market economy. This again affected the production relation in the otherwise acephalous tribal societies. Much of the rhetoric of neoliberal land reforms have centred round privatisation of land resource either for commercial agriculture, industrial use of land or for land speculation through sale, purchase, lease, mortgage. The neoliberal land reforms programme has emphasised computerisation of land records (CLR) and individual land titling. This is, as Saxena wrote, not to correct the record of rights (ROR) but to store whatever is contained in the ROR (Saxena 2005: 317). What was not taken into account was that the system of shifting cultivation in the hills was never record-based and chain-measured. Even the British could not record such lands to give individual titles and the survey operation could not extend to these areas with much success even today. (Although the Orissa government decided to confer ownership rights to all the persons in the Scheduled Areas cultivating it upto 30 percent hill slopes and to carry out a special survey of the unsurveyed hill slopes in the Scheduled Areas) (Saxena 2005. 315).

The Plantation sector was tagged with the trade regime under the WTO. A project was sponsored by the Northeast Regional Agricultural Marketing Corporation and the Ministry of DONER in 2008. A detailed project report on setting up procurement centre of horticultural products at Roeing at Lower Dibang Valley District of Arunachal Pradesh was prepared by Omeo Kumar Das Institute of Social Change and Development, Guwahati, in 2008. This report let loose the fear that the sanitary and phyto-sanitary measures (SPS Agreement) were now being used for crafting trade distortion and were used for protectionist ends. The Agreement on the application of sanitary and phyto-sanitary measure emphasised on the institutional and legal mechanisms across the wide spectrum of the WTO member countries.

The crop conditionalities, including the Agreement on Trade Related Aspects of IPR perennially annihilated the tribal subsistence farmers. Therefore, from the regime of primitive accumulation to the regime of accumulation by dispossession, communal land has been subjected to various institutional restructuring that scrambled the land-community symbiosis to privilege the market forces. The post-liberalisation policies in this way converted the "Zameen to commodity" (Dasgupta 2014). Penetration of the market economy proved perilous to the customary rights of land in Northeast India and threw challenges not only to the social policy of the state in respect of communal land but also threw challenges to the credibility of the Sixth Schedule.

The trouble of customary land rights in Northeast India is to be understood with reference to two diametrically opposite economic and ideological roots of land systems—the communal and the capitalist. The surplus-oriented agricultural economy defended a permanent and transparent individual right regime that was feasible only through reversal of the community ownership of land. The neoclassical economic arguments against communal ownership were not paltry. These included denial of community as a "Person; under-developed factor market; absence of formal production in shifting cultivation; lack of modern technology and capital input and so on" (Roy and Kuri 1998: 57; Nayak 1988: 89-96). This diluted both the concepts of 'public purpose and the land-based ontology of the tribal people. This affected the tribal areas more than elsewhere. The state also promoted the corporate interest and as the Article 300A (1978) of the Constitution provided that 'no person shall be deprived of his property save by the authority of law, the state could acquire any land by making a law in this regard and might well pave the way of accumulation by dispossession.

The fetish nature of land and labour was de-humanising that led to annihilation of the communal land system and 'fell into the impersonal process that appear as alien forces beyond their control' (Marx 1967, I, 71-83; III, Chap. 48). On the other hand, re-enactment of the community as artifactual community provided the first tract to the private accumulators, destroyed the uni-class and egalitarian community and helped class-market punctuation in the tribal societies of Northeast India. The neoliberal hexes dispelled the archaic communal institutions and provided a policy berth to the *artifacatual* communities for the down side administration/management of natural resources that could attract the investors' choice to invest in communal land and accumulate wealth out of it. This New Public Management (NPM) approach in the neoliberal economy charged the methodological inadequacy of institutional economics that annihilated the anthropological construct of land. NPM reinstituted community neoliberal construct once again, where it made a departure from the colonial *'dismissal mode'* to *'cooptional mode'* of the community to capture the communal land resources. A World Bank study conducted jointly with MoDONER patronised the NPM approach (The World Bank 2006; Ray 2005: 320-321). Subsequently, the Community Forestry Alliance for Northeast and NEHU joined the band. Their advocacy for 'green capitalism' recast their demands within the World Bank-IMF agenda of neoliberal conservation that went parallel to extraction of land, water, forest and mineral resources from the region. This approach oscillated towards a pseudo-cultural anthropology and moral economics. Such a 'community portrait' was used as the safe mode of accumulation by dispossession.

The enormous consumptive value progressively reified and fetishised the communal resources, including the land, water, forest and the mineral resources. Reification and commodity fetishism in the tribal societies of Northeast India made only an episodic appearance in the immediate pre-colonial tribal society, where exchange value was yet to take the form of its own and it was bound up with use-value in which case, the nature of exchange was largely ritualistic. But the use-value no longer remained use value and assumed exchange value when both the land and the labour associated with this were fetishised and both these went out of the control of the tribal communities till the latter became the non-possessors. This process began with their contact with the outsiders in the past when the colonial agents, businessmen and labour recruiters, during the First World War, for example, threatened the land economy of the tribes, including the Kukis of Manipur and Nagas of Nagaland (Ray 1990: 81; Vashum 2000: 65) which had serious disintegrative effects on the land economy of the tribes. This process continued till communal land progressively assumed a fetish character and market economy penetrated in all aspects of the tribal societies. The market process broke the organic unity between the land and the community and separated the use value from exchange value of land.

The states of the Northeast region started to acquire land for private, corporate and foreign investment in the pretext of public purpose and incorporated 'deregulation' and 'policy subsidisation' to satisfy the conditionality clauses for FDI and corporate investment on natural resources and usurpation of the same from the region. The hill region, to be the preferred investment destinations, was enclavised for industrialisation, infrastructure building, urban expansion and resource extraction. It once more trivialised the communal land system and the in-built regulatory and customary mechanisms associated with the land system. In the FDI regime, territorialisation of land became an easy mode of land grabbing which shifted discourse from land to territory. Das stated that land turns into a territory when it is 'monopolised, captured and colonised by any state and/or nation when the state enjoys superseding power over communal land' (Das 2009: 41). Once land is territorialised, the community loses all its stake over it which, in turn, disjoins the community both from the land resource and the products of it. This distinction between land and territory helped us to explore another trajectory of privatisation of communal land in Northeast India in the FDI regime.

Fielding in the land-centric debate in the neoliberal Northeast India became problematic. On the one hand, some kind of spatial fix was required for capital investment and for infrastructure building that necessitated space annihilation of the community. The Asian Development Bank and the World Bank, became the critical players in Northeast India for spatial fix of capital along with many private corporations. Eventually, this caused massive displacement of the forest dwellers, cattle graziers, fishermen, indigenous tribal groups and caused extensive environmental damage and political conflicts in many parts of North Eastern region. Given the public outrage since 2007, there were moves for comprehensive amendment of the Land Acquisition Act of 1894 (Wahi 2013: 49-51). On the other hand, the regional elites tried to make a space for themselves by mobilising the community people for territorial movement either for state or for Sixth Schedule, while a section of them chose to thrive under their protectionist patrons, including the corporate cronies, concessionaires and private entrepreneurs as *pariah capitalist* by making their presence felt in the speculative land market of *sale-purchase-lease-mortgage.* Chakravorti has stated that for the last couple of decades, the state has become a 'rent-seeking state' for which land is the biggest source of rent. The rent-seeking state sheltered the leaders and real estate politicians, who extract value from land when the use changes from agriculture to something else. At the local scale, the small actors derive money rent from land while at the regional and national scale, land is the source of a different kind of rent of political significance. (Chakravorti 2015: 38-39). In this case, following Chakravorti, the small actors are those, involved in speculative land market of *sale-purchase-lease-mortgage* and the big actors are the politicians engaged in territorial movement, who derive rent from land for political mileage.

The Lockean defence of privatisation made the communal land a contesting space of the three players—state, market and the community, the latter standing at the defeated court. This scrambled the very taxonomy of land, annihilated the social function of it, made it a major market good and created a fluid land market. The re-meaning of land also de-essentialised the constitutional and the judicial meaning of land to re-institute a post-liberal *sui generis* land right that found place in the country policy and legislations. This invited a great crisis of the *Gemeinscaft* and delinked the tribal community from land. In recent times, C.K. Prahlad became the greatest advocate of such a delinking project through his "Bottom of the Pyramid" economy, E-Choupal and the entrepreneurial model, etc. that he argued, could act as an antidote to poverty. This gave further impetus to the RNFS economy. His thesis sought to reverse the agricultural practices from production of staple to commercial species and his agricultural model was tailored to fit in with the needs of the market by removing trade barriers and protectionism (Ray 2012: 290-292). Production of commercial species was pushed by myriads of seed companies and bio-tech farms promoted by the MNCs, corporate seed farms and the private companies.

In 2007, under the Prime Minister's initiative, the Ministry of Commerce and Industry accorded approval of two Special Economic Zones in Nagaland. A Multi-Product Special Economic Zones was promoted by a private company on acquiring over 400 hectares of land on the outskirts of Dimapur. An agro-food processing SEZ was earmarked as an export promoting industrial park with 125 acres of land already acquired by the government. The Nagaland Industrial Development Corporation (NIDC) acquired estates covering a total area of 40 acres with 25 acres already built with standard factory sheds and area for a small industrial plot at Dimapur. There are also two integrated infrastructure development centres in Kiruphima and Longnak, each with 50 acres of land, both of which were to be undertaken by the government. In the ongoing process of liberalisation and privatisation, the state of Nagaland, without in-depth perusal and consideration of the local realities, threw open the doors to the foreign investors (Longkumar and Jamir 2012: 50).

The methodological individualism of neoliberal institutional reforms and surrogate state celebrated freedom of the market and trade that reflected, as Harvey noted, "the interests of private property owners, businesses, multinational corporations, and financial capital" (Harvey 2005: 8). Retreat of the developmental state and its facilitator role reflected the ongoing mechanisms of primitive accumulation that the state machinery began to enforce through the liberalisation agenda (Vasudevan 2008: 42). This initiated a paradigm shift towards land concentration in the hands of the elite class, middlemen, land speculators, state agencies, and not the least, the custodial right holders in the tribal areas. Property right was linked up with market rationality and profit maximisation principles that invited a triangular trade-off between the tribal communities, state and market. Annihilation of space by time progressively eliminated the ethnic labour and its relational character and turned them into the lumpen class while it offered entry to the exogenous agencies—the state, corporate and the alien—into tribal lands. The Enclave economics of neoliberalism reconfigured and re-regulated the community space and obliterated the natural space of the multitudinous ethnic groups.

The dramatic shift from protective insulation to market-driven strategies made corresponding shift of capital from production function to speculative function. In the hills of Northeast India, that is why the practice of sale-purchase-lease-mortgage became common for the land speculators, who cashed in on the speculative practice in a big way. Lease markets in Meghalaya and Mizoram progressively came up. An integrated IT park on a plot of 80 acres of land at Mawdiang, near Shillong, was set up in PPP mode. There are many more examples of this sort in the hill areas of Northeast India.

The colonials made bifocal theorisation on the same landscape—the non-economic social theorisation on the one hand and the individual-right theorization on the other—that marked the threshold of a perpetual contradiction between the tribes and the colonials. The individual-right theorisation scotched the customary usufruct rights with the twin jurisprudential principles of *lex loci* and *res nullius*. These principles created a trans-historic path dependency on positive law and annihilated the communal land, the process of which remained unabated even in the post-colonial and post-liberal tribal societies in Northeast India. The state reproduced the colonial theory of private property and individual rights and made private property, the fulcrum of development. The Indian state also rooted the institutional economics regime, where private property contravened the golden canons of the egalitarian tribal economy in the same way as the colonial state did. This trivialised the combination of the social theory and the state-managed *modus vivendi* between community and land. This trivialised the *once-proposed* prolegomena to a moral rationale for an otherwise non-capitalist and contingent land economy in the hills. The modernist legal paradigm, in reality, also went against the moral economy notwithstanding the owner-lineage, clan ownership or custodial-ownership of communal land in Northeast India. The longitudinal state policies facilitated usurpation of communal land resources and invited tension between the social optima principle in communal land and profit maxima principle of global capital. The neoliberal political economy sought for 'Pareto Optimal' investment in the land sector for individuation of benefits either through legal or extra-legal/illegal means. This, once more, signalled the peril of the community; unveiled the universal truism of perennial dispossession and caused *cathexis-dislocation* of the tribal people from both land and identity in the hills of Northeast India.

REFERENCES

Administrative Report of Manipur, 1896-97 and 1898-99. Imphal: Old Secretariat Archive.

Amavilah, Voxi Heinrich (2010). Introducing Anthropological Foundations of Economic Behaviour, Organisation, and Control, Working Paper 20100501, Resource & Engineering Economics Publications Services, May 26, 2010 http://mpra.ub.uni-muenchen.de/22921 posted May 28, 2010 6:18 UTC Munich Personal RePEc Archive (REEPS), USA.

Baruah, Sanjib (2008). Territoriality, Indigeneity and Rights in Northeast India, *Economic and Political Weekly*, March 22.

Bordoloi, Manasjyoti (2014). Impact of Colonial Anthropology on Identity Politics and Conflicts in Assam. *Economic and Political Weekly*, May 17, Vol. XLIX, No. 20.

Chakraborty, Gorky (2012). Roots and Ramifications of a Colonial 'Construct': The Wastelands in Assam, Occasional Paper 39. September, IDSK, Kolkata.

Chakravorti, Mahadev (1989). The New Zealand Baptist Mision and the Beginning of the Christian Missionary Activities in Tripura. Shillong: Proceedings of Northeast India History Association, Tenth Session.

Chakravorti, Sanjoy (2015). Land Acquisitioin and Rent-Seeking State. New Delhi: *Seminar* 674. October.

Chin Lushai Conference (1982), No. 3. (1892). Calcutta: Fort William. January. (Sections 4 & 5).

Das, S.K. (2009). Land, Identity and Conflicts: A Plea for Rebuilding Civil Society in Manipur, in Ch. Priyabrata Singh edited, *Tribalism and the Tragedy of the Commons–Land, Identity and Development: The Manipur Experience*. New Delhi: Akansha Publishing House.

Dasgupta, Sejuti (2014). Zameen to Commodity: Post-Liberalisation Policies and Class Consolidation in Rural Chhattisgarh and Kerala. Seminar on Return of the Land Question: Dispossession, Livelihhods and Contestation in India's Capitalist Transition. Organised by Faculty of Arts, Australia-India Association, University of Melbourne, IDSK-Kolkata and IIM Kolkata, 6-8 March.

Datta, B.B. and M.N. Karna (eds.) (1979). *Land Relations in Northeast India*. New Delhi: People's Publishing House.

Dutt, R.C. (1996). Economic Administration: Its Unsavoury Features, *The Indian Journal of Public Administration*, July-September, Vol.

XLII, No. 3.

Elwin, Verrier (1964). *A Philosophy for NEFA*. Shillong.

Elwin, Verrier (1969). *The Nagas in the Nineteenth Century*. UK: OUP.

Engels, Fredric (1972). *Ludwig Feurback and End of Classical German Philosophy*, Marx and Engels. (1972). *Selected Works*. Vol. 3. Moscow: Progress Publishers.

Fowkes, Ben (Translated). (1990). *Karl Marx, Capital: A Critique of Political Economy*, Penguin Books (Reprint).

Gangopadhyaya, D.K. (1990). *Revenue Administration in Assam*. Guwahati: Government of Assam.

Geisler, Charles (2012). New Terra Nullius Narrative and the Gentrification of Africa's "Empty Lands", *Journal of World Systems Research*, Vol. XVIII, No. 1.

Gough, Kathleen (1990). Anthropology and Imperialism Revisited, *Economic and Political Weekly*, Vol. XXV, No. 31, August 4.

Guha, Amalendu (1991). *Medieval and Early Colonial Assam: Society, Polity and Economy*. Calcuta: K.P. Bagchi & Co.

Guha, Ram Chandra (1999). *Savaging the Civilised*. Delhi: Oxford University Press.

Handique, Rajib (2012). Colonial Forest Policy and Land Resources in Assam in Editorial Board edited, *Aspects of Land Policy in Assam*, Guwahati. Vivekananda Kendra Institute of Culture.

Harvey, David (2005). *History of Neoliberalism*. London, New York: Oxford University Press.

http://dic.dlib.indiana.edu/dic/bitstream/handle/10.

Humphreys, S.C. (1969). History, Economics and Anthropology: Works of Karl Polany. *History and Theory*, Vol. 8 (2)

Hussain, Ebadat (1983). *Marxbader Bichare Rammohan* (in Bengali). Calcutta: Saptarshi.

International Encyclopedia of the Social & Behavioural Sciences.

Karlsson, Bengt G. (2011). *Unruly Hills, Nature and Nation in India's North East*. New Delhi: Orient BlackSwan.

Khouthonjam, Indrakumar and Homen Thangjam (eds.) *Location, Space and Development: Development Trajectories in India's North East, Centre for Alternative Discourse*. New Delhi: Concept Publishing Company.

Lewis, Diane (1973). 'Anthropology and Colonialism', *Current Anthropology*. Vol. 14, No. 5, December.

Lodhi, A.H. Akram (2007). Land Market and Neoliberal Enclosures: An Agrarian Political Economy Perspective, *Third World Quarterly*, Vol. 28, No. 8.

Longkumar, Lanusashi and Toshimenla Jamir (2012). *Status of Adivasis/ Indigenous Peoples Land Series-6, Nagaland, Land Alienation: Dynamics of Colonialism, Security and Development.* Delhi: Aakar Books.

Lyngdoh, Alfreda L. (1992). Land Use Pattern and Changes therein in West Khasi Hills District: A Case Study of Mawthawniaw Village. Assam Sachivalaya, Guwahati: Institute of Social Change and Development. (Mimeographed).

Maini, Darshan Singh (2000). *Encyclopedia of Anthropology, Vol. 6, Political Anthropology.* New Delhi: Mittal Publications.

Marcuse, George E. and Michael J. Fisher (1999). *Anthropology as Cultural Critique: An Experimental Movement in the Human Sciences.* 2nd edition, University of Chicago Press.

Mathur, Hari Mohan (1989). *Anthropology and Development in Traditional Societies.* New Delhi: Vikas Publishing House.

Misra, Bani Prasanna (1979). Agrarian Relations in a Khasi State. *Economic and Political Weekly,* Vol. 14, No. 20. May 19, 1979.

Misra, Bani Prasanna (1983). Society and Politics in the Hill Areas of North-East India in B. Datta Ray edited, *The Emergence and Role of Middle Class in North-East India.* New Delhi: Uppal Publishing House.

Misra, Bani Prasanna (2014). Facts, Fads and Fantasies of Globalisation, Seminar on 'Ideology and Social Science' organised by OKD Institute of Social Change and Development. Gwahati: November 27-28.

Mukhopadhyaya, Prabhat Kumar (1972). *Rammohan O Tatkalin Samaj O Sahitya* (in Bengali), Shantiniketan: Viswa Bharati.

Nayak, N.C. (1998). Institutional and Sociological Constraints of Agriculture in M.C. Behera edited, *Agricultural Modernisation in Eastern Himalayas.* New Delhi: Commonwealth Publishers.

Pemberton, R.B. (1991). *Report on Stern Frontier of British India.* Guwahati: Department of Historical and Antiquarian Studies, Reprint.

Proceedings of Annual Conference of Northeast India History Association (1987). Kohima: Northeast India History Association.

Puffenberger, Mark. Draft Discussion Paper, Forest Sector Review of Northeast India, Community Forestry Alliance for Northeast India.

Ray, Asok Kumar (1990). *Authority and Legitimacy: A Study of the Thadou Kukis in Manipur.* New Delhi: Renaissance Publishing House.

Ray, Asok Kumar (1992). Christianity and Manipur in Soumen Sen edited, *Religion in North-East India*. New Delhi: Uppal Publishing House.

Ray, Asok Kumar (2005). *Revisiting Northeast India in the Era of Globalisation*. New Delhi: Om Publications.

Ray, Asok Kumar (2012). *Political Economy of Inclusive Growth and India*. New Delhi: Om Publications.

Roy, Niharranjan (1972). Introductory Address in K.S. Singh edited, *Tribal Situation in India*. New Delhi: Anthropological Survey of India.

Roy, N.C. and P.K. Kuri (1998). A Model Institutional Change of Land Ownership in Arunachal Pradesh, in M.C. Behera edited, *Agricultural Modernisation in Eastern Himalayas*. New Delhi: Commonwealth Publishers.

Roy Burman, B.K. (1995). Indigenous and Tribal Peoples and the UN and International Agencies. New Delhi: RGICS Paper 27.

Rymbai, R.K. (1993). Christian Mission and the Indigenous Religion of the Khasi Pnar Soumen Sen, edited. (1993). *Religion in Northeast India*. New Delhi: Uppal Publishing House.

Saxena, Naresh C. (2005). Updating Land Records: Is Computerisation Sufficient? *Economic and Political Weekly*, Vol. 40, No. 4.

Sen, Soumen, edited (1993). *Religion in Northeast India*. New Delhi: Uppal Publishing House.

Siyemlieh, D.R. (1983). The Cherapunjee Experiment (1829-1834). Barapani: Proceedings of Northeast India History Association.

Syemlieh, David (1990). *A Brief History of the Catholic Church in Nagaland*. Shillong: Vendrame Institute Publications.

Thomas, M.M. (1969). *The Acknowledged Christ of Indian Renaissance*, London: SCM Press.

Vashum, Reisang (2000). *Naga's Rights to Self Determination: An Anthropological-Historical Perspective*. New Delhi: Mittal Publications.

Vasudevan, Ramaa (2008). Accumulation by Dispossession in India. *Economic and Political Weekly*, March 15.

Wahi, Namita (2013). Land Acquisition, Development and the Constitution. *Seminar*. February.

White, Major Adam (1988). *A Memoir of Late David Scott, Esq*. Compiled by S.K. Bhuyan. Guwahati: Department of Historical and Antiquarian Studies in Assam.

The World Bank (2006). New Delhi: World Bank in India. Vol. 5, No. 3 November.

Index